Rooms To Grow

Natural Language Arts
in the Middle School

Rooms To Grow

Natural Language Arts in the Middle School

Second Edition

Deborah Butler
Tom Liner

Carolina Academic Press
Durham, North Carolina

428
B9 85

ISBN   0-89089-697-6
LC   98-87687

Printed in the United States of America

Carolina Academic Press
700 Kent Street
Durham, North Carolina 27701
Telephone (919) 489-7486
Fax   (919) 493-5668
E-mail   cap@cap-press.com

Contents

Acknowledgments

For these friends we are grateful:

For Philip Menzies and Andrew Wilson, our editors, and the good folks at Carolina Academic Press.

For the support and encouragement from Wabash College, for members of the Wabash Faculty Development Committee who graciously funded my travels. For Debbie Polley, Interlibrary Loans.

Likewise for the help and well wishes from the Dougherty County School System in Albany, Georgia, for Dr. William Gardner and Dr. Alfredo Stokes and Helen McCorvey and Gloria Ammons.

For the Crawfordsville, Indiana, School System, for Dr. John Coomer and Principals John Tidd and Don Fine. For the school system of Warren Township, Indianapolis. For Principal Teresia Wynns.

For Albany Middle School and Principal Ted Horton. For Pat Bradley and Mamie Fulmore and Jerry Holmes and Murlene Jones and Malcom Mercer.

For Creston Junior High and Deborah Bova and her seventh grade team members.

For Dougherty Middle School and Principal Larry Medlin. For Paul Gainer and Donna Thomas.

For Hose Elementary School, Pat Stull, and her colleagues.

For Merry Acres Middle and Dr. Mike Manning, its principal. For Linda Clark and Linda Darrah and Melissa Moore and Virginia Monroe.

For Radium Springs Middle School and Principal Jim Ramsey and Linda Waters.

For Tuttle Middle School and Mike Barton and Tambra Cambron and Debbie Hatke and Gary Linn and Brad Mullendore and Sally Remaklus and Sheridan Hadley and Susan Streetman.

For Jeanneine Jones and Janet Thompson at Western Middle, Alamance County, North Carolina.

And for dear colleagues at Model Lab School, Eastern Kentucky University, Mary Davies (Strubbe), Margaret Graham, and Mike Wavering.

And for all the kids, those whose words appear in these pages—and all the others who generously shared with us and there just wasn't any more room in the chapters. And for the parents.

For Jeff Fletcher, photographer and teacher.

For Tom and Myrna, our best friends, and our families.

We are blessed in our friends.

Rooms To Grow

Natural Language Arts
in the Middle School

1

A Language Arts Ecology: Whole Language in the Middle

"Tell me, and I'll listen. Show me, and I'll understand. Involve me, and I'll learn."

Lakota Sioux

"To become a good middle grade school requires a change in vision about the possibilities of educating young adolescents."

Joan Lipsitz, 1984

"What we need is an ecological approach to change, which is still uncommon rather than common sense for too many people."

John Mayher, 1990

Ecological Romance

It's morning and the sun is out. Our classroom windows filter the light through a painted blue sky, white clouds, and single rainbow—the writing class's latest composition on glass. John lies on the floor under the painted rainbow which colors his shirt. He's stretched out reading a Cormier novel. Several others around him read different books from the corner classroom library—I see Blume, Hinton, Zindel. They're propped easily against the air conditioner, or in chairs, one primly in her desk, but all reading intently.

In a few minutes John will bring the book to me, and we'll talk about his impressions. Jeremy, who finished it yesterday, will join us. Right now, he's at the art station at the other end of the room creating a book card ad for Cormier's book. It's a visual ad with a written blurb on the novel; he liked it and wants to share it with the others.

He hopes they'll read his enthusiastic comments and want to read it too.

Another corner holds two tables. At one a small group shares their writing. In quiet tones, they take turns reading and reacting to each other's writing. The other table's kids plan a dramatic presentation, group writing the script, getting ready to practice. Against the wall in the back, a student works at a writing lab station reviewing some skills she needs more work on.

The room is rich—filled with tables, chairs, cushions, artistic and informational posters on the walls, both kid and teacher-made, bulletin boards that are little publishing houses for kids' works. It's filled with bodies in all positions, with movement in all directions. It hums with thought being transformed into talk, writing, art.

It's different. Clutter. Talk. Movement.

What does it all mean? We think this is an ecology working. It's people doing language together in an ordered environment. We see purposeful activity, purposeful communication, oral and silent. Each part depends on other parts. It is a natural language environment. John will finish his book and will be able to use his teacher's responses and guidance to gain more insights—as will Jeremy. Because the parts of the room are functional, too, Jeremy can extend his writing-reading prowess and can inform his peers of his discoveries. As a consequence of these interactions of parts, because they will read, write, talk and listen, both John and Jeremy will think a little more deeply, will come away from a language experience with fewer missed and mistaken ideas. And because they are a little richer in language and thought, they have more to give back to the other kids as classroom give-and-take evolves. Ultimately, all the parts together, that is, all the students with the teacher in the room, the learning experiences, and the relevant resources, make a whole and healthy ecology of language growth for middle school kids and their teachers.

In nature, an ecology is the set of relationships between organisms and their environment. It's a set of mutual bonds, dependencies, which if working well, spawns healthy, growing alive-to-the-ultimate life. Our language arts ecology is about a different nature—a nature made of the relationships among the classroom itself, the people who live in it each day, and their unique plans for doing language together. That classroom may indeed appear a little chaotic, but if we can just observe carefully the *links*, the bonds between people, their activities, their aims, their learning needs, the room's resources, and not just see the isolated *parts*, we might discover the sources of all learning. It was John's and Jeremy's *interaction* with each other and their teacher about reading the book and about John's designing and writing a book ad that tied all the parts together and promoted language growth for them. Yes, the space for the table, the students, their separate written pieces, their communication, were all the necessary parts for reaching the goal of language improvement. But really the fact that all these objects, people, and events interacted smoothly, purposefully—this experience promoted healthy language growth. So, a classroom ecology is like the best modern art; it's not the objects in space that have meaning, it's the spaces themselves that complete the artist's purpose.

Creating your own ecology, not duplicating ours, is what we hope this book is all about. There is a model here, a way to go if you care to draw it out and replicate it. In fact, we want to present a path to the teaching role described here and suggest some plans for getting there. But more than that, we want to clearly describe images of language arts teachers who are autonomous, yet collaborative, instructional leaders and empowered professionals who make independent decisions based on informed assumptions about kids, language, and schools.

So you'll find mostly options here, offered within the boundaries of our own beliefs about middle schools, kids, and language. And our beliefs, in some cases, might be a little different from yours. We just have to remember that the teacher's work has got to be informed by sound assumptions. Ultimately, we hope that suggestions in these pages might help you tend to a healthy ecology for your own kids, your own classes, and yourself. That is why we have built in an extra feature throughout all the chapters—a "teaching journal." These short reflections ask you to interact with the ideas you are reading, to interject your own thoughts and plans into the process of becoming a natural language teacher.

A natural language arts classroom is a healthy classroom ecology. When language is being learned naturally, both students and teachers are empowered partners in the learning process. They both have choices in their learning. When students learn language naturally, they read whole pieces of literature, not basal readers. They write constantly and with confidence, real messages for real audiences, trying their hands at many kinds of writing. They do this with a teacher who writes and reads with them; they show each other how. The classroom exudes the attitude that meaningful reading and writing will constantly get better in the flexible room of a caring teacher-coach. It will get better as everyone talks and listens to each other. And what we all talk, read and write about is not always the subject matter of "English," but the interdisciplinary subject of life.

Some Guiding Assumptions About Teachers and Students Learning Language Together in a Middle Level School

While Tom and I believe in the power of the teacher's knowledge, values, and judgments, we also believe that there are basic principles that middle school language arts teachers assume and acknowledge as they go about developing and implementing appropriate experiences with kids in their rooms. Some of these are principles of language, some are truths about middle level students, and some are about the schooling ideas that support their learning best.

1. *Teaching middle school is different from teaching at any other level—elementary or secondary.*

I really get upset when I read national reports, or well-known journals, or see a decree come from the federal government, or even a statement from a prominent reformer who should know better, which refers to K–12 education as "elementary and secondary grades." Middle grades education (roughly grades 5–8) is not the same as elementary school, and it is certainly not the same as high school. Anyone who thinks so hasn't been in a school with 10–14 year olds in a long time—maybe not ever.

What makes these grades and the schools that house them so different is the 10–14 year old people we teach. At no other time, except perhaps during the early years of life, is change of such similar magnitude that the self is altered forever. Just opening our eyes tells us that many of this age group are going through puberty with all the attendant changes in body, sexuality, sense of identity, and intellectual capacity. Most go through this in time and quite well, but the passage can be risky. Enough of this here. For some developmental lessons, wait for chapter 2.

What educators who see this as a special time of life have tried to do to help the middle level learner through this transition is to create a special third level of schooling. Middle level schools are staffed by knowledgeable, sensitive educators; they offer a relevant, yet challenging curriculum, packaged inside a schedule responsive to the needs of both kids and the adults that educate them. The most successful features that seem to reach these needs are flexible scheduling, integrated or multidisciplinary curricula, and interdisciplinary teaming. Exploratories and teacher-advisories are often part of the scheme. But these are certainly not "the only ways" a good middle level school can work. Your students can develop their language abilities with you even if you teach in a traditional junior high. The important point is that there is little in that list that is part and parcel of the elementary school, and even less that characterizes most high schools now. Reformers like Ted Sizer (1992) would like to change that, but it has not happened yet.

Good teachers at the middle level, regardless of their schooling situation, know their students are different, they acknowledge and accept it, learn about the age, and challenge themselves and their teams, if they have one, to constantly find ways to engage kids in learning. Good middle level teachers are familiar with what's happening in middle level education and in language arts. They are up on both. They appreciate the uniquenesses of the job and they like the challenge of balancing all of it and helping the classroom remain an ecology. Tom tells you more in chapter 3 when he writes about middle level language arts teachers. It takes a while to become a good teacher. Most people just don't land in a middle level classroom and become excellent right away. I could have used the help of someone, or even some guidance from a decent text when I first began teaching language arts at the middle. I have always wished someone had bothered to teach me about the unique developmental changes these ten to fourteen year olds experience, and the differences a good middle level classroom can make for them. My students' experiences and my first few years would have been better. Turns out the middle level ideas were already out there, but no one in my state was paying much attention then. Certification covered grades 7–12. Every adolescent was the same.

2. *The teaching in a middle school has to be appropriate for the metamorphoses of kids and their language growth.*

And that statement brings us to this issue of what really does go on in middle level classroom interactions between language arts teachers and learners. Just having a sign over the school door, or out in front in the schoolyard, one that says "middle school," does not mean that education proceeds any differently inside than it did when the sign read "junior high." In fact, those labels may mean nothing. Anyway, plenty of good instruction goes on, including real natural instruction, in schools that are called junior highs.

Even if a middle level school is organized and scheduled into interdisciplinary teams, multi-age student groups, and flexibly scheduled days complete with thematic units broken up by student advisories, good and appropriate instruction still may be a truant member of the middle level recipe for student success. Nancie Atwell (1987) said that a curriculum puts limits on both kids' and teachers' learning. She's right. Just having the good structures in place and good curriculum designs does not mean that much learning is going on in classrooms. Too often I have walked into a middle level school with all the above trappings and found in classrooms the traditional, factual lecture, exclusively textbook-based reading, recitation and drill practice sessions, memory-work, and worksheet after worksheet after worksheet. This is not to say there is never a place for some of these activities, although I frankly cannot think of many genuine uses for them. But, a steady diet of them turns language learning into nothing but a series of "dummy runs."

That is not my term. James Moffett (1983) used it to describe the traditional ways we English teachers have tried to teach kids their own language. I bet you remember these practice sessions, even if you don't teach like this yourself. They usually go like this lesson:

1. The teacher introduces "the apostrophe," not because it is a problem for many writers in the class, but because it is next in the text, or next in the system's curriculum guide.
2. There is usually some question and answer—designed to determine understanding of the rules of apostrophe usage, maybe some oral examples and drill.
3. Then every student practices this new concept using the *same* 10 sentences in the *same* book as everyone else, whether he needs it or not, whether she understands it or not.

Almost everyone finishes this lesson quickly and in the remaining class time, Roger writes Susie a note about his new dirt bike. There is not a trace of an apostrophe in the writing. Angie opens her private journal and continues a story that may need a few apostrophes. She will never know though because she will never read and share it with anyone, nor will it even get to a stage needing careful editing. Probably the talking and listening going on during the lesson was more sophisticated then the content of the lesson itself. Certainly the writing and reading in these couple of examples is far more sophisticated than reading and writing those practice sentences. The stuff will need teaching again, but only after the test. Everyone is that wise at least.

So many chances exist for real language learning in middle level instruction. We learn the conventions when the really important writing and reading calls for it. Even when the best middle level exteriors exist, too often instruction remains a matter of "dummy runs," and real language has to get smuggled into class and developed in the cracks and crannies of the school day. School is sometimes like practicing all afternoon, then sitting on the bench, waiting out the game, watching from the sidelines, never getting a chance to really play.

If there is a single most important challenge for language arts teachers in middle schools now, it is achieving this shift from the traditional instructional paradigm to one that is based on beliefs in active, meaningful involvement in one's learning. John Mayher (1990) calls it going from "common sense" (what traditionally has been done in schools, generally based on faulty assumptions about kids and learning) to teaching using "uncommon sense." According to Mayher, these are the key elements: "learners going beyond the information given; language being learned in use; the power of narrative in learning, in memory, and in development; the normally creative use of language; and a focus on learning, not teaching" (p. 3). Other terms, like "apprenticeship," "whole language education," and "meaning-making" are phrases lining up on the uncommon sense side of the world, too.

I think that there are shining moments lighting the landscape of language arts teaching. Most of these are from natural and whole language learning classrooms with their emphasis on real, relevant language use and development, their emphasis on integrating knowledge like the real world does, their emphasis on working together with students who have choices in generating their own learning directions.

Look at that description closely and go back and look at the natural language environment I described a few paragraphs before. Both mirror what middle school educators have always *said* kids should *do* in classrooms. If ever a ripe convergence rose on the horizon, it is melding these notions together right now. Natural language principles can bring to chronically anemic middle level instruction what it has been looking for. The middle school concept, with its key components grounded on student-centeredness, is the schooling environment most fertile for whole or natural language, for learning naturally.

Teaching Journal

In your teaching journal, divide a page into halves. At the top of one half, write "common sense ideas" and "uncommon sense ideas" on the other. Think about your own teaching in your own classroom. Jot down what you think are experiences based on "common sense," then those that you and your students do that would be based on "uncommon sense." For now, just let the lists alone. You may want to come back to these first thoughts later after reading this chapter and reflect again on what changes you believe you might make in the classroom.

3. *Language growth is developmental itself. It occurs differently for different kids.*

Years ago, in his pioneering study *Language Development: Kindergarten through Grade 12* (1976), Walter Loban told us clearly that a child's use of both oral and written language parallels his (or her) cognitive development. His findings on oral and written language development, for grades 6-8, could be informative to us still:

- that the steady growth in language through elementary school hits a "slower pace or plateau in grades, 7–8 . . .";
- That before grade 7, oral language evidences more words per unit than written, but that situation equals out in grades 7–8;
- that because kids are generating hypotheses and envisioning consequences, more complex sentences and clauses and connectives and auxiliary verbs appear in both writing and speaking;
- that the stage of thinking appearing in both writing and speech now is usually applied to things of the "here and now," not to ideas and relations quite yet;

The message here is that kids have a readiness for speaking and writing with certain structures in their own good time; they should be "pushed" in Arthur Powell's terms, but not pushed off the edge into a land of permanent failure. "Push" according to Powell and other authors of *The Shopping Mall High School* (1985) refers to a quality of a demanding and relevant curriculum. Often we are not demanding enough because we don't expect a lot—especially from our "unspecial" or average kids. We do need to expect a lot of middle school kids. And even more recently, James Beane has brought the notion of relevance for all middle graders home with his radical notion of curriculum restructuring for the middle level (Beane, 1990).

But kids, like ecologies, are full of delicate balances. So, at the same time, we have to nurture their growth, looking at their developmental capacities realistically, helping them make successes out of failures, remembering that other studies on middle school kids and learning processes suggest that this age span is a critical break-point for future school successes or failures. The natural language teacher tries to keep that balance.

4. *Reading and writing are always best taught when related to each other. This is also true of other subjects.*
This is definitely a statement from the "uncommon sense" side of teaching. Not all that long ago, everyone knew that the language arts, or the subject of English, was the summary of separate components—little ABCs under the big Roman numeral I. Language arts was the elementary subjects of handwriting, grammar (English), vocabulary, and spelling. Reading was something altogether separate. And writing? It was assumed that kids had not learned enough of the parts of the language yet to do much of that. Creative writing was a fun throwaway when it was done at all.

On the other end, at the secondary level, English was three separate things: composition, grammar, and literature. We hurried through traditional grammar and usage in the first two six weeks, and composition (types of essays) during the next one so that we could all spend the rest of the year on literature.

Where was English or language arts in the middle? Well, since for a long time the level itself was not recognized, what the language curriculum was depended on whatever went on from one school system to another. Language arts had no definition since kids and teachers in the middle were not recognized. We had no home.

Somewhere in the mid to late 1960s, there came to be some rumblings of dissatisfaction with all this subject separateness. James Moffett (1968) tried to give language arts a new definition grounded in a theory of discourse and thinking, and a definition of English that *integrated* reading, writing, speaking, and listening with other disciplines. The theory conceived of language growth across childhood, adolescence, and young adulthood. Most radically of all, he advocated a personalized, student-centered curriculum. He even developed a series called *Interaction* (1973) to help teachers. But nothing changed a lot in English teaching. Maybe it was too much all at once.

But by the early 1970s, Steve Judy had written a green paperback book, *Explorations in the Teaching of English* (1972), that challenged secondary teachers to think about English in these kinds of radical new ways. Traditional grammar teaching was out, although not language study, and while literature and writing were still separate, they were a lot more personalized and relevant to teenagers. Young adult paperbacks were "in." Ken Macrorie (1968) was already telling us to give up "Engfish" and write real words and sentences. Peter Elbow (1973) began telling us how to center the teaching of writing on our students. Daniel Fader (1968) had been reading real trade books with students and integrating reading with writing. He was having good success with teens in reform schools. Already Elliot Wigginton was integrating writing, reading, and language study as well in a personalized curriculum marketed as the *Foxfire* (1967) books. Fader and Wigginton were proof of the theory of transformation in action.

At the same time in the 1970s and early 1980s on the elementary level, Donald Graves (1981) had been watching young writers and readers, observing and writing about the natural connections between the two. Frank Smith (1971) had already been writing about the reading process, while Ken and Yetta Goodman (1978) were putting these insights to work in elementary classrooms. In all, the 1970s and 1980s saw a wealth of study on writing and reading processes and their interdependency was becoming readily apparent.

Based on all this study, it is no wonder that you can hardly pick up a language arts or English "how to" book anymore and not find the emphasis on teaching reading and writing together, especially through reading and writing workshops in a whole language environment. Jane Hansen (1987) says it for the elementary grades. Nancie Atwell (1987) and Linda Rief (1992) for the middle. Even secondary level teachers are practicing more integration of reading and writing. Read John Mayher's excerpt on the teacher portrait of Dan Kelly in *Uncommon Sense* (1990). While the whole language movement seems new on the educational scene, it has really been coming for a long time. The insights behind a natural language ecology have been developed over a long number of years.

You will notice that some of the teachers above blend reading and writing purposefully not only because their classrooms are set up as workshops, but because their teaching integrates these functions around important themes and questions for the students. Linda Rief works with an integrated study of generations. Dan Kelly worked with a study of "Growing up in America," an American cultures and literature study. These two are just a couple of examples. Clearly these cases go beyond the integration of the language arts to the blending of discipline areas. The examples above use themes that are language arts and social studies. A lot of the language arts teachers you will read about in later chapters of the book work on interdisciplinary teams where the subject becomes part of thematic or integrated studies including science or related arts. And this kind of broad interdisciplinary curriculum has been the legacy of the middle school movement since the 1960s on. In fact, its development parallels the development in language arts somewhat, a fact I will talk more about in chapter 4.

It is not enough to think about our language arts classrooms as environments for natural learning. The whole curriculum needs to provide such an ecology, too.

5. *Reading and writing are complex processes: they are not a series of steps from a writing or a reading textbook.*

I once thought I retained a clear memory of being taught "how to write." In 7th grade I learned parts of speech and how to diagram sentences. I received A's on the tests and on the all-to-brief and seldom assigned short papers. Therefore, my logic told me, I had learned to write well.

But I was wrong. Later my 12th grade English teacher told me I couldn't write well after all. Not directly, but I failed my first papers, so it was clear I really learned nothing in the 7th grade. We seniors wrote madly, in solitary confinement, and often. Formal papers handed in came back corrected in red with criticism. Most who survived the class felt they had finally learned to write and were better prepared to do college writing. We probably were, unfortunately for the Ken Macrorie's out there.

In assuming I could pinpoint when I learned to write, I forgot that I had accumulated a trunk full of original stories by the end of my third grade year, all written outside of school, all written because I wanted to, all read by numerous, usually appreciative family members and neighbors. I had forgotten my neighborhood newspaper, my short stories written in junior high.

Because I believed I knew when and how I learned to write, my first years of teaching junior high followed those part-to-whole, teacher-centered methods of my 7th and 12th grade models. I taught fiercely using that image.

Luckily, I was a constant reader. As I sank exhausted into bed each evening, I found time to read Judy, Elbow, and others; and I began to question my memories. The trunk rose from my memory unbidden.

It was possible that I didn't develop writing ability in the 7th and 12th grades from studying grammar, passing tests, or finding the right formula for a canned essay. Maybe, as Elbow was saying, people grew their writing, maybe it cooked, and became open, honest, real, and full of voice, written because there was a desire to write, shaped to a real audience. So, I experimented a little with writing workshops with kids, trying to make writing a more natural verbal occurrence for them in school, trying to accommodate the immense complexities of writing. I read all I could on writing processes and "process approaches to teaching writing." These ideas seemed to promote cooking, growing, struggling, creating.

Three years and a dissertation later, I came away with a sense of understanding finally how I and others might really write and have learned to write. Even then, I had only a beginning understanding of the complexity of writing processes, one which ripened and developed after more years of working with young writers.

I came to understand that it is really not important to know when I learned or exactly how, only to know that the conditions somewhere, sometime were right—and to try to provide the same good atmospheres for fledgling middle school writers. I wish that I had had then Brian Cambourne's (1988) explanation of the conditions for learning language. Based on the conditions under which we all learn oral language, Cambourne advocates recreating as closely as possible the conditions of immersion, demonstration, engagement, expectation, responsibility, approximation, use, and response in the reading and writing classroom. These are the conditions under which oral language thrives and grows; we can develop literacy classrooms based on these, too.

That reading is as equally a complex and mysterious act, that it, like writing, is driven by inner processes of making meaning opens vast opportunities for teachers, and ought to make us question our past practices of teaching reading, too. Frank Smith's work (1985) clearly explains the complexities of the processes at work just as Louise Rosenblatt's work (1968) on responding to literature helps us appreciate the complexity of the reading act, those transactions among readers, texts, and writers. They, among others, offer us a language to realize our own reading processes, a framework to appreciate that of our kids.

If we cannot create a healthy language ecology based on learning the parts of the language, the names for words, and functions, or by writing sentences or even paragraphs without purpose, then how can we help a nation of would-be readers by assigning basal skills and comprehension exercises?

Like many teachers, I have always been a reader; I can't remember being taught to read any more than I really can remember being taught to write. My friends, Bob Canady and Shirley Raines, long-time teachers of reading and language arts teachers, say this is why I'm still a reader. I learned, through desire, from personal purposes, from models, within the right environment. Like writing, growth in reading was so natural, I just can't remember it happening. Bob would say I'm one of the lucky ones. Tom and I are concerned that middle school kids are this lucky.

But while reading and writing are complex inner processes and their strategies and workings are individualistic, there are still, paradoxically, "shared features in the ways we write" as Emig says in *The Web of Meaning* (1983), or shared components in our processes of writing—and reading. These shared features are the visible outer signs of inner working processes. Teachers can use these shared features to guide their work with middle school readers and writers. They can help kids come to sense, develop, then rely on their own inner strategies for making the processes work. Our teaching of writing and reading may be linear when we all work together as a whole group, but we cannot lose sight of our goal to help each writer's internal language abilities to grow wildly. We middle school language arts teachers have got to live with another paradoxical situation in the middle. We have to acknowledge the linear features in our teaching, but continue to remember the non-linear complexities of these two mental processes. This is why the creation of reading and writing workshops is ultimately the healthiest classroom structure because multiple abilities and paths can exist simultaneously, and kids' individual growth patterns can be accommodated much more easily. Tom describes how to set up workshops and how they work in chapters 5–8.

Teaching Journal

Take out your journal again. Write your own history as a reader and a writer. Are there insights in your narrative that you can bring to your own teaching? Reflect on these in your journal and what difference they can make in your classroom.

6. *Good reading and writing learning is based on the model of how we learn to talk.*

Loban and his researchers found also that most kids needed to develop and practice syntactical complexities in speech before they could use them in writing. Even earlier, James Moffett (1968) told us that putting thoughts clearly into coherent oral language was a prerequisite to writing. Surely, based on these two men's work and that of others, classroom ecologists long ago should have accepted this dependency, and therefore included oral language as a legitimate curriculum component.

If they alone don't make the point, then re-read Brian Cambourne's (1988) conditions for learning that I just pointed out in the last assumption. Cambourne's eight conditions are directly based on how he perceives children naturally learn their language as they grow in the early years of life. In his book, *The Whole Story*, he spends over 30 pages in chapter 5 describing those conditions and how they might translate to literacy learning in schools. It is another helpful blueprint for setting up this kind of natural learning environment Tom and I are advocating.

Finally, as Nancie Atwell so aptly pointed out in *In the Middle* (1987) the kids are at an age where they are talking to each other constantly anyway; social development is dictating behavior codes. Why not use their natural development for the purposes of good language instruction? It makes sense to us. The implications of all of this? A silent language arts classroom is as deadly as one without any print—or video. A natural language teacher's classroom is likely to be noisy with purposeful sound.

7. *We all talk, listen, read, and write for different reasons naturally; it is the teacher's job to set up conditions to let this happen in schools.*

Just as most of us realize multiple audiences exist, we have also accepted the notion of purposes for writing. Really, those purposes are largely defined by writer intention, intended audience, and by the shape of the traditional genres. A sixth grader writing a diary knows his audience is only himself, so he writes messages allowing that knowledge to fully shape his style and content. But his message and style change dramatically if he knows the letter written in your class will be published in the editorial column of the local paper. Most middle school sixth graders came to my class ready to write personally; they enjoyed keeping a journal as a form of personal diary. They enjoyed the personal responses to classes, to an event in school, to a piece of literature—especially if they got to share these orally!

It is the formal, and sometimes creative realms, that middle schoolers are shaky about. They've got some experience writing poetry and stories and even group novels, and almost always very little experience writing expository pieces. In fact, for many, any expository writing form is synonymous with "lines copies from the Britannica Encyclopedia last week." But as Marvin Klein pointed out in his section on middle school language arts in the *Development of Writing in Children, Pre-K through Grade 8* (1985), because of the cognitive growth occurring during this age span, emphasis changes at least slightly to logical and analytical writing. I would only add that I think the change in increased ability for more abstract writing should also be mirrored in the reading, speaking, and listening experiences we offer our kids in our rooms.

Klein is also quick to point out the continuing need for personal writing experiences. And the kids need plenty of time for personal discussion and reading. While middle graders are becoming capable of experimenting with and handling more abstract discourse choices, they are still inexperienced enough to need the security of personal writing opportunities, especially kids with pretty undeveloped language abilities. I don't think we can ignore the fact that the insecurity born of personal changes during these chaotic years of identity-seeking demands a continued use of writing and reading as personally therapeutic experiences. It's an age which needs a push into the world, but also needs the safety of personal journals and reading opportunities that may even engage readers in much needed bibliotherapy.

8. *For kids to grow best as language users, the teacher cannot be
   the only audience.*

Traditional kinds of audiences, like oneself, peers, or teachers, ought to sound very familiar to those of you who are steeped in James Britton's (1975), Nancy Martin's (1976) and their co-authors' earlier work with kids and writing. Of course, if you will remember further, they found that kids mostly wrote for one audience in school—the teacher. Naturally, given that real writing is done for a real purpose with a real audience in mind, they assumed this one dimensional and artificial treatment of the writing act was unsuitable for true language learning. The suggestion, and rightly so, is that we should allow kids opportunities to write often, to many audiences, for many reasons, trying on and taking off the various rhetorical and linguistic differences among all shades of discourse.

Certainly this is easy enough to do, as Tom hopes to show you later in chapters 7 and 8 on writing. And certainly, it is time to do this with many middle schoolers because many are ready to start moving away from their egocentrically centered views of reality; they are more ready now to stand back mentally and look at their writing from another point of view. They may not be ready on their own, but ready to be helped to begin.

Although many writing experts talk about audience and writing, we would like for you to think about audience in light of teaching *language* because "audiences" applies to speaking, listening, and reading, too. It is helpful, for both writing and reading, to help kids think about reading audiences (was the author writing to her brother? Her husband? Was he preparing this for an anonymous public? Avid readers of science fiction? How does audience make a difference in the writing?). And certainly, the acts of speaking and listening can differ tremendously. If you're the speaker, your talk depends on how big your audience is; if it's a small audience, how intimately you know the persons there makes a difference in your delivery. If you're the listener, listening levels depend on how motivated you feel, or are made to feel, who the speaker is, what the context is for the listening. Speaking and listening are a fundamental and inescapable part of a natural language classroom and I will bring them up again when I talk about ecology and oral language in chapter 9.

9. *Everyone on a teaching team, especially the language arts teachers, needs to remember that natural language—talking, listening, reading, and writing—are ways of discovering and making meaning.*

Many of us, as middle grades teachers, are teaching or will teach as part of interdisciplinary teams. As the fundamental schooling concepts behind middle school education take hold increasingly, team organization of teachers and students becomes a staple of everyday classroom life.

This thought scares some people—teachers who have not taught in this structure, and even those that have, where, for many reasons, it didn't work out. I'm asked occasionally to talk with teachers in schools preparing to make a move from the traditional junior high to middle school with its more student-centered organization. I always tell them that I have taught in both a traditional junior high English classroom, and in a middle school as an interdisciplinary teacher in charge of language arts. And I tell them that I like being part of a team better.

They think I say this because I'm hired to do so for that day, but I really mean it. I would never again desire the isolation, of both the kids and myself, that teaching in a traditional junior high encourages. Team-teaching brings you in close contact with other professional adults, increases communication about subjects and shared kids, spawns endless creativity, and cushions inevitable daily pain and frustration of living in a school. This is not even mentioning the safety benefits of teaming to kids—staying with a block of peers for most of a day, and being known well by a small group of adults, being able to benefit from the connections among knowledge areas that interdisciplinary teaching brings about.

More about these benefits when we talk about kids and teachers in chapters 2 and 3 and about teams in chapter 4. For now, I just mean to say that one benefit of teaming is that a language arts teacher can see clearly how language is used to explain, understand, and talk about other disciplines. She gets to bring this up in her classroom—a way to touch her kids' lives through the rest of the schoolday. And she gets to influence those other colleagues—by sharing ways that writing and reading to learn can work in science or math journals, or by combining efforts with the social studies teacher on library group research projects. The ideas are endless and Tom and I will share more in later chapters.

Mostly though, she comes to see how kids explore language, using language in a much larger ecology than that of her own classroom— and she gets to influence that larger ecology in ways that insure the health of the whole group.

10. Language skills are really learned in the context of sending real, whole messages to a real audience.

I cannot resist briefly commenting on the evils of teaching grammar and usage as isolated skills activities. We have systematically killed and buried our grammar books and curricula as long as I've been in this profession, only to watch them rise from the grave upon the full moon of back to basics hysteria. Why we, as a profession, have not driven home the wooden stake once and for all and ended this deadening cycle is a topic deserving a monumental analytical effort by an expert social historian.

In spite of our knowledge of research, which has been telling us since the turn of the century that teaching grammar and skills in isolation teaches nothing except how to pass the grammar and skills tests, we insist upon resurrecting the dead body of grammar at the first sign of public unrest with education. But direct teaching of grammar and skills apart from any meaningful context violates a language arts ecology.

This does not mean that skills teaching is of no value to middle schoolers. It just means that learning language skills ought to be accomplished within the context of real messages purposefully sent and received. Our teaching aims should include usage correctness in speaking and writing, and proficient understanding in listening and reading, but those skills are just simply better learned by developing and comprehending whole messages, not by drilling, or doing exercises with the pieces of the whole. Learning how to assess individual kids' language needs, carving out time to hunt up (and cut up) resources necessary to create and manage an individualized classroom language lab are teaching skills far more requisite to helping kids develop their language abilities. They are more useful than a knowledge of English systems of grammar and usage rules which are often simply watered down and presented to kids' flat bored eyes day after day.

11. Reluctance to read and write is a real issue.

As an eighth grade teacher, I sat in a graduate class and heard that kids could read and wouldn't. I was dumbfounded at first. But a part of me knew it was true. I knew a lot of my kids were not very able readers, still, they literally could read. That they didn't was because it was such an unrewarding activity.

While none of this about less able kids surprised me, being forced to admit that many of my "average" and "above-average" (we were tracked then) kids who read perfectly well just never did pick up a book unless it was assigned was disheartening.

But this was an accurate insight too. Writers have been telling teachers this for a long time. We have gotten good at ignoring studies on children which find that, because of our overdependence on phonics, testing and basals, kids who have looked forward to the magic of reading before school are often turned off and become disinterested in reading by the time they're in the third grade (Bettelheim & Zelan, 1982). And they're not middle schoolers until fifth or sixth!

Some educators have even been telling us for years how we might keep the will to read alive and well. Witness Fader's and his colleagues' work with kids in reform school that I mentioned briefly earlier. In *Hooked on Books* (1968) 27 years ago Fader and his friends described how saturating the even "tough to crack" kids with books, letting them choose literature freely and begin to read real works for their own purposes, could stimulate the diffusion of the reading act—indeed, the value of reading itself. And even more recently, in a regular school atmosphere, Nancie Atwell has outlined a unique reading workshop that works—clearly a model of integrated language learning.

I think kids also know how to write and they don't do that either. Kids know the basics of writing. They may not spell everything well or have the mechanics down. But they can write coherent messages when they want to or have the need. They are just inexperienced, fearful of trying to develop their abilities, too used to being corrected to even try serious writing in any form. So they don't write. I myself stopped filling my trunk during these middle level years.

According to Gabrielle Rico, author of *Writing the Natural Way* (1983), the middle grades years are a breakpoint at the edge of adult success or failure for many developmental concerns. For her, the ability and will to write either takes root and blossoms or withers and dies.

Clearly, thoughtful people in our own profession have given us the authority to stop working against kids' learning needs and development. We don't have to stay with commonsense notions; we have permission to use our uncommon sense. We have many respectable people telling us good ways to free ourselves from diseducative curricula and how we might begin to structure our own learning environments.

12. We learn the language applications in electronic media just like we learn them in other settings.

We probably all accept now, whether we are great media users or not, that technology is not the panacea for all educational ills. Media can be used badly or well, just like books or writing lessons. Once upon a time, films and filmstrips, and more recently videotapes, seemed to be such hot items. They were the answer to the TV generation's waning interest in the classroom. But we've all seen these media used to perpetuate the separation between teacher and students, the gulf between teaching and learning. We've seen kids stay in the passive learning mode to the point that when lights go out, the heads go down in automatic response.

Not even the computer is a panacea. I cannot now imagine doing the work I do without my computer and my favorite wordprocessing programs, but if the words in these pages do not sound right, the fault is in my mind, not in the computer's memory. It does not create or think for me; it does what I tell it to do. Even if the human relationship with the computer is really more an interactive process than that, it is still "me" that instigates the creative interaction, it is "me" that perceives the insights made available by the computer. The computer is a powerful tool, no doubt, but it is still that—a tool that assists composing and comprehending, one that we use to help us learn, that we can use to design interactive ways for our students to learn.

If we can keep this in perspective, the computer integrates itself powerfully into our instruction. There is one further "separation" that computers have brought about though—the existence of the computer lab. Labs are wonderful, except that computers don't need to be taught all the time as just computers. They don't need to be turned into a subject like we have done with Reading class. Computer labs and classes are necessary, but the machines need to be made available to all kids for some of the school day as they grow into literate language users.

The best media usage to me is when kids actually use the media to create their own works—visual, verbal, or combinations, as individuals or in groups. Tom and his students used to use home movie cameras to make their own films. They did what the filmmaker did; they became artists and explored the mode. My students used to plan and make video docudramas and TV shows. In Tom's friend, Tom Dickinson's room, the social studies classes made slide shows set to music. All of these projects take a lot of research on a topic, a lot of storyboarding, scripting, and a whole bunch of creativity. "Involve me and I'll learn," as the Native American saying goes. We did and they did. Tom has more to say about involving kids with media in chapter 10.

13. Assessment and evaluation are part of everything we do.

When most people think of assessment and evaluation, images of SAT or CTBS scores, of objective tests, or even of psychological tests, come to mind. If these immediate images aren't already changing in your mind, we hope they will after chapter 11.

Images like those tests keep the ideas of assessment and evaluation separate from what we do in classrooms. They keep us thinking that assessment is part of some formal endpoint of instruction. Under the old "common sense" model, the teacher delivered instruction to students and students delivered it back on a test or paper at varying degrees of correctness and success on the bell curve. Under this system, those images fit exactly what teaching is about. Or what we thought it should be about.

But if you have been reading all the sections up to now, and if you believe any of them, then you are aligning yourself with some pretty "uncommonsense" stuff: writing and reading are complicated, recursive processes; they are enhanced by talking and listening, and active involvement in learning *with others*; subjects share integration points; people work well together, learning from each other by collaborating, and on. Part of the "uncommon sense" notions is the idea that assessment and evaluation are on-going processes in the natural classroom, too. As teachers in such rooms where these principles operate, you constantly watch, record, give feedback, set and reset goals with individual learners and for small groups. When teaching is responsive, teachers must "kid-watch" (Goodman, 1978), collecting information and analyzing it in order to know best how to create and re-create the appropriate language arts ecology.

These are the principles we believe in. In classrooms of those natural language teachers I have known, many of these assumptions, these basic beliefs, were the deep structure to the surface structure of everyday discourse. They were the fertile soil of all learning experiences. The ideas that sprang forth were healthy because they were well based in theory; decisions were solid, experiments with kids and language, daring but safe. Inescapably, the knowledge and absorption of sound language theory is critical to your ecology.

Teaching Journal

Use your teaching journal to reflect on what *you* believe about 10 to 14 year olds, about middle level schooling, and about language learning. Just let yourself think and create your own list of assumptions that cover those topics. Don't compare your list to ours; instead look back over your list and ask yourself which ones might rest on "common sense" principles and which ones rest upon "uncommon sense" ideas of teaching and learning. Which support the notion of a classroom ecology and which may not?

Middle School Language Arts Classrooms: Rooms to Grow

These 13 principles can be put into practice in your classroom regardless of the kind of school you work in. You can create a natural language ecology almost anywhere. Which reminds me of a story. When I taught middle grades curriculum to aspiring teachers in North Carolina, we studied the classic components of middle level schooling, and as a culminating event, I took the class half way across the state to see an exemplary middle school in action. This was Western Middle School, an open space school complete with teaching teams at all grades levels and interdisciplinary instruction. The building was modern, new, and carpeted with great open spaces; it suited the kind of flexible arrangements that students and teachers needed. When we left, one of my students looked at the building, shook her head, and said: "But you know, you could do it (the middle grades concept) in an outhouse just as well."

Natural language too can adapt to any physical space; it is teachers and students and how they help each other learn that count. But you do need to think about making whatever physical environment you have as friendly to your classroom as possible. Tom and I have seen many classrooms—all as different from one another as the people in them are. About all they have in common are four walls, a ceiling and a floor, and sometimes, not even that.

Consider my friend Lynn's classroom. Lynn lived on the same junior high hall right next door to me when I took my first middle level teaching job in Hampton, Virginia. Hers, like the rest of ours, was a room on a traditional hall, filled with standard issue metal and wood desks. A traditional teacher's desk domineered the front; hard tile floors, green blackboards against three walls, complemented by a single cork bulletin board and a lone window on the other, filled out the rest. The window was closed; we were air-conditioned. The front of the room boasted a miniature American flag on top of the squawk box.

I used to think about those hard, awkward rooms in that junior high when I, in another teaching assignment years later, helped John, Jeremy and their peers keep up our middle school classroom. It, too, had four walls, a floor and a door, but the carpet, the tables, and the wall of windows just waiting for rainbows freed our spirits, our imaginations, and our curriculum a bit more easily.

And that old junior high room was vastly different from the open-space language arts classrooms I saw at Western Middle School even later with my education students. Western, located in central North Carolina, is dubbed a highly successful school for young adolescents. Its open spaces house three grades of students (sixth, seventh, and eighth) along with their teachers, who work in teams, the administration and support services, and special academic programs and facilities. My college students were amazed as we entered the second floor, eighth grade wing of the school. As our guide herded us around a corner, we gasped as dozens of students in that huge expanse jumped into our view. In that light, airy, carpeted and spacious area, the language arts groups were invisibly walled areas. They were tiny islands of kids in a sea of other eighth graders studying science, math, or social studies simultaneously and quite audibly.

But a natural language arts ecology could work in each of these very different physical settings because it's never dependent on architecture, but on what the people, students, and especially teachers, do with and within the room's boundaries. In the junior high, it took Lynn very little time to cover her walls with posters and student writing, to line her cement walls with butcher paper for kids' wall-writings, and to collect old magazines from the library which became fuel for the students' thematic bulletin board, a collage of colorful scenes. It took her little time to paint old industrial spools and lay them sideways for tables, to break down rows of chairs into groups of circled desks, and to shove her own desk off center-stage and into the corner. More important, it took little time for the students to feel at home, to feel ownership of that classroom. There was really no loss of structure, just a shift from one of authority to democracy, from school to home. When I think about how she and her students transfigured that room, and how, young novice that I was, I tried to transform mine in like copy, I see the roots that gave rise to the flexible structures of John's and Jeremy's middle school room.

And Western Middle's open spaces did not mean *no boundaries*. A closer look revealed that bookcases, personal cubbies, a portable blackboard rolled around at the proper angle, interesting projects surrounding the language area along with a teacher and students comfortable with each other all prescribed a space structured just for language arts. But the structure allowed visibility, flow, and connection with the rest of the subjects, too. The kids were comfortable and in touch.

So in junior high we teachers broke down the formality into livable rooms; in the middle school, we used the informal space for both learning and comfort; and in the open-space, teachers built up some formality to insure order. In all three places, the language assumptions could remain the same—the environment was supposed to support kids and language growth.

What we all did in these classrooms was not only to create a flexible, but structured place for learning, but also a place that felt good, like home, because it was friendly and shared by everyone. They were all places where kids could feel daring, but safe, and feel a sense of stability. And if there's one overwhelming need a middle schooler has during this time of intense personal chaos, it's the need for a stable place and an ordered routine. However invisible to others, this paradox of "structured flexibilities" offers middle schoolers chances to experiment safely, places to risk and to fail, but with no harm done. A middle schooler's development requires such a classroom environment to exist. While going from the safe world of childhood to the adult world of risks, middle schoolers must be able to experiment widely, but safely. We adults reluctantly acknowledge their needs for social and emotional experimenting, but we sometimes forget that this need exists for their language growth as well as for personal growth.

We teachers forget, too, that we can help build a sense of structure, not by adapting space only, but also by manipulating the organization for learning. In John's and Jeremy's classroom, reading and literature were always done two days a week, with two days for writing workshops on related issues, and one day for work on individualized skills. This routine dominated, but was abandoned for special talks, seminars, major group research, dramatic activities, or personal reading and writing. Kids didn't have to walk in wondering "What are we going to do today?" And this is only one way among many to pace the curriculum. In many natural language rooms, students may choose to work on reading and writing in their own ways nearly all the time; the structure resides in the management and pacing as each student works with a teacher consciously aware of his needs and goals.

Structure—through class routines, instructional patterns, room management—might help meet the young adolescent's need for stability, but a behavioral paradox exists here. Middle school kids have notoriously short attention spans and are easily bored. It seems they need both structure and variety.

Solutions tend to encompass paradoxes, like the dilemma. The class environment has to both stimulate and offer a variety of routes to a goal, that is, optional choices of activities. It has to be a safe haven but also tease and dare kids to try anything and everything.

In John's and Jeremy's classroom, everyone helped feed the paradox by dressing and undressing the structure regularly. They washed the windows every two weeks, sometimes repainting scenes, sometimes letting bare sun, earth, and sky dramatize the outside. They changed book cards, filing them. Posters came down, new ones went up. A few posters, mainly directions for projects, stayed up, but basically the walls changed colors endlessly, a restless kaleidoscope.

In Lynn's class, I remember seeing folk-singers come and sing folk-tunes when they studied poetry. Next door, in my room, I invited local writers who talked about how they struggled and sometimes agonized as they wrote. The kids sat and wrote outside; they brought the outside inside too, and wrote even more. These "happenings" were necessary "moments of surprise" in the curriculum, a way of counteracting the stability of even flexible routines.

To balance the paradox, I think, takes a certain attitude about teaching, and an appreciation of what experiences middle school kids need. A lot of the experiences you will see in teacher's rooms in this book are the heart of the book in chapters 4–12. In and out of all those chapters you will meet many more teachers Tom and I know who are even now trying to work with natural language principles, who are trying to make the schoolroom into a natural (physically and intellectually) place to learn. It is these critical factors—these teachers and their understanding of their students along with their constant search for appropriate unique opportunities to experience language—that undergird a natural language ecology.

The Book As a Whole

In chapters 1, 2, and 3, Tom and I try to explain what a natural language arts class might be like. We try to share its "uncommonness" along with the uniquenesses of 10-14 year old student learners and the necessary unique characteristics of the teacher. These are the foundational chapters for the rest of the book.

Chapter 4 not only talks about the natural language arts teacher's place on a team, but, through describing many "rooms" we've seen, it gives you ideas on natural language study. It points to the power of natural language teaching across a whole team's learning experiences.

Chapters 5 through 11 really give you the nuts and bolts "how to's" of teaching language naturally in any setting using reading and writing workshops (chapters 5-8), integrating all kinds of oral language experiences into the day (chapter 9), and making media (chapter 10) a natural part of language learning. Because we believe that assessment and evaluation are normal parts of instruction, we have tried consciously to weave ideas for them throughout all of chapters 4-10. But chapter 11 makes more concrete some assessment tools and ideas necessary for a continued healthy language growth.

Chapter 12 deals with all the "well but" and "what if's" you may have remaining with you at the close of the book. We hope it resolves enough of any lingering doubts you have so that you will go ahead to chapter 13, the resource chapter. Here you should find sources for many, many more examples of experiences and ideas to create more "rooms to grow" in your school. Ultimately, that is what we hope happens after this book. That your classes make even more room for the growth of middle level language arts students.

References

Atwell, N. (1987). *In the middle: Reading, writing, and learning with adolescents.* Upper Montlcair, NJ: Boynton/Cook.

Beane, J. (1990). *Middle school curriculum: From rhetoric to reality.* Columbus, OH: National Middle School Association.

Bettelhelm, B., & Zelan, K. (1982). *On learning to read: The child's fascination with meaning.* New York: Vintage Books.

Cambourne, B. (1988). *The whole story: Natural learning and the acquisition of literacy in the classroom.* Auckland, NZ: Ashton Scholastic.

Elbow, P. (1973). *Writing without teachers.* New York: Oxford University Press.

Emig, J. (1983). *The web of meaning.* D. Goswami & M. Butler. Upper Montclair, NJ: Boynton/Cook.

Fader, D., & McNeil, E. (1968). *Hooked on books: Program and proof.* New York: Berkeley Publishing.

Goodman, K., & Goodman, Y. (1981). *A whole language comprehension centered view of reading development* (Occasional Paper No. 1). Tucson, AZ: University of Arizona, Program in Language and Literacy.

Goodman, Y. (1978). Kid-watching: An alternative to testing. *National Elementary Principal, 57*(4), 41–45.

Graves, D. (1978–81). *Final report: A case study of observing the development of primary children's composing, spelling, and motor behaviors during the writing process.* Durham, NH: University of New Hampshire.

Hansen, J. (1987). *When writers read.* Portsmouth, NH: Heinemann.

Judy, S. (1972). *Explorations in the teaching of secondary English.* New York: Harper and Row.

Lipsitz, J. (1984). *Successful schools for young adolescents.* New Brunswick, NJ: Transaction Books.

Loban, W. (1976). *Language development: Kindergarten through grade 12.* Urbana, IL: National Council of Teachers of English.

Klein, M. (1985). *The development of writing abilities in children, pre-K through grade 8.* Englewood Cliffs, NJ: Prentice-Hall.

Mayher, J. (1990). *Uncommon sense: Theoretical practice in language education.* Portsmouth. NH: Heinemann.

Moffett, J. (Ed.) (1973). *Interaction: A student-centered language arts and reading program, K–12.* Boston: Houghton Mifflin.

Moffett, J. (1968). *Teaching the universe of discourse.* Boston: Houghton Mifflin.

Moffett, J. (1983). *Teaching the universe of discourse* (2nd ed.). Boston: Houghton Mifflin.

Powell, A., Farrar, E., & Cohen, D. (1985). *The shopping mall high school.* Boston: Houghton Mifflin.

Rico, G. (1983). *Writing the natural way.* Los Angeles, CA: J. P. Tarcher.

Reif, L. (1992). *Seeking diversity: Language arts with adolescents.* Portsmouth, NH: Heinemann.

Rosenblatt, L. (1968). *Literature as exploration* (rev. ed.). New York: Appleton Century.

Smith, F. (1971). *Understanding reading.* New York: Holt, Rinehart, and Winston.

Smith, F. (1985). *Reading without nonsense* (2nd ed.). New York: Teachers College Press.

Wigginton, E. (Ed.). (1967). *Foxfire.* New York: Doubleday.

2

The Middle Schoolers

"Know the children."

Donald Graves, 1983

What I didn't tell you about Jeremy and John and their other friends in chapter 1 is that John is a 12 year old who could easily be taken for a junior football player at the high school, and Jeremy, although 12, could physically be his far younger brother. Mandy, a good friend of theirs, writes stories practically non-stop and they're developed and correct and get oooh's and aaah's from us all. Sandra often sits isolated at the back table, mostly doodling and gazing out the window while her partner Mandy is spinning out those neat stories for us. Raoul is just starting to gain confidence speaking out, now that he knows we listen to him and not to his home dialect. The most striking thing about all of them is how different they all look and behave.

Teaching Journal

To prepare for this review of young adolescent development, use your journal to free-write about your own early adolescence. Think back to when you saw the world as a ten to fourteen year old. Pick a year, a grade, or perhaps a period of time in those years made unforgettable by some memory related to your development. Think about the way your development made you feel different from everyone else (physical, intellectual, social-emotional, moral, or just a memory).

What other concerns or issues or high points makes early adolescence return to your thoughts? Continue writing about two or three of these reflections. Try to think about more issues that were important to you.

Early Adolescence—A Diversity of Youth in Transformation

Early adolescence—now there's a stage of life embodying a lot of contradictions. If we were to look for a one or two word summation of it, "diversity" sums it up pretty well—a diversity of outsides and insides. Diversity in physical and social development (and thus behaviors), intellectual, moral, emotional, and identity development. Diversity in preferences for learning modes. Diversity in societal and family contexts. Diversity in race, class, ethnicity, gender. The diversity of the "differently abled," those exceptional children including gifted ones, who are "included" in all classes. Diversity created by where you live— urban, rural, or suburban. Diversity caused by media images, reflecting back pictures of who you should be, could be, or who they want you to be. And diversity in language—standard and dialect. Diversity in preferences for talk, reading, writing, or just listening. Diversity is not just synonymous with early adolescence, it is the *essence* of early adolescence.

It's also another word—metamorphosis, or maybe transformation— because with middle schoolers, *even the diversity is diverse*. All those different places and stages students exist in are changing all the time; it's the age of transformation. It's about growth in one's own time.

I like one of Carol Gilligan's (1990) new metaphors, "voice," for understanding the nature of the growth going on through early and later adolescence. Her term seems to describe best the complexity behind this diversity in metamorphoses. By being sensitive to differences in the "voices" of both genders, especially by listening and honoring girls' and women's differences, she and her researchers have widened the ways we can consider all diversity. Their work makes us sensitive to the complexities of growth.

Yet another of her proposed metaphors for understanding developmental change could replace the linear, visual metaphors of progressive stage-like growth we are used to. Gilligan proposes that we consider development as musical form, perhaps as a double fugue. A fugue is a musical term elaborating multiple themes, with these themes co-existing contrapuntally, and developing with more complexity as the piece progresses. In effect, different "voices" work together in ever more complex harmonies or melodies. If we listen to basic themes or principle melodies in middle graders' development, we can hear through each unique voice how he or she works out these basic developmental issues as each one actively constructs and elaborates development (Gilligan, Rogers, and Brown, 1990, pp. 320-321).

Gilligan's recasting of development in metaphors of unfolding themes already in existence, and the continued elaboration and growth of them, is helpful to me. It captures the complexity of the individual's growth process by asking us to *hear* the myriad "voices" in the developmental areas of early adolescence. For those who want to *see* the complex networks of development, Chris Stevenson (1992) has a helpful visualization of the intersecting domains of developmental areas, one which stresses the reciprocal nature of these domains as they continually influence kids. And he points to Hill's (1980) more complex three dimensional visualization of three basic developmental areas (biological, psychological, social), and their intersection with environmental influences (family, for example), and how the particularities of that interaction impact on basic themes of early adolescence (achievement, for example). Any way you look at it, or *hear* it, the message behind young adolescent development is about complexity suitable for diversity.

As language teachers, the best thing we can do for Jeremy, John, Mandy, Raoul, and Sandra is to get some impressions of the inner and outer developmental diversity going on with our young students. What I really want to do in the rest of this chapter is create contexts for hearing all those differences, all those metamorphoses we see everyday in the classroom. And, in keeping with the metaphor of development as fugue, or an adaptation of it, I want to talk about the developmental areas, capturing within each area a diversity of voices, voices made richer and more melodic or harmonious by differences of gender, class, race, or place. We need to review those areas of development and use them as frameworks for understanding our students.

Teaching Journal

Switch from your own memories now, to visions, or "soundings," of your own kids in your own classes. Write in your journal about "who your students are," being as sensitive as you can to differences that you see, hear, know about, or feel among them. You might pick a handful of "cases," or just write short, quick portraits within or among your classes. Or, you could just take one outstanding case and explore this very different young adolescent.

Hearing Young Adolescents: The Voices of Growth

Physical Development: Moving to a "New Key"

The most visible area of development in early adolescence, and the one that inevitably strikes across gender, class, and race, is the onset of puberty, the development of primary and secondary sex characteristics. It's an outer change, a sure index of growth for the adult looking at the young adolescent, and seemingly one which is pretty cut and dried. As teachers, we remember from human biology or human growth and development class what changes occur in height, weight, and secondary sex characteristics. We see everyday the unevenness of the growth spurt, the awkwardness of the young adolescent getting around through the day. We know, too, that girls tend to hit puberty before boys, and that there are early and late maturers, and that all of this is affected by a complex interaction of diet, heredity, and health issues. On top of that, perceptions of how well the growth is going are tempered by everyone's individual and broader cultures.

A quick list of key changes serves as a reminder of this age, and may also enlighten us about different young adolescents:

- girls tend to enter the growth spurt (height and weight) around age 11 and boys around age 13; after 15 years of age, this physical advantage girls have is lost forever (Hillman, 1991, p. 4);
- the progression of growth during puberty for boys and girls is the same for all ethnic groups (Brooks-Gunn & Reiter, 1990, p. 28);
- the timing of maturational changes seems to be similar in ethnic groups unless nutrition has been a problem (Brooks-Gunn & Reiter, 1990, pp. 28–29);
- early maturing boys seem to have better experiences than later maturers during this period both academically and socially. This may be especially true for lower socio-economic status boys (Brooks-Gunn & Reiter, 1990, p. 41);
- however, early maturing girls may not be served very well compared to later maturing girls. They may have poorer emotional health and may tend to be depressed more (Brooks-Gunn & Reiter, 1990, p. 42). Forced to socialize with older peers they may not be ready emotionally for the tasks of early adolescence (Hillman, 1991, p. 4);

- while the age for the onset of puberty became lower over the last century, that trend seems to have stopped (Hillman, 1991, p. 4).

As teachers, we're aware of what Elkind calls "the perils of puberty"—the issues that arise for kids and the ways that puberty and physical growth make our Jeremy's and John's and Mandy's and Sandra's feel. From my own memories, I can recall the perils posed by menstruation and the impending encounters with sexuality and adulthood that this obviously conjured up for my parents. In fact, one of my clearest memories of being twelve and in the sixth grade, a self-contained elementary classroom, was seeing "The Movie." This was a quite dull black and white documentary on women and menstruation. No one was comfortable just telling us about our bodies; just a flick of a switch took care of it all. This was the film that the boys couldn't see, but they all seemed to know about it anyway. It was the first time my own gender differences impacted on my affect—I knew that I was different now from the guys I loved to play kickball with, but now I knew I was different and in a lower, somehow inferior way. The stares and the snickers from the boys as we girls re-entered the classroom parted us forever and set up an insidious superior/inferior feeling.

Somehow, viewing this movie was very soon followed by the real event. My mother's personal culture dictated that I learn to play the piano and my very first period surprised me during a beginner's lesson. The hushed lessons in sanitary napkin usage and disposal brought back the feelings engendered by the movie. I never did learn to play the piano.

According to several researchers, whose insights are detailed below, many young adolescents, but especially females, may associate their physical changes negatively with their changing sense of self-image during the pubertal process. The capacity for a new sexuality especially opens up new possibilities, and kids confront these with a mixture of fear, excitement, guilt, and worry. Many of us don't like to remember these times, but it is good to keep a few things in mind as we watch our young adolescents share language each day:

- by grade 6, girls are already more vulnerable than boys to negative self-esteem (Simmons & Blythe, 1987, p. 63);
- girls tend to perceive their bodies with greater dissatisfaction as early adolescence continues (Benson, Williams & Johnson, 1987, p. 59);

- there seems to be a clear connection between the onset of puberty and the beginnings of the adolescent's sexual activity (Katchadourian, 1990, p. 337);
- higher achievement in academics and more motivation seem associated with a delay in sexual activity; thus there is a higher incidence of early sexual activity in adolescents who are lower in academic achievement or who do not have many educational goals (Katchadourian, 1990, p. 339);
- with regard to sex and love, gender differences are seen even before early adolescence with girls putting more emphasis on commitment and caring in friendships and "boys learn[ing] about sex first and about its relational components later" (Katchadourian, 1990, p. 344).

Anyone could go on about the particular perils caused by sexuality—masturbation, homosexuality, or incest (Elkind, 1984). In fact, there are some very good recent sources on development that are particularly sensitive to the diversity of the 10-14 year olds who are out there, and you can find out more about them by checking Chapter 13, the resource chapter. The resources would be worth following up on to broaden this slice of life I've just jotted for you. But it is also enough to remember these themes as they are played out very differently by young people as they read, listen, talk, and share writing with us and each other. It is important to remember, too, that their physical development will always reciprocate with that core developmental theme of these years—the redefinition and reforming of one's identity as a person.

Intellectual Development: "Thinking in a New Key"

While reading up on material for teaching a course on middle school curriculum, I encountered a classic piece by Jerome Kagan (1972) on early adolescence and cognition. When I read about the young person's new "cognitive competence," that something deep in biology and cognition that "clicks" at the onset of early adolescence and transforms the world, I remembered personal examples of becoming a more formal thinker. It made me remember being in seventh grade language arts class.

Being smart on the intellectual playing field of junior high school was different from elementary school. For the first time, seventh grade meant I could not rely on my memory alone to be smart, or to even get by. Miss Moore taught us language arts; and as the paradigm went at that time, the curriculum went "part to whole," or grammar rules, to a tad of writing, to literature (or "boring to fun" as we put it). I just couldn't get the grammar, especially the diagramming of all those complex sentences teachers swear we speak and write. I wept at night over my exercises, and called the older neighbor girl next door for help. I was paralyzed by my fear of diagrams of complex sentences.

Suddenly, it "clicked" and I felt smart again. What "clicked" I now realize had something to do with that luckily timed capacity for beginning formal and abstract thinking. Even my post-Sputnick NASA math curriculum stayed fun until ninth grade geometry, then somehow "clicking" failed me.

Elkind (1984) talks about this time, too, calling it "thinking in a new key," a new time in the growth of abstract thinking. What's really happening here, as we know from Inhelder and Piaget (1958), is that the capacity for formal thinking, that is, for thinking about thought, about knowledge, for thinking in "if . . . then" hypothetical possibilities, and of the future, becomes possible if this new competence is nurtured in an appropriate environment. Young people need an environment where adults are knowledgeable, aware, watchfully caring, and encourage with just the right push, the right challenge. They need to be in a natural classroom ecology which invites curiosity in a comfortable zone for taking risks.

Middle schoolers in our classes will share in common more intellectual characteristics we should remember:

- as we know from Piaget, from 10 to 14 years of age, most middle schoolers will be in transition from concrete operations to abstract thinking, a qualitative change in the ways of reasoning (Inhelder & Piaget, 1958; Hillman, 1991, p. 5);
- from 10-11, youngsters may use more concrete problem-solving capacities; from 12 on, most kids begin to think hypothetically and abstractly as well as more idealistically (Hillman, 1991, p. 5);
- with the expansion of thought comes broadened horizons of topics to think about, like religion or justice (Benson, Williams, & Johnson, 1987, p. 35);
- with the new abilities in thinking comes the possibility of Elkind's idea of adolescent egocentrism. That is, with the idea that one can take another's perspective, one might also be the focus of the

other's perspective most of the time, thus, the existence of the "imaginary audience" and "personal fable" syndromes (Keating, 1990, p. 71; Elkind, 1984, p. 33, 36);

- from early adolescence on, thinking tends to become relative about knowledge rather than dualistic. It becomes more self-reflective and multi-dimensional. But, these are potentials and not necessarily habits of everyday thinking (Keating, 1990, pp. 64-65);
- capacities to process information, including memory and paying attention, increase (Hillman, 1991, p. 5). Not only is capacity intensified, but efficiency in processing is heightened (Keating, 1990, p. 60);
- during early adolescence, the ability to think about one's own thinking and monitor and evaluate it for consistency and quality begins to appear (Keating, 1990, p. 76).

This is the time, as both Atwell (1987) and Elkind (1984) remind us, that most kids are able to enjoy puns, understand the punchline of a joke, see the irony and appreciate the symbolism (without always being told). They speak, write, and read in tongues. But because they can do these things does not mean they can analyze the short story you just read for the implicit existential themes. They are in transition.

And again, not everyone will "metamorphose" in the above ways all at once. It happens for some learners at one time and not everyone all at once on the first day of the sixth grade. Timing is a great individualizer, too, along with some other parts of the melody, like individual ability and exceptionalities, cognitive learning style preferences, multiple intelligences, and the varying language facilities kids bring with them. All of these factors intertwine around the individual's intellectual path, shaping the particularities of intellectual growth, especially during the maturation of abstract thinking.

The other great shaper is the external social and cultural situation of each middle schooler. While common sense tells us that these situations are bound to influence intellectual growth in some way, it remains important to remember that "there exists no firm empirical basis from which to infer inherent differences between groups in terms of cognitive competence" (Keating, 1990, p. 79).

Individual Differences and Intellectual Growth

Now a little more about the differences related to and impacting on intellectual development—the different voices in the fugue. The voices in this section arise from particular groups; those of differing abilities and capabilities, differing cognitive preferences, and differing stages of language growth.

The voices of our students who are classified with "different abilities" can become very problematic. No one who has read Jeannie Oakes, *Tracking: How Schools Structure Inequality* (1985) or Anne Wheelock's *Crossing the Tracks* (1992) can re-enter a classroom satisfied that there is definitely a natural ability difference among students in tracked classes. In fact, the data in both books point relentlessly to the high probability that the middle schoolers in various tracks may very well be there because the system has never allowed them to experience their growth potentials. Early negative labeling, early lowering of expectations for certain learners, possibly based on a lack of developmental readiness in early school years that could have been rectified, may cause some apparent intellectual differences among "slow" and "fast" kids. And those labeled "gifted" have often had just the opposite kind of labeling because of high expectations imposed in early life both at home and in school. Their environments, unlike that of many slower students, reflected back a positive intellectual image.

When I taught eighth graders in my first teaching job at Lindsay Junior High in Hampton, Virginia, my favorite classes became the "average" and the "basic" tracks. The reason? They were always full of surprises. Those students knew a lot, and many of them could really think very well. They were so surprisingly insightful about all kinds of issues that came up in class. And sometimes what was surprising about the very advanced or "gifted" classes was their real need to remain children, their real problems thinking through a challenge or puzzling material. They were afraid of being wrong.

Of course, none of this is to say that there are not mainstreamed or included students with diagnosed disabilities that we must respond to individually, and there are very gifted students who need our most challenging planned experiences. They are really there beyond the tracking system, but they are there along with every other student who also has truly unique abilities and gifts. All our kids must be included. All should receive our best expectations, our most challenging and effective instruction.

As if the differing dimensions of ability, whether they have been socially imposed and learned or not, were not enough to add to their "voices," middle schoolers will come to intellectual tasks with their own preferences developed for learning styles and with differing strengths in the various types of intelligences. Regardless of what learning style approach you may use to gather information about kids' differences, whether it be Witkin's field independence/dependence framework (1977), Dunn and Dunn's (1978), Kolb's (1984), McCarthy's (1980), or Gregorc's (1979), all of them will underscore the diversity within the classroom for individual learning preferences.

I routinely give a learning style inventory based on McCarthy's notion of learning style types to one of my junior teacher education classes. Generally, this instruction class is quite small, anywhere from six to eleven students. Never once in four years has there been anything but a wide spread across all the learning style quadrants—even in such a small group! It is interesting to keep in mind that the literature on learning styles shows some correlation between preferred learning styles and culture as well as gender (Anderson & Adams, 1992).

Arguing for a continued understanding of diversity in intellectual growth is Gardner (1985) with his notion of "frames of mind" or multiple intelligences that many kids show some preference for even before the middle level years. The seven intelligences he highlights (linguistic, logical-mathematical, spatial, bodily-kinesthetic, musical, interpersonal, and intrapersonal) can diversify our classrooms. In a powerful way, they suggest to us ways we can facilitate successful intellectual growth. By not paying exclusive attention to the linguistic intelligence orientation, we language teachers could create an environment for language growth that includes chances for movement and communication, for music and communication, for personal and issues-oriented talk, and for sharing. We can build on all our young adolescents' strengths as they grow in language.

Certainly, they bring all kinds of language into our classrooms, and sometimes we wish they wouldn't. We should remember a few truths about their language though. First, language growth to a certain extent is developmental, too. I mentioned this in Chapter 1 when I wrote about the Loban study (1976), a K-12 longitudinal study which traced language growth in oral and written expression. And it's interesting to go back to that study and to note the raggedness of development. It's never all steady growth, but a process of spurting forward, and falling back, of testing, and getting usage under one's belt, of slow and quick growth, particularly during the "junior high years" (p. 80). It's also interesting to see that a characteristic development for 10-12 year old language users is the increased use of "if . . . then" phrasing in sentences along with increases in sentence length and complexity, a phenomenon reflecting the same increased complexity in thought processes for many kids.

The Loban study, even that long ago, wisely cautioned us about letting language usage differences, including dialect differences, suggest ability difference among groups, especially among ethnic groups. One of Loban's researchers said: "There is no a priori reason for thinking that the relative complexity of a child's grammar correlates with intelligence, social background, or anything else . . . so every child's language is adequate for his communicative needs at the moment the language is sampled. . . . What we do find is that those who use the full resources of language usually come from families with reasonably good socioeconomic status" and it is "social injustice, not genetic differences, [that] account . . . for the larger number of our minority subjects with lower socioeconomic backgrounds" (Loban, 1976, p. 87). We might also be careful to add to these cautions the issues of gender differences in language. So many young girls' audible voices differ from young boys' even at this age, and girls too often are silenced by our collective ignorance of these differences (Sadker & Sadker, 1985).

All these differences that both impact on and reflect intellectual development, that sum up the diversity of middle graders in our classrooms, is knowledge that the caring teacher knows. He makes his agenda for observing and guiding students while remaining sensitive to these issues.

Making Decisions "In a New Key": Moral Development

Just as Piaget serves as a foundation for understanding intellectual change, it's probably still Kohlberg (1983) and Gilligan (1982, 1988, 1990) whose ideas about intellectual development and moral issues paint the backdrop for understanding multiple voices of moral reasoning in middle schoolers.

A quick overview from Kohlberg can begin to refresh our memories on the moral development range possible at middle years. Generally, of the six hierarchical stages in Kohlberg's moral development scheme, three stages may characterize many of the young adolescents we see (George & Lawrence, 1982, p. 49):

Stage 2: In this pre-conventional stage, young people reason about moral issues using practical self-interest and occasionally fairness to those who treat them well as a basis for judging right action.

Stage 3: In this stage, considered conventional thinking, what is right action is determined by what pleases others or is approved of by others.

Stage 4: Correct moral action in this conventional stage aligns with following rules and laws that are seen as appropriate authority to preserve society.

Generally, Kohlberg's post-conventional levels are reserved for older adolescence although the stages are not age-specific any more than Piaget's. Even in the conventional level, some element of abstract thinking is required for conventional moral reasoning.

Carol Gilligan challenged Kohlberg's "voice of justice" in moral reasoning in the late 1970's and early 1980's. Competing with the "justice perspective" of the Kohlberg scheme was the "care perspective," the latter more typical, although not exclusively so, of female reasoning, while the former seemed more typical for males (Gilligan, 1990). In her developmental scheme, the care perspective focuses on connection and response in relationships as a person reasons about solutions to moral dilemmas, while the justice perspective focuses on equality, reciprocity, and fairness in determining the rights of self and others. From this perspective, development in moral reasoning proceeds through a kind of selflessness in relationships to a reasoning based more on caring and protecting oneself, a kind of self-assertion. At the most sophisticated level, reasoning becomes based on caring for oneself balanced with meaningful responsiveness to connection in relationships with others (Gilligan, 1982).

Because Kohlberg's research underlying his moral reasoning categories was based on listening almost exclusively to male subjects, females were judged based on the criteria for those stages, too. Because they predominantly value care and connection throughout development, women were often found wanting, or "stuck in stage 3," and seemingly less capable of sophisticated moral reasoning. Gilligan's alternative conception reveals another path to elaborate moral reasoning, one which re-empowers females as the moral equals of males.

What this may mean in our classrooms is this: just at the point where developmental models suggest dramatic movement toward an increased individualism, separation, and autonomy which meets established individual and social goals, girls in particular may balk. In fact, they may be downright resistant to this definition of development as some researchers like Gilligan (1990) and Hancock (1989) are finding. As teachers we need to remember that the issue of development in a social context which rewards separation and autonomy, coupled with the female's attempt to keep a focus on the importance of self-in-relationships, creates a critical growth dilemma for young girls beginning in early adolescence.

As we hear our students' diverse voices while they talk about each other's writing, share perspectives and ideas on the literature they read, and as they make decisions about goals important to them, we need to be sensitive to these moral voices in the fugue. And we need to keep a few other things in mind too:

- both moral voices are present in the reasoning of both genders, but one perspective is usually more dominant in males (justice), one (care) in females. Both genders can use either perspective in certain situations (Johnston, 1988, p. 49);
- diversity in living environment may be important in either gender's moral reasoning. Urban youth from lower income neighborhoods, for example, show use of "care perspective" in moral reasoning more often than other groups (Bardige, Ward, Gilligan, Taylor, & Cohen, 1988);
- the transition to abstract thinking invites increased idealism which becomes applied to moral thinking. Thus we see frustration and despair sometimes in all of our students over issues of inhumanity and injustice (Hillman, 1991, p. 5).

All of this may seem academic on the surface, but creating classroom contexts for all young adolescents in which they can speak and hear other voices on moral and value issues may be most critical—and most do-able for us as language arts teachers. For these are the years during which the capacity for developing empathy is especially strong for both genders (MacLean, 1990), for all diversities in our classes.

Identity Development: The Self "in a New Key":

"I ain't what I ought to be, I ain't what I'm going to be, but I ain't what I was."

Erikson, 1959

Where all this ultimately leads is to the redefinition and elaboration of the middle schooler's identity. The physical changes, the intellectual capacity to notice them and others' reactions to them, to suspect and to feel the transformation not only in body and mind, but of self in relation to self, peers, family, school, community, society, world—all of this inevitably brings up the critical question "who am I?" in a new way. Each person's identity is suddenly up for grabs.

Just as there have been a few special spokespeople for previous developmental areas, there are a few on identity development too. Erik Erikson still gets the major focus on personality development; it is he who is most often credited with establishing that it is at adolescence (and early adolescence) that the main crises points occur around both "industry vs. inferiority" and "identity vs. identity diffusion" (Erikson, 1950, 1968). These are probably the major developmental tasks in early adolescence. Elaborating on Erikson from a gender perspective are researchers like Jean Baker Miller (1984) who reminds us that female developmental tasks may be different. Others, detailed later in this chapter, add to the voices considering the impact on identity of race, ethnicity, class, and social factors. And various other researchers like Simmons and Blythe (1987) have looked at additional issues impacting on identity for young adolescents of both genders. As always, there are multiple pathways to forming an identity.

Yet there are probably some general characteristics of identity-seeking cutting across all our students:

- younger adolescents (around 10 or 11 years) are probably grappling more with industry vs. inferiority, or defining oneself by what one can do and be recognized for accomplishing well (Stevenson, 1992, p. 81). Stevenson makes the point clearly that a student's self-esteem can be irrevocably damaged if she comes to see herself now as unsuccessful, as a failure at any number of tasks or roles (p. 82). Noting accomplishments, giving opportunity for successful accomplishments, are all things we can make sure happen for all middle schoolers;
- in beginning to grapple with identity and self-concept, young adolescents "can construct abstractions about the self," but "they cannot yet cognitively compare these abstractions" until around 14 or so (Harter, 1990, p. 359). This conflict at the end of the early adolescence phase over one's inconsistencies in attributes may diminish in later adolescence for boys, but not so for girls (Harter, 1990, p. 360);
- in the slightly older young adolescent, the attempt to synthesize a self from choices and roles propels the middle schooler on a

journey from identity to identity diffusion to moratorium and
back to identity formation (Hillman, 1991, p. 7; Harter, 1990,
p. 379);

- the adolescent self concept incorporates attitudes that significant
others hold about the middle schooler; it is a "social construct"
(Harter, 1990, p. 356).

All of us have our own individual stories of this time of new self-
definition. Just writing this calls up a whole river of memories during that 10-14 year old period for me, memories of who I was and
who I was becoming. But before I plunge down memory lane, perhaps
you should too—as a way of empathically "being there" with our
young adolescents.

Teaching Journal

Re-read your first journal entry for this chapter where you
recalled a memory related to your own development during your
10-14 year old period of life. Carry that memory further, or re-
read your other concerns, issues, or highlights during those years
and free-write now another vivid memory of yourself as a young
adolescent.

I was 10 and 11 in the fifth and sixth grades. Fifth grade was sin-
gularly pleasant. It was the late 1950's, and I spent that year in school
in the usual single room elementary classroom with the typical separate subject curriculum. I did well at it and felt like my accomplishments were noticed and praised. My teacher had a pony-tail that
bounced blondly. I sported a long pony-tail in imitation, but was flat
unlike her. Climbing trees and playing kickball and football with the
guys was more fun than trying on brassieres anyhow. I remember
though being in love with one or two mainstay boyfriends during fifth
and sixth grades, enough that I would occasionally hope for rain so
recreation could be spent inside square dancing with favorite partners.
Although sixth grade brought "The Movie" and the inkling that I was
somehow different now, not a whole lot changed. School was still elementary. I did have my first male teacher ever; he was the only one
in the whole school. He seemed shyer about it than we were—our
curiosity was all boldness to his embarassment.

Seventh grade brought the big traumas. It was "junior high" and
the year of many new tensions summed up in three words: Sputnik,

guys, and hair. Junior high brought separation into class groupings. Sixty of us were isolated in two blocks of thirty to be experimented on with new math and science curricula along with 'smarter' social studies and language arts. Our NASA math was so new our books were mimeographed and stapled together.

My competition with guys had always been friendly and on the physical playing field more than the intellectual one. I had always done well, and nobody seemed to care then that I was a smart girl. Boys cared more about whether I was physically tough enough to play on their teams. Everyone played together in school, ran races together. Junior high was different. Suddenly there was "gym" class, and boys and girls were in different physical worlds. Reluctantly, I ran girls' track now. The intellectual field, never important before, became our only in-common playing ground and the competition was keener. But, it took another year for me to feel that being smart and a girl was not necessarily good news.

Junior high marked a break from my parents both intellectually and socially, and maybe morally a little too. I had called my friend next door to bail me out in language arts because mother could no longer recall the more sophisticated concepts. As I entered base systems, algebra, and geometry, I left both parents behind. Their points of view about politics and religious beliefs all seemed problematic to me, and many Sunday dinners and evening suppers were spent in debate over God, the age of the world, metaphor, and who could lead the country best. I was leaving them, necessarily so, I suppose, but at the time, it just seemed to hurt and make me feel scared and alone.

By eighth grade, I did not want to compete on that intellectual playing field anymore with the guys. New hair styles my mother had forced me to get in seventh grade, which I sported ungraciously then, became a focus for many weekend hours of preparation. How did she get so smart so quickly? I didn't want to compete in girls' track anymore either. I discovered I wanted to be a cheerleader instead and earn accolades like "Miss Personality" instead of "Most Likely to Succeed." I wanted to be asked on dates, to be someone's companion and admired because the boy I dated was cute and popular. I don't know how all this happened, but everyone seemed to expect it and dismissed it as "normal" if a little regrettable. In the eighth grade, I wrote my last voluntary short story, one the teacher liked. Unlike the impact of acceptance on Tom, as he will tell you about in chapter 3, it wasn't enough to outweigh both culture and development. At least I went out on a high note. As a writer, I quit before my first rejection notice.

Researchers on identity development in girls (Gilligan, 1988, 1990; Lyons, 1988; Hancock, 1989) have noted that something happens to the autonomous self, the risk-taking girl, before 12 years old, the girl Emily Hancock calls "the girl within." She is that being who was competent, capable, and self-possessed before the culture redefined her as female and not quite a person. She loses her "true identity," her authentic "voice," perhaps for a while as adolescence progresses, perhaps until well into adulthood, perhaps forever. Gilligan (1990) puts it bluntly, "Adolescence seems a watershed in female development, a time when girls are in danger of drowning or disappearing" (p. 10). This critical juncture in identity formation at adolescence blocks the way for one gender, perhaps for half our young adolescents in our language classrooms. It is a significant issue we must as teachers be sensitive to.

Not that boys have it easy either. The researchers listed below also look at the gender differences in self-perceptions related to identity questions for both boys and girls, and these conclusions might serve as issues to be sensitive to as we establish good language arts contexts:

- parents and teachers tend to evaluate boys lower than girls (Simmons & Blythe, 1987, p. 96);
- although boys do not rate themselves lower on intelligence or competence in school, they do earn lower GPA's in school and score lower in verbal achievement (Simmons & Blythe, 1987, p. 96);
- some research shows that boys may be more vulnerable than girls to depression (Rutter, 1980), although the discrepancy between girls' self-perceptions and desired images often causes high incidences of depressions for them, too;
- boys show a greater involvement than girls in sexual activity now, but it is girls who receive more parental guidance. Boys also need it, perhaps even more (Benson, Williams, & Johnson, 1987, p. 59);

On the other hand:

- some findings indicate that the experience of the identity crisis may be different for females and males (Harter, 1990, p. 380), and the task of identity "exploration and commitment may be more complex for females than males" (Harter, 1990, p. 381);

Some of these findings may contribute to this difference:

- some evidence exists that girls score lower on measures rating self-esteem (Simmons & Blythe, 1987, p., 63; Harter, 1990, p. 367);
- girls also score lower than boys on self-consciousness, perceptions of their body images, and attitudes toward their own sex (Simmons & Blythe, 1987, p. 64; Benson, Williams, & Johnson, 1987, p. 45).

There is also some evidence that race and ethnicity, additional voices of diversity needing to be heard, complicate the Eriksonian "identity crisis" in special ways too. Over a dozen years ago, Geneva Gay (1978) noted that the particular period of development known as early adolescence, with its numerous psychologically important tasks, was very important for ethnic and racial minorities like African-American, Hispanic, Asian American, and Native American young people. For many, this was the first time of "conscious confrontation with their ethnic identity" (Gay, 1978, p. 650). For example, new perceptions of self based on culturally accepted and often narrow standards of beauty weigh heavily on some young adolescents from diverse racial backgrounds, and they become more cognitively conscious of the place of their particular minority groups in the society at large (Gay, 1978, pp. 651-652; Spencer & Dornbush, 1990, p. 132).

Other issues pop up to complicate self-esteem and identity formation:

- for some ethnic minorities, a severe conflict in values occurs between role models; for example, American role models exhibit behaviors and beliefs antithetical to those of some immigrants such as Chinese families (Spencer & Dornbush, 1990, p. 131). Another example involves a lack of successful role models which may exist in the case of African-American youth in urban cities (p. 131);
- the task of balancing between value systems (and language systems) of one's own group and that of the white majority adds a complicating feature to one's developing identity, too (Spencer & Dornbush, 1990, pp. 133-34), forcing the young adolescent to begin a parallel journey to resolve his or her marginal status as a minority person (p. 135);
- more work has been done on African-American children and the role of self-esteem in forming identity than on other groups (Harter, 1990, p. 369). Work in this area has found that these adolescents' black communities and black role models can send positive messages about the self and can even screen out harming effects of the racist messages from the larger society (Harter, 1990, p. 369).

With all these different types of situations impinging on identity development, it is no wonder that many of our boys and girls run the risk of developing what Elkind (1984) calls a "patchwork self," especially those from lower socio-economic groups, minority groups, or girls who are white or of color. The person with "a patchwork self has acquired a set of attitudes, values, and habits that are more or less unconnected . . ." (pp. 168-69) and these often conflict. These kids especially may be the ones having problems with self concepts. Instead of beginning to integrate the self into a more stable identity, they may become characterized by anxiety, over-conformity, anger, or self-punishing behavior which may include suicide attempts, overly competitive behavior, or extreme fright (pp. 170-76). They remain locked away from true identity formation. All of this does not even really address the impact on identity development of other filters like peer groups, family units, cultural groups, or societal media images.

In Language Arts Classrooms: Harmony Revisited

What do we do about all these students and their different voices? The male, the female, the majority or minority students, the urban, the rural, those of varying socio-economic classes, of varying abilities and learning preferences—what difference does all this diversity make for the teacher of language arts?

It all means one thing for the teacher of language—teaching "naturally," doing language "whole," being real, creating the ecology while constantly reflecting on these real pictures of young adolescents. The term "natural" links with the concepts of "diversity" and "metamorphosis" because all three undergird the thriving climate and context of the language classroom. All these differences within and among young adolescents are natural; all affect the realities kids bring into our language arts classes. Each person has a need to feel at home, to feel she is on natural ground there, to feel he is a normal and necessary part of the ecology. Each needs to find himself or herself in a place to grow and be nurtured. So, what should be the natural classroom for such diversity?

As I said in chapter 1, it's natural to keep using language in the context of the variety of real worlds our students represent. We need to give choices in writing, in reading, and in speaking. There needs to be real audiences for all of these language engagements. Natural writing honors everyone's messy process, and acknowledges that everyone has something important to say. Natural talk honors the process of groping for ideas, encourages chances to listen and to hear each other's perspectives on personal and public issues as we learn from each other's differences. Natural reading offers choices among real books, ones which reflect back positive images of gender, cultural, racial, and ethnic differences. Offering multicultural literature, interesting and challenging genres, and various authors, all of which authentically engage different genders, races, and classes, and abilities and which challenge prevalent stereotypes about our differences, is critical for those whose developmental paths are "alternatives" to the mainstream. Naturalness builds sensitivity to difference, acceptance and tolerance. Again, this is the stage of life to develop empathy. And it's also natural and timely to integrate other subjects and other multiple strategies for learning which can capitalize on our students' learning strengths.

We're really talking about natural language, which does have the aim that the teacher is trying to build on the early language acquisition and development through which younger kids have naturally progressed. And we're talking about a total classroom ecology where expansion and growth does keep on going. This is another reason why Gilligan's metaphor of development as the growth, the unfolding and elaboration of what's already there, is so apt.

We need to remember that comprehension and composing are functions of the young adolescent's pre-existing schemas, which are always culturally, experientially, and contextually created. This is a theme running through multicultural instruction, feminist pedagogy, radical pedagogy, and whole language. That goes for language use too; each middle schooler's natural home language ought to be accepted, honored, and acknowledged within a framework of language learning and growth.

And while offering the spectrum of discourse (Moffett, 1983) is really important in the language classroom, it's especially important for young adolescents to have many opportunities for personal and reflective writing, reading, and talk that's listened to by us. I alluded to this in our first chapter, but now that a clearer picture of middle school learners exists, it makes sense to think about this once again in light of intellectual, moral, and personal transitions.

For such a diversity of kids, acceptance and tolerance, modeled by the teacher's behaviors and empathy along with her classroom environment and resources, are bolstered by challenging chances to work, share, and hear all the voices. This classroom, filled with metamorphoses, requires a teacher and a natural environment concerned centrally with affect, the connections between emotion and intellect.

That's why I like what Sharon Rich (1989) has said about whole language classrooms and the teacher. She speaks of the importance of affect as the driving force behind it all. These are special classrooms because, as Rich says, doing whole language is an attitude, and not a matter of methods. The teacher is as unique as each of her kids and is also growing and learning. She plays Peter Elbow's (1981) "believing game" when it comes to kids' abilities and wills to learn what's good and necessary. She understands what's going on developmentally with them, and co-creates the language environment with all of them. Her classroom is a "creative dance of learning" (Rich, p. 228). She is truly what Belenky (1986) calls the "connected" teacher who, Rich says, supports the growth of her students' thinking and feeling, trusts it, and helps it expand in a classroom open to taking the good risks to grow.

Who else is this middle school teacher? That's what Tom is about to tell you more about in Chapter 3.

Teaching Journal

Now that we've talked more about diversity in middle grades classes, switch your thinking back to your own students. Go back to your portraits of "who your students are" and add to them, or expand on the kids you wrote about. Try to hear other voices of difference in your classes, or to hear the same voices differently.

References

Adams, J., & Anderson, M. (1992). Acknowledging the learning styles of diverse student populations: Implications for instructional design. In L. Border and N. Van Note Chism (Eds.), *Teaching for diversity* (pp. 19-33). San Francisco: Jossey-Bass.

Atwell, N. (1987). *In the middle: Writing, reading, and learning with adolescents.* Upper Montclair, NJ: Boynton-Cook.

Bardige, B., Ward, J., Gilligan, C., Taylor, J., & Cohen, G. (1988). Moral concerns and considerations of urban youth. In C. Gilligan,

S. Ward, J. Taylor, with B. Bardige (Eds.), *Mapping the moral domain* (pp. 159-173). Cambridge, MA: Harvard University Press.

Belenky, M., Clinchy, B., Goldberger, N., & Tarule, J. (1986). *Women's ways of knowing: The development of self, voice, and mind.* New York: Basic Books.

Benson, P., Williams, D., & Johnson, A. (1987). *The quicksilver years: The hopes and fears of early adolescence.* San Francisco: Harper and Row.

Brooks-Gunn, J., & Reiter, E. (1990). The role of pubertal processes. In S. Feldman and G. Elliott (Eds.), *At the threshold: The developing adolescent* (pp. 16-53). Cambridge, MA: Harvard University Press.

Dunn, R., & Dunn, K. (1978). *Teaching students through their individual learning styles: A practical approach.* Reston, VA: Association for Supervision and Curriculum Development.

Elbow, P. (1981). *Writing with power.* New York: Oxford University Press.

Elkind, D. (1984). *All grown up and no place to go: Teenagers in crisis.* Reading, MA: Addison-Wesley.

Erikson, E. (1950). *Childhood and society.* New York: W. W. Norton.

Erikson, E. (1959). Identity and the life cycle. *Psychological Issues, 1,* 18-164.

Gardner, H. (1985). *Frames of mind: The theory of multiple intelligences.* New York: Basic Books.

Gay, G. (1978). Ethnic identity in early adolescence: Some implications for instructional reform. *Educational Leadership, 35,* 649-655.

George, P., & Lawrence, G. (1982). *Handbook for middle school teaching.* Glenview, IL: Scott Foresman.

Gilligan, C. (1982). *In a different voice: Psychological theory and women's development.* Cambridge, MA: Harvard University Press.

Gilligan, C. (1988). Remapping the moral domain: New images of self in relationships. In C. Gilligan, J. Ward, J. Taylor, with B. Bardige (Eds.), *Mapping the moral domain* (pp. 3–19). Cambridge, MA: Harvard University Press.

Gilligan, C. (1990). Preface: Teaching Shakespeare's sister: Notes from the underground of female adolescence. In C. Gilligan, N. Lyons,

& T. Hanmer (Eds.), *Making connections: The relational worlds of adolescent girls at Emma Willard School* (pp. 6-27). Cambridge, MA: Harvard University Press.

Gilligan, C., Rogers, A., & Brown, L. (1990). Epilogue. In C. Gilligan, N. Lyons, & T. Hammer (Eds.), *Making connections: The relational worlds of adolescent girls at Emma Willard School* (314–329). Cambridge, MA: Harvard University Press.

Graves, D. (1983). *Writing: Teachers and children at work*. Portsmouth, NH: Heinemann.

Gregorc, A. F. (1979). *Student learning styles: Diagnosis and prescribing programs*. Reston, VA: National Association of Secondary School Principals.

Hancock, E. (1989). *The girl within*. New York: Fawcett Columbine.

Harter, S. (1990). Self and identity development. In S. Feldman, & G. Elliott (Eds.), *At the threshold: The developing adolescent* (pp. 352-387). Cambridge, MA: Harvard University Press.

Hill, J. (1980). *Understanding early adolescence: A framework*. Carrboro, NC: Center for Early Adolescence.

Hillman, S. (1991). What developmental psychology has to say about early adolescence. *Middle School Journal, 23* (1), 3-8.

Inhelder, B., & Piaget, J. (1958). *The growth of logical thinking from childhood to adolescence*. New York: Basic Books.

Johnston, D. K. (1988). Adolescent solutions to dilemmas in fables; Two moral orientations—Two problem-solving strategies. In C. Gilligan, C., J. Ward, J. Taylor, with B. Bardige (Eds.), *Mapping the moral domain* (pp. 49-85). Cambridge, MA: Harvard University Press.

Kagan, J. (1972). A conception of early adolescence. In J. Kagan & R. Coles (Eds.), *Twelve to sixteen: Early adolescence* (pp. 90-105). New York: Norton.

Katchadourian, H. (1990). Sexuality. In S. Feldman and G. Elliott (Eds.), *At the threshold: The developing adolescent* (pp. 330-351). Cambridge, MA: Harvard University Press.

Keating, D. (1990). Adolescent thinking. In S. Feldman & G. Elliott (Eds.), *At the threshold: The developing adolescent* (pp. 54-89). Cambridge, MA: Harvard University Press.

Kolb, D. (1984). *Experiential learning: Experience as the source of learning and development*. Englewood Cliffs, NJ: Prentice Hall.

Kohlberg, L. (1983). *The psychology of moral development.* New York: Harper and Row.

Loban, W. (1976). *Language development: Kindergarten through grade 12.* Urbana, IL: National Council of Teachers of English.

Lyons, N. (1988). Two perspectives: On self, relationships, and morality. In C. Gilligan, J. Ward, J. Taylor, with B. Bardige (Eds.), *Mapping the moral domain* (pp. 21-48). Cambridge, MA: Harvard University Press.

MacLean, P. (1990). *The triune brain in evolution.* New York: Plenum Press.

McCarthy, B. (1980). *The 4MAT system: Teaching to learning styles with right/left mode techniques.* Arlington Heights, IL: Excel.

Miller, J. B. (1984). *The development of women's sense of self.* (Work in Progress, No. 12). Wellesley, MA: Wellesley College. Stone Center for Developmental Services and Studies.

Moffett, J. (1983). *Teaching the universe of discourse.* (2nd ed.), Boston: Houghton Mifflin.

Oakes, J. (1985). *Keeping track: How schools structure inequality.* New Haven, CT: Yale University Press.

Rich, S. (1989). Restoring power to teachers: The impact of whole language. In G. Manning and M. Manning (Eds.), *Whole language: Beliefs and practices, K-8* (pp. 220-228). Washington, DC: National Education Association.

Rutter, M. (1980). *Changing youth in a changing society.* Cambridge, MA: Harvard University Press.

Sadker, M., & Sadker, D. (1982). *Sex equity handbook for schools.* New York: Longman.

Sadker, M., & Sadker, D. (1985). Sexism in the schoolroom of the '80's. *Psychology Today, 88,* 54-57.

Simmons, R., & Blythe, D. (1987). *Moving into adolescence: The impact of pubertal change and school context.* New York: Aldine de Gruyter.

Spencer, M., & Dornbush, S. (1990). Challenges in studying minority youth. In S. Feldman & G. Elliott (Eds.), *At the threshold: The developing adolescent* (pp. 123-146). Cambridge, MA: Harvard University Press.

Stevenson, C. (1992). *Teaching ten to fourteen year olds.* New York: Longman.

Wheelock, A. (1992). *Crossing the tracks*. New York: The New Press.

Witkin, H., Moore, C., Goodenaugh, D., & Cox, P. (1977). Field-dependent and field-independent cognitive styles and their educational implications. *Review of Educational Research*, 47 (1), 1-64.

3

The Middle School Language Arts Teacher

"He teaches from the center and not from the fringe. He imparts an understanding of the basic principles of the art before going on to the meticulous details, and he refuses to break down the . . . movements into a one-two-three drill so as to make the student into a robot . . . . A Master teaches essence. When the essence is perceived, he teaches what is necessary to expand the perception."

Gary Zukav (1979)

Who were the best teachers you had in the middle grades? Do you remember their names? For some of us that's reaching back quite a few years. Names dim in my memory and faces blur out of focus. One of the things that humbles me as an educator is when I try to remember what my teachers taught me.

Fort Hill Junior High School, more years ago than I like to think about. My fifth grade teacher was a white haired lady who looked like everybody's grandmother and who taught me how to draw. I had chalk or pencil or crayon in my hand all year long. With few resources and pitifully underpaid, she brought us the bright colors we scratched and splashed across the paper and hung proudly in her room and the halls of the school. Somehow she made the connection for me between the colors and the drawing and the books in the school library and even the big Carnegie library downtown. I've loved books and libraries ever since that year. She taught us to *see* with our hands and our imaginations. My sixth grade teacher taught us how a water pump works, and I brought her a coffee can full of snakes. More hands-on experience than she wanted, I think. She was a pretty, dark haired lady who smiled bravely if a little squeamishly when we brought her turtles and crawdads and spiders and lizards and other treasures. I prowled the creek banks, read everything about animals I could get my hands on, suffered through math, and fell in love for the first time. The sixth grade was quite a year for me.

So was the seventh grade. Miss Crutchfield was my English teacher, and I fell in love with her. She was stern and beautiful, an irresistible combination for a twelve year old boy. I would have died for her gladly. She also taught me to write and created for me one of those grand and shining moments, to use Eliot Wiggington's (1985) apt phrase, teachers sometimes give us unaware and we carry with us from then on. The assignment was to write a story. We had been reading Poe. My favorite time of the week was Friday night at 11:30, when *Shock Theatre* came on Channel 2. My head was filled with dark and creepy houses, full moons, pale and sickly heroines and strangely possessed heroes, and foul, bloody, and violent deeds. All of that stuff got into my story. Mercifully, I don't remember the narrative, but I do remember reading it out loud to the class. I was a shy boy. I sat in the back of the room, and I read my story last. My hands shook and my voice quavered, but I made it through. It was a moment charged with fear and pride. I had worked hours on my Gothic masterpiece and I wanted desperately to please my teacher. When my voice finally stopped in the growing silence of that room, she smiled at me. I don't remember what she said, but I remember her smile. I have been a writer ever since.

I remember no shining moments in the eighth grade, and one ignominious one when my father was called to the school because of his knotheaded son. I was in trouble a lot that year. Coach Smith helped some. In his class my love for science and curiosity about the world around me grew. But his PE classes were an ordeal from the painful shyness of the adolescent dressing room to my humiliating awkwardness on the playing field and gym floor. It's a year I really would rather forget.

Ninth grade I went to the high school across town. Still suffering the onslaught of puberty, I was not ready. But there was no choice. I was "grown up." But that's another story.

That was Junior High in the fifties, and that was a long time ago. We are better teachers than we once were. The things I remember from the years at Fort Hill Junior High School—like the things you remember from your school years in the middle grades—were not the only things that stuck certainly, but they are telling. What I remember illuminates what was, and is, most important to me. They are memories of relationships, relationships started with me by important adults in my life. Except for that one shining afternoon in Miss Crutchfield's room, I remember almost no lessons, no assignments, only one book. It was called *The Earth for Sam*, and it was from the school library, not the classroom. I do not remember a grade I made on a single paper or for any subject. What I do remember are a handful of grownups who cared about me and who let it show.

Teaching Journal

Try this. Make a jot list of the teachers you remember from your middle years in school. List the names down the left margin of the page, skipping a line or so between them. For important teachers whose names have fallen out of your memory, a descriptive phrase works for me, e.g. "Miss Magnolia," "the Bear," "Wonder Woman." To the right of each teacher write words and phrases recalling the most important memories you have of him. It should not surprise you that most of the memories are personal rather than academic.

Share some of your memories with understanding colleagues and with your students. Write at least one memory in your journal.

Good Middle School Teachers

Don't put your journal up yet. Make a list of middle school teachers you admire. Don't worry about what they teach. Just put them down. What is that special something each of them has?

I work with a lot of middle school teachers in eight schools. And I'll bet you two things are as obvious to you about the people on your list as they are about the ones on mine. First, good middle school teachers are restless, maybe a little zany in some good ways. They are different from other teachers. They are brave and easily bored with routine ways of doing things. They are always looking for another way to do it. Never satisfied, they are genuinely innovative; and they are innovative every day. They are constantly re-creating their teaching worlds. Secondly, no two people on your list are alike. They share many attitudes toward teaching and toward kids. You may think of them as liberal, humane, enlightened, spiritual. Yet they are as mixed a bunch of personalities as the students they teach. Diversity and change are always part of good middle grades classrooms.

Teaching in the middle is a unique job, like no other in education. Middle school teachers are individuals. Patience, tolerance, acceptance, love of children, a tendency to praise rather than criticize, more than the normal dose of energy they share with other good teachers, although maybe in larger amounts. But in some ways they are just different because middle school teaching demands the difference.

Deloris Spears. The school is old with high ceilings and tall windows like the ones I remember from my boyhood. Only these windows are filled with the glare of an August South Georgia sun. First period and it's already hot. The school is not air conditioned. It is a beautiful old building. It is a good school with a small student enrollment, an intelligent and involved and demanding principal, a faculty who know how to work together. This is my first month in the school system, but I already know this place is special.

I'm headed upstairs to Deloris Spears' room. I notice again the gentle grooves worn in the stone steps. In the big room ceiling fans drum in the still air, but the kids don't notice. There is a buzz of activity. Quiet voices and rustling papers and turning pages. Under the tall ceiling the short woman standing near her desk in deep conversation with a couple of seventh graders seems even smaller. But it takes only a moment to sense her presence in this place and to know it is totally hers. She is the hub of all this activity and she directs it all.

Deloris Spears is the softest voiced teacher I have ever known. Yet her students hear her. When the conference ends at her desk, she is among her students, directing one with a word or a gesture, answering a question, getting a gangling boy back on task with a touch on the shoulder—and praising, smiling, approving, questioning, responding, showing how. Everybody seems to be doing something different, but there is no confusion. It is not one of those completely individualized classes either. There are just lots of choices for students. What keeps everybody working and all the related activities working together is the cheerful energy of the short black woman moving among the desks.

It takes me a while to notice something else about her room, so obvious I miss it for a while. Almost every kid in her room is black. They come from the projects and the inner-city neighborhood around the school. These are street kids, deprived, some of them abused, and tough. So the principal tells me. I can't tell it in Ms. Spears' English class. They are just kids, busily and cheerfully at work.

That was when I first knew Deloris Spears ten years ago. Today she works in our system's Alternative School in a worse neighborhood. Instead of teaching seventh graders, she teaches sixth, seventh, and eighth graders and some older kids too. The school is ugly, the ceilings are low, the place looks and sometimes feels like a jail. And I have that same amazement at the enthusiasm and hope I sense when I come into her room and see her students, with her in their midst, reading and writing and sharing and publishing. Learning from a quiet voiced small black woman who believes powerfully they can do it.

Malcolm Mercer is another case altogether. I describe my friend Malcolm as a traditional teacher and a good one. He teaches in a school that is really a junior high with a name change. Almost all junior highs in Georgia became "middle schools" because of regulations from Atlanta. Well, it is his place.

Like Deloris, he is good with street kids. He has taught his share of them. He taught in the school's reading lab for years and is probably the best lab teacher I've seen. He should be, he designed the lab himself. Bored with that routine, he moved back into the English class a few years ago.

I stand in the doorway of his room watching him teach for a few minutes before he is aware of me. The desks are precisely spaced in rows facing front, the aisles carefully aligned. His lectern is large, and he sits on a stool and leans over the top. The room cracks with his energy. He talks and listens, pushes and prods and challenges, shares and laughs. He questions and praises, then takes the talk further into the subject, testing ideas, putting things together, questioning and questioning again, and always in touch with each student in the room. It is important for him to know where each one is, checking and clarifying and explaining.

He is not behind the lectern long. The rows of desks break apart into working groups, and he is among them. Malcolm is in touch, wary of the kid who falls behind or misses something.

He is proud of his school, its record, his colleagues, and his eighth graders. He wants them to do better than anyone else. They usually do. When test scores slip or assignments falter, he wants to know why. He worries about his kids and he pushes them.

Malcolm is back at the lectern, talking about the library assignment Monday. The desks are back in perfect rows. He questions and listens and answers questions in his rapid-fire style. Watching the faces, alert for missed ideas, watching for understanding. Listening for light in the voice of an adolescent.

Janie Martin. Across town is a very different school, one that looks like a cross between a Motel 6 and one of those movie theatres that have eight shows at once. Here Mrs. Martin's room is a scene of cheerful clutter. I'm quick this time and I get maybe six steps in the door before she spots me and interrupts the writing conference she is in the middle of to pull me over to a three-sided, six foot tall display of student poetry and drawings.

There is no empty wall space in the room; it is all covered with student work. All of her students' writings and many of the graphics are computer printed. Janie is the computer wizard of the school. The tap-tap-tap of keys and blip of the machine, whir of disk drives and *scree* of the printer are background in her room. Publishing is routine in her class.

I believe Janie has the biggest smile of any teacher I know, and she will not let you come into her room without showing off her students. Before I leave today she makes sure I read every wall, including the "grammar poetry" and the science projects and properly appreciate each piece. It's easy to do, and her eighth graders beam with pride. The lady's enthusiasm is catching. I'd like to inoculate everyone in the county with it, and with her smile.

Diversity in classrooms and uncommon teachers. Mary Howe has animals in her room. The sixth graders bring them in, snakes and turtles and baby squirrels. The shelves are crowded with skulls and turtle shells and bones and hornets' nests and other treasures. Aquariums and terrariums are as much a part of the furniture as desks or book shelves. Watch your step in her room. A box turtle may lumber out from under one of the desks or a flying squirrel sail off the light fixture. Ms. Howe looks like everybody's idea of a school teacher. She is tall and thin, her grey hair pulled up in a bun. She smiles at you over wire-rimmed spectacles. Debbie Kuykendahl is young and pretty and looks like a model. Her sixth grade boys are enthralled by her dark eyes and long, long hair that whips around her waist. You will find her up to her elbows in newspapers with scissors, markers, posterboard, and glue close at hand. Cutting and pasting and writing, reading and discovering and creating.

Individuals. Joyce Durham is tall and straight and white haired, with a youthful sparkle in her eyes as she jokes with her seventh graders. The walls of her room are covered with pictures, posters, and writing. I usually surprise Pat Dunlap head-to-head with an eighth grade writer, deep in a conference over a story. And you'll see red-headed Barbara

Engram hugging a sixth grader and bragging on him until he blushes crimson. Teresa Freeman teaches in the biggest reading lab I've ever seen and somehow keeps it all going and keeps up with everybody in there. And Mamie Fulmore who always says "Yes, you can" and "Yes, you will" and "No, I won't let you quit"—staring down her street wise eighth graders who know she's just as tough as they are and who know she loves each one and will not let them fail.

Middle school teachers are diverse, various, unique. Individuals. Sometimes outlaws in the best sense of the term. Sometimes saints.

Teaching Journal

Identify a good teacher in your school who is different from you. Find one who does not mind your hanging out in her room. Go visit. Take field notes of what you see, concentrating on exchanges between teacher and student. Then reflect on your field notes and write your impressions, hunches, questions, discoveries.

Take the time for three or four visits and share your journal reflections with your friend.

The Compleat Middle School Teacher

Old Izaak Walton (1653) knew about compleat fishermen and used the term more as a statement about attitude and the quality of the experience than anything else. His Piscator was a teacher, at least of novice fishermen. What about compleat middle school teachers? What is the common ground of experience and attitude they share? How do we know one when we see him? How do we become more compleat in teaching middle school kids?

1.First, the compleat middle school teacher knows adolescence as well as adolescents.

The teacher knows how middle school kids develop and understands what growth processes mean in the classroom. She understands the changes taking place in her students and the physical, intellectual, emotional, and social importance of those changes. Especially the social importance since school can be a big and bewildering world for the young adolescent. She does not impose arbitrary abstract assignments on students who are not ready for them, nor does she keep the student in concrete tasks who is ready for formal thinking. She knows how children grow to adulthood and how to help their growth.

Which means if you skipped Chapter 2 to get to this one, you need to go back and read what Deb says about the metamorphosis of the middle school student. It also means if you have been "getting them ready for high school" and are frustrated with your teaching and want to be more effective, you will probably find some help in the area of adolescent development. Or if you were trained for high school English teaching and find yourself starting a middle school job, you will want to study all the information on growth in the middle years you can get your hands on.

Yes, they are different. They are supposed to be. Don't try to figure out what works and doesn't work teaching middle school kids by instinct and trial and error. That's bad for the kids and will only frustrate you. Spend some time in the *Resources* chapter at the end of the book. Join the National Middle School Association and read the *Middle School Journal,* especially the articles by and about other teachers. It won't take you long to get a feel for the real stuff.

2.*The compleat middle school teacher is a natural language teacher.*

He knows what natural language learning is, and what it isn't. And what it is, folks, is an attitude.

Natural language teaching is really very simple. The natural language teacher teaches books and poems and plays and stories rather than chopping reading up into thousands of isolated skills. He teaches real literature that kids read because they want to rather than the controlled vocabulary and controlled rate mush offered up in basal readers. He doesn't use basal readers. He teaches writing with a confidence that kids can write if he lets them and shows them how. He knows their writing will get better through working together in editing groups, lots of sharing in class, and publishing. He is a writer among apprentice writers, just as he is a model reader among younger readers. He makes sure speaking and listening have a natural place in his classroom. And he looks for ways to teach everything in related and mutually reinforcing ways.

3.*The compleat middle school teacher is a member of a team.*

Whether her school assigns her a group of kids along with three or four other teachers and they teach classes together with flexible scheduling according to the needs of students and curriculum, or if she has a traditional junior high schedule with forty-five or fifty minute periods changing at the bell, she collaborates with her colleagues about what and how to teach all of the students in their charge. The term **collaboration** is a good one for her working style. She is an independent thinker about language arts. She knows her specialty, and she communicates what she knows about language learning and kids to her colleagues as she learns from them.

She is something of a diplomat, a quietly assertive leader in matters concerning language teaching, always a learner, a teacher who enjoys working with other teachers. She is the teacher in a traditional school with a rigid schedule who goes down the hall to involve a friend in a project. And she is the teacher on a middle school team with a flexible schedule who says things like, "What if we tried it this way?"

4. The compleat middle school teacher has a special kind of confidence.

He has to reach inside for most of the satisfactions that come from the job. Elementary kids are warm and cuddly and huggable. Good high school kids are intellectually stimulating and challenging and sometimes brilliant. Middle school kids are a mess. Elementary teachers have students returning year after year to bask in the golden glow of childhood memories. High school teachers have students back from Harvard or the state college or the Marines who talk grown up stuff about books, careers, and living. Middle school kids don't come back.

What young adult wants to remember the eighth grade? I don't. How many high school valedictorians mention middle school teachers by name? How many Star Students in your school system picked middle school teachers as their Star Teachers? See what I mean?

The compleat middle school teacher draws his satisfaction from the healthy growth of his students, and that growth can be phenomenal. And as Nancie Atwell (1987) says, because they are funny and fun to work with. And there is an element of missionary zeal in the job as well.

5. Deborah says "the compleat middle school teacher is someone who wants to 'save them all.'"

She is almost a missionary of learning and humane values and emotional well being. She is an anchor in their emotional storms and a guide through the most difficult years of their lives.

The middle school teacher is a listener, a confessor, a cop, a coach, an advisor, a trouble shooter, a confronter, a counselor, a friend, sometimes a savior. For all students this is a hard time, and for some it is the last chance they will have academically. In an age of booze and crack and abortion and teen suicide, it's the last chance some will have, period.

Your students face a world where 60% of the jobs haven't been invented yet. They will see space stations on both the moon and Mars. Missionary zeal seems perfectly in order to us.

6. *The compleat middle school teacher is not a high school teacher stuck in the middle grades waiting for a promotion.*

What we are concerned with is the schools' Great Pecking Order. This is the kind of attitude that says what we really want is to work in high school because it's somehow better because the kids are older, the ultimate goal of the English teacher being to teach nothing but twelfth grade and to teach them nothing but College Prep English. The result of the Great Pecking Order, in addition to being a pretty silly notion and backwards to boot, is to turn middle school language arts teaching into a temporary position and to prevent any real professionalism in the middle grades.

There are some people who can't stand middle school kids, and some of them are even very good English teachers. That's OK, I think. We all try to serve where we are best suited. But if you are biding your time until you can "move up" to the high school, we hope you get there as soon as you can.

7. *The compleat middle school teacher is grown, not made.*

Think about it? Why are you a middle school teacher? How did you get where you are? The fact is, very few readers of this book started out to be middle school teachers. Deb began teaching eighth grade at Lindsay Junior High because she was offered a job. She intended to move "up" to the high school when there was an opening. Instead, she fell in love with teaching young adolescents and has been in the middle ever since. Her experience is typical. Some of you may have moved into middle school teaching from the lower grades. State certification regulations can be quirky.

Teaching Journal

Think about how you got into middle grades teaching. As quickly as you can, jot your reasons in your journal. Don't try to be eloquent, just make the list. Make another list of things you learned about teaching your first year. Then write about your reasons for teaching middle grades kids and the lessons your teaching has taught you. You may find the contrasts interesting.

Read it to a colleague.

Only in the last fifteen to twenty years has formal training for middle school teachers been available. Certification is confusing and contradictory in many states, reflecting the educational establishment's ambivalence and uncertainty about the middle school. If your language arts training in undergraduate school was like ours, you majored in literature with a few methods courses and student teaching thrown in. Not very good training even for high school. The only recognition that middle school even existed were a couple of days in the Ed Psych class devoted to the havoc caused by all those hormones and another dull chapter in an overpriced textbook. Think about how you would feel if your family doctor were trained with the same care.

We believe middle school training is a crucial first step, but middle school teaching is still a job you grow into. There is no way to learn enough to teach middle school in four or five years of schooling. It takes at least a year in the classroom with a good friend down the hall to complete the apprenticeship.

References

Atwell, N. (1987). *In the middle.* Portsmouth, NH: Boynton/Cook.

Walton, I. (1653). *The compleat angler, or the contemplative man's recreation.* Ed. J. Major (1844). New York: A.L. Burt.

Wigginton, E. (1985). *Sometimes a shining moment.* Garden City, NY: Anchor Books.

Zukav, G. (1979). *The dancing Wu Li Masters: An overview of the "new" physics.* New York: Bantam.

4

Building Blocks: The Language Arts Teacher on a Team

"I have come increasingly to recognize that most learning in most settings is a communal activity, a sharing of culture. It's not just that the child must make his knowledge his own, but that he must make it his own in a community of those who share his sense of belonging."

—(Jerome Bruner, *Actual Minds, Possible Worlds*, 1986)

An Interdisciplinary Memory

Model Laboratory School, Eastern Kentucky University. I was the language arts person on a four-teacher interdisciplinary team with 88 multi-age grouped seventh and eighth graders. We were all settled in a small city in the midst of rural Kentucky. The kids were mostly white, but there were large variations among socio-economic class in our groups. They were blocked in our team's academic subject times all morning from 8 to 11:15 a.m. We were the usual teachers: along with me there was Mike in science, Margaret in math, and Mary in social studies. Exploratories and advisories took up the other parts of the school day—for us and the kids.

I remember that our team planned for our interdisciplinary unit in the late spring. We were all familiar with the middle level's concept of flexible scheduling, grouping, and interdisciplinary team organization, but this coming year was to be the first to set the goal of doing an interdisciplinary unit each of our four nine week terms. But set it we did!

As lab school demonstration teachers and supervisors, we were charged with developing and implementing experimental curricula. And in 1980-81, there were many fewer models of the teaming process and of interdisciplinary curricula in existence. There had been some writing in the 70s but no blueprint for the process, or books with pictures of how to do it, until George and Lawrence came out with their *Handbook* in 1981 and Alexander and George with the *Exemplary Middle School* in 1982. Noe Middle School in Louisville, Kentucky was our closest similar school and it was half a state away. It might as well have been on the moon. I wouldn't know about Western Middle in Alamance County, North Carolina until a year later when I moved to that state. We felt like explorers in very new, unopened territory. Mary, our team coordinator, was ready and eager to guide us through, thank heavens.

By the end of the spring, the team agreed to systematically build in interdisciplinary approaches all year long the next year. We'd do four major two or three week units in our nine week terms, probably at the end of each term. We'd each complete our separate subject agendas in six of nine weeks. For me, that meant I would continue language learning and development into the three week unit, somehow weaving it into the theme.

We spent a lot of time designating our first unit. It means more to me to talk about using parts of my anecdotal journal I kept then.

An Anecdotal Journey of "The City" Unit

Tuesday, August 7

Well, I guess it makes sense that I'm keeping the team journal on this first unit. Everybody knows my kids keep two journals, one a class journal, one a writer's notebook. Why not one more for me? And, as Mary noted, since my daughter Cortney is on our team, I'll see and feel it all from a different, unique, and close-up perspective. You bet.

All this started in May when Mary asked us to set our yearly team goals. This year, we'd design four interdisciplinary units, starting with an elaborate one lasting three weeks in late September and October.

And sure enough, that's what Mary got us started on in today's meeting. We spent some time brainstorming themes and we've fairly quickly decided on one. The kids aren't here yet, but we've got to move. It would be better to check it out with them, but that'll have to wait for the other units. We needed to plan something potentially personal and relevant. Why not focus on our city, Richmond, Kentucky? Why not the place where we all live? Why not begin to see it in a new way? Our small-sized city has become the thematic focus for our combined subject area goals. And those goals are what we have to work on next.

Thursday, August 9

Good discussion today and yesterday. I didn't write yesterday—figured I'd wait until we hashed through what real interdisciplinary goals we shared.

Problem-solving and inquiry—that's the overarching linkage among us. It seems intellectually where the kids need to develop. I think this is a pretty fair summary of where we ended up for now. We want the kids to:

—understand what these interdisciplinary units are, what we're doing for this first one and why;

—think about the theme and some of our topics and questions for research (not done yet!). These have got to be real questions that individuals or small groups could explore, that could involve the whole class;

—make responsible choices and intellectual commitments;

—generate, find, and use sources for gaining information. These would be books and beyond—like people, events, places;

—find out and share something of significance about our community;

—learn a structure, a plan for inquiring;

—learn to assess their own efforts and others'.

We also talked a little about format over the last two days. It seems that the students might get at these goals best by going in-depth on one project. It's probably going to emphasize one academic area over another. This would also help us regroup them with us. We can best assist each kid according to our particular expertise although we'll use our generalist backgrounds enough! Mike reminded us though that even if each kid focuses on an individual exploration, peers should always be able to help each other brainstorm, think over problems, and read drafts of work. We all agreed. This is not going to be quiet work, but I know that's not new in my language arts class. Mary wants us to brainstorm possible research questions from the slant of our subjects for the next meeting, plus we're not through with defining and refining goals yet!

Monday, August 13

Thank heavens for weekends. A chance to relax and not work. But the old unconscious worked on us all a little because we all brought in our beginning questions. We didn't even get to the list of language arts possibilities today—which is OK. Mary's list from social studies looks like it could hook with some kids' interests well. She's preparing the whole list, about 30 options allowing kids to explore the community, to research, interview, write, talk, think, and share their knowledge.

Then Margaret asked for help with math. It was harder to think about math as part of the interdisciplinary unit, so we all spent part of this meeting brainstorming with her. A few more ideas came out which she took away and printed up along with her own thoughts.

Something else came up today, too. A little more of the unit's shape emerged. We want all the kids to experience Richmond from various cross-disciplinary points of view, too. Yet another goal! So we're going to weave threads of each disciplinary perspective into the three weeks. All the kids will probably participate in a nature/geology walk around the city, joined by all team teachers and led by the science teachers. We'll take tours of local historic city homes, complete with guides and historical information. Mary will coordinate this. And, we'll all attend a reader's workshop led by two local authors. Margaret and I will coordinate that.

Next meeting, we look at Language Arts and Science lists. Mine has made me wonder though. What about my language learning goals for my kids? Will they get lost?

Wednesday, August 15

My turn today—and Mike's. We talked through my list of possible explorations for kids. I had generated about twenty ideas, and Mike about a dozen explorations for science.

I broached my concerns about language learning. As we talked about this, it became clear that as the kids would make choices and move into their own quests, an awful lot of language development would naturally go on as part of the unit process.

All of our ideas had been designed to have extensive communication components:

—talking and listening were built in with the frequent opportunities for teachers and students to conference with peers and adults.

A lot of kids would be developing interviewing skills. More formal opportunities could occur if oral presentations became a part of the project.

—massive amounts of reading and writing naturally flowed through the research process. Kids would be generating interview questions, transcribing parts of tapes, taking notes, looking up words, terms, phrases, and slogans they didn't know, writing drafts, creating original dramatic or narrative pieces or research reports, photographing or creating poster art and writing captions for these.

After we talked and these language arts processes surfaced, I think I realized how powerful the unseen and natural learning really was, how pervasive it was even though a behavioral objective didn't hit right on it. This would be interesting, I thought. One more planning meeting and we're ready to see the kids!

Thursday, August 16

Today we got down to business and Mary led us in brainstorming final organization questions:

—How are we going to present this to the kids and invite them to be involved?

—If the three weeks are a balance of group and individual things so far, how much of each?

—How are we going to learn from each other's individual inquiries? How will we share?

—What sort of evaluation would be called for?

We tossed around more ideas and finally it seems we'll all spend the first week of three in our separate sections focusing on the city from our perspectives. This is where we'll see our writers. Our tours and our field trip will have to wait though until week two. The second week and part of the third will be time for individualized research, with a couple of days at the end for sharing and evaluation. I know I'm going to start the nine weeks right away with a unit of folk literature and folklore in general and narrow it to our city during the seventh week or the first week of the interdisciplinary time. Not everyone else is going to do this. We split up our jobs for "set up." We'll meet to check all this next week. In the meantime, we'll all talk to the kids about the project and get some of their topic ideas. We'll start involving them and see how things change.

I charted the possibilities for me:

Week I
Monday—Friday—Stories and fables on folklore
                —Writing our own

Week II
Monday—Friday—Choosing topics
                —Scheduling research time, interviews and
                  collecting data
                —Field trips

Week III
Monday—Friday—Completing research
                —Making final products
                —Sharing and evaluating

Monday, September 24

"Interdisciplinary" unit must be too hard for the kids to say. They're always talking about the neat "block" project we're ready to start. Especially today. They are so excited! My own daughter Cortney bubbled over at dinner: "Mother, I love this block." Everybody had assembled in the advisory groups early this morning and we gave the kids the revised lists of possible inquiry topics along with their project choice sheets. Choice sheets are real simple and they look like this:

> Student Name:
> Subject Area:
> Possible Project Choices:
> (1)
> (2)
> Additional Comments:

They've got all week to make a decision about what to emphasize and explore while we do our special discipline focus on Richmond. I've told my groups to talk this over with themselves, friends, and parents. On Friday, we want their options so we can schedule groups.

In each of my sections, we moved from general folklore to folk literature of Kentucky and Richmond. They seem like they're looking forward to a look at the local traditions, crafts, and storytelling all week. I wonder how many of them will want to follow this up for the rest of the unit. We'll see by Friday.

Friday, September 28

Well, after school today, we eagerly read through the kids' choices in team meeting. This first week was so good. It was filled with the energy of charged up, emotional kids, very excited kids. It was neat watching their decision-making processes all week. They were so serious; none made quick decisions. We heard them talking to each other. Some came to us. They wanted to tailor projects, establish new ones, or just check for understanding.

As we looked through the choices, it was clear that interest was the dominating reason for choice. We had been worried that friends would be the reasons behind them! There seems to be little of that. But out of about 50 projects, they seem to be selecting 10-12 more than others: the science "action" projects, historical homes, grave-rubbings, interviewing and study of local crafts, family trees, and supernatural topics top the choices. Upon reflection, the choices didn't seem too odd though. They chose topics that allowed active, physical exploration, or movement to other settings, or that explored personal identity. Everything you think of when you think of young adolescent development, we thought. These were all explorations they were unlikely to get in our traditional school curriculum.

We divided them up to manage the projects before leaving. Science seemed to work out OK. Language Arts and Math took some projects with Social Studies emphasis. They were similar groups though, so we could group them for mini-lessons if we needed to. Twelve of 22 kids did one of the language arts projects. A lot were crafts, some stories. I'm looking forward to learning with them. That's exciting for all of us. I don't know what they're going to find out either.

Monday, October 1

Today, we met in advising groups early, and all the kids got their topic, room, and teacher assignments. We immediately rescrambled our rooms. With four rooms on the same hall, traffic back and forth was possible. Peers and other teachers could all help everyone. Normally rotating the group among four subjects, we suddenly had one inquiry group all morning in a workshop, a more elementary-like classroom. What an interesting and neat feeling for some of us former secondary people like me!

I told Mary that afternoon that I thought this was probably the most important day we'd all spent together. The same thing went on in all our rescrambled sections. The goal had been to try to help a lot of still excited, very motivated kids get organized enough to explore their inquiries. Specifically, the goal was to get them to process enough to fill out the contract form outlining their question, the research process they planned to take, the kind of product outcome and how they'd want to share it—go public, or publish it in other words. The students really had to get a seven or eight day calendar together to pace themselves. And we had to teach and help.

I think the hardest part for me was helping them focus their questions. They just couldn't automatically take the topic and reframe it in a problem-solving question or questions. It must have taken half the morning explaining, giving examples, having them try framing the question, testing it in groups, reading them aloud and to each other, getting class feedback, re-asking questions, getting help from me. A lot of thinking, problem-solving, a lot of talking and listening intently.

Brainstorming for sources of information was fun though and my small groups worked easily and well. I dropped in on them, added suggestions, quelled a few of theirs ("No, David, you can't go to Lexington one morning to interview your artist, but you might be able to set up a telephone call from the school office, or even from home."), and took notes to go mull over other unknown sources with the librarian, the principals, or other teachers. Most could get an idea of whether they'd wind up with a story, a tape, or some combination of products, but we had to leave it tentative as we did the sharing for a few days. Sometimes it's hard to see the end before you're in the middle of it. But everybody did hand in a rough daily timetable today. Cortney's looked something like this:

Tuesday—Check library references on local crafts for background.

Wednesday—Work on notes and interview questions—compose them, check them with groups, Dr. B.

Thursday—Set up interviews with craftsperson—either go then or go in p.m.; work on Tuesday/Wednesday if not finished.

Friday—Begin sorting and transcribing notes to use from interviews.

Monday—Same and begin free-writing drafts.

Tuesday—Write introductions and drafts; read drafts with friends, with Dr. B.

Wednesday—Organize tape selections; write overview; make poster.

Thursday/Friday—Sharing session; prepare talk (outline).

It'll get changed, filled in and more detailed as we work, as everyone's will, I thought. And, this one, and others like it, made me remember that they would all still have to budget time for the science/geology walk and the social studies tours!

Tuesday, October 2

Whoops! We forgot some things! Like the fact that we needed a system for checking kids in and out of school and getting to the phone, getting parent permissions for leaving school, etc. Most of our meetings now look like they're going to be what I call "ventilations" and "synchronizations." The latter is the policies and guidelines we forgot to make; the former is really letting down our hair!

Thursday, October 4

What a day to watch those language goals in action. Some kids have primarily interviewing to do to collect information from university professors, public officials, the local mortician. Some are off today doing library work; they're using ours, the public one, or the university one. Some need to observe and take notes in the courthouse. Some needed to visit other workplaces, or go to local sites and collect data for their science inquiries—they'll analyze it later in Mike's room. Each day, they're writing a summary of where they got today in the quests.

The sign-out sheets and the permission slips are really busy. Boy, are we relying on parent help a lot. I've never met so many. It's better than back-to-school night would ever be.

Speaking of parents, I took a nervous Cortney for her interview today with the local potter whose work she chose to study. He was so patient with her tape and questions, and even showed us his kilns and explained how they worked, kind of the science behind the craft. We bought pottery and he gave Cort samples for her display. I hope no parents complain to me about doing this with their kids!

Monday, October 8

I guess I'd better do a little reflection on other projects in the room—leave a little record of how the kids and I are spending time together this new way. The amount of interviewing and library research to do spawned a lot of quick, impromptu lessons. My small group interviewing craftspeople got together last week for about 20 minutes while I gave them pointers and a handout on asking good questions. We helped each other brianstorm, then took our questions and rewrote, reordered them for "the real thing."

I sat with my two short story writers part of one morning last week. They were both creating pieces of historical fiction about people in the area. We talked about character, plot, scene possibilities. They free-wrote. We looked at how some writers of historical fiction worked so we could get a sense of how this fiction works. I left them talking while I checked out tape players to kids for their interviews. I browsed over their questions in conferences and gave pointers as I did with my story writers.

Some kids are writing biographies of local people. I signed them out to the library with suggestions to scan some other bios for models. Talk to the librarian, too, I told them.

I try to see their directions, anticipate their resource needs in particular. I've been bringing in my own books—*Foxfire*, collections of folklore and tales—I've made up quickie handouts, prepared 5-10 minute talks for small groups on report-writing.

We've moved, interacted, laughed, and marveled over artifacts, stories, real findings and new knowledge that's walked back into our room. I think even now, before our sharing phase at the end of this week, a lot of learning just naturally flowed across the workshop. I'm tired, but exhilarated.

And we keep learning from each other in our "ventilation" and "synchronization" meetings when we ask each other who can work with Tracy or Kyla better than we can because they're driving us crazy!

Wednesday, October 10

Whew! Another fast two days. And another two days where I could see kids doing a lot of thinking, a lot of synthesizing and evaluating, a lot of honing their reading and writing skills through editing together or with me. We've all spent a fast two days helping with proofreading, editing pieces of transcripts, reports, coaching oral presentations, assisting with posters. Everyone's helping with all this writing for publication. I'd hoped so! We are all teachers of language arts right now.

The kids are excited about the sharing phase, if apprehensive. Now's the time for learning from each other and for a celebration of what each kid has learned.

Friday, October 12

Open house and sharing is over. But you should have seen us all leave today. What an odd feeling to leave school on a Friday anything but tired, full of pep, energy, confidence, and talking about school, not the weekend!

We managed to have all four groups spend time with the projects of each of the others, plus display and explain their own, too. When you weren't displaying, you were being an audience. We all did this a little differently. My kids and I set up similar independent stations and let our audiences come by each one and spend time with us. Mary's group each presented formally to each audience and left a few minutes to peruse projects. While I think we all wanted to hear and learn from each other, the most fun were the two blocks of time that were "open house," one for families who could come, administrators, high schoolers—anyone, and a special time for the 5th and 6th graders. This chart says it visually:

Thursday:
    8—8:30—Set up projects and displays
    8:30—8:55—Share with your own group
    9—9:25—Group A to Group B
             Group C to Group D
    9:30-9:55—Group B to Group A
             Group D to Group C

And so on, through Friday, where all groups sat with their projects while the other school groups and parents came.

This afternoon's final advisory period found us all reviewing our two days. Kids shared peer evaluations and we began to make our own evaluations of our groups.

Peer Evaluations

	Yes	Somewhat	No
1. Is the information clearly presented?			
2. Did I learn anything new from this project?			
3. Is the display attractive?			

Individual Evaluation

Name: _____ Evaluator: _____

	Wow!	Neat	OK	Ho-hum	Yuk
1. Depth of research (collection of data)					
2. Appropriateness of conclusions					

3. Appropriate use of time
4. Clarity of presentation
5. Neatness
6. Overall evaluation
Comments:

I wanted my students to do self-evaluation in their journals on Monday. I gave them these questions to think about for a focused free-write on Monday:

—What was your question? Did you need to modify it as you went along? How did it change?
—What learning stands out for this three weeks—about self, the city, or skills?
—How did you like learning this way? What was good and bad about the interdisciplinary focus?
—What did you learn from your peers as they shared?
—What other things do you want to tell us?
I wonder what they'll say.

Teaching Journal

Cluster a list of goals you and your students share for developing language abilities in your class. You might use the ones begun in Chapter 1 as a start. Cluster these goals tightly in the center of a page in your journal.

Then, for each goal, do another clustering level focused on ways that goal could be shared with other disciplines, ways it could be learned through shared activities. Do this for each goal. When you have thought of what you could, share your ideas with colleagues in other subjects, whether they are on a team with you or not. Find out what other ideas they could suggest.

If you are on a team, talk to some team members about doing some of these experiences together. If you're not, think about ways you can integrate other content meaningfully into your own curriculum and absorb these perspectives into your reading and writing experiences.

Interdisciplinary Curricula and The Language Arts: "The Team is Us"

I went into that interdisciplinary unit a subject specific language arts teacher and came out as one with a difference. My room had long been one inviting active learning and encouraging process. I was convinced by educators long gone, by people like John Dewey and Earl Kelley, that learning was an active process and natural for everyone. It needed to be facilitated and grown in an open, active, real environment by a helper, a guide, a knowledgeable, student-centered teacher. What I was learning in the 1960s and 70s about teaching language arts supported those ideas. Writing was a process and the way we taught writing ought to promote that process. Reading and writing had always been a part of my life. They were natural processes and led to satisfying products, too. I tried to share that. I tried to let it happen for others, too.

But the interdisciplinary unit made me grow as a language teacher. Unlike my fears whispered, I didn't have to give up my language arts-ness, those goals that were important in my kids' development. I just had to share them. They just spread from my room to everyone else's. Kind of like real language in real life. Knowledge is not separate; it's not static. I believed the theory. Now, I felt its power and reality. Like the kids, I looked forward to the next interdisciplinary adventure and wondered why school couldn't be like this all the time. I still wonder.

Subject integration, multi-disciplinary teaching as a team, finding interdisciplinary threads, being flexible and personal, allowing study directions to arise from students—these words and phrases come alive in many of the units teams do. These are words and phrases that middle school educators have known for a long time support the metamorphoses of young adolescents. They call for creative daring and caring from middle school teachers. The "team is us" was a matter of both fun and survival for all of us in our Richmond unit. We shared ourselves as an interdisciplinary team of kids and teachers. We shared space, a wing of a building with enough rooms for a math, a social studies, a language arts, and a science lab room! We could move about with each other quickly, closely—like living in a big house. There's space for quiet and separation, but the connections of halls to other rooms, other people—other family—was there.

We teachers shared time—time to brainstorm and work and assess at the end of the day. Time together and apart from our own special hourly time to be alone, to think, to plan language arts.

And, we and our kids shared each other—about 88 7th and 8th graders who were blocked with us in the traditional academic subjects all morning, taking exploratories in writing, physical education, art, music, or vocational studies during the other parts of the day. Our advisories only met once a week at that time, a small, worthwhile bite out of a morning schedule during the middle of the week.

We came to share more goals, goals going beyond special subject objectives, the ones our subjects had in common, ones like those for the Richmond unit.

The "team is us" has become an increasingly more common team framework because it seems to meet so many student and adult needs as well as curricular learning goals. It is one of the classic models that you can find in lots of middle school literature like George and Lawrence's book (1982), or Lounsbury and Var's (1978). Elliott Merenbloom (1985), along with Tom Erb and Nancy Doda (1989), have some very recent books describing this kind of team (among others) and the ways people work together with success. In fact, they talk about how even more fully inclusive teams are becoming, how teams now include the unified or related arts, physical education, or special education teachers as fully integrated members, how teams are enfolding their exploratories and advisories in one integrated effort, for example. These are good informative books, worth taking a longer look. Essentially, they all say that the interdisciplinary team is:

—a group of professionals from various subject areas bound as a team of adults, anywhere from 2-5 people or more;

—who share a common group of kids in classes, advisories, and sometimes exploratories;

—who share a common schedule (block, period, modular, whatever) that can be flexibly used;

—who may be grouped in houses, or common spaces in a building;

—who try to integrate their curriculum and instruction as much as possible, or at least to correlate this across subject areas, striving to reinforce the common academic, social, and personal goals of students even when they are not teaching and learning together in an interdisciplinary thematic unit;

—who model caring, close, adult-student relations made possible by the increased chances for small group, individual, and personal interactions.

Ultimately, a team is a way of working and living together which puts the diversity of young adolescents centermost, and releases the creativity of the empowered middle level teacher.

"Teams are us" groups might not share all those characteristics above, and they are still teams. There are lots of different ways to do it. This pattern is one that seems to help teams function really well.

Well, so what? You might say, "What's so great about this structure for teaching and learning? For kids? Especially for kids learning language?" You may be working on a team and still say this if you don't have chances to use its structure for your kids or yourself.

For the language arts teacher who wants to teach naturally, who wants to provide a positive place and to help kids keep developing language naturally during this difficult time, the interdisciplinary teaming idea can be a real boon. For one thing, it presents the opportunity for flexibility, for theme and project teaching. And that's a natural way to break down separateness in curriculum, even in one's own subject. That's what happened to my reading and writing goals in Richmond; they became everybody's. They were still there; they just didn't belong to me only.

Since teaming is a structure promoting topics and themes as organizers, it's relational. It forces disciplines to relate, to find commonality, wholeness. It forces them into *use* (active), not *being* (passive). It forces knowledge to touch kids' lives—if the themes are at all relevant. Frankly, I think teaming is one of the most natural school organizations supporting the natural language classroom. That is what I came to realize beginning in that first interdisciplinary unit I was part of so long ago.

Recently, I stumbled across a wonderful example of the strength of teaching language naturally as part of a team—Deborah Bova's team at Creston Junior High in Warren Township, Indianapolis, Indiana. Thirteen years after my initial experiences with teaming and my beginning transformation as a language arts teacher on a team, Deborah is there to agree with me strongly. Not only does she agree that teaming promotes relations among subjects and breaks down those artificial barriers, but she's convinced that language arts is, as she puts it, "the pivotal part" of the team. Far from being afraid of losing something as the subjects (and the subject teachers) blended, she embraced the naturalness, built on it, and found her strength in it. When Warren Township decided to move from the junior high system to the middle school concept, Deborah saw the consequent move to teams as a way to infuse meaningful writing and reading processes across the curriculum of her interdisciplinary team. Her story is a good way to share with you a vision of where teams with natural language teachers are headed.

It's a Monday afternoon. I am on my way home, tired at the end of a long semester. But, I've got one important stop to make coming through Indianapolis—at Creston Junior High, currently still a 7-9 junior high on the east side of the city. Deborah Bova teaches language arts there as part of a seventh grade team made up of a math, social studies, science, and a P. E. teacher. About 125 heterogeneously grouped kids pass through their rooms each day. Creston is not totally detracked; there are some gifted classes, but it's close, and inclusion is an important concept.

I met Deborah in Greencastle, Indiana, as she talked at a roundtable session about doing whole language, not just in her room, but throughout the whole team. I was elated. I needed to know more.

Creston Junior High is part of Warren Township schools. A school of 1300 kids, it draws from a diverse population just at the edge of Indianapolis. Of the 1300 students, 17% are from minority groups. Right now, the seventh and eighth grade teachers work on teams as they will when the school becomes a 6-8 middle school.

The school lies low and flat, sprawling on its wide corner at the crest of a hill. A second floor of classrooms juts from part of it. It sits on 20 acres in the middle of farm fields. Indianapolis really is only a few mile west, but you'd never guess it out here. Built in 1962, it's got the typical flecked tile floors, lockers in halls, and classrooms on the outside of the hallways where windows line the exterior of the rooms.

They are all open in every classroom today. It's a hot, dry one in Indiana, early for this 88-degree temperature at the beginning of May. There is some air-conditioning around, and it is struggling unsuccessfully to reach the classrooms.

I hang around outside Deborah's room until a final bell dismisses a flurry of kids. I know enough to stand out of the way. Backed flat against the wall, I watch them bounding out the door, scurrying to lockers and out of doors.

She doesn't see me come into the room. I blend in even though I'm heading "upstream" through the few stragglers left. I like her room. You can hardly tell the walls are institutional green; there are so many posters, so much student work on the walls, and the bulletin boards are colorfully covered. The front boasts the usual blackboard with a huge cart filled with books, a lot of YA literature. A duplicate cart sits in the back. I'd love to spend all day browsing. There's one computer against the back wall next to her paper-covered desk; beside this there are cabinets built into part of the wall, a place for art supplies which literally spill out into the room right now. In front of these is a big rack with single carpet squares, and a big four-by-six foot cardboard box filled with more. The floors are broad green-flecked tile, so I guess that kids create their own comfort. When I see the big rocking chairs spaced around the room, I know this is true.

A table sits in the middle of the room with supplies, papers, book samples. Kids are finishing up, leaving late, and Deborah is piling stuff up. At last she sees me.

"My room's a mess!" she says. I think it feels comfortable and like home. When I came into this room, I somehow left the hard surfaces of a junior high and sensed the transition to all that a middle level experience should be for kids.

Even though there's a fan there, it's too hot to talk. We're off to the computer room, where the air-conditioner works and it is fully carpeted. We spread out her team activity sheets on the floor and begin to talk.

Deborah tells me that her team plans together during team planning time three times a week. Those planning sessions, plus their rooms being clustered (except P.E.) allow them chances for exchanging ideas and information. "Communication is absolutely necessary for integrating the curriculum successfully," she says.

Even though language arts spreads across the subjects and the other subjects flow back into language arts, Deborah starts her year with less integration and more "alone" time spent developing the notions of reading and writing workshops, especially the writing process. The kids on her team spend the entire first grading period learning the format of writing workshops. They experience revision, conferencing, and editing—all with real writing. (Deborah cringes if you mention grammar or spelling taught out of context.) Dialogue journals become a staple. She structures some of her class periods to balance reading and writing, but the students are, at the same time, learning to use class time effectively, learning to plan and be responsible for decisions and to take the consequences of their choices. Then the rest of the team's reading and writing assignments become opportunities to use the language arts workshops productively and realistically since the atmosphere in her class encourages kids to find their own topics and develop strategies to use time wisely.

The curricular flow within the team is steady. The other subjects don't dominate language arts at the same time that social studies, science, or math-focused topics may be the subject of a kid's writing or reading time in English. "Our team meetings are usually brainstorming, sometimes trouble-shooting about kids, and we don't force themes or issues approaches. We just try to integrate everything naturally."

Deborah tells me that what we have spread out on the floor in front of us is a "common team calendar" which was part of their team log last year. That's why it's only four academic subjects without the P.E. I had been looking at this in puzzlement, but she explains.

"Events, mini-units, spur-of-the-moment ideas, projects, whatever, can start with any team member and spread throughout the whole team. We just added the integrated work we did all year and this calendar or flow chart is a record of one year's work for our interdisciplinary teaching."

We take a few pieces of it, so I'll get a better idea. Some slices are two team members working, some three; sometimes it's all four.

An example of four, with Social Studies taking the lead from a Cultures Unit:

English	Social Studies	Science	Math
line 10-poetry forms are introduced	Japanese poetry forms; African poetry; Chinese poetry	element poetry	syllables, patterns, meter in poetry

An example of two, with English taking the lead from Drama:

English	Social Studies	Science	Math
line 24-IRT visit to **Gift of the Magi**	study of the culture of homelessness; the value of giving; citizenship	collection of clothing and personal items at school for Dayspring Center and figuring recycling values	

An example of three, with Science taking the lead from a Heredity study:

English	Social Studies	Science	Math
line 25—invent a race; use heredity material	invent an environment for the race	Study of principles of heredity	

An example of four, with Math taking the lead with a seasonal unit topic:

English	Social Studies	Science	Math
line 26—ransom note writing; press releases	maps via scripts; master suspect charts	evaluation of evidence via lab; deductive reasoning	Who Stole Cupid Valentine's Day unit; logic boxes eliminate suspects; fingerprint patterns; counting ransom

As I piece these together and I listen to her elaborate, I see how language arts as whole language really can work for the whole team. Deborah believed fully what I was allowed to see in my own team experience as a glimmer of a promise for the future: that middle school kids need purposeful writing and reading, not fragmented and disconnected from the rest of their learning, from the rest of the subjects. And, that teaming is the fundamental support structure that can extend writing and reading to the rest of school life, a kind of natural combination.

Deborah bounds on with this year's accomplishments and plans. "When we studied families in social studies, the students researched and created their family trees. As a way to integrate a writing/reading focus, I asked them to get a recipe that had been passed down in their families from generation to generation. Some actually derived from old slave dishes! The kids put the recipe together and they illustrated it. Then, at home, with their parents, they were asked to prepare the dish and everyone was invited to come on the morning we shared dishes. We used this as an opportunity to remind kids of social graces in social settings. We related it to math (fixing the recipes for such large groups required some mathematical figuring!). We then put the illustrated recipes together in a large book. Everyone signed their recipes and the books were given as Christmas gifts."

The P.E. teacher has played an important part in this year's units, too. "We'll have an Olympics which will be correlated with all the subjects on the team. I will do some sports literature, and we'll write stories. Math will deal with scores and scorekeeping, science with sports medicine and the physics of sports. At the actual Olympics games culminating the study, each physical activity will be paired with an academic one. For example, jump rope competitions might be paired with a language arts contest, or running events paired with a Math relay. We feel like this gives everyone a good chance to succeed, a real place in the Olympics, not just the physically adept kids."

Read-ins for parents and kids, Young Authors publications and celebratory readings, visiting storytellers, compilations of all writings into anthologies, a "Parents Sharing Books" evening once a month, an event meant to encourage parents and kids to read and to use literature and writing to deal with adolescence—all these flow out of this curriculum, connecting not only all of the kids and teachers on the team, but all of them with the schools, their parents, and the community. And clearly, language arts is the hub as the way everyone makes sense of it all. It's not the place of isolated lists and worksheets, but is the very heart of total communication.

If there was any doubt about this, all I had to do was just read what kids have to say about natural language, the language arts workshops, and integrated instruction. Deborah asked all the kids to write her letters about what they learned this year as part of the seventh grade team:

Kelli Taylor:

"... The writing workshop helps me especially in social studies and science. I can use what I have learned in English and add spice to my reports and projects. No longer are they your typical four page, boring report. They have additional, fun things, such as fact sheets, poems, etc. It helps me musically also. I could re-do a song or make a song a parody with what I have learned.

It helps me in Math because I understand Math concepts better with story problems and I can understand them better with English. It helps me in Foreign Language a lot. It helps to know and understand English when trying to learn a second language.

English and writing workshop also help me understand school in general. You learn a lot through writing about something. ..."

Tiffany Hogue:

"... One advantage is that we learned how to write a simple essay in this class and that could be used in other classes. ... During writing workshops in this English class, we went to the computer lab and learned how to use the computers. . . ."

Erica Wells:

". . . In this class we write about what we know. Some examples are how to cook a certain menu in home ec. or writing about levers and pulleys from learning in science.

No matter what we write about we should dare to be different. Individuallity [sic] gives a certain uniqueness for a person. . . . Learning to be good writers by writing different things like a business letter, a friendly letter, or a humerous [sic] limerick. I when I think about it, English is kind of like physical education. We are always excersising [sic] our minds to be good writers."

Stephen Pearson:

". . . I learned about how to write to others in DJ's [dialogue journals] about books I was reading. I think reading other people's DJ's has inspired me to want to read more."

Josh Laisure

". . . I have learned to express feelings on a book. I have learned that a book is not just to read, but to write about it."

And one other student said:

". . . I now know the difference between revising and editing. You have to change sentences and you cannot revise on a machine. You can edit on a computer and it's more like changing spelling and fixing punctuation. . . . I also know that conferencing is when you talk or discuss what you're going to write about."

And on they went with not just positive, but some of the most enthusiastic energy I've ever seen for end-of-the-year assignments. These letters show us that the students in a natural language team environment learned what many of us have missed. They came to appreciate some deeply sophisticated concepts about curriculum, about reading and writing, and about learning. They learned:

—that powerful writing starts with what you know;
—that just the sheer act of writing helps them learn more about themselves, school, and life;

—that reading and responding increases your liking for more reading;

—that revising is not editing and that talking about your reading and writing is part of growth;

—that reading and writing spring naturally from each other;

—that there is a relationship between what they learn in language arts and the learning in other subjects;

—that as language users, they are unique and individual and that this is powerfully liberating.

Not a bad year's worth of learning.

Teaching Journal

Take a few minutes with one (or several) of your classes and ask them about what they learned about language arts last year, have learned so far this year, or learned during this last year with you. Perhaps, as Deborah did, have them write you a letter sharing their insights and realizations. Read the letters and make a list of the common learnings in your journal. Do their responses echo the learnings of a natural language classroom? And assuming this is where you are headed, what steps can you take, based on what they have said, to begin to create more of an environment that encourages growth of positive views of reading and writing? Enlist helpful suggestions from teammates or friends from the other disciplines.

Curriculum Questions: Then and Now

The team organization and team teaching ideas have long existed in middle level education as ways to provide a structure which ensures healthier, more natural relationships between teachers and kids, and between kids and the curriculum. This was known well before my own experiences and Deborah Bova's nearly a dozen years after. At least since mid-century, a lot of middle school leaders have been advocating approaches to middle level curriculum that rely on teaming. Its flexible scheduling and grouping rely on a more natural school, not just a classroom. Folded inside one of these schools, the natural language arts teacher ought to find kindred spirits in other disciplines like Deborah has.

But this natural relationship between the whole language ecology and the school curriculum in the middle deserves a little more of a look. So even though this is a language arts book, here's a little bit more history.

Earlier I mentioned that from mid-century on, educators had been advocating teaming along with flexible scheduling and grouping as ways of meeting the young adolescent's needs. They also talked about different curriculum organizations, too. Not the traditional separate subjects, but organizations tempting more interest from kids and teachers, more friendly to the interdisciplinary nature of knowledge, more natural for the language arts teacher.

Of course, the traditional curriculum had been the separate subjects. After all, the junior high was just a little high school wasn't it? And the high school had always been separate disciplines. A lot of middle level schools still have a curriculum like that. You might be a language arts teacher in one. I know I started out teaching English in a junior high conceived of just like that. If you live like this, we talk about you soon enough. Even now, you can be in a building called a middle school and it feels just like a junior high.

But along about the 1960s and 70s, people like Donald Eichorn (1966), William Alexander (1969), and John Lounsbury with Gordon Vars (1978), started using similar terms to describe a better curriculum organization for young adolescent needs. Middle school people heard words and phrases like "variable," "continuous progress," or "individual needs and interests," "core, block, and interdisciplinary designs," even "fusion," and "correlated" curriculum. Even then, not all these words were new. If you dust off enough books, you'll find that child-centered schooling and integrated knowledge go way back to educators in the 1800s, and are definitely traceable to John Dewey in the early 1900s. But these curriculum terms had a new ring when the sign on the door started saying "middle school" somewhere in the 1970s and early 1980s. These words usually referred to partial ways to organize a curriculum. They were about joining subjects and joining individual kids' learning rates and interests to knowledge.

About the same time, in the late 1960s and 70s, the field of English teaching was getting a bit of a jolt, too. The late 1960s produced Macrorie's *Uptaught* (1968), Murray's *A Writer Teaches Writing* (1968), and Moffett's *Teaching the Universe of Discourse* (1968). All of these thinkers told us that writing and reading were complicated processes that people developed naturally if they had something real to say to someone real. Reading and writing deserved better than definition by worksheet. Moffett especially advocated a student-centered curriculum which integrated knowledge around the basic thinking and skills core of English. Steven Judy wrote his first edition of *Explorations in the Teaching of Secondary English* (1972) soon after, a radical book which based English teaching on personal growth, relevance, and processes of reading and writing. It changed my thinking about teaching English forever.

Both the middle school and the English educators highlighted personal and social development and academic learning as equally important. Definitely not the traditional "junior high way." Some middle level curriculum models, like Alexander's and Eichhorn's, did stress the academic subjects. Science, social studies, math, and language arts made up the knowledge domain of their usually three-part total school curriculum. While they both saw the interdisciplinary teaching possibilities there, in Lounsbury and Vars' (1978) model, the knowledge area was actually proposed as a problem-centered, core block. Knowledge was integrated and kids could examine in depth both personal and social issues that were important to them. This model had its echoes in Moffett's and Wagner's handbook for teachers, *A Student-Centered Language Arts and Reading, K-13* (1976). It would take until 1990 for Lounsbury and Vars' model to dominate the middle school field's thinking and become metamorphosed into something even more integrated. It would take the rise of the whole language movement in the 1980s to call up memories of Moffett's and others' ideas on a more holistic language arts.

Those middle school curriculum organizations are what Paul George called those of "the first path" (1992, p. 82). "First path" visions paved the way for educators to think about fitting the curriculum to the needs of young adolescents. They are all a good stretch away from separate subjects, a giant leap from the old junior high pattern. Their curriculum is based on the realities of the young adolescent learner, not on subjects. I was lucky enough to have moved in the early 1980s from a junior high/mini high school to a school trying to become "middle," trying to make interdisciplinary teaming and curricula a fact of life for teachers and students. I was also lucky enough to be getting an English education which steeped me in the thought of Moffett, Judy, Emig (1971), Britton (1975), Murray, and Macrorie. The "first path" middle level visions were the backbone of happenings like the "Richmond" interdisciplinary unit. But, it too was really a kind of bridge from the first path to the new one of the 1990s, what Paul

George calls the "second path," or "new visions of the middle school curriculum" (1992, p. 88).

The last decade brought the first of many reform reports, a *Nation at Risk* (1983), and it saw states rising up in defense of our country by adding more hours to the school day, more subject requirements, and more testing so we would not lose THE RACE with the Russians, nor our economy. That's worked, right? The late seventies and eighties are called a "back to basics" time even though the watchwords have been *reform* and *restructuring*. Thirty-some odd reports came out in the eighties to tell us all how to teach better so the schools could save the nation. Some people saw the threat to the "first path" and sounded alarms; the middle school concept was a "notion at risk" (Melton, 1984).

At the same time there was a call to save "the notion" of middle schools from top-down reformers, there were new challenges to the "first path" ideas, even more radical ones which might drive a back-to-basics person as silly as the simultaneously burgeoning whole language movement must. They are new visions which the language arts teacher, alone or with a team, in a middle school or a junior high, ought to be aware of. Just as the middle level and English curricula of 1960s and 70s were in part reactions to the program rigidity caused by the Cold War, so are these newer ideas reactions in part to short-sighted top-down reforms from the President's and the Governor's office.

Other reasons buoy up the "second path" middle level visions though. They are very similar to the assumptions behind the whole language movement:

—knowledge is constructed actively; it's not sets of isolated information;

—processes are important—the process of thinking, writing, reading, and of inquiring;

—developmental appropriateness is "where instruction is at";

—subjective and objective, affect and cognition are inseparable. Translation: the personal concerns of young adolescents are central to education. The whole of the learning act is important, whole people in natural environments learning about self and others in an unfragmented way across an integrated day.

The middle school educators clearing the "second path" in the 1980s and 90s build on those roots from the 60s and 70s, those first steps away from separate subjects. Likewise the whole language movement and process language arts teachers of the 1980s and 90s who base their ideas on Kenneth Goodman (1986), Donald Graves (1983), and Nancy Atwell (1987) also build upon the personal relevance and integration thrusts in the field of English during the 1970s. At the middle level, Chris Stevenson (1992), Ed Brazee (1992), John Arnold (1985, 1991), and James Beane (1990) all lead us down a new path toward a curriculum world where problem and theme-centered inquiry and process dominate the kid's whole day. They are applauded by some of the same people on the first path like Lounsbury (1991) and Vars (1987) whose knowledge domains always focused on core and interdisciplinary ideas. They are compatible with natural language classrooms inhabited by Deborah Bova and her colleagues. These voices all join together, and we hear in most of them the possibility of interdisciplinary approaches becoming the totally integrated curriculum.

Most of the middle school second pathers don't go in for diagrams of curriculum organizations. Chris Stevenson in fact said there is no one curriculum model or framework (1991). But they're pretty big on lists of principles to help us out. They agree on a few more ideas beyond those I listed earlier. I don't think you'll find these ideas incompatible with teaching language arts naturally either:

—The curriculum must deal with, even center on, the young adolescent's questions, significant ones about adolescent and societal issues, or about problems and moral concerns. Questions integrating self and world are the basis of curriculum. And these significant relevant questions form the basis of intelligent inquiry, of a problem-solving approach to knowledge which merges intellectual development and academic learning inside healthy, curious exploration.

—Such a curriculum depends not only on the beliefs that knowledge is interdisciplinary and it's actively made by the learner, but on a teacher who knows these kids and who values the integrated focus on real world, relevant concerns, who values the notion that skills are learned by "doing" purposeful application and are means to ends, who values the belief that all individuals learn differently and that the curriculum must be flexible enough for this.

—Such a curriculum may lead to integration of the whole, that is of the advisory, the exploratory and academic/skills learnings aspects of the whole kid's whole day.

While some of the second pathers push to retain a place for the subjects (Arnold, 1991), at least one of them, James Beane (1990), thinks about total integration nearly all the time. He says the middle school should ultimately be a "general education" school, a place where the total curriculum is one based on "emerging needs" and "social problems" approaches to curriculum (George, Stevenson, Thomason, and Beane, 1992). Departing a little from the others, Beane does draw us a graphic version of this vision. Probably the most radical of the new visions, his curriculum embraces the themes arising from the intersection of personal and social concerns, and these themes always connect with and help develop personal, social, and technical skills along with the kids' concepts of democracy, human dignity, and cultural diversity. Those are pervasive ideas embedded throughout the curriculum. And teachers are integrating their curricula this way. For some slices of this reality, check out Chris Stevenson's and Judy Carr's *Integrated Studies in the Middle Grades: Dancing Through Walls* (1993).

The focus is still on creating schools and classrooms which meet the needs of diverse emerging adolescents. Whatever the path, it keeps headed that way. It's a good direction, the only one for us. The middle school curriculum just keeps getting friendlier to the natural language teacher. It's the place to be.

Just like the new curriculum visions, whole language ideas for the 1980s and 90s argue for a program arising from kids and teachers, real books, and real writing, not texts and ready-made programs. Whole language argues, too, for skills developed naturally as kids explore with language what means most to them. If integrated curricula and interdisciplinary teaming can offer a structure to relate language arts to everything, certainly a flexible curriculum pushes us all in more natural learning directions, too.

But, if you do teach in a different framework, the rest of this book is for you, too.

Other Patterns, or "The Team is Me," or "The Team is We Two"

Many natural language teachers I see seem to work by themselves in their own classroom. Sometimes they work in a departmentalized junior high, middle, or intermediate school with 6-8th, or 6-7th grades. Sometimes they work in an elementary school and have their 5th and 6th grade young adolescents for nearly the whole day in a self-contained room. Sometimes they work in integrated dual subject blocks (usually language arts and social studies, with reading thrown in). They do the integration themselves. Occasionally, there's a two-person team doing that.

None of these patterns is really new. I even remember being a seventh grader in a team in 1962. We had four academic subjects blocked in the morning and early afternoon, with two teachers sharing us. One taught science and language arts, one taught social studies and math. I don't remember any integration within blocks, any interdisciplinary teaming, or even a little correlation. But the chance was there.

Any of these arrangements allow us to offer an integrated approach to our subjects. We can focus on topics, themes, concerns, or projects. We can come closer to kids' interests, concerns, and development if we value the spirit of interdisciplinary work and natural language.

Portraits: The "Team is Me"—Part I

If you haven't picked up Linda Rief's book, *Seeking Diversity: Language Arts with Adolescents* (1992), you ought to add it to your shelf right next to Nancie Atwell's *In the Middle* (1987). I mentioned both of these in Chapter 1 and I have a longer summary on them in Chapter 13. Linda Rief is an 8th grade teacher at Oyster River Middle School in New Hampshire. She doesn't work on an interdisciplinary team. She and her kids manage in her room day after day to live and love language. Her classroom is different from Atwell's, as it is from all of ours. Her title reminds us about diversity. She, her kids, her school, her community, are different. They're unique.

Her classroom is clearly a natural language one. Her kids are immersed in reading and writing. They read literature, together and individually, and are read to by their teacher. They write about it, write to real people about real events and emotions. They're often out in the community where they talk to people and share their works beyond the classroom. They read each other's journals, write letters to authors, submit their best writing from their portfolios to literary magazines. And get accepted. They help maintain their own classroom library, even bind their own books occasionally. They do art. There's a continous self-assessment process. They feel successes and they grow. As far as I can tell, they do this without the crutch of the traditional textbooks, workbooks, spelling and vocabulary lists, and reading comprehension drills.

A version of integration happens here, too, even though her "team" is herself and her kids. For one thing, some of it revolves around themes which blend social studies concepts with language arts. The kids seem to really get caught up in one called "Generations." That focuses a lot of the reading, writing, and oral language on both an exploration of the elderly and on adolescence, their own time of life. They visit homes, write and read, give oral talks, play simulations and choose their own topical literature to read. Lots of growing empathy develops through many chances to compare lives and to come to understand one another.

Some projects come from the individual student, projects which integrate disciplines naturally as kids explore important interests. It's sort of like the individual interests and continous progress kind of curriculum that the middle school experts talked about. Topics like "Indians and the American West" (Ch. 6) seem to draw together another culture, another history through reading literature and doing all kinds of writing. The kids' questions drive these options. Their need to explore, communicate and develop their thinking and language does this. A kind of combination of the "personal" domain of curriculum with the "academics" and "skills" domains happens.

If you are alone, with no team, and teaching language arts, you can focus on topics and questions too. While this may not be an integrated curriculum in some senses, it helps you and the kids touch each other's lives. You can at least point the way to integration. And if the class is natural, it will be about exploring real questions with natural talking, reading, and writing. Bottom line, natural is what really counts.

Portraits: "The Team is Me"—Part II

Pat Stull is a fifth grade teacher at Hose Elementary school in Crawfordsville, Indiana. Her classroom is on the very back of the school at the end of a hall. It's nice. She's either next to or across from the combined third-fourth grade class, the other fifth grade, and the Music teacher. She's also next to the wide end door leading to a large field outside. A perfect set up. A combination of possible company and an easy route to freedom.

The first morning I came to observe Pat's class, the room was already buzzing with chatter of happy, busy fifth graders. Fifteen 10 and 11 year olds moved around her room or wrote in their journals before school—eight boys, seven girls.

The room is carpeted an aqua green. There are desks, but they are long, rectangular, and very moveable. Right now, the desks are arranged in squares facing the front where a long board rests on the wall, framed by the big curriculum integrating theme of the fifth grade year, "Freedom."

Pat and many of her colleagues in the city system's K-12 Accelerated and Enriched program organize the curriculum around overarching themes. They generated this integration device all together, led by their system director of A & E programs and borrowing from the work of Adler and his syntopican (1952). The K-12 theme is "The Human Quest for Understanding" and there are specific themes at each grade level, all serving as focuses in some way on the main K-12 theme. The specific organizer for the fifth grade's curriculum is "Freedom." That's why I'm looking at the word now dominating the front bulletin board in its big red letters. It stays visible all year. Both these overarching frameworks help link all subjects to one focus.

Each nine weeks, the subjects are dominated by a different generalization related to "freedom." For language arts, the four nine weeks' focuses are: (1) People search for freedom; (2) Freedom allows exploration; (3) Preservation of freedom requires courage; (4) Independence is obtained through conflict. Each of the other subjects' generalizations overlap with each other each nine weeks. They may be stated slightly differently but the central idea spans everything.

For example, the second nine weeks Pat tells me is dominated by *exploration*, the third by *courage*, and the fourth by the role of *conflict* in becoming independent. So not only does the curriculum hark back to "freedom," but it uses materials, activities, and projects to focus on freedom through exploration, through courage, through conflict resolution. Not everybody uses the thematic focuses to integrate the subjects, to blur the lines between social studies, science, language arts, and math, but the promise of and ease for integrating traditional subject lines always exists.

Pat and the kids working during the second nine weeks reveals a good example of a combination of multidisciplinary and integrated thematic teaching. The fifth graders have moved into a new aspect of their thematic study dealing now with the injustice and intolerance some people face when striving for freedom. Pat's class will be multidisciplinary and integrated from two perspectives:

—The theme easily correlates language arts with social studies. As a group, the kids will be reading some Bradbury and Dickens and studying ancient Central and North American Indian cultures. Research-focused journal entries and discussion highlight the themes in contemporary times, Victorian England, and ancient ages, sending the message of common humanity across the school day.

—Reading and writing specific to social studies projects weaves through the day, too. Groups of fifth graders might pursue research on one of the ancient cultures they choose to study, but the processes of reading for meaning and drafting, revising, and editing for presentation or publication will take an equal seat in teaching and learning. Like Deborah Bova's seventh graders, the fifth graders will draft, redraft, use peer editing, and conference with Pat as they prepare their writing. They'll read only real sources, real literature, and not basal texts. In this case, the thematic focus allows a fully integrated approach to occur.

Perhaps language keeps growing in a third way, too. Not every single solitary aspect of classroom life revolves around the thematic focus. Individual readers and writers continue to grow in their own directions, with their own interests, their own rates of growth, their own needs. Individual reading and writing still goes on, gets logged in reading folders or placed for later scrutiny in working portfolios along with unfinished research and report drafts on the theme. The portfolio itself is an integrating mechanism.

I watch one afternoon as groups of kids work together, researching information on a Central or North American Indian culture. The five groups each work on proposals first—what they expect to find, in what composed form they expect to present it and teach it to the class.

Lists of ideas and materials needed to work on visual aids come in to Pat. Groups mill around, trying to settle at their tables, trying to ready themselves to research.

There are dozens of books at each table, each grouping on one particular culture. One group is off to the library to collect more books. Some are promising to use the CD-Roms at the libraries. Everyone's chosen a specific assignment within each group. They read aloud to each other as they take down information.

Days later, groups are ready and have scheduled themselves for the class. In every case, it's a multi-media exhibition: long written reports, visual aids including overhead material, charts, maps, re-created artifacts. Everyone in each group takes part.

On another afternoon I'm there, Brad, Brian, and Christy teach us about the Mayans, while the rest of the class listens and then evaluates the group's presentation. Each has an oral explanation drawn from their group report. The class is busy jotting notes—and comments. It's very quiet. Brad explains the Mayan migration from Asia to Central America using the group's chart. A clay diorama allows them to demonstrate the cultural custom of sacrifice. They handle questions at the end, showing even more detail about what they learned.

Evaluation is quite simple really. It's positive peer feedback for each group. The rest of the class evaluated "one thing the group did well" in "content" and "presentation" skills. Everyone writes self-evaluations, too, all of which Pat considers as she generates a more comprehensive evaluation.

Reading and writing for purposes, researching and problem-solving, discovering, talking, listening and planning—these common threads pull language and other contents together normally as I discovered with my team's interdisciplinary unit and as Deborah Bova discovered with hers. And in some ways, if "me" is the team and the students are with me for flexible and lengthy amounts of time, everyone moves even more smoothly and quickly toward integration of self and knowledge.

Portraits: The "Team Is We Two"

Tom says he has seen interdisciplinary teaming develop naturally from two teachers on a team spontaneously deciding to team teach a unit. No one mandates a certain number of interdisciplinary or multidisciplinary units, or fully integrated studies across the school day. But teachers he works with often naturally gravitate to teaming.

A lot of formally organized teams in schools are two person teams— usually one person is a math/science teacher, another is a language arts/social studies one. Jeanneine Jones swears by two person teams. If you read the *Middle School Journal* at all from 1990-92, you would probably remember her "Teacher to Teacher" column. She often wrote in her column about the natural language learning opportunities they gave their students. Jeanneine was that language arts/social studies teacher on a two-person team at Western Middle School in Alamance County, North Carolina. That's a school I mentioned briefly back in Chapter 1 as an exemplary middle school.

Often Jeanneine integrates her own subject focuses, language arts and social studies, such as when kids compose and write stories as part of her "Recording Cultures, Recording Memories, Recording Self" integrated unit. This is when kids create stories of a fictional person. They draft, revise, peer edit, then edit the story for mechanics. And, Jeanneine brings this natural focus on language, this process approach, to all the work she and teammate Janet Thompson do with their kids.

In one of her columns, Jeanneine describes an interdisciplinary unit Janet and she did that integrated reading and writing naturally in an interdisciplinary study of the Desert Storm war (1991). In a fashion true to naturally taught interdisciplinary units, this one grew out of student needs and concerns and lasted as long as the kids needed it. Their plans included all the disciplines: obviously social studies, but also a study of oil and its abundance in the Middle East integrated a science focus, too. And reading and writing was significant and natural—from researching the life of Hussein to compiling, as small groups, these readings into a bibliographic portrait of the Iraqui leader. Journal responses helped clarify readings and fed discussions, and activities like the class press conferences encouraged listening abilities. In this unit, neither Jeanneine nor Janet sidestepped the importance of dealing with emotions on a substantive but highly relevant topic, and language growth occurred as kids used their opportunities to read and write meaningfully. Pick up the article and read the whole thing. She's eloquent about what they all realized and learned.

Jeanneine and Janet created other interdisciplinary units, many times spontaneously in response to student interest and needs. And even when the focus shifts more toward Math or Science, natural writing and reading weaves through the curriculum. Another unit on the 1989 San Francisco earthquake was brief but made heavy use of student journals. Janet outlines a few of the ways:

(1) Students come into the team-room the first day and immediately see a fault-line running down the middle of the floor. A TV monitor plays footage of the quake in the background. Students write "instant reaction" journal entries.

(2) Students write about their experiences from the point of view of someone in San Francisco. They choose their own views and compose their own situations.

(3) These personal responses are the beginning of a self-composed booklet constructed over the course of the short unit. Lectures, speakers, and readings from *National Geographic*, all of which sharpen thinking and writing, continue the unit along with more journal entries across the next topics and next days.

(4) Another reading-writing focus is library research on nearby earthquakes (involving a Math focus), which also becomes part of the booklet.

(5) The final part of the unit is putting together the book. A partial table of contents reveals that both process and product is valuable:

—Writing: drafts and final copies;
—Final research paper from magazine article, and notes gathered along with sources used;
—math papers;
—student evaluations of the IDU;

For Jeanneine's and Janet's kids, the work is relevant, meaningful, and responsive. The language growth happens, sometimes without a lot of overt attention being paid to it, without a piece of paper with "9/10 correct" marked on it.

When I think back about the times when our "team is us" worked with just "we two," it was manageable and still exciting. On some units only Mary and I worked together. One spring, we agreed to teach an integrated social studies-language arts unit on famous regional biographies. The kids were to select a famous Kentucky person, a list which would be brainstormed by them with Mary in their social studies hour. I would teach them lessons on using the library, research skills, and documentation. Both of us decided to block our class section together, making a two hour long section available to kids, so that, as they plowed into the reading, researching, and drafting, they would have a longer period of time to really get into their explorations—and they had more time to work with Mary, me, and with each other.

My students already experienced writing as a process and reading real pieces of literature. We had spent the earlier part of the fall free-writing, brainstorming, cubing and looping for ideas and learning our ways into topics and journal-keeping along with learning to respond to each other's writing helpfully by using Elbow's (1973) helping circle model. Our students knew they would draft and revise their work, work many of them were interested in because, even though it was a class project, it was self-chosen exploration. And they had us and each other to help.

Doing the "team is we two" was natural, normal, and fun. It was easy. Our rooms were next to each other; we had come to know each other well and to feel comfortable supporting each other's instruction. We had come to see that reading, writing, talking, thinking, problem-solving, and researching were not just the province of social studies or language arts, but were acts of human communication and literacy in social settings, acts which permitted growth in society and knowledge and appreciation of our common history.

Sometimes, as we see, people organized as teams help reinforce each other's curriculum. But too often the language arts teacher settles for ladling out the right skills to use for everyone else's project, for forking over agreeably the vocabulary needed by the science or the social studies teacher. We need to change that. We need to witness to the power of doing language actively and naturally in all disciplines. Just like Linda Rief and Pat Stull did when their classes focused on the exploration of real issues, supported by real reading and writing. Just like Jeanneine and Janet at Western Middle. And most of all, consciously integrating it, teaching it to the team like Deborah Bova did with her team at Creston Junior High. Maybe more of us can help people see the power of keeping journals, of keeping student writing of all kinds, in all stages of the process, in folders, in portfolios, wherever it can grow over time. Maybe they can taste with their students the thrill of reading excitedly, of researching real questions, of talking about interesting things to each other, of testing and growing our thinking everywhere on the team.

It just seems that when there's a natural language teacher involved, that the language growth seeps through those classroom walls and starts to permeate those science, social studies, and math classes. Learning logs grow overnight in science or math. Kids start writing narratives in science—stories mind you, not reports or labs. Math journals become commonplace. I know this happens; just listening to Deborah Bova talk about her team called up all these thoughts for me. If you are all set to do this, but feel you are lacking all the natural language tools you need, then you really need to pay attention to Tom's next four chapters carefully. They are your blueprint for creating reading and writing workshops, for creating a language arts ecology, which, once growing and vibrant, can spread healthy and lively language growth to the rest of the team.

Teaching Journal

Go back to your first journal entry for this chapter. Select one experience, topic, or unit idea that could integrate content in your own class, or that could be a shared theme you might work on with a friend as a twosome or that your team could create. Try it out and keep an anecdotal log as the teaching/learning process unfolds.

Come back to your journal at the conclusion of the project and reflect on the experience. What differences did this approach make in your students' interest, in their language growth, or in their knowledge growth?

Beginnings

Tom and I will leave you now like Charles Kuralt used to on *Sunday Morning*—with a picture. Sometimes, language arts teachers work in a total way with the total school with all the kids.

It's sometimes still cold in Indiana in April. But that's when Earth Day comes, so that's the period when students and teachers at Tuttle Middle School participate in a school-wide Ecology Unit. Rain or shine, cold or hot, for two weeks the whole school relates its studies each day to ecology. Teams of teachers and students decide how to integrate ecology themes and contents. They decide how much, whether there are total interdisciplinary projects planned and explored, or whether each teacher on the team will simply integrate her subject with the themes. Within this one unit focus, we might see multidisciplinary or fully integrated curricula from any team perspective I have talked about.

Some cross-school projects do occur: Everyone attends the opening convocation on "The Environment: It's Where We Live," provided by the Bureau of Lecture and Concert Artists; the whole school participates in a recycling project; all kids do a community trash pickup project, supervised by police and Park and Recreation officials, and coordinated with the Sanitation Department; ecology posters go up all over the school; the morning announcer's daily trivia questions promote ecological awareness; the whole school throws a picnic, with careful cleanup stressed of course; and there's usually a final celebratory school slide show of kids doing varied ecology unit activities across the whole curriculum. It's set to music with scripts written by the language arts classes. But mainly teams of teachers and students decide where on the ecology continuum they will fall from year to year.

I come in from the rain on the first day of this year's unit. Debbie Hatke, one of Tuttle's special education teachers, coordinates the school-wide unit's progress. She's waiting in the library to give me an overview of what I might see teachers and kids doing, in language arts as well as across the school.

"I coordinate the unit," she explains, "because I have students in all grade levels. I can see all the projects going on. I'm in touch with everyone anyway, so I have a natural overview of plans."

She talks about the unit's inception. "We didn't want to mandate curriculum for teams beyond having a school-wide theme with some in-common activities."

The "we" she's talking about are the teachers and administrators who put together the unit's database, the resource unit which serves as a starting point for many teams. "There were 12 of us who worked on compiling the resource unit one summer. We tried to pick at least two people per grade level (sixth, seventh, eighth) and there were two administrators." Teachers spanned academic subjects, teams, and related arts and were paid for two weeks in the summer to plan and put together ideas.

"So we could focus on ecology each year, we had to generate subthemes. The sixth grade focuses on the Rain Forests, the seventh on Conservation and Water, and the eighth on Alternative Energy Sources. Related Arts focuses on other ecological applications in their fields."

Since it's the first day of the unit this year and Debbie's really busy, she leaves me with the resource unit while she's off to work.

The Ecology Resource Unit is hundreds of pages! It's entitled "An All-School Ecological Interdisciplinary Unit for Tuttle Middle School." The rationale is followed by objectives and then sections of unit themes for teams and grade levels.

Language arts suggestions depend on and foster inquiry about the environment. Many ideas allow the kids to pose their own questions, to search independently or in groups for potential and possible solutions.

Some from the sixth grade include:
—selecting a profession dependent on forests, then preparing questions for interviewing resource people. Gathered data is shared in a self-chosen, original way;
—analyzing media and its messages about the environment;
—surveying adult attitudes in the community and analyzing and writing up results for sharing or publishing;
—creating and keeping across time a naturalist's journal, complete with sketches and descriptions of local nature;

Seventh grade project opportunities also promote student inquiry:
—selecting local concerns on water or pollution issues and researching these. Letters to the mayor and the health department are part of sharing the results.

And eighth grade, too:
—exploring and analyzing the community's use of energy sources, which includes conducting interviews of local industrial workers and professionals. Products include anything from letters to children's books composed to create awareness of the issues.

On all three levels, language arts, alone with ecology, or integrated with other multiple subjects on this theme, leads to many products: debates, talks, essays or papers, books, journals, or poetry. And lots of literature possibilities for discussion spill out of the resource book: stories, books, film, all for individual choice or small or large group reading.

One year, Sally Remaklus, the eighth grade language arts teacher and team leader, along with her kids decided to make a time capsule. They wanted to show people 50 years from now what kind of ecological measures Montgomery County sponsored in the 1990s. Sally wanted to test the idea, so she suggested it to one of her classes, intending to broaden it later to them all. The class was really enthusiastic about it and had their own ideas about what to do, too! She also talked to the science teacher on her team. He agreed to have the kids construct a wooden box and vault for the time capsule artifacts everyone put together over the next two weeks.

"We [the class] talked a lot the first week. In fact, we spent the first two days brainstorming all possibilities we could think of doing. The third day we spent discussing what we'd collect for the time capsule, which people in the community we'd interview, what we'd read and write about, who'd take pictures, and what trips all or some of us might need to make. We also decided on an evaluation process for the unit's work." Sally did spend time helping kids make choices, but after that, people came to class every day and worked on what their planned schedules dictated.

"Kids conferenced with me on what they were reading and writing—from questions to other's pieces. Whenever students needed to, they went to the computer lab to wordprocess the writing there."

"We stored two kinds of things: artifacts and a group-composed booklet of our own writing about the community. People brought in flyers from stores, recyclable containers, posters, catalogues, recordings, tablets with recyclable paper—all kinds of artifacts."

We flip through a copy of the big book they all made. "The book we put together contained an opening essay on the city composed by one girl in class, poetry on the earth and the environment, news stories, articles on Wabash recycling, on waste management, and on Pace Dairy. Copies of student newspapers made during the unit for each grade level, and various other descriptions along with written interviews made it into the book. We actually infused a lot of writing not only from my other classes, but from other grades, especially the sixth grade," she says pointing to their poems. The whole book contained community pictures taken by student photographers showing environmental conditions and pictures of Tuttle's celebration of the ecology unit. "The real book is in the time capsule," she explains, "along with the artifacts we placed there."

And so, 50 years from now, the time capsule will be opened and other readers of other times will read and view, and see and feel, the ecology of the 1990s. They will do so because of the writing efforts of eighth graders 50 years before. And the pieces in the capsule, like Betsy Enenbach's poem, will call up a personal ecology of memories for these middle schoolers then turned middle aged.

The Wabash College Chapel

It is a silent place,
Filled with dreams.

Beyond the great alabaster doors,
Footsteps, ringing across the black and white linoleum,
Bring one through another pair of doors.

The chapel itself lies here,
An ancient hum giving life to its walls.
The smell of dust and memories fills the air,
Penetrating the crackled paint on the ceiling.

Dust particles, glittering in beams of light,
Dance about like the elves of a forest.
Sunlit trees outside the windows and their red velvet curtains
Wave in the same breeze which carries birdsongs in
with the sigh of the opening doors.

Archaic white pillars rise on the sides of the stage,

Guarding the red curtained arches which in turn flank
The flowing crimson velvet in the center of the hall.
A white ledge runs around the wall, behind which
Is a backroom on either side of the stage, once buzzing with life
But now disguised with dimmed green EXIT signs.

The music of years past haunts the chapel,
Echoing off the walls and flowing down the
Scratched, rolling brown linoleum.
Faces of presidents past
—Of decades ago and those of my childhood—
Peer down from the balcony at the endless white rows of pews
Under which I used to crawl.

The lonely lights hanging from the soaring ceiling
Remember warming the stage with their circumradiant glow.
The steep, white, creaky steps to the belltower innocently expect
To be climbed forgetting the door at their reach is locked.
Outside a balcony window, down below, a small courtyard
In perfect sight is somehow forgotten.
Overgrown steps lead to a birdbath.
In which somebody has planted flowers.

Below the steps from the balcony,
Past an ever-locked door of unknown contents,
Beyond the stage entrance,
Even further into the depths of the chapel,
There breathes a basement.

In the hallway ahead, old wood tables sleep atop worn brown
    carpet.
Hundreds of ancient posters ornament the bulletin board
Above the blue doorways; above the old bandroom
(Filled with black music stands with
WABASH stenciled on them in red),
The old violin room, and above the open threshold
To what was my father's office.

Outside the violin room, where I used to crawl out the window
During lessons, a drain stained with green leads a path

To dark, fearsome, medieval gated arches.

At the end of the hallway, the old lobby,
Cluttered with a coffeetable and old seats,
Holds a lingering memory of its former inhabitants
In wooden plaques near an ageless lap.

At the other end of the hallway lies a door,
Beyond which is an isolated path lined with
Several bushes and a large spruce basking in sunlight.

Elisabeth Enenbach

References

Adler, M. (1952). *The great ideas. A syntopicon of great books of the western world.* Chicago: Encyclopedia Brittanica.

Alexander, W., Williams, E., Compton, M., Hines, V., & Prescott, D. (1968). *The emergent middle school.* New York: Holt, Rinehart, and Winston.

Alexander, W., & George, P. (1981). *The exemplary middle school.* New York: Holt, Rinehart, and Winston.

Arnold, J. (1985). A responsive curriculum for emerging adolescents. *Middle School Journal,* 16 (3), 14-18.

Arnold, J. (1991). Towards a middle level curriculum rich in meaning. *Middle School Journal,* 23 (2), 8-12.

Atwell, N. (1987). *In the middle: Writing, reading, and learning with adolescents.* Upper Montclair, NJ: Boynton/Cook.

Beane, J. (1990). *A middle school curriculum: From rhetoric to reality.* Columbus, OH: National Middle School Association.

Brazee, E. & Capalluti, J. (1992). Middle level curriculum: Making sense. *Middle School Journal,* 23 (3), 11-15.

Britton, J., Burgess, T., Martin, N., McLeod, A. & Rosen, H. (1975). *The development of writing abilities (11-18).* London: Macmillan Education Ltd.

Bruner, J. (1986). *Actual minds, possible worlds.* Cambridge, MA: Harvard University Press.

Eichorn, D. (1966). *The middle school.* New York: The Center for Applied Research.

Elbow, P. (1973). *Writing without teachers.* New York: Oxford University Press.

Emig, J. (1971). *The composing processes of twelfth graders.* Urbana, IL: National Council of Teachers of English.

Erb, T., & Doda, N. (1989). *Team organization: Promises and possibilities.* Washington, DC: National Education Association.

George, P., & Lawrence, G. (1982). *A handbook for middle school teaching.* Glenview, IL: Scott Foresman.

George, P., Stevenson, C., Thomason, J., & Beane, J. (1992). *The middle school—and beyond.* Alexandria, VA: Association of Supervision and Curriculum Development.

Goodman, K. (1986). *What's whole in whole language?* Portsmouth, NH: Heinemann.

Jones, J. (1991). There's a storm in the desert: Keeping our children safe. *Middle School Journal, 22*(4), 44-46.

Judy, S. (1972). *Explorations in the teaching of secondary English.* New York: Harper and Row.

Lounsbury, J. (1991). A fresh start for the middle school curriculum. *Middle School Journal, 23* (2), 3-7.

Lounsbury, J., & Vars, G. (1978). *A curriculum for the middle school years.* Columbus, OH: Charles E. Merrill.

Macrorie, K. (1968). *Uptaught.* Rochelle Park, NJ: Hayden.

Melton, G. (1984). A notion at risk. *Middle School Journal, 15* (3), 3-5, 9.

Merenbloom, E. (1985). *The team process.* Columbus, OH: National Middle School Association.

Moffett, J. (1968). *Teaching the universe of discourse.* Boston: Houghton Mifflin.

Moffett, J., & Wagner, B. (1976). *A student-centered language arts and reading, K-13.* (2nd ed.) Boston: Houghton Mifflin.

Murray, D. (1968). *A writer teaches writing.* Boston: Houghton Mifflin.

National Commission on Excellence in Education. (1983). *A nation at risk.* Washington, DC: U.S. Government Printing Office.

Rief, L. (1992). *Seeking diversity: Language arts with adolescents.* Portsmouth, NH: Heinemann.

Stevenson, C. (1991). You've gotta see the game to see the game. *Middle School Journal, 23*(2), 13-17.

Stevenson, C. (1992). *Teaching ten to fourteen year olds.* New York: Longman.

Stevenson, C., & Carr, J. (Eds.). (1993). *Integrated studies in the middle grades: Dancing through walls.* New York: Teachers College Press.

Vars, G. (1987). *Interdisciplinary teaching: Why and how.* Columbus, OH: National Middle School Association.

5

Reading and Writing Connections

"I have learned to find out a student's goal before I help. How else can I help?"

Jane Hansen

Look for ways to put them together. That's a simple idea about reading and writing Deborah and I keep before us every time we teach. Students naturally relate reading and writing; all literate people do. Reading and writing are learned in similar ways, basically the way we learned to use language in the first place when we learned to talk. Schools tend to separate them, for convenience mostly; so we look for ways to enhance the relationship between them and to make it visible to students. And to connect reading behaviors and writing behaviors in natural and interesting ways.

That's the kicker—natural and interesting. We really prefer to teach both reading and writing without a textbook. A lot of the publishers are making claims about Whole Language, and I will admit most stories in the textbooks are interesting again. But basals always chop learning into isolated skills. Textbooks give us exercises instead of reading. No matter how the composition book proclaims that it teaches "the writing process" (five steps, you know), there are those traditional grammar exercises. They may be disguised, but there they are. Days and weeks spent on skills and drills instead of writing. We would rather have a handbook like *Write Source 2000* (1990) on the shelves, dictionaries in the room, thesauri. A literature anthology perhaps, but we really prefer to have several handy. We can do without the teacher's manual and the blackline masters, thank you. What we really need are lots and lots of paperbacks. And there are some good paperback collections of short stories and poems and plays better than the stuff in most reading or literature books.

Natural and interesting. That's simple enough. But it may not always be easy. In a normal year you will have kids who are confirmed non-readers. You will have others who tell you sincerely they cannot write, and prove it to you. Some of them will be the same kids who can't read. You will have other kids who panic when they don't have work-sheets instead of reading and others who are terrified when they are told to write instead of "underline the simple subject once and the simple predicate twice." They will be "A" students.

It does us no good to badmouth the teacher they had last year or complain about lost opportunities. Often students come to you poor-ly taught for one reason or another. They come with all kinds of other problems too. Big deal. You've got them. Teach them the best you know how. We don't like saying things in a negative way, but let us suggest some things not to do when you are faced with the non-read-ers and non-writers and worksheet addicts and grammar grubbers.

Don't believe them. Yes, they can read and, yes, they can write. It just takes a little extra cleverness on your part. Expect it. Insist on it. Put things in their hands they want to read. Show them how to write. I know it is not always easy, but it is possible. Make a beginning with your hardest case and you will be amazed at how much he grows. Believe they can do it. The job is showing them that they can.

Do not teach phonics. It simply does not work at this age.

Do not put the kid in a lower grade basal. All that does is humil-iate him. Forget his "reading grade level." Find something he's very, very interested in.

Do not put the kid in a lower level basal. More humiliation. No mat-ter how well meaning, as soon as we do that we confirm her low opin-ion of herself. We prove to her she's dumb and that she can't do it.

Do not use "High-Low" paperbacks. They are just lower level basals in smaller form. I don't care if they are about rock stars and basketball players. The kids are not fooled. It's just another well intended way of telling them they cannot read. Give them something worth reading.

Do not start the year with the parts of speech. They've done that every year since the second grade. It doesn't stick and it doesn't make them effective writers. Put up the grammar book and those empty exercises and teach them to write and read.

Do not give in to them. Or their parents. They will want the secu-rity of a basal. They will demand to know when you plan to get out the grammar book and "do some real English." That insecurity is nat-ural. Expect it, but remember. You are the professional.

Parents can be a bigger pain than their kids. Listen to them. Inform them. Educate them. Be patient with them. You are still the professional.

Do not teach about reading instead of reading.

Do not teach about writing instead of writing.

Do not teach badly because the teacher next door does. Or the one your students will have next year. You are not obliged to teach sentence diagramming or vocabulary lists because your colleagues teach them. I don't care how long they've taught at your school. If your students read instead of doing basal exercises and worksheets and if they write instead of doing grammar drills, some of your fellow teachers will not understand what you are doing. That is a sad but true commentary on our profession. Some will see your success and want to learn from you. Share with them. Others will be threatened. Their disapproval can be uncomfortable. Ignore them if you can. We have found it does little good to argue with such people. Don't ever be afraid to teach your students well.

Do not teach writing one way and reading another. We state it that way carefully. The reverse is also true, but this mistake is more common. Jane Hansen in *When Writers Read* (1987) describes the situation this way. "Writing instruction rests on certain principles about how people learn, and if we believe in them we need to reassess our reading instruction. If what we know about writing doesn't bring changes in our reading instruction, then we don't really understand writing. Typical reading instruction cannot exist alongside writing instruction; they are philosophically incompatible. Unless we change the way we teach reading, in time, writing instruction will falter in our classrooms because we do not believe in it and do not reinforce it when our writers read the work of other writers." This is the nub of the matter. **Real writing** and **real reading** share the same processes and require the same conditions for learning.

Teaching Journal

We want you to think back to how you studied reading and writing in the middle grades. That takes most of us back some distance in our lives, but do the best you can remembering whatever experiences you can. Reflect on them in your journal in contrast with your own teaching.

There is a method in our madness. All of us tend to teach the

way we were taught, or we react against the way we were taught
when we teach. Think about it.

Time, Choice, and Response

Hansen tells us there are three conditions for growing readers and
writers, **time, choice,** and **response.** I like her list. It's simple, easy for
me to remember, powerful for teaching. Readers, just like writers, need
class **time** for reading, thinking about, and talking about books. For
most of our students, if it doesn't get done at school, it won't happen.
If we want them to be readers, we have to make time in the school
day for them to read. That is another reason why it is so important
for our students to be engaged in real reading and real writing instead
of wasting precious time with drills and seat work.

Students need the **choice** of what they read and what they write.
Making their own choices will be new for many of them, and they
may not know where to begin. "I can't think of anything to write
about!" "I don't have anything to read!" They can be so pitiful, and
I'm tempted to take the choice away from them one more time and
just tell them what to do. Write this. Here, read this book. It's easier
that way. Nope, I won't do it. What are you interested in this week,
kid? Sports? OK, here's a shelf of books; pick one out. Try it. Put it
back and get another if you don't like it. Nothing to write about?
Perfectly natural; all writers get stuck, you know. Keep that list in
the front of your journal of interesting things to write about? Nothing
looks good now, huh? Well, look it over carefully. It's your list. Review
your reading list on the back page, too. There is probably something
the pros have done you want to try? Still no luck? Look through this
file of published pieces from the class. You remember them when they
were read in the circle. A lot of good ideas in there, and they're not
used up.

But you do not have the choice of not reading. And you may not
not write. It may take some work, but we will get you unstuck.

The choice of what to read and what to write must be genuine. Not
another sugar-coated exercise. Not a choice manipulated by the teacher. You can spot a phony and so can your students. If we want our students to know the joy of reading and the thrill of writing, and to carry
these gifts with them throughout their lives and share them with others, then we must trust them to grow to choose books and choose writing tasks for themselves. You can model writing for them, sharing the

different kinds of writing you do and all your tricks. You can read to them and read short pieces with them, pointing out and making visible for them the things the pros do. But they must have the choice of the writing. You can fill your room with exciting books, a variety of books, books popular with adolescent readers, easy and hard books, long and short books. You can give them a taste of many of them, reading aloud and talking about them. But the choice of what to read, finally, must be theirs.

And they will know from your **response** if they can trust you. When the choice is genuine, this is the crux of the matter for the teacher. I am always working to be a better responder for my students. I may never master it. I am also constantly working to make them better responders to each other. Adolescents need both responses, their peers' and yours. Yours is the most important. You control the peer responses. You create the routine and the atmosphere for them. You also show them how to respond—the **showing** is more important than any instructions. You model responding for them every day. But beyond that what your students want more than anything is to please you. No, they don't act or talk that way all the time. Some try very hard not to show it. But it's true. And that is an awesome responsibility.

Responses that grow readers and writers have to be honest and kind. Sometimes we are so kind we are phony. That doesn't work. And I have seen, and used, honest criticism so cruel it stopped learning altogether.

This matter of kindness is very important. Perhaps your models for teaching English and reading and literature were bad ones like mine were. No, I am not ungrateful. Those dedicated people taught me many things. I owe them a great debt. But I was ten years into my career before I saw a good model teacher who showed me **how** to teach this stuff. I've been learning how to do it ever since.

As an adolescent reader, when I read I was examined and my answers critiqued. When I wrote, my errors were pointed out to me in bold red ink. As I grew older the critique got harder and the red marks spread. English and reading and literature as school subjects were gauntlets I had to run through more and more dangerous ordeals. We've got to quit teaching the language arts that way. We simply must stop it. We treat our students wretchedly, and they hate us for it—and they hate to write and they hate to read anything in school.

Mistakes are part of learning. Photographers and potters and bird hunters and trout fishermen know that. In some ways the mistakes are the learning. They are not mortal sins. I learned this teaching writing, finally. I am beginning to learn it as an adult reader with younger readers. I am the master craftsman in that room. I teach the craft to apprentice writers, and we share together the workmanship of excellent writers better than any of us are. There is no place in it for damning criticism. The worst I say is "Try it again."

It is a community trip. They need your response, first and last. And they need the response of their peers. What you seek to create within the environment of the school is a family of writers and readers who share with each other and encourage and help each other to dare more challenging tasks. It is exciting and fun and we all learn better and faster in a group that supports us and pushes us at the same time.

Teaching Journal

What do you believe about teaching reading? You know what we believe. What conditions do you think are necessary for your students to grow as readers? Spend some time talking it over in your journal. Do the same for writing.

Making Connections Between Reading and Writing

So much for theory. We know the conditions of time, choice, and response are necessary for both reading and writing in our classrooms. Now in the real world of the middle school, how do we put them together?

Teach Reading and Writing at the Same Time, If You Can

I try to remember that the divisions between subjects and the arrangement of the day into classes is for the convenience of teachers and not because the divisions and the classes help students learn. Dividing Reading Class from English Class is particularly arbitrary and artificial. We shouldn't separate them. Period.

Many middle schools teach a Language Arts block, typically about

90 minutes long. Grades may be given for English and Reading, or only one grade for Language Arts. It's really not a problem either way. If you teach in a school with such an arrangement or work with a team of teachers and an interdisciplinary schedule, count your blessings. Insist that your team not divide the language arts or, in a school with separate subject periods, ask that the language arts be taught together. That's a start anyway.

Another word about teaming. Remember that with your team reading and writing need to connect with all subjects, not just English and reading. As the language arts specialist, you will probably have to take the lead in showing your colleagues how to connect them. Planning units and projects and programs of study together, you will not find this difficult. Reading and writing, after all, are part of all learning—or should be. Your sharing with your friends will also have its effect. We do teach more by example than what we say anyhow. If you want more information on writing to learn in particular, Ann Gere's *Roots in the Sawdust* (1985) is a good source of useful and useable ideas.

Use Reading and Writing Workshops

But you may work in a school where the classes are separated, and that's the way it's going to be until there is a more enlightened regime. Paul Gainer teaches English and reading to seventh graders at Dougherty Middle School. His classes are divided, and he has a mixed schedule. One group of students report to him for both subjects but have their schedules divided into English class first period and Reading class sixth period. He teaches another group of kids whom he sees only third period for English class. Hardly an ideal schedule for a teacher who teaches language the natural way. In addition, he teaches in a conservative system with curriculum objectives prescribed by the state.

This is what Paul does. He likes the workshop approach to teaching, and he spends time with his students at the beginning of the year training them to work in this environment. Each class begins with a mini-lesson of about ten minutes, no longer than fifteen. Early in the term many of these deal with procedural matters. Students used to basal readers and worksheets in reading class have to be trained to choose and read, talk and write about real books. Students used to traditional grammar exercises and a weekly vocabulary list have to be trained to write and share their writing with their peers. Members of his Reading Class choose their own books from a wide variety of paperbacks in the room, read them in class, share them with their peers in book talks and informal sharing sessions, get his response in conferences both during and after the reading, write about and sometimes do projects on the books they choose. Once the class routine is learned, and it is slightly different for each class depending on its size and personality, his mini-lessons shift to subjects dealing with the needs he sees in his students. Some deal with how to read different kinds of things, from books for pleasure to official forms to textbooks. Some with how to read faster. Some with vocabulary. Some with literary devices. Some with standardized reading tests, what they do, how they are written, and how to cope with them. Many deal with favorite authors and with the books read by his students and Paul himself. He is an avid young adult literature reader and enjoys swapping books with his kids.

Students in his Reading Class write to him about their books at least once a week in their journals. Books do not go home; neither do the journals. They write him a letter. He spends several mini-lessons during the term teaching them how to write about their reading, showing them the kinds of things you can say about what you read without summarizing or saying things like "It's great" or "It's boring" or "I really liked it." He puts a length requirement on the letter, and he writes them back. They also write letters to each other; and there is a lot of informal sharing about what they are reading, what they enjoy and have trouble with, favorite episodes and situations, and especially favorite books for individual interests.

Paul keeps a daily record of each student's progress—what they are reading, who is writing a response, who is ready for an end-of-book conference, who will do a book talk during the class, who is looking for a new book, who is doing a project on a book. He does this for roll call as he starts the period. He conferences with each student in-process as they are reading. His intent here is to get to each kid at least once while he is reading the book. But he does only one or two conferences during a normal period. Most of the time after the mini-lesson he is reading with his students.

How does he grade them? How many books do they have to read? He checks each student during the period to make sure she is reading. She gets so many points a day for actually reading, and he deducts points if she is off task. There is no set number of books required. The journal, end-of-book conferences, book talks, projects all share in the grade.

If you have never taught a reading process workshop, it is not as daunting as it sounds. Establishing the routine is important, and kids will have to be taught what you expect. So you have to think it through carefully. Do not neglect the mini-lessons. The class needs time to read and choice in what to read, but they also need to be together each day as a class and they need you. Paul describes himself as not being particularly organized, but this kind of record keeping and fairness in grading suit him. If you are worried about grading and record keeping, take a look at the examples Deborah gives you in Chapter 11.

Paul's English Class is a writing workshop; and it operates similarly, with well established routines and the same feel to the pacing. And the same high interest and motivation in the students. His students write to publish. The processes established in the class to foster natural writing, and to manage thirty kids, parallel the processes for reading. Together they look something like this.

Writing Journal	Reading Journal
Getting Started	
Jotting, verbal head scratching, re-reading finished pieces and unfinished journal entries	Reviewing favorite books and writers
Browsing files of published writings	Browsing the book stand, library
Talking to peers,	Talking to peers,
Conference with teacher, if needed	Conference with teacher, if needed
Getting It Down	
Writing a fast exploratory draft	Reading the first chapter
Finishing a draft—time varies	Reading the book—time varies
Checking It Out	
Peer response group	Reading journal response
Getting It Right	
Editing for publishing	
Publishing conference with teacher	End-of-book conference with teacher
Showing It Off	
Publishing in various forms	Book talk to class
Reading to the class	Sometimes a book project

The diagram is crude and does not show in-process conferences in both writing and reading, but you can see how classroom management and routines are similar in two activities that are mirror images of each other.

The kids he sees only third period pose a problem for Paul because he still wants to teach them in full reading and writing workshops. He is not comfortable with the compromise of three Writing Workshop days (Monday, Tuesday, and Friday) and two Reading Workshop days (Wednesday and Thursday) a week. He is most concerned with students' having more reading time at school. But he likes the workshops and his kids really like them. They work for him in that setting, and he sees a lot of growth. Most of his students are poor, and many come from some pretty rough situations. A lot of them have known little success in school by the time they get to him. His workshops work.

Teaching Journal

If you do not teach the language arts in a workshop setting, this is your chance to start. Workshops take planning. Think it through carefully. Study portraits of middle school classrooms in the sections between the chapters. What physical changes do you need to make in your room? Melissa Moore at Merry Acres Middle uses tables. Paul Gainer uses three corners of his room for student conferences. Plan the class routine, including mini-lessons, for the first week in detail. Remember you will have to train students about routines and your expectations.

As you begin the workshop, keep a daily log for the first term. Reflect on problems and aggravations. What is just not working and how do you want to fix it? And record your successes. What parts are the most fun?

The Response Journal

I come to reading as a writer. It is natural for me to think on paper about what I am reading or have just read. It is a way I have of validating the experience and making the novel or poem or whatever I am reading mine. So most of the time when I connect reading and writing, a lot of the instruction has to do with asking students to respond to what they read and then showing them how. It all goes in the journal.

Most responses are intended to be quickly written, tentative, exploratory. They are intended to be written down thinking, and we share the insights they give us as we talk about the story or poem or novel or essay or play in class. I want these responses to be as non-threatening as possible. Usually they are short.

I use the responses to lead students to writings of their own. When the response journal works well, a cycle is established that relates what we read to what we write, which then very often prompts the next thing we read. A kind of rhythm is established as natural as talking and listening, watching and thinking, breathing out and breathing in.

I use several different kinds of journal responses depending on the class, the kinds of reading we are doing this week, how I feel, and our need for variety or routine.

The creative response is my favorite because it leaves all of the choices of what to write up to the student. The instructions are simple. Write anything you want to about the piece, but please do not summarize it or evaluate it. The writing must be something of your own. I deliberately do not give them a lot of instructions about how to do it; but if students are really uncomfortable starting with this kind of freedom, I will brainstorm with them a quick list of possibilities. The list might look something like this.

Change the opening.

Change the ending.

Change the genre. Write a poem about a story or a story about poem or a dramatic scene from either.

Write another stanza to the poem you just read or another episode to the story or dramatic scene.

Talk to the author.

Talk to a character.

Ask questions of the writer or the characters. Why did you put this part in? Why did it end like that? Why did you do that? Why did you say that? What does this mean?

Make a montage of quotations from the piece. Put them together in different ways.

Psychoanalyze one of the characters.

Become the narrator and tell something else.

Change the narrator in a scene or incident.

Script a scene for TV.

I do not want an analysis. The point is for the reader to rub up against the piece, look at it from a different perspective, and mainly to create something of her own. To be a writer talking back to another writer.

Creative responses do not always have to be written. There will be a young artist in your class who responds to the piece visually. That's OK. If he does it every time, nudge him to write about what he has drawn.

One visual creative response I ask for sometime during the term is the **illustrated map**. The notion is to "map" the action of the story with small simplified illustrations (stick figures work just fine) and label the episodes. Narratives that involve journeys work well for this one. Novels like *The Hobbit* by J.R.R. Tolkien, Peter Beagle's *The Last Unicorn*, or Twain's *The Adventures of Huckleberry Finn* work well. But so do stories like Ernest J. Gaines' "The Sky Is Gray" and Thomas Wolfe's "The Child by Tiger" or self-contained pieces from longer works like the *Odyssey* and some of the other Greek myths or the story of Jumping Mouse from Hyemeyohsts Storm's *Seven Arrows*. Students have also chosen to map the neighborhood of such narratives as Walter Dean Myers' *Scorpions* or S.E. Hinton's *Rumble Fish*.

Les Parsons in his fine little book about *Response Journals* (1990) emphasizes the **personal response** to independent reading in an early chapter. It works a lot like what I call the creative response. He also talks about helping students get started who are not used to the freedom of their own response. He uses what he calls "queing questions," open ended questions to suggest ways of thinking about a piece of literature that will make the response their own. I will not give you his complete list of questions, but paraphrase a sample to stimulate your own questions for your students. And remember his point that students should be weaned from the cueing questions as they become independent and are able to take responsibility for their own reading and writing and learning. These sample questions are for books, but you can see how the notion can be adapted to any kind of reading task.

Why did you choose this book? Have you read this author before?
What does the title and the cover tell you about it?
What will happen when you pick the book up again? How will the hero get out of this one?
What surprised you in the part you read today?

If you changed the setting to your own neighborhood or community, how would the story change?

Which character is your favorite? Why do you like her?

Do you know anyone like the characters in the book? Are any of the characters like you?

Are there any situations in the book that make you mad? Or sad?

Free Writing

Free writing is a skill I teach kids early. It is as basic to me as a language arts instructor as teaching the proper stance is to a football coach or the proper use of a band saw is to a shop teacher. I have taught only one student who could not free write in some fashion, once he understood and believed what I was asking him to do. Free writing is not flashy; it is not brilliant—it just works. We will talk more about it in Chapter 7, where we talk about writing and the private self. Right now look at it as a tool for reading response.

I use free writing very often as a response to in-class reading. Because it is simple, effective, and quick. You read the piece and immediately free write—write fast without stopping or correcting for a set period of time, usually ten minutes. Done routinely, amazing things will appear on the page. Students will see their ideas literally taking shape under their hands, and they will find insights into the reading they did not know they had. You can see that discovery in this excerpt from the journal of one of Melissa Moore's students. Paul's talking leads him inevitably into thinking about the popular movie based on his book.

Dances with Wolves by Michael Blake is one of the best books I've ever read so far. Michael Blake seems to do a very good job at describing how one might feel alone in the wilderness. He constantly switches points of view to keep the story well-balanced and full of suspense. The first day I started reading the book, I read 80 pages. I think that shows alot about how well Blake writes.

In the movie, I think Kevin Costner does a good job with his role of Lieutenant Dunbar because Costner is good at seeming lonely. I think Blake also did an excellent job of the soldiers' impatience, worry, and boredom before they abandoned Fort Sedgewick. The movie was also very good, but I think if I had a choice between reading the book and watching the movie, I would read the book. There is always some element that movies can't capture but books can. Maybe it's the fact that, if you read the book, you can imagine the scenes as you wish, and no one can throw popcorn at your private screen in your head and say, "It's not supposed to go that way!" It's really a great story.

(Paul Black, 7th grade, Merry Acres Middle)

"...and no one can throw popcorn at your private screen in your head and say, 'It's not supposed to go that way!'" Nice. I wish I'd said that.

The learning really is in the writing—or at least in the dynamic between the reading and the writing. Students make sense of their reading and make sense of their own perceptions and thinking powers as they write.

When the free writings are read over silently and additions made so they read without gaps (we think faster than we can write), then shared in class as in-process writings, learning about the literature and the writing, and the thinking, increases. It is surely a better way to study literature than for me to ask questions for which I already know the answers to bored students trying to guess "correct" responses. Good literature teaching, if nothing else, begins with the interests and feelings—the response—of the kid.

And there is no way to do it wrong.

My favorite way of using the **focused free write** is to begin with a quote from the reading. I usually do not choose it for students, but ask them to pick their own and use the quote as the starting point in their thinking as they begin the ten minute free write. Then we can share our writings or just the quotes themselves.

10-6-92

Reading

Behind the Attic Wall by Silvia Chase

"Wait, I'm coming!," she cried and she ran back along the hall with the key pressing it's babyteeth into her hand."

This caught my eye because at first I couldn't understand if it was a simily or metaphor or neither. And I went up to Miss Moore and asked her about it and she said it was a metaphor. Anyway, I like the way it sounds about the baby teeth of the key. I mean, I can almost feel it and it used concrete image that helped me understand it better and visualize it better. It also tells me what kind of key it is cause if it had "baby teeth" it would be kind of old fashioned. You know this type—   —bad drawing!— Like the type they used in castles and stuff. And it must be pretty important, too, or she wouldn't be running with it. So there's some foreshadowing there.

(Lauren Haire, 7th grade, Merry Acres Middle)

10/6/92

English

"Your eyes are blue daisies flapping in the wind."
    This sticks out to me because it is a beautiful description of the girl's eyes. The girl's eyes aren't really daisies, but they look like daisies in the boy's eyes. This metaphor is used to describe the girl's eyes. This could be better because I've never seen a blue daisy. But I guess the boy thinks they look like flowers. This author in my book [Paul Zindel], *Confessions of a Teenage Baboon*, has a wonderful knowledge of similies & metaphors. He is always using great ones that make you stop and think about it for a few minutes. This is the best author I've ever seen. He makes the story go by much smoother by using these metaphors and similes. It's not like he uses a metaphor or simile every other sentence. He just sneaks them in. That's what I like about this book.

(Charles Clark, 7th grade, Merry Acres Middle)

Notice I said the quote is the starting point only. As in any free writing, it is perfectly OK for their writing to wander off the subject. "Let your writing go where it wants to go" is what I tell them. Are the responses aimless? No, almost all do, in fact, go somewhere. And there are a lot of nice surprises. What I want to do when I write about something is discover what I've got to say about it.

You can also use the focused free write to direct students' thinking to whatever aspects of the piece you want them to consider. Reading Poe's "The Black Cat"? Read the first few paragraphs aloud and free write about the narrator. Free write about him again when you finish the story. Ask a question, free write responses to it, share the responses.

Tom Dickinson taught me how to do that. I've seen him stop in the middle of a heated discussion in a social studies class, or when his kids are stuck and can't grasp the point he wants them to see for themselves. "Get out your journals and give me five minutes," he says. Out come the journals, his too. They free write together on the question or problem. After five minutes he calls a halt to the writing (a student can come back to it later) and starts calling on students all over the room. Usually in the sharing the class will find the answer—or several answers. He has found the teachable moment. Because it comes from them, the learning is theirs. And it works just a well in the language arts class.

Writing Before You Read

This is something I am working on. I don't do a very good job getting kids ready to read. My tendency is to say, "Just read it." Then we write about it and talk about it. But when we read a short piece together in class—or when I read something to them—I know it is helpful to make some connections before the reading. Setting up a novel before they read it in groups or individually also makes visible the things experienced readers do without thinking much about them. Focused free writing is handy for that.

Deb and I call this kind of writing **pre-reading responses**, a term that really doesn't make sense if you think about it. Nevertheless, my pre-reading responses often have to do with helping students relate their experiences to the text. I use the writing to focus their attention on some experience, relationship, or feeling of theirs that will help them relate to the work. I like Have-you-ever questions with free written responses.

Have you ever lost anything and found it the same day? We write about that for five or ten minutes before we read "The Purloined Letter."

Have you ever gotten into trouble with an older person who was not your relative. Free writing about that is a good lead-in to *Won't Know Till I Get There* or "Thank You, M'am."

Have you ever wanted to fly? We write before we read *Jonathan Livingston Seagull* or the myth of Icarus or William Carlos Williams' poem about Brueghel's painting.

Have you ever been sooo cold? We write about that before reading "To Build a Fire."

So you see, focused free writing is a handy tool before the reading to grab their interest and get them into the text, during the reading at any point of confusion or to highlight the author's skill—likewise during class discussions of a piece—and of course responding to the piece after it is read.

Graphic Organizers and Other Stuff

Although not writing experiences, graphic organizers like **Story Mapping, Semantic Mapping, Time Line Charts,** and **Webbing** are fun to do in the journal and fun to share. Don't turn them into a right or wrong exercise where students try guess the "right" answer you expect. The point of any graphic organizer is to make visible the thoughts and questions of the reader. Demonstrate the ones you like to use and keep them in the journal.

Story Mapping is a favorite of several of my friends. Frankly, it's a little too linear for me, but that's OK. The form is a simple outline. I'll use Ray Bradbury's "A Sound of Thunder" (1959) to illustrate it.

"A Sound of Thunder"
Ray Bradbury
Setting: Prehistoric time travel!
Characters: Eckels the hunter (?)
        Travis the Hunting Guide
Time: 2055 AD and when the dinosaurs lived.
Situation: Hunting Tyrannosaurus Rex
Action: The deal
        Time Travel
        Hunting Safari and the warning not to get off the path
        Eckels panics
        Fight with the Monster!
        Return and surprise!
Conclusion (if any): The butterfly

The **Time Line** is similar, except it is only a list of the story's events in order. Do not dismiss it as too simple for your students. I find it helpful in my own reading to jot things down in my journal. Often there is a detail, an insight, an image, or an irony I miss until it appears on paper and I share it with a group.

Semantic Mapping is a way to diagram a story (or poem or novel or play) in terms of major ideas and their relationships with each other. It's fun to play with.

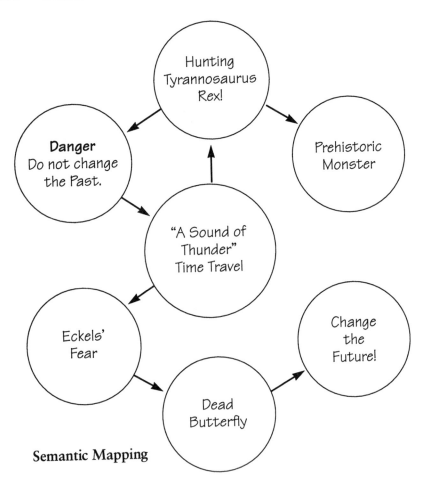

Semantic Mapping

Like other visual interpretations of literature, you may do yours differently than mine; but there is no way to do it wrong.

I think of **Webbing** as the reverse of **clustering**, the pre-writing technique made popular by Gabriele Rico (1983). We illustrate clustering a little later in the chapters on writing. Webbing, however, is a way of looking at and thinking about a piece already written. Unlike Semantic Mapping that looks at broad ideas in a whole piece, Webbing is specific and is a good tool for close analysis of a passage or section. Really it looks at relationships in the way the author uses language.

My favorite passage in "A Sound of Thunder" is a paragraph that describes Tyrannosaurus Rex moving out of the jungle mist toward the terrified time travelers.

It came on great oiled, resilient, striding legs. It towered thirty feet above half of the trees, a great evil god, folding its delicate watchmaker's claws close to its oily reptilian chest. Each lower leg was a piston, a thousand pounds of white bone, sunk in thick ropes of muscle, sheathed over in a gleam of pebbled skin like the mail of a terrible warrior. Each thigh was a ton of meat, ivory, and steel mesh. And from the great breathing cage of the upper body those two delicate arms dangled out front, arms with hands which might pick up and examine men like toys, while the snake neck coiled. And the head itself, a ton of sculptured stone, lifted easily upon the sky. Its mouth gaped, exposing a fence of teeth like daggers. Its eyes rolled, ostrich eggs, empty of all expression save hunger. It closed its mouth in a death grin. It ran, its pelvic bones crushing aside trees and bushes, its taloned feet clawing damp earth, leaving prints six inches deep wherever it settled its weight. It ran with a gliding ballet step, far too poised and balanced for its ten tons. It moved into a sunlit arena warily, its beautifully reptile hands feeling the air.

Ray Bradbury (1959)

See the next page for one way to draw a web of this passage.

Because I learned to cluster first, I like to use arrows for Sematic Mapping and Webbing. Some teachers and students prefer simply to draw lines connecting the elements. Don't get hung up on details. Both are only visual aids to thinking about what we read. Except for particularly elegant maps or webs you will want to display, keep them in the journal and keep them fun.

Please note: We use three graphic displays with one short story only to show you how they work and to contrast the activities. We would not use all three with any story. Use the one you like best.

Do not overlook **brainstorming** for thinking on paper about literature. Often for me the simplest approach can be the one that helps me see more in the story or poem or novel than I would see otherwise. Show your students how to brainstorm questions, words, phrases, ideas that strike them as they read or immediately after reading. It is simple, quick, effective, and another one of those things you cannot do wrong. The secret of brainstorming, in fact, is to suspend our critical faculty entirely and put down whatever strikes us, no matter how silly or obvious.

Like other reading journal techniques, the best way to teach it is to read something together and model it with the class on the overhead or blackboard.

Webbing

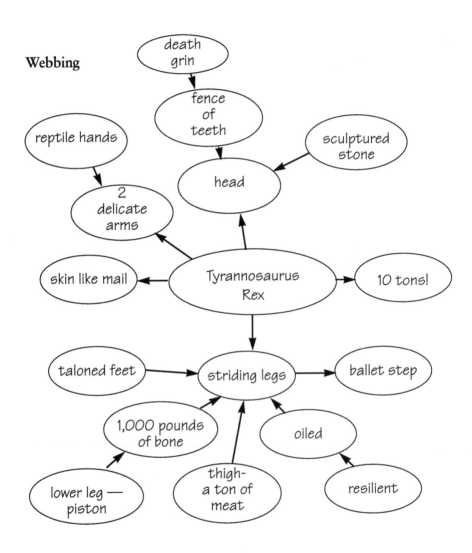

Double Entry Journal

The **Double Entry Journal** is a technique I learned from an article by Susan Reed (1988) in the *English Journal* a few years ago. I especially like it for book reading and response. I've used it for short stories, essays, and poetry; but when I am reading a book it gives me a chance to have a continuing conversation with the text over several days or weeks. It works well in the Reading Workshop where everybody is reading his own book, and it works for me in those situations where everybody reads the same book.

The idea is simple. On the left hand side, I jot down a quote from the chapter I am reading, and on the right hand side I respond with my own writing to the quote or the thinking it stimulates about the chapter or the book as a whole up to that point. I ask for a minimum of one quotation for each chapter of the book. Students may do more, but in most young adult fiction chapters are short and I am satisfied with one. The response may run no longer than a page. Most are rather short. The quotation does not have to be the main idea of the chapter or even very significant to the action or theme of the book— just one that strikes the kid's fancy. But I do ask students to give me enough in the quote so that I get some idea of what it is talking about.

Flowers for Algernon
Daniel Keyes

"April 16 Today, I lerned, the comma, this is a comma (,) a, period, with a tail,, Miss Kinnian, says its importent, because it makes writing, better, she said, somebody, could lose, a lot of money, if a comma, isn't, in the, right place, I don't have, any money, and I don't see, how a comma, keeps you, from losing it,

But she say, everybody, uses commas, so I'll use, them too,

I thought it was funny how he used the comma so much to show how important it was.

I chose this because it had irony. He was trying to make his writing better but it made it worse. I think the author worked very hard on this particular progress report to do it wrong. He might have gone overboard just a little on the paragraph.

(Carla Branden, 7th grade, Merry Acres Middle)

I find it easier to write the quotation on the back of the previous journal page on the left and the response on the right hand page rather than in two columns on the same page. It just gives me a little more room. I do like the quote and response side-by-side, instead of putting the response under the quote as I have done in the past. This way, I get the feeling of talking back to the book.

And that is my purpose really, to set up that dialogue between book and reader. It moves students closer to the text. They read more carefully, and see more in the reading.

Be patient when you start the double entry journal. You will have to teach students how to do it at first. I find it helpful to make xeroxed copies of a double-page opening of my journal to show them how I do it. I talk about the quotes I choose and my responses to them. I know when I start it that I will have to teach some students not to give me snippets of dialogue from the text for every entry. Some think that is what I mean when I ask for a "quotation" from the chapter.

We share "quotable quotes" from our double entry journals in class regularly, sometimes with responses and sometimes not. The sessions are good literary discussions among readers involved with their books. Otherwise, the double entry journal gives me a window into their reading, thinking, understanding, and responding. Students like it once they get started, and I like it because it involves them closely with the text and it keeps me in touch with their reading and understanding.

Teaching Journal

What book are you reading for pleasure right now? Is it one you are comfortable sharing with your kids? Do a Double Entry Journal of the first several chapters just the way we have described it here. Xerox it and share it with your students.

Grading the Literature Journal

So how do you grade personal letters, creative responses, free writings about literature, double entry journals, semantic maps, webs, and all that kind of stuff?

Don't.

I'm tempted to end the chapter right there. The kind of reading and written responses we describe do not lend themselves to right or wrong answers. There are no wrong answers. Nor do you red mark student journals if you want your students to grow. Most of these written responses will not be published. They will merely be shared as part of the experience with reading things we really like. Traditional grading practices just don't work very well in a natural language classroom. As a profession, I think we've let ourselves become more than a little grade crazy anyhow.

But still, at some point a grade will be expected by the school, by your students, and certainly by their parents. You've gotten some notion of what Paul Gainer at Dougherty Middle does. He gives his students credit for doing the work he requires. Melissa Moore at Merry Acres Middle checks the activities off on her clipboard. The student does everything she's asked to do, and she makes a good grade. Basically you make yourself a check list of what you want your students to do and check them off either each class period or on some kind of regular schedule to make sure they're doing the required tasks. It takes some thinking, and you have to come up with the list and make sure students understand it. But it's really easy, and it works. Deb will tell you more about performance grading in Chapter 11.

I keep grading as simple as I can, although it tends to complicate itself somehow. What I try to keep in mind is that the grade belongs to the kid. He earned it. I want it to be simple, and I want him to understand it instantly. The easiest method for me is a point grading system. Each activity in the journal or daily assignment is worth ten points. Projects and other big assignments are worth more. Grades are easy to calculate: divide the number of points you have by the total assigned (and posted across the top of the grade book). Simple and easy.

That gets the grade out of the way and we can get on with the more important matters of reading and writing together, sharing and learning and celebrating the written word, ours and the masters.

References

Bradbury, R. (1959). A sound of thunder. *Twice 22*. New York: Doubleday.

Gere, A.R. (1985). *Roots in the sawdust*. Urbana, IL: NCTE.

Hansen, J. (1987). *When writers read*. Portsmouth, NH: Heinemann.

Parsons, L. (1990). *Response journals.* Portsmouth, NH: Heinemann.

Reed, S. (1988). Logs: Keeping an open mind. *English Journal.* 77(2): 52-56.

Rico, G. (1983). *Writing the natural way.* Boston: Houghton Mifflin.

Sebranek, P., V. Meyer, and D. Kemper. (1990). *Write source 2000.* Burlington, WI: Write Source.

Jason's Reading Journal

Dear Miss Moore,

I have just started a new book called The Outsiders by S.E. Hinton. It is about a heroic territory of youth and belonging.

Hinton makes sure you don't know too much about the situations in the story so that they don't bore you. She makes sure you know how the characters feel and think before the gang fights. She writes about real life in a gang.

Every time I hear the name S.E. Hinton, I think of violent stories. She captures or projects the reality of suspense in real life happenings. She keeps your eyes on the people instead of the background unlike some authors. It's easy to tell a lot of details about a story that is so great. To find out more, check into my next few teacher letters.

Jason Hampton

Dear Jason,

You have certainly touched on Hinton's style. Her characters do seem very real. Her stories also seem real. Keep her technique in mind as you write. Try to make your writing as realistic!

M.M.

January 28

Dear Paul,

The Outsiders is truly a well written and wonderful story. S.E. Hinton is not like other authors. She expresses the feeling of the people and the people themselves.

I know, Paul, that you have already read the whole book, so would you kindly answer these few questions?

1. What is the name of the gang?
2. What is your favorite part of the story?

3. Is this the best book you have ever read?
This story needs to be sold all over the world so people can have something suspenseful to read in their spare time. I am going to read this book more than once, I can tell you that.

Yours truly,
Jason Hampton

Jan. 30

Dear Jason,
As for your letter, I thought it was pretty good. I think you should compare her writing to other writers though. She wrote this story when she was in her teens, so she had to have had a lot of spunk and knowledge of the type of stories people were looking for. As for your questions, I have some answers.
1) There is no particular name for this gang. They are just a bunch of working class kids who gang up on more privileged kids. Typical street talk for such a gang would be "greasers," referring to the large amount of grease in their hair.
2) I think my favorite part of the story would be when the last rumble occurs. That's when people start getting tense, because they know that something has to give before they are finished fighting, and as it turned out, a few people die. They might not die because of the rumble, but that is one of the problems they must face.
3) I wouldn't say this is the best book I have ever read, but it is a good one. I feel that it can only be compared to her other books.

Your friend,
Paul

Feb. 4

Dear Miss Moore,
I've been reading S.E. Hinton's The Outsiders for three weeks now and it has been a thrill. I am almost finished. I have five more chapters to read. I can't wait to find out the ending. So far I know that Johnny, a character in the book, is in critical condition from being shot in the stomach. The nurses said there were to be no visitors because Johnny may go into shock hearing his friends talk

even. Johnny got shot in a gang fight that lasted an hour. Many other boys got hurt besides him. This and many other parts of this book are what make it so good to read. In other words, this is the best S.E. Hinton book yet.

Sincerely,
Jason Hampton

Dear Jason,
   How many books by Hinton have your read? Can you put your finger on exactly what Hinton does to make the book so enjoyable?

Feb. 12   M.M.

Dear Paul,
   I've been aiming to ask you if S.E. Hinton's books were your favorite kinds of books. Do you think they are the best? Well, I'm on chapter nine in about the middle of it. Ponyboy, Soda, and Danny are on their way to a big rumble with the "Socs." It was long and hard but they and the "Brumbly Boys" scared the "Socs" off. The details of the fight came from broken noses to bloody faces and broken ribs. It a was very good and tremendously suspenseful chapter. Even though Johnny was still in the hospital, the boys still won the fight. It took some guts and lots of will power to do that.

Sincerely,
Jason

Dear Jason,
   I also thought that chapter 9 was very interesting. S.E. Hinton always does a good job narrating fights. She gets the facts and motives for fighting straight before she gets into the pushing and shoving to stabbing. About the stabbing part, she doesn't have the fighters throwing pine cones or wielding bazookas, she gives them realistic abilities and real-life weapons. She skilfully points out the fighters desperation for protecting themselves by saying that they will fight with whatever they can get their hands on. In Rumble Fish, people use knives, heaters (slang for guns), bike chains, broken bottles, even zip guns in the fighting. Can they do that and not get hurt—no way!!! For her ending, she does this, not following overdone plot lines and writing methods. Hinton's style is very

unique, and it was very good for a teenager—and a famous author. I know there are people like Ponyboy.

Your friend,
Paul Black

Feb. 17

Dear Miss Moore,
   I am now three chapters away from finishing The Outsiders, and it has been great. In my last letter I told you about Johnny, the character in the book who was in the hospital. Well, he is out with only a few bruises left on his body. In the book it has been three weeks. Johnny just got out of the hospital to hear about the big rumble, a big fight in the story. He had heard that some of his friends were dead or hurt really bad.
   Anyway, if a person reads The Outsiders and doesn't notice the suspense, they need to try to read another book. There are plenty of action packed pages in The Outsiders.

Sincerely,
Jason Hampton

Feb. 24

Dear Paul,
   Last night I rented the movie of the book The Outsiders. There were so many scenes that were missing in the movie that were in the book. This happens a lot. For example, the last letter you wrote to me you talk with me about Dances with Wolves and how it was different from its book.

Your friend,
Jason

(Jason Hampton and Paul Black,
7th grade, Merry Acres Middle)

6

Book Stuff: The Ins and Outs of Outside Reading and Reading Inside

"How do you know a book is good before you read it?"

"Those of you who don't like to read, it's harder to act like you're reading than it is to read."

—Paul Gainer, teacher
Dougherty Middle

"It stuck in my mind....It just stood in my mind. I read the whole chapter, and did not find anything that stood out more."

—Michael Huff
7th grade, Merry Acres Middle

Reading is best taught using authentic literature. The real stuff. Books.

Think about it. When you read just for yourself, what do you read? Books, magazines maybe. Except for your professional reading, do you ever read an anthology? Probably not. Or if you do, your personal reading is maybe like mine. The collections I read are related by subject. My favorites are either nature books or, more likely, fishing books. The book I'm reading now is typical, written by one author, John Gierach in this case. (If you like fly fishing, you'll like Gierach.) Subject—my interest—is the key. I have a love for fly fishing that borders on obsession, and that's part of a greater love for the outdoors and all natural and wild things. So I like books with trees in them, as Norman Maclean (1976) described the genre. You may like books with cooking or movie stars or politics or murders in them. Deb and my daughter Anna have long conversations about Stephen King, all his novels and even his short stories. But he scares me. See what I mean?

Our goal is to teach life-long readers. Real readers read books. We read them because we are interested in the subject or we like that writer or a friend liked the book and loaned it to us. We also learn from the reading we do. Sometimes we learn a great deal really, and the learning itself is a lot of fun, too, and part of what makes it all interesting. When we hook a kid on reading, we hook him on learning.

Teach your students with this in mind. If they are going to read at all, they will have to have the opportunity in your class. Don't send them home with a book and expect it to get read. You may want to check out books they can take home later, if you have enough available, once they are readers. But most of your students need the class time you will plan for them to grow into the kind of readers you want them to be. The classroom is also where you model reading behaviors and where mutual sharing and responding go on.

It sure beats those dull exercises from a basal reader.

Teaching Journal

Spend a little time with your journal and sketch your Reading History. What books and experiences have been most important to you over the years? Why are they special? You may want to free write your history as a narrative, or do a rough time line in note form.

Look over your Reading History and concentrate on your adolescent years. Brainstorm as many favorite books as you can. Grab a friend or two and brainstorm a list of favorites together.

Reading Survey

You will be building a classroom library, and you will want a pretty clear notion of your students' reading histories—their likes and dislikes, their reading experience or the lack of it—as you start. An informal Reading Survey like the one at the end of this chapter will fill in some of the gaps for you. After they fill it out—and you do one with them—it is also the basis for a good classroom discussion of books and our experiences, good and bad, with them. Keep the surveys in the students' folders and ask them to do another one at the end of the year. The changes in their responses may surprise you, and them.

After your classroom library is building, the survey is still a good way to start the year. It will help you get to know your students, and you and they will be talking about favorite books and reading experiences from the beginning. The end-of-the-year survey is the one you will use to update your library.

Building a Classroom Library

Your goal is to immerse kids in reading, to literally surround them with books they cannot resist. Eventually your room will have five hundred to a thousand paperbacks in it. If you are just starting, don't panic. It will take a little time to build up that kind of collection. With a limited budget—or no budget—how do you get started?

First, don't be discouraged, and do start. Don't wait until an enlightened school board gives you a paperback budget for your reading program or you have scraped together enough for a hundred books from the used bookstore downtown, or for fifty books or even twenty-five. Scrounge what you can, bug your principal, go to the PTA, get your school media specialist to bring a book cart to your room of the latest YA titles, ask your neighbors and friends for books they have read, bring the books from home you can bear to part with—but start. Get some books in your room and into the hands of your kids.

Ask your principal or your system language arts coordinator if you can use your portion of the textbook allocation for paperbacks. Some states and systems allow this; others make it more difficult. Linda Rief (1992) tells parents about her eighth grade writing-reading workshop and asks them to donate books they've read to her classroom. She suggests they give a favorite book to the class in honor of their sons and daughters' birthdays with an appropriate inscription inside the cover. She involves parents in the growth of her students, and she builds her classroom library.

We mentioned Paul Gainer at Dougherty Middle in Chapter 5. He obviously is an outstanding Reading Workshop teacher. But he did not have an easy time getting started either. He does not teach in an affluent school, and there was no money. Still he went ahead and made a start, and he scrounged books anywhere he could get them. Paul was blessed with an energetic and knowledgeable media specialist in the school's library. Donna Thomas knows middle school kids and young adult writers, and she wanted to help. She checked out books from the library directly to his classroom. That way, five classes of students had access to them instead of a few kids being sent to the library to "check out a book and come back." She also helped introduce his students to many of the young adult fiction writers who became their favorites.

At Paul's school the budget is always tight. Getting and replacing paperbacks is still not easy. I know he would like to have three times the titles he has now. I think he has done everything to get books except a bake sale, and he might try that. Don't be discouraged. Good books in your room for your students are worth the effort.

Booklists

If you are just starting this adventure, what books do you choose? Which writers will really grab your kids? At the end of the chapter is the booklist of **Seventh Grade Favorites** from Melissa Moore's students at Merry Acres Middle. They put their favorites on the "Rate A Book" poster she keeps on one wall of her room. Any student who wants to puts up the title and author of the book by her name, rates the book from one to ten, and jots a very brief note about it. When the poster is full, Ms. Moore wipes it off so new titles can be added. Particular favorites of this year's class are marked "***". Take a minute and scan the titles and authors.

It's quite a list! Everything from *Deathwatch* to *Hamlet. Sweet Valley High* meets Charles Dickens. And you need to know that's OK. You want that kind of range and that kind of choice. Don't worry about them. When students have real choices, they read everything—and their choices amaze me. Just like your choices, and mine. I'm looking for my copy of T.E. Lawrence's *Seven Pillars of Wisdom* to share with my daughter (*Lawrence of Arabia* was on the cable channel last night), while I'm reading Pat McManus' *Never Sniff a Gift Fish*. See what I mean? Real writers do that. And, yes, *Little Women* and Nancy Drew and Jack London still make the list. That surprises me a little, but it's kind of nice.

Also at the end of the chapter is a shorter list of **Fifth Grade Favorites** from Pat Stull's students at Hose Elementary. We include it for those of you working with younger kids.

Don't leave out the giants of literature. When Bobby wants to read Melville, I cheer him on. I don't know why Erin wants to read *Great Expectations* (I certainly don't!)—but I know she can and will read it. The great fun of the whole business is sharing my favorite writers and special discoveries with young readers and enjoying the ones they share with me. Include the books you don't want them to miss. Just don't insist they read them.

Do not worry about reading grade levels.

Most of your books will be Young Adult novels with some nonfiction. Nancie Atwell (1987) and Linda Rief (1992) have good lists of favorite books from their eighth grade students. Like the books from Melissa Moore and Pat Stull's classrooms, we like their suggestions because they come from the kids. You may also want to check out the booklists in the NCTE catalog.

NCTE
1111 Kenyon Rd.
Urbana, IL 61801
1-800-369-6283

You can get Alleen Pace Nilsen's *Booklist for Junior High and Middle School Students* (1991) from NCTE. The listings are annotated.

Another booklist you will want to have is the Newbery Award books. The Newbery Medal has been given each year since 1922 to an author of an outstanding book for children. Many of these are young adult titles. We've marked recent Newbery winners in the **Seventh Grade Favorites** list with a capital N. You can get the current list of titles from the American Library Association.

Newbery Medal Books
Association of Library Services to Children
American Library Association
50 East Huron St.
Chicago, IL 60611
1-800-545-2433

Some of the teachers I know like the BMI catalog. It has a good selection of teen fiction, and you can order grade level sets (again, don't be too concerned about levels) or titles grouped by themes like supernatural tales, science fiction and fantasy, murder stories, funny novels. But what I like best about their catalog are sets of titles by some of my favorite authors, people like Judy Blume, S.E. Hinton, M.E. Kerr, Walter Dean Myers, Gary Paulsen, Paul Zindel.

BMI Educational Services
26 Hay Press Rd.
Dayton, NJ 08810
1-800-222-8100
BMI will usually get books to you in a couple of weeks.

I have worked in a community where library resources were limited, especially for adolescents, and where there were no book stores. Unlike Linda Rief's school, nobody would consider letting me spend scarce textbook money for paperbacks. There the Troll Book Club was a life saver.

Troll Associates
2 Lethbridge Plaza
Mahawah, NJ 07498-0001
1-800-526-5289

There are other good companies out there. We list **More Sources of Paperbacks** at the end of the chapter. Check them out. And the media specialist at your school should have a bunch of catalogs for you to prowl through. Don't be shy about calling companies and asking for your own copy. The book stores in my community are helpful about ordering books for me, and they give a good discount for all books I buy for the classroom. I also save a little by not paying sales tax. We also have a good used book store in our city. Don't forget your local sources.

Teaching Journal

You can guess what's coming in this Teaching Journal. Start your own booklist for your classroom. If you are just beginning your library, use the sources we suggest here, or some of your own. Check with your media specialist and brainstorm with your kids to make a wish list of titles you will seek. If you've made a start and there are some paperbacks in your room, it's time to get organized. Linda Rief keeps her booklist on a data base for the computer in her room. That's a good idea, if you have access to a machine. If not, I suggest a card file of titles, authors, publishers, and prices.

Keeping It Going—Adding to Your Library

One reason we talk so much about paperbacks—besides the fact they are cheap and kids love them—is that they are supposed to wear out. Linda Rief does cover hers with clear contact paper to make them more durable, but paperbacks are just not going to last. They are not supposed to. The appeal of most young adult writing is that it is **new**.

You add to your classroom library all the time as your students and you make exciting new discoveries. That's part of the life of a reader, and it's a lot of the fun. Melissa Moore uses her "Rate-a-Book" poster to find new titles for the next school year or whenever money is available. Paul Gainer surveys his kids about their favorites at the end of the year and asks them to list for him what they recommend for "the sixth graders who'll be in our room next year." Linda Rief asks her students at the end of the year to "list three books I should absolutely not be without for the next year." You will already know their favorites, but it is helpful to make the list.

The *English Journal* reviews ten or a dozen young adult books in every issue in the "Books for the Teenage Reader" column. The *EJ* comes with your NCTE membership. The address is listed in this chapter.

Donna Thomas, media specialist at Dougherty Middle, tells me her favorite source of reviews of young adult books is *The Book Report*. A lot of the media folks use *School Library Journal* as their source for new books, but she likes the selection and reviews in this one better.

The Book Report: The Journal for Junior and Senior High Librarians
Linworth Publishing, Inc.
480 E. Wilson Bridge Rd. Ste. L
Worthington, OH 43085-9918

Ask your media specialist if he has a copy you can browse through.

One of the outstanding features of our local language arts journal in Georgia is Patti McWhorter's "Book Corner." She reviewed over 20 titles of books for kids in the last issue alone. Her reviews cover new book for primary, upper elementary, middle school, and high school (almost all of the high school titles you can use). Patti teaches at Cedar Shoals High in Athens, Georgia, and has done the column for several years. I don't know how she reads so much or keeps them all straight! Now she is also co-editor of the quarterly journal itself.

Patti McWhorter
160 Valley Road
Athens, GA 30606-4178

Check out the local English Council journal in your state or your state's middle school publication to see if they include reviews of new YA books. If not, maybe you and your students could start reviewing for them?

Now that we're reading all these books, what do we do besides read them?

Deborah reminds us in Chapter 9 that speaking and listening are natural ways we extend our experiences with print. After all, the first thing I want to do after I finish a good book is tell somebody about it. If you've read it, too, our conversation can be a special sharing. I don't want to overlook opportunities for good talk about the books we enjoy and the ideas in them, in groups or with the whole class or with individuals. It's a wonderful thing to see the excitement in the eyes of a student who has read a favorite author of mine for the first time. Take another look at what she says about cooperative learning, and especially her section on **Other Oral Language** Connections with Reading. Book talks can be everything from formal presentations with props to casual dining room table talk with a group or partner, or between teacher and kid. You'll find an outline for a brief individual book talk a little later in this chapter. I know several teachers who like that approach. Oral reading is the lifeblood of the language arts classroom, and a day shouldn't pass without something being read aloud. And you will find Deb's other suggestions equally helpful.

Chapter 5 talks about different ways to use writing and reading together. So if you skipped it, you may want to back up and pay particular attention to the example of Paul Gainer's teaching and to the section on the Response Journal. You have a glimpse of how a good reading journal can work with **Jason's Reading Journal** just before this chapter. If you are just starting the adventure of teaching reading and writing the natural way, you will find they come together easily and, once you get your class going, opportunities present themselves without your having to look for them. And remember.

Your students' writing becomes part of the literature they read in your class. When you make them authors, they write good stuff their peers want to read. And their writing will reflect the best things they read among the young adult writers. Melissa Moore tells me her seventh graders have been studying foreshadowing, flashback, and irony the last couple of weeks because "without knowing it, they used them in their writing. So we talked about them and gave them names."

Writing-reading connections are easy for me. I am less adept at seeing opportunities for such things as classroom drama, skits, video taping, visual and musical arts. And I think these responses to literature are important, deepen our involvement with the work, let us express ourselves and share ourselves with each other, help kids grow, and are just plain fun. Melissa Moore's kids like to do video book presentations in groups. Her students also like to dress up and become a character from a book for individual sharing. The costumes and the acting are often impressive, and always fun. Like almost any group of kids, several of Paul Gainer's seventh graders like to draw in their journals. And I like watching them draw, and seeing through their eyes just a little bit of what they see when they read. I always encourage visual responses to reading. These responses may be as simple and private as sketches in the journal or elaborate public displays of drawings, paintings, or mixed media.

A lot of students like to do collages, so many in fact we recommend you limit the number your students can do for credit. Good ones will knock your socks off, but looking at one collage after another can get boring. I try to get students to be a little more original than just pasting magazine photos and words on poster board. I like mixed media myself, and collages with unusual shapes and sizes. "Think of something to make it different. You don't want it to be just part of the background. How can you make it jump out at me?" Like any worthwhile project, brainstorming and planning before grabbing the scissors and the magazines go a long way.

If you are a camera buff or have a media specialist at your school who likes teaching kids to use one, slide-tape presentations are good projects. While tape recorders are easy to come by, if your students are going to make slides from magazine and book photographs, that will require some special equipment, a copy stand and some special lenses. Also, any kind of photographic project takes time. If you are interested, there's a section on photography in Chapter 10.

Students who are audiophiles—and what student doesn't like music?—can make powerful statements about the books they are reading with cassette tape. Encourage them to do sound collages in response to their reading. Really, I think a more accurate word here is **montage.**

The idea is to put snippets of songs and instrumental music together to make a statement or create an atmosphere. Two tips from my experience. Insist students script the sound collage, and set a time limit on the production within fifteen minutes. And if the work is done at school, you will need some equipment for taping, a place to work, and **headphones** for your junior sound engineers.

One more simple but effective idea from Melissa Moore's classroom. Displayed on one wall of her room are **BQ's**—Book Quotes. Her students type up on the computer, or print up neatly, with appropriate illustrations their favorite quotations from the books they are reading and their responses to them. These are backed with colorful construction paper and hung on the wall. It is an attractive display, and a good place for students to browse who are looking for a new book to read. The possibilities for responses to book reading are limited only by your students' imaginations and what you encourage—and sometimes by what your principal will allow.

Teaching Journal

For one week, plan with your class to do responses to reading that are not written. You might work with groups to demonstrate several different kinds of responses during the week, e.g. drawing, photography, video taped skit, sound montage, slide tape, reader's theatre, dramatization. Enlist the aid of your media specialist and the art teacher and your colleagues who are camera and recording hobbyists. Do your planning well in advance and give yourself and your students lots of time for this one. Make the week a celebration of media.

Keep a log of the planning, work, and results in your Teaching Journal.

Don't forget the reliable Book Talk

The Book Talk is not as original as some other activities. It may not be flashy. But it gets the job done and is a good way for students to get up on their feet and share the books they are reading with each other.

I suggest you keep them brief. Limit the time to five minutes and coach students on not giving away the ending. A simple outline helps, and that also gives you and the student a record of the book talk in the journal.

Book Talk

Title: [Show the cover.]

Author:

Main character and central conflict or situation:

Why I like this book: [What is different about it?]

Read an excerpt (pages?):

Other books by this author or on this subject:

Remember that you teach the Book Talk like everything else, by showing them how. Model Book Talks in your mini-lessons and introduce your students to some of your favorite books at the same time.

What if I'm not comfortable with the Reading Workshop approach to teaching?

You may not want to teach like Melissa Moore and Paul Gainer teach. You may not be comfortable with the management of a full blown Reading Workshop that Nancie Atwell describes in *In the Middle* or the Reading-Writing Workshop Linda Rief uses in her classroom in *Seeking Diversity*. That's OK. Don't give up.

Your principal may require you to use the basal reader adopted by the school system. Don't despair. And don't give up.

Don't give up on using authentic literature in your classroom. Our goal is to make life-long readers. While Deborah and I like the Reading Workshop and believe in it, we recognize that everyone is not going to teach that way. What we do strongly recommend is that you do whatever you can to make good adolescent reading available to your students and that you encourage them to read books habitually.

I believe kids should have a choice of what they read. But it's OK for all of us in the classroom to read something together. Linda Rief describes how she and her students read a play based on Anne Frank's *Diary of a Young Girl*. "We read fine literature in many ways: kids choose their own books, we read different books to each other, and sometimes we read the same book together. I think we need to get at reading from all those angles. I like choosing books to read by myself most of the time. But occasionally I like to read the same book a number of people have read, or even the whole class has read, and get into a good discussion about it." Anne Frank's diary in dramatic form is a particularly good choice, I think. And you'll want to check out what she and her students do with the story and the Holocaust theme.

Rief reminds me of my friend the late Sue Gilmer, who used to teach at McIntosh Middle. Every April she taught her sixth graders Irene Hunt's *Across Five Aprils*. On my bookshelf I have a worn paperback copy of the novel she gave me. I can't open it without hearing Sue's clear strong voice reading to her rapt students. In case you were worried you would have to give up that special book you and your students read together each year, or every other year—don't. Keep your special loves to share with them.

A required basal may be an aggravating situation, but not insurmountable. I know of no modern basal reading program that does not provide for book reading. The publishers want to sell you their supplementary paperbacks (most today do have titles and authors you will recognize), but you will quickly see where other titles fit the broad themes in the textbook just as well. Stress this point with parents and with your administrators: the purpose of any basal reading series is to get kids to read. And ask them to fill your room with books.

What about the classics?

Sure, you can teach the old favorites, and you can teach your students to read challenging books. There are a few titles on Melissa

Moore's **Seventh Grade Favorites** list that surprise me. Our suggestion is to make your favorite writers available to your students, read aloud to them from the pages you love, encourage them to read Frank and London and Lewis and Tolkien and other time-honored authors—but give them the choice.

A notion we would like to dispel is that young adult fiction is inferior somehow to the canon of accepted writers in the literature anthology. The anthologies are fine. But we want our students to read books, and they probably are not going to be very interested in the ones you read for your literature professors in college.

Students read because of interest. It's just that simple. Young adult literature is literature in the finest sense. There is no reason for you to feel self-conscious about it or apologize for it. This is the literature most appropriate for your students.

Why all this reading in class? What about homework?

Middle school students need school time to read for several reasons. If we are going to hook them on books, we have to work with them at school. Paul Gainer spends a good bit of class time talking to kids about books that are in his room. It's the easiest way to get the kid and the book together, and give the kid a good push toward reading it. Paul takes two days a week of his seventh grade English classes for reading in class in the Reading Workshop. That means he has to get everything else into three days. That's a pretty tight schedule, but he wants his kids to read. He checks books out over the weekend, and students can read their own books with his approval. Reading in class keeps the books in his room available to all five classes.

Reading in your classroom is the easiest way to model reading behaviors for your students. Reading is important to them when it is important enough to you so that you read when they read. It works the same way it does with writing. Modeling is the most powerful thing you do in your classroom. Your interest in books, your sharing, and your reading before them make them readers.

Allowing time for reading in your classroom also helps relate reading and writing in natural ways, and it encourages group projects on books students read together. Melissa Moore has two class periods to work with her seventh graders, and I think you can see in the description of her students' Journeys how strong the relationship between reading and writing are in her room. Once they get started, her students do a lot of reading at home; but they have a lot of time at school with books also.

Linda Rief's homework is thirty minutes of book reading and a journal response each evening. I like the idea. I do wonder how many books go astray between home and school. Middle school kids lose things. When journals and books stay in the room, they are more likely to stay around. That is no guarantee, as you know. Any middle school student worth his salt can lose anything, big or little, between the bookcase and his desk. And books that are used get worn out, used up, and sometimes go missing. That's how you know which books are the really good ones.

Can we read magazines?

If you want to keep your life simple, tell them no. Magazines will complicate your program. But many good teachers of the natural way do use them.

Nancie Atwell does not let her kids read magazines. She wants them to become book readers, and that's what her Reading Workshop is about. Melissa Moore's classes run the same way. Lots of choices of paperbacks to read, but you will read books. Paul Gainer does not include magazines until later in the year. He wants them reading books first. Then he lets them bring in magazines for class credit. Paul goes a step further. He is a comic book enthusiast, and he is the one who brings in the comic books!

First, I want kids to read books. If you yourself are an avid magazine reader, as I am, and want to use them in your classes, I think Paul's approach makes sense. Get your Reading Workshop going well with books before you add magazine reading.

What about censorship?

It's going to happen sooner or later in today's school climate. Somebody's daddy is going to scream bloody murder because of a book you let his precious darling read. Forgive my sarcasm, but we are not talking about logic or even common sense in these kinds of cases. The last time it happened to me, I simply forgot those poems and that word were in one of Richard Brautigan's books I handed to a young man. His father called me late that night, and he was mad. It was a dumb mistake on my part, but it will happen. The student came in Monday with a copy of *Helter Skelter* (you remember the paperback a few years ago with blood splashed across the front of it) and a permission slip from his father. Sigh!

If you love books and make books available for your students to read, you need to be prepared for complaints. Here are some things you can do before an irate father is at your door with fire in his eyes or you're summoned before the school board.

1) Communicate with parents from the first day of class. Send home a letter explaining the Reading Workshop with a list of favorite authors. Invite them to your classroom at every opportunity. Get parent volunteers to help you with response groups and book projects. And assure parents their sons and daughters are not required to read anything that offends them.

It is a lot easier for me to talk to a parent who knows me and my program than deal with a midnight phone call from a stranger.

2) Don't panic. If the complaint has already gone to your principal, the school board, the superintendent, be prepared to follow your school's procedure for challenged materials.

Make sure, by the way, that your school has such a procedure. If not, information is available from NCTE and the American Library Association with suggested guidelines. Two books you may find particularly helpful from NCTE are Henry Reichman's *Censorship and Selection* (1990) and James Davis' older book, *Dealing with Censorship* (1979).

3) If the complaint appears to be coming from a well organized group, talk to your principal early and keep her informed. There are some fundamentalist religious groups who simply object to almost any adolescent literature and who really do seek to disrupt the public schools. These cases are very rare. Your school system has a lawyer on retainer and a school board to deal with these kinds of situations.

If it comes to that, let your principal and the lawyer and the school board talk to the reporters.

4) I am always prepared for a student to read another book instead of the one questioned. The Reading Workshop with a free choice of what we read saves a lot of grief in this area. I don't have to defend Cormier or Blume or Zindel or any writer. I just tell the kid to pick another book, and guide him toward one by another writer or on another subject.

5) As much as possible, know the books your students are reading. I know that *Fallen Angels* will probably get me into trouble in my community because of language, but that Walter Dean Myers' *Hoops* is OK. I know that *A Hero Ain't Nothin But a Sandwich* is not a good choice for some seventh graders (language again, on the second page), but *That Was Then, This Is Now* also deals with the drug problem and they can read that.

No, I haven't read them all. But I read them because I like them, first, and want to be able to talk to kids about good books they will be interested in. And because I know many of the books and writers, I can talk to that mother or father about them.

6) I use permission slips myself. Yes, it can be a hassle, and check it out with your principal first. Some principals I know don't like them and say they draw fire. But I don't use them as a cynical exercise (I know students sign them for each other when they know they won't get the grade without them), but as another means to communicate with parents. After all, I like to know what my daughter is reading so I can talk to her about it.

This is the form I use, and comments are for parents and for me.

Reading Permission Slip

My son/daughter_____ has my permission to read the book_____. I am familiar with its contents and language.

Signature_____

Date_____

Comments:

Unless they study reading skills, won't students do poorly on standardized tests?

We know you feel a lot of pressure from standardized tests. We talk about them in Chapters 11 and 12. But keep this in mind. Our goal, first and last, is to make lifelong, independent readers of our students. Years of experience have taught us that teaching isolated reading skills does not do that.

And one more thing. I see the enjoyment, and the joy, in the faces of the students I know who read books they choose from good classroom libraries. I hear their excitement when they talk about the books they are reading, and I see them sharing their favorite books with each other in many ways, from leaning across the isle to point to a page to elaborate classroom presentations. And I see the stuff of the YA writers they admire as it shows up in the kids' writing. I cannot measure those things, but I know what they mean.

Don't worry about them. They'll do OK on the tests.

Reading Survey

Name_____ Date_____

1) What is your favorite book or writer? What kinds of books do you like to read? What are your favorite subjects?

2) How many books have your read this year? (Guess if you need to.)

How many did you read this summer?

3) How many books do you personally own?

4) How many books are there in your home?

5) How do you choose a book to read? (Movie, friend liked it, teacher, parent?)

6) Do you read magazines? Which ones?

7) Are you a newspaper reader?

What parts of the newspaper do you read?

8) How did you learn to read?

How old were you when you started reading?

9) How do you feel about reading?

Seventh Grade Favorites, Merry Acres Middle

(N) indicates a Newberry Award winner, ** indicates a student favorite.

Louisa May Alcott. *Little Women*
William Armstrong. *Sounder* (N)
Fran Arrick. *Tunnel Vision*
Lynne Banks. *The Indian in the Cupboard, The Return of the Indian*

Judy Blume. *Are You There, God? It's Me, Margaret, Freckle Juice, It's Not the End of the World* **Superfudge ** *Tales of a Fourth Grade Nothing* ** *Then Again, Maybe I Won't*
Robin Brancato. *Winning*
Sue Ellen Bridgers. *All Together Now*
Beth Brown. *The Wonderful World of Horses*
Betsy Byars. *Summer of the Swans* (N)
Mary Higgins Clark. *A Cry in the Night, A Stranger Is Watching, Stillwatch, While My Pretty One Sleeps*
Beverly Cleary. *Dear Mr. Henshaw* (N)
Daniel Cohen. *Southern Fried Rats and Other Gruesome Tales*
Caroline B. Cooney. *The Cheerleader, Freshman Dorm, The Return of the Vampire*
Susan Cooper. *The Dark Is Rising, Greenwitch, The Grey King*
Richie T. Cusick. *April Fools, Fatal Secrets,* ** *Trick-or-Treat*
Maureen Daly. *First a Dream*
Paula Danziger. *Can You Sue Your Parents for Malpractice?* ** *The Pistachio Prescription, There's a Bat in Bunk Five*
Charles Dickens. *A Christmas Carol*** *Great Expectations*
Lois Duncan. *I Know What You Did Last Summer, Killing Mr. Griffin*
Thomas J. Dygard. *Halfback Tough, Rebound Caper, Running Scared*
Phyllis R. Fenner. *The Hunter and the Hunted*
Paula Fox. *Slave Dancer* (N)
Susan Fox. *Black Sheep*
Anne Frank. *Diary of a Young Girl*
James Garfield. *Follow My Leader*
Jean George. *Julie of the Wolves* (N), *My Side of the Mountain*
Fred Gipson. *Old Yeller, Savage Sam*
Bette Greene. *Summer of My German Soldier***
Shep Greene. *The Boy Who Drank Too Much*
Simon Greene. *Robinhood*
John Gunther. *Death, Be Not Proud*
Virginia Hamilton. *M.C. Higgins, the Great* (N)
Robert Hawkes. *This Stranger, My Father*
Patricia Hermes. *My Girl*
S.E. Hinton. *The Outsiders*** *Rumble Fish*** *Taming the Star Runner, Tex, That Was Then, This Is Now*
Irene Hunt. *Across Five Aprils, Up a Road Slowly* (N)
Norma Johnston. *Whisper of the Cat***

Carolyn Keene. *The Bungalow Mystery, The Double Horror of Fenley Place, Fatal Attraction, Secret at Lilac Inn*

Helen Keller. *Story of My Life*

M.E. Kerr. *Dinky Hocker Shoots Smack, Gentlehands, If I Love You, Am I Trapped Forever?*

Stephen King. *Children of the Corn, Cujo, Graveyard Shift, Lawnmower Man, Misery, Night Shift*

E.L. Konigsburg. *Jennifer, Hecate, Macbeth, William McKinley, and Me, Elizabeth; From the Mixed Up Files of Mrs. Basil E. Frankweiler* (N)

Lewis L'Amour. *Bowdrie's Law, High Lonesome*

Madeline L'Engle. *Arm of the Starfish, Many Waters, Ring of Endless Light, A Swiftly Tilting Planet*** *A Wrinkle in Time* (N)

Gaston Leroux. *Phantom of the Opera*

C.S. Lewis. *The Lion, the Witch, and the Wardrobe*** *Voyage of the Dawn Treader*

Robert Lipsyte. *The Contender***

Jack London. *The Call of the Wild, White Fang*

Lois Lowry. *Anastasia at Your Service, Anastasia Krupnik, Anastasia on Her Own, Number the Stars* (N)

Patricia MacLachlan. *Sarah, Plain and Tall* (N)

Luriene McDaniel. *Six Months to Live, So Much to Live For, Time to Let Go*

Patrick McManus. *Grasshopper Trap, Never Sniff a Gift Fish, They Shoot Canoes, Don't They*

Ann M. Martin. *Missing Since Monday, Stage Fright*

Harry Mazer. *The Last Mission*

Norma Mazer. *After the Rain*

Herman Melville. *Moby Dick*

L.M. Montgomery. *Anne of Green Gables, Anne of the Island, Emily of New Moon, The Story Girl*

Farley Mowat. *Never Cry Wolf, A Whale for the Killing*

Walter Dean Myers. *Fast Sam, Cool Clyde and Stuff, Hoops*** *Motown and Didi, Outside Shot, Scorpions, Won't Know Till I Get There*

Scott O'Dell. *Island of the Blue Dolphins, Sing Down the Moon* (N)

George Orwell. *Animal Farm*

Barbara Park. *Skinnybones*

Francine Paschal. *Sweet Valley Saga*

Katherine Patterson. *Bridge to Terabithia* (N), *The Great Gilly*

Hopkins, Jacob Have I Loved (N), Master Puppeteer, Sign of the Chrysanthemum
Gary Paulsen. Canyons, Dogsong, Hatchet**, The Island
Susan Beth Pfeffer. The Year without Michael
D.C. Porter. White Indian
Russel Ramsey. A Lady, A Healer
Wilson Rawls. Where the Red Fern Grows
Nancy Robinson. Just Plain Cat, Mom, You're Fired
Thomas Rockwell. How To Eat Fried Worms
William Shakespeare. Hamlet
Mary Shelley. Frankenstein
Barbara Silverberg. Kit and Caboodle
Robert Silverberg. Mutants
Elizabeth Speare. Sign of the Beaver, Witch of Blackbird Pond
Armstrong Sperry. Call It Courage
Jerry Spinelli. Maniac McGee (N)
Robert Louis Stevenson. Dr. Jekyll and Mr. Hyde, Treasure Island
L.M. Schulman   Winners and Losers
Mildred Taylor. Roll of Thunder, Hear My Cry (N)
Corrie ten Boom. The Hiding Place
Eve Titus. Basil of Baker Street
J.R.R. Tolkien. The Hobbit** The Fellowship of the Ring
Cynthia Voigt. Dicey's Song (N), Izzy, Willy-Nilly **, Tree by Leaf
E.B. White. Charlotte's Web **
Robb White. Deathwatch
Alieda E. Young. Is My Sister Dying?
Paul Zindel. Harry and Hortense at Hormone High, My Darling, My Hamburger, The Pigman**, The Pigman's Legacy **, The Undertaker's Gone Bananas

Fifth Grade Favorites, Hose Elementary

Mary Jane Auch. Kidnapping Kevin Kowalski
Bruce Coville. Jeremy Thatcher, Dragon Catcher
Gery Greer. Max and Me and the Time Machine
Carolyn Keane. The Secret of Shadow Ranch
Madeline L'Engle. A Wrinkle in Time
Lois Lowry. Number the Stars
Ann M. Martin. Babysitters Club Books

Frank Peretti. *The Door in the Dragon's Throat, Escape from the Island of Aquarius, The Tombs of Anak, Trapped at the Bottom of the Sea*

Lee Riddy. *Shark Pit*

Willo Davis Roberts. *Sugar Isn't Everything*

Laura Ingalls Wilder. *Little House on the Prarie* Series, *The Long Winter*

Betty Wright. *The Ghosts Beneath Our Feet*

More Sources of Paperbacks

Avon Books
1350 Avenue of the Americas
New York, NY 10019
1-800-238-0658

Baker and Taylor
P.O. Box 6920
652 East Main St.
Bridgewater, NJ 08807-9990
1-800-526-3825 Eastern Division
1-800-435-5111 Midwestern Division
1-800-241-6004 Southern Division
1-800-648-3540 Western Division

Follett Library Book Company
4506 Northwest Highway
Crystal Lake, IL 60014-9986
1-800-435-6170

Scholastic Inc.
P.O. Box 7502
Jefferson City, MO 65102-9968
1-800-325-6149

In addition, Donna Thomas, media specialist at Dougherty Middle, and some of the other media people I know tell me they prefer books with the special hard covers because of their durability. We do not recommend them because they cost twice as much as regular paperbacks and the tendency is to enshrine books in your collection instead of adding new titles as you and your students discover them. And the kids are really attracted to the colorful covers of the paperbacks. They choose the paperback because of its cover and because it's not a "textbook" with the hardback copy of the same book right beside it time and time again. Merle Jones, media specialist at Albany Middle, covers her paperbacks with contact paper, as Linda Rief (1992) reports she does. Nevertheless, we give you the addresses of two of the big companies who furnish paperbacks with the special hard covers. They do offer discounts for orders of 25 or more books. Their listings of young adult fiction are extensive and up to date. Besides, your school's media specialist may want suggestions for adding to the school library.

Econo-Clad Books
P.O. Box 1777
Topeka, KS 66601
1-800-255-3502

Perma-Bound Books
Vandalia Rd.
Jacksonville, IL 62650
1-800-637-6581

References

Atwell, N. (1987). *In the middle.* Portsmouth, NH: Heinemann.

Davis, J.E. (1979). *Dealing with censorship.* Urbana, IL: NCTE.

Maclean, N. (1976). *A river runs through it.* Chicago: University of Chicago Press.

Nilsen, A.P. (1991). *A booklist for junior high and middle school students.* Urbana, IL: NCTE.

Reichman, H. (1990). *Censorship and selection: Issues and answers for schools.* Urbana, IL: NCTE.

Rief, L. (1992). *Seeking diversity.* Portsmouth, NH: Heinemann.

Reading and Writing Our Way to a Story

In my school district in Crawfordsville, Indiana, there is a community-wide publishing project called Dial-a-Tale. The project itself is handled through the town library, and local kids write stories for telephone audiences in the kindergarten through third grade or so range. They're usually fantasies or humorous stories. The stories produced are submitted to local raters who select ones to be programmed for use in the Dial-a-tale bank of stories. Younger kids call the right phone number and can select a story to listen to over the phone, a story produced by other young writers who shaped the narrative for this even younger audience. The creation of the tale itself is an illustration of kids thinking, writing, revising, conferencing, and celebrating their products. A neat one this year was Steve's and Aaron's.

Composing the piece took most kids from January until April. They kept taking it in and out of their working portfolios during their writing workshops or anytime they could and wanted to work on it.

Besides, they started thinking about it by talking about good books they'd read when they were little and what had made those books so good. I watched beginning discussions in late January, when Pat pulled the class together just to talk for brief times. The students were all telling Pat favorite titles when I slid quietly into class on the first discussion day.

Pablo: "I liked *Green Eggs and Ham.*"

"And a good one was *Where the Wild Things Are.* It's about a weird-looking monster and a boy," says Aaron.

John liked *The Wish-Giver* but the rest of the class thinks it's very long.

Abigail and Sheila remember favorite books about animals like Garfield.

"*Everyone Else's Parents Said Yes* was a good one," says Cameron. It's a real life-like story. That's why he liked it.

Ashley remembers *Penelope's Dirty Feet,* a book about a little girl getting her feet dirty coming to school. It was real, too.

As they bring up books, Pat asks if they liked their favorite children's book because of the pictures or because of other things. She's leading up to orally reading a short children's book called *Sylvester's Donkey*, a book she asks them to listen to and then to evaluate based on whether or not the story is interesting without pictures.

We all listen to poor Sylvester's exploits attentively. After the story, Melissa says, "Well, at the beginning, it does tell you he's a donkey outright."

And someone adds, "The writer uses words well. There's a lot described well and there are lots of descriptions." Aaron says he could picture the story very well.

Brad: "I think the book is better than the pictures."

Pat reads a second story, one meant for just audio. It's an adventure story about a peach.

Afterwards Brad says, "I think this one would be fun for little kids."

"Why?" asks Pat.

A chorus of answers. "It's imaginative; it's got good description; I like the food processor guns." They start to pick out vivid, memorable parts.

"Why do you think this would be good for a younger-aged reader?" Pat probes.

Pablo's quick to respond. He has a younger sibling. "It's funny. And it uses lots of objects like they were alive."

"About that age, they imagine things like that," Aaron comments sagely.

"It really helps them use their imaginations," says Sheila. "These are common objects so they can visualize the story."

"Well, it was written two years ago by Jonathan Reidy who won the Dial-a-Tale contest."

Pat gives some other suggestions for thinking about creating a tale while everyone mulls over the invitation to create a tale to submit. (Not everyone will submit something of course.) "You might want to call the library number, or you might want to read a few more storybooks to get some ideas about books without pictures." The kids can co-author or not; certainly they can collaborate with other peer authors at any time.

The next time I'm in the room, the kids are still mulling over what makes the audio tale really work. Brad's reading a simple story to the rest of the class as I sit down at the back table.

But most of the kids are already beginning to incubate ideas on paper. Pat encourages them to list ideas, to do a story-map, to "cluster" their ideas.

I notice that some of the kids are working by themselves and some are collaborating authors. Some are up and around; some look at the book Brad finished; some want to do a little research.

Beside my round table, a twosome has stretched out on the floor side by side, one notepad between them as they brainstorm some ideas. I've been listening a little to all the authors, so I come in on the middle of theirs.

"It could be the computer is choking." They're doing some freewriting of ideas and helping each other at stuckpoints.

"Or the chalk and the markers could be bad. But someone has to be the computer's friend."

"Should we even have rulers? What about paper?"

I think they're writing some kind of object-fantasy, but I don't want to interrupt to find out.

Pat wanders by and its cornered by Steve. He recounts to her the plot so far. It's catch-up time for me, too. It seems that at midnight each night, certain objects in a classroom come alive. Some have good qualities, some bad. They're brainstorming good and bad objects and qualities while they're thinking up plot possibilities, too. Pat listens carefully and just nods. She likes this. She's got a clipboard that's she's making notes on about kids' work.

> Clock - Mother, tells them when to wake up.
> Desks - Big, fat, and jolly, beds for others
> Chairs -
> Markers - Bad, they do Graffiti
> Pens - Change Teachers paper, bad in with markers
> Pencils - Cops, Correct Pens
> Paper.
> Chalk
> Erasers
> Computer
> Disks
> Books

A while later, Pat asks the whole group if they would stop and share what they're working on with each other. Erin's is on a caterpillar family and its first encounter with snow. Melissa and Sheila are doing a story about a girl and a dog. Ashley's not quite sure, but she knows there's a cardinal in it.

Aaron and Steve have formulated a little more of a possible plot in addition to their list of characters and qualities. "A clock wakes up at midnight and does things," they tell the class. "So do a lot of other objects."

Another day, Pat knows Aaron and Steve are going to take some time to work on their story, so I appear, too. When I come in, quite a few are busy on this story or others. Brian and Pat are talking a little about revision being an ongoing thing. Megan's going through her red working portfolio, looking for her draft. I sit down near Steve and Aaron, again stretched out on the floor. They somehow misplaced part of their initial writing of the story, so they're remembering and jotting. But also imagining some new things, too.

"The pens can change the teacher's papers," says Steve, ascertaining the "bad guys" of these objects.

"But the pencils are cops. They correct bad English," says Aaron. And soon, "Oh, let's start writing the story."

They do have a piece of the original story. "Look at all this we've got, Aaron."

Aaron works on their joint draft, with Steve reading and reminding him of details. Aaron composes aloud. "It's midnight," opens the story. Steve listens to what they have so far:

> "Rise and Shine," said the clock, "It is ~~███████~~
> Midnight.
>   All of the desks, Chairs, Markers, Pens, Pencils,
> Chalk, erasers, and books, began to stir around.
> The classroom suddenly burst out as everything
> came to life. Thats right, everything did come
> to life.

Aaron thinks they need to tell the reader now that this is a classroom coming to life. They talk about this. "What can we say next?" he asks Steve. Steve takes the writing pad from Aaron and begins to write silently. Aaron reads over his shoulder. "O.K.," says Steve. They both re-read everything.

And revision begins even now. Aaron says, "Don't you think this seems a little forward?" Steve has written in an altercation between objects. Aaron continues, "I just got through saying that no one knew this. This [the altercation] would be later, don't you think?"

"Rise and Shine," said the clock, "It is ▓▓▓▓ Midnight.
   All of the desks, Chairs, Markers, Pens, Pencils, Chalk, erasers, and books, began to stir around. The classroom suddenly burst out as everything came to life. Thats right, everything did come to life. Little did the teachers, and other people that go to this classroom know that at Midnight every night, their classroom came to life. A young Pencil made fun of some markers so they blew their top and went to work with their grafitti on the walls.
   I'm Phil the pencil, I am a cop. here

"I think you want to tell who everybody is first. The adventure would be later." They decide to leave it for now; it might work. They can decide later. "Maybe we should take a character and be it. Maybe a pencil because they're cops. What's a good name?"

They talk about this. Finally they agree on Phil. "Phil the pencil," Aaron quips, playing with the accent on the last syllable and smiling at his rhyme.

Steve's writing now. They're stuck on how to inject Phil into the narrative. Aaron says, "Let's use something like, 'I've had many adventures being a cop and I want to share one with you.'"

Pat's been with other writers. But now she comes by and sits down with them. She asks them to read what they have so far. She listens carefully, and tells them she likes the focus on the new character, Phil. It's a brief exchange, but all that's necessary now.

Other days of talking, writing, reading to others, brief revision conferences with Pat, and some revising, pass by while I am not there. An editing workshop later in April was a little more structured than the constant conferencing and revising earlier.

Authors and co-authors edited themselves when they believed they had a nearly final draft. Three questions for Aaron and Steve and the others were paramount:

—Did the story make sense?
—Did the authors use descriptive language?
—Were mechanical elements correct so the story was readable?

After Aaron and Steve word-processed a draft, a peer editor then used the same three questions when reading the story and gave feedback to them. Some peer partners read and gave verbal feedback; some gave suggestions or comments in writing. They cleaned up the copy. For some, it was simply editing; sometimes more revising occurred. Aaron and Steve were at the editing stage.

Pat looked at the papers again, but this time giving suggestions for cleaning up the language, style, and mechanics.

Steve and Aaron did decide to submit their story to Dial-a-Tale, and although they did not know it yet late in April when Pat whispered the news to me, the panel selected their story as one included in the story bank. When younger audiences phone and ask for it, this final draft submitted to the library is what they hear.

Classroom Catastrophe

"Rise and shine," said the clock, "It's midnight."

All of the desks, chairs, markers, pens, pencils, chalk, erasers, and books, began to stir around. The classroom suddenly burst out as everything came to life. That's right, everything did come to life. Little did the teachers and other people know that at midnight, every night their classroom came to life. A young pencil made fun of some markers so they blew their top and went to work with their graffiti on the walls.

I'm Phil the pencil, I am a cop here in the classroom. I have solved many crimes in my life and would like to share one with you. A long, long time ago, two years to be exact, I was walking along my normal patrol. I was just arriving at the teacher's desk and under the table as usual, when I least expected it I heard a blood-curdling yell. The sound was coming from the chalkboard area, all the way across the classroom. It was not my area, but I decided to check it out anyway. At first I thought it wasn't anything serious, but when the scream came again, this time louder and longer, I rushed as fast as I could to the scene. When I reached the area I heard a gun shot and cries of "Stop! Police!" I turned the corner in the alley and met another police officer. The evil pen gang looked up and took off with the sacred eraser 2000. This eraser can erase whole chalkboards in a single swipe. The other officer and I called for backup and started after the gang.

We heard reports that they were heading for the door to the hall. If they made it there, it would be up to the school police to catch them. After all, we were only classroom police officers. The reports turned out true and just as we arrived the gang slipped out the door into the hall. I knew I would get into trouble, but I had to go after them. Lucky for me the other officer had left to go and meet the backup.

I ran toward my hiding place, where my bookmobile was. I hopped in and pushed the starter button. I had an advantage, as I had a book, and they didn't. I sped out the door and went after them. I did not see them so they must have already gone around the corner. Then I did something I had never done, I pressed the turbo button on my bookmobile. I blasted after them, and almost had them but they turned around and went back towards the classroom. I was hot on their trail when I thought of something. If I could only chase them into the classroom where the backup was. They were going to turn away from the room with the backup in it so I had to think fast. I launched an eraser missile at the door to their hideout where they wanted to go and hoped that it would force them to take the route I was hoping for. To my surprise it worked from what I could tell. When they got to the classroom they spun around and shot at my tires. Then they announced that they wanted me to come out with my hands up. Little did they know, the backup was right behind them. All at the same time as if in unison the backup arrested the pen gang handcuffing them and reading them their rights.

Finally the whole gang was put in jail. The eraser 2000 was rescued and put back to work. Case closed.

By: Aaron Schaefer
    Steve Dunn
    Hose Elementary, Grade 5

7

Writing: The Private Self

"It's not the teacher up here and students out there. It is classrooms that are communities in which students and teacher work together on problems interesting to all of them."

—Beverley Shoemaker,
Instructional Supervisor of Mathematics

"I drove an English teacher half insane making up jokes about bicycle spokes and red balloons."

—John Prine

Writing is risky. Or I should say, good writing is risky. When I write something that is real and genuine and revealing of myself—and all good writing has that honesty to it—I don't really know how you will react. You might not like it. You might not like me! You might laugh at me! I fear your rejection and your ridicule more than anything in my world.

But, oh, if you like it! Then my heart really does sing. Life is good and sweet, and I am **SOMEBODY**. And that essentially is why I write.

Good writing always takes a chance with its reader. And good writing flourishes in a place where there is shared trust and respect, and lots of acceptance. A place where mistakes are a natural part of learning and everyone is expected to do wonderful things.

If you want your students to be excellent writers, then you must do three things. You must create a safe writing community. You must model writing before them. You must publish them.

Almost three decades of experience are distilled in those three statements. There are a lot of other things you can do to make writing instruction exciting and motivating and fun, many clever approaches you can take. The experiences you provide your young writers are limited only by your imagination. Still, the safe community, teacher modeling, and publishing are the necessary conditions if you want

171

them to write and write well. It's really very simple. But not always easy.

Deborah and I talk about publishing in Chapter 8, "The Public Self." This chapter mainly deals with the journal. We want to be as practical as we can. You have already seen how the Classroom Ecology works and how important a supportive, it's-OK-to-make-mistakes atmosphere is where teacher and student share the kind of wonder in discovery Beverley Shoemaker describes in the good math class. You've seen how outstanding teachers create and sustain learning communities. Each different, individual, and very successful. Good writing teachers use the journal as one of the tools in building that community. The reasons are simple. Journals foster daily writing, making it easy and convenient in the busy world of the middle school. My journal lets me keep up with my writing easily, and in it I can mark my progress and also follow the unfolding of a particular piece of writing. The journal gives me continuity and a real sense of growth. The journal is inherently private, protected, safe. My writing is better because I do not reveal it to you too soon. The daily journal, after a few weeks, gives me lots and lots of choices of pieces to continue working on toward publication. Choice makes for ownership, and ownership makes for strong writing. My journal is very portable. And journals are easy to grade.

Journal Dos and Don'ts

The journal is a writer's tool; it is not a magical object for creating writers fully grown. Like all tools in the hands of an apprentice craftsman, what makes it effective is a lot of work and healthy doses of common sense.

The classroom journal is not a dairy. It is the writer's workshop, her sketch pad, her place to try things out, to get writing going, to experiment, to tinker, to draft and redraft. I tell students it is personal, and I respect that, but it is not the place for secret writings. Do that at home. While we do not share everything from our journals and I certainly don't read everything in students' journals, its purpose is to create things that will be shared. That is an important distinction.

What if they have never kept a journal? Or what if the inexperienced teacher last year let them keep a secret journal with no real sharing and no publishing? Share your journal with them. Show them how.

Set limits for the journal. The first year I taught I really did tell kids, "Write anything you want to in your journal." Don't do that. It will get you into all kinds of trouble. Today I try to be frank with students about what I don't want to see in their journals. I don't want any profanity. I don't want to know about their sex lives, nor am I interested in their boyfriends and girlfriends. I do not want to know if they have committed—or are now committing—any felonies. And I do not want any personal attacks. And that's about it for me. My students still enjoy the freedom of the journal, and I can be comfortable reading and sharing with them.

Protect their privacy. Although I stress the fact the journal is not to be a diary and that much of what we write in it we will share, still it is a personal and safe place for writing. And I try to safeguard that. My rule is simple: You cannot read anyone's journal without his expressed permission. That is just good manners, for one thing.

In the past, I have told students to fold down pages they did not want me to read. I don't do that anymore, but ask them not to write anything in their journals they would mind my reading. Sometimes still a student will be self-conscious about an entry, and I tell her to tear it out or mask it. That rarely is necessary.

The permission rule holds, by the way, even when students are asked to share journals. When partners are writing letters to each other in one another's journals, for instance. And journal writings are shared aloud in class at least on a weekly basis, usually more often.

One of the things I often do during the first two or three weeks of a class is type up and run off excerpts from journals for in-class publishing. I want students to see their stuff printed and shared as early as possible. But I am very careful to get their permission before I run it off for the class. It is a simple matter to ask them to mark selections they would like to share when they turn in journals weekly.

The student's writing belongs to the student. I treat it with respect.

Keep journals in the room. Middle school students lose things. Ross managed to lose his journal with a complete draft of the term's big writing project in it in Melissa Moore's room at Merry Acres Middle during one class period!

By the way, Deb and I have tried every kind of reasonable format for the journal over the years, spiral notebooks, loose-leaf notebooks, folders, multiple notebooks for different tasks. Melissa Moore actually uses two journals with her seventh graders, a "P.J." (Personal Journal) and a "L.J." (Literature Journal). Keeping up with two of them would drive me crazy. I use one notebook, and it is the old mar-bled Composition Book you see in elementary schools. Tom Dickinson suggested it to me. It is a convenient size, stacks neatly on a shelf with no wires to tangle, has 100 pages sewn into it, and is made with heavy cardboard backing that makes it good for field work. Use what you and your kids are comfortable with, but you might want to try it.

Set clear expectations for number of entries and length. I want students to write in the journal every school day, so I plan that in. Writers grow by writing. If I scan a journal and it has three entries in it from a kid who hasn't been absent, I know instantly we have a problem. After years of trying all kinds of clever schemes to get the writing experience I want, I find it fair to ask most classes for a minimum of a page for each entry. That is simple, easy to remember; and students accept the requirement without too much moaning and groaning.

The rule of thumb is a page a day in the journal in most classes. Some kids may have to start with half a page a day. The important thing to me is that students write every day.

Respond to journals weekly. Do not bury yourself in journals to read and write notes back to the kids in. I used to do that, spending every weekend with a stack of 150 journals to plow through, reading every entry and thinking up clever, supportive things to say in each one. I don't recommend it. Tom Romano, in *Clearing the Way* (1987), a good book about teaching writing in high school, says he does not read journals at all. What he does is make sure students get plenty of response in other ways in his classroom. He makes sense, but I want to see the journals regularly myself. And I want to interact personally and on paper with each kid, writer to writer. Think it through and be realistic about your time.

I have tried two schemes that worked for me. One is simply a staggered schedule for turning in journals. Group 1 turned theirs in every Monday, Group 2 on Tuesday, and so forth through Thursday. No journals on Friday. My weekends are my own. The other approach to journal responses I've taken is to ask kids to flag one or two entries they want me to respond to in writing. The others I do not read. That also directs them back to their journal for a few minutes to re-think at least one thing they have written.

Keep in mind, my weekly journal response is in an atmosphere where there is a lot of reading aloud and conferencing. I have already heard their stuff when I respond to their journals.

Melissa Moore responds to journals every two weeks, and she staggers the schedule. But she also requires students to write letters to each other in their partner's journals once a week. She reports the peer response is probably more important to most students than hers. She reads it all very quickly. "I know it. I've already heard it several times by then."

Students do need regular response to their writing. My suggestion is some kind of a response from you or their peers regularly. But plan carefully and be realistic about your own time.

Keep grading simple. The first thing I do when I pick up a student's journal is count the pages. A page a day at 10 points per page is my grading scheme. I put that down in the grade book, and I can sit back and enjoy the reading and responding. I use a point grading system because it is easy for me, and I put a heavy emphasis on the journal. 50 points a week add up to a substantial part of their grade by the end of the term.

As I mentioned, the page-a-day scheme lets me know instantly if a student hasn't done her work and we need to talk. Otherwise, I work in an evaluation conference with each student every two weeks. We open the journal and the folder of finished writings and talk about how it's going. I take the number of points she has in the book, divide by the number assigned, carry it two decimal places—and that's her grade at that moment. It's quick, and it's fair. And we identify unfinished and missing assignments and talk about makeup work before it's the last week in the term. I keep my grading scheme as simple as possible for the kids and for me.

Do not red mark the journal. I read your journal and respond to it. I encourage you to share writing in-progress from it aloud to your peers. I talk to you about it, reflecting what I hear when you read selections to me. I help you edit pieces from it for publishing. I do not mark errors in your journal; I don't care how egregious they are.

If you want to kill your writing program, mark up your students' journals with the red pen. Sit on your hands if you have to. Talk to them all you want. Do mini lessons on subject-verb agreement and spelling and pronoun reference and punctuation and capitalization and all that good stuff—but do not mark errors in their journals.

Look at it this way, if I correct your errors, who is learning?

Don't be nervous. There is a place for correctness. But the journal itself is one place where ownership in the writing is unquestioned. I want you to write and I want you to share. I want you to try what I ask you to do. We will do it together. I want you to read to me and talk to me about what you've written. And I will give you credit for doing so because schools demand that kind of accountability. But as much as possible, your journal is yours. I know my response is important—especially my spoken response—but I keep my hands to myself.

My personal rule for responding to student journals is simple. I will write in your margins—comment on what I like, use ! marks and ? marks, draw ☺, ask questions. I will write you a personal note. A brief one, there are many journals to read and other things to do. With your permission and a clear understanding, I may highlight with a florescent marker words, sentences, and paragraphs that are really powerful writing. With your permission, I will excerpt sections for class publications. In those I do silent editing so you will not be embarrassed. We will talk about anything and everything in your journal in head-to-head conferences. **I will not mark your text.**

Journal Assignments: What Do We Put in It?

Really any kind of writing you and your kids want to. In many very successful classrooms, teachers choose neither topics nor writing approaches for their students. They merely require that they write. Choice, remember, is essential to growing young writers and readers. In a safe place where there are lots of good books to read, daily sharing with peers and teacher, and teacher modeling, it is actually easier than you might expect. Getting started is the tricky part.

You may not be comfortable with the write-anything-you-want-to approach common in true writer workshops. That's OK. You don't have to go back to writing "How I Spent My Summer Vacation" on the board the first day of class either. My suggestion is to direct the kind of writing but not the topic, similar to what Melissa Moore does with the Journey that you will see in the portrait of her after Chapter 8. That way you control daily class activities, but your students have the choice of what to write about.

What I have tried to do here is collect from outstanding writing teachers some of their favorite kinds of writing.

Free Writing

We talked about free writing already in Chapter 5, *Reading and Writing Connections*. I list it here with a different emphasis. Many teachers begin class with journal free writing. This may be focused or unfocused. Melissa Moore puts in one corner of her board for each class as they come in two or three "Life's Little Instructions." She takes them from H. Jackson Brown's book (1991). One that caught my eye is number 32—"Once in your life own a convertible." And I like number 43—"Never give up on anybody. Miracles happen every day." The kids like them too. It's a good way to start class.

Other teachers use quotations from various sources, sometimes from the reading the class will be doing or from one of the books being read. I frequently start class reading something I like to them. Sometimes it is related to the lesson; often it is not. I start a lot of classes with music, with lyrics or without. Unless I am working on a particular song-writing connection, like Harry Chapin's "Flowers Are Red," for instance, I tend toward instrumental music for journal free writes.

But I recommend starting kids with unfocused free writing if they are not accustomed to doing it. That leaves them to their own devices, listening to nothing but the language in their heads. I do not want them dependent on music or a quotation I give them. They will be their own writers. Every writer learns to face the blank page. Once they are practiced free writers, then I am comfortable using quotes and music and other stimuli.

As I have said, free writing is a basic tool of the writer. It is a part of drafting any kind of writing. I always teach kids to free write.

Life Maps

My friend Dan Kirby (1988) taught me about Life Maps, and I like to use them with kids. *Write Source 2000* (1992) also includes instructions for doing them. The idea is not to draw a real map but to draw a line tracing the ups and downs of your life with simple illustrations along the way representing important events.

Misty Peeples (see her Life Map on the next page) is the student of Becky Flanigan, who teaches ninth graders at Westover High. Becky starts the year with her young writers by showing them her own Life Map and talking about some of the episodes. Students draw their own and share them with the class, omitting any personal stuff they are uncomfortable sharing. And the maps are posted around the room. That leads to their first long writing, a memory piece from one of the events they have shared.

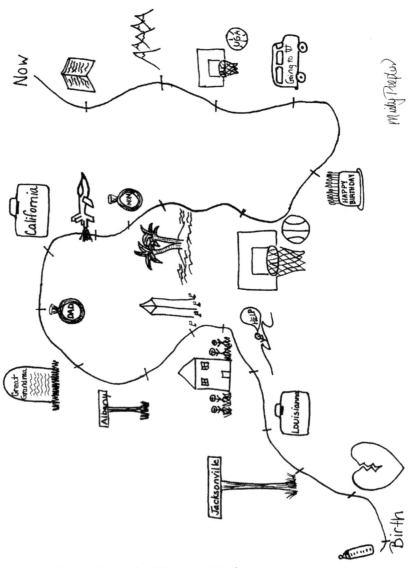

(Misty Peeples, 9th grade, Westover High)

Life maps are fun to do, are a non-threatening way to get students to share with each other, and make good resources for writing topics.

Linda Rief in *Seeking Diversity* (1992) describes the "Positive-Negative Graphs" she has her eighth graders draw. It is another way to display the significant events in their lives and give them a ready source for writing. Like the Life Map, I enjoy using the Positive-Negative Graph. But I would not use both with the same class.

Teaching Journal

Alright, you know what's coming. Draw your own Life Map, and use it as a model with your students. No, you don't have to be an artist. Stick figures work just fine. You've seen the example of Misty Peeples' Life Map, and there is another example by Jay McAfee in *The Anatomy of a Memory* section in Chapter 8. It really doesn't matter, but when I draw mine on unlined paper, it makes a neater job for xeroxed copies to share with students.

People Photos

When a class gets restless, I like to take them people watching. This is one of my favorite journal activities, and we do it just for fun—and to hone their observational skills. Instructions are simple. Go some place where people congregate, the mall, a basketball game, MacDonalds. Sit to the side where you have a good view of their comings and goings, but don't be obvious. You don't want to be noticed. Make quick word-sketches of people who catch your attention. The object is to catch the genuine and telling detail. I ask students to do several. Then it is easy for them to share their best ones. As always, their writing is better when I share some of mine with them first.

Eavesdropping

This is my favorite activity for teaching dialogue, and it's easy. I send them out to be quiet, even sneaky, and listen to other people and jot down quickly interesting conversations. You will have to give your students instructions about not using names (it's more fun with descriptive titles anyway—"the Hat," "Tattoo," "Mac the Marine," "Cool Dude") and not collecting obviously embarrassing, or incriminating, conversations. They collect several in their journals during the week and pick the best one and write it up as a dialogue on Friday.

Encourage them to use as little scene setting and as few tags (the he-said, she-said explanations) with their dialogues as possible. My object is for the conversation to stand on its own. Also look at how their favorite authors handle dialogue and talk about dialogue with action, that characters in good fiction rarely just talk but talk as they are doing something. Of course, you are also teaching punctuation and para-graphing at the same time.

If you have tolerant colleagues and a patient principal, eavesdropping is fun to do at school. Do warn your friends and get permission from your boss ahead of time. But I am sensitive to the possibility of embarrassing another student or teacher and monitor carefully what students share.

Word-Sketching

You can probably tell that I like little field trips, to the local mall, to the cemetery, to a park near the school, or just outside to a part of the campus with trees or where a PE class is playing soccer or softball. I have learned that the success of the excursion depends on how clear instructions and expectations are before we go out. As always, modeling is important. I share mine with them and talk about my experience with this kind of writing. I go observe and write with them. And I share my journal along with them when we finish.

Like People Photos, most of the experiences I want students to write about involve close observations and Word-Sketching. These can be set up in different ways. My friend Dan Kirby does what he calls Walking Compositions where students collect sensory details in five columns and bring them back to the classroom for writing. Students can work in pairs or go out with the instruction to separate while they collect observations in the same location. You can send students on a Nature Walk in their neighborhoods, including a map of their walk. One of the most successful Word-Sketching experiences I've seen was a team project between science and language arts teachers. After several Nature Walks, students took their journal observations and turned them into poems, some of which were eventually published by one of those big textbook companies in their science series.

Although we are talking about journals and how to use them in this chapter, the comment about publishing is worth noting. While a lot of our People Photos and Word Sketches stay in the journal after we share them aloud in class, many of them are chosen to work on in editing groups and publish, just like any other kind of writing.

Zen Drawing

The idea for this experience came from a book for artists by the same name I flipped through at a book store in the local shopping mall while I was waiting for my wife. I'm sorry I cannot remember the writer's name, if I noticed it at the time. I read none of the text, merely admired the delicate and beautifully detailed drawings. At the same time, I was frustrated with much of the writing in my classes. We were all writing every day and sharing and publishing, but it had gone a little flat. A lot of it didn't get down to the nitty gritty. I wanted something real, something you could touch. This notion grew out of those two feelings.

Zen Drawing is something you do with experienced students who have been with you for a while. It requires them to focus on a small close observation and to edit and publish the writing that results.

The instructions are simple.

Find something small and alive (a leaf, a flower, a clover, a stone) and look at it very, very closely.

Draw it. No, this is not an activity for artists. Just try to draw what you see. But keep it small. Don't try to draw the tree; draw one leaf. Don't draw the boulder; draw the pebble.

Continue to study the object you have drawn and jot list or cluster as many details about it as you can. If an association with something else or an experience suggests itself, include it.

Free write a fast zero draft of whatever writing suggests itself. If you are stuck go back to your drawing or your jotting until you grab a hook.

I always like to read these aloud right out of the journal as soon as we finish zero drafts. It is a good sharing session. Then we go on to fix them up and publish them.

For some reason, our Zen Drawing writings are not very long for the work we put into them. To give you an example to help you get started, this one is mine, copied straight out of my journal. I was sitting on the front steps of an old school building and drew only a corner of one of the marble blocks. The Zero Draft is transcribed with minor editing.

In the old cemetery where my grandmother is buried (somewhere in rural Tennessee) over in a cedar thicket are the old stones. They say they date from the Revolution, I don't really know. They are tall, the few left standing, dark (granite perhaps) and bare of inscriptions—

except for grey lichens. But if you run your hand over the wind-smoothed surface of a stone and **listen** hard to your fingers, you can hear the stone talking.

1980
10/1

Zen drawing —— observation
steps of library — dreamer

veins in stone, sketching of grey in a 'white' marble block
it's worn little by time — edges rounding a little, comfortable
not really cold-looking, and there's something living here. (they say rock breds; folds; moves' — 'living' perhaps only in the sense of changing however slow
or maybe it's the veins that —make me think so, I don't know.
a red ant stiff-legs it past, perpendicular in her ant-way — she seems intent upon private business, an lean a-twiddle (tasting the rock?)
ah, an apple-core down there. That's her concern

"Someone was here, toiled, raised kids, fought the Creek Indians, was in love maybe, suffered, died young. And except for the cedars, the sky, the winter wind, and you—was forgotten to the earth and the days turning under the Tennessee sky."

The cedar thicket is dark but not a lonely place, a rare feeling for a cemetery (almost always the loneliest of places). I don't like graves and I don't like tombstones and I don't like cemeteries, but I like those old anonymous stones, standing crookedly together in the dark cedars, and I don't mind thinking about my grandmother's stone, white and grey marble now a little weathered too, being there.

I encourage all kinds of drawing in the journal, as long as kids write about what they draw. I draw a lot in my own journal, and we have something to share in that way as well. The only time I ask for it is in activities like Zen Drawing where the object is seeing more closely, not the drawing itself.

I have personally enjoyed Clare Walker Leslie's *A Naturalist's Sketchbook* (1987), a book by a naturalist- artist whose subject is keeping a sketchbook/journal of quick drawings from observations. These are sort of Zero Drafts for the artist (or sketcher, if you are like me.) It reminds me again that the writer and the visual artist have a lot in common.

Character Sketches

Character sketches can be ten minute free writes about your younger brother or carefully crafted and edited pieces. Melissa Moore and her students write what she calls the Portrait. I sometimes combine Character Sketching with people watching and ask students to watch and take covert notes on one member of their family. Try to see things you haven't seen before or haven't seen as clearly. Study them. How do they talk? Capture some of their speech on paper. Their mannerisms. Do a thorough list of physical characteristics. A psychological profile. Then write about your Character in a situation. I find that writing about a person in action is better than a description without a context.

Teaching Journal

Look back over the five kinds of journal writing based on close observation—People Photos, Eavesdropping, Word-Sketching,

Zen Drawing, Character Sketches—and choose the one that most interests you to try with your students. Share your own observing, sketching, and writing as a model. Also, watch your students as they work and record your observations of the experience with them.

Poetry, Poetry, Poetry

We haven't said anything about poetry yet. And it certainly is an important part of the writing going on in your room and in students' journals. Let me mention a few things that work well.

Name Poetry

Name Poetry is the only kind of acrostic poetry I like. Write your name down the page and start each line with a letter. As I do with all poetry, I ask students not to rhyme it; but some do anyway. That's OK. I always put mine on the board first. If you are brave, get your students to help you compose it.

Teaching writing joy
Only wondering
Miracle of words

Living one singing day
Intense with listening
Never alone
Eager to learn and serve
Remembering my God

I ask students to do two things with their Name Poems, to tell the truth and to be positive. Ask your students to try one with a single descriptive word for each line, then another one with phrases. Sometimes these tell a little story. Then they have a choice of which one to put on construction paper and put up in the room.

That's why I like them. Name poems are quickly displayed.

Teaching Journal

Do your own name poem and put it up in the classroom with

your students' poems. If you are brave, do the poem on the board or the overhead in front of them with their help.

I Remember...

This idea comes from the first chapter of Florence Grossman's nice little book about writing poetry with kids, *Listening to the Bells* (1991). It is a book I am still reading and trying to make a part of my teaching. This writing is a good starting place for a poem with reluctant poets. All of us have a memory. Instructions are simple: write down in your journal as many statements as you can starting with "I remember..." Here is the way the list started in my journal.

I remember running on the beach with Dad
I remember flying a kite with my brother Steve
I remember football practice at DHS
I remember fly fishing on the White River
I remember Robin, my dog
I remember Fort Hill Jr. High
I remember Old Carl
I remember when JFK was shot in Dallas

The list can get pretty long, and I want it to. We mark the memories we want to share with each other. I share mine with the class, and we talk about them. They share in groups or with a partner.

Then we pick one statement and begin the poem with that "I remember..." line.

I remember Carl
big lumbering glasses-wearing Carl
sad sad face and slump-shouldered walk
long arms swinging like a go-rilla
big old ape-ugly Carl

Too big for eighth grade
slouching slow-moving slew-footed Carl
his shadow fell across my life
on the hard playground like a rat-plague
clumsy old Carl

Always made the best grade
teacher's pet, he'd snitch on you
Asthma, he said, didn't have to dress out
suffer the locker room or the gym
old sissy Carl

Lumbering through my days
squint-eyed baggy pants proper Carl
wheezing down my neck in English
always first in Math, A-plus
dang Carl!

Old Carl, my shame
that hard afternoon on the hard ground
he squinted at me, square-jawed
hands knotted at his side
looking sad

I pushed old Carl
and called him a name, a bad name
the playground hooted and hollered FIGHT
and I hit him first...
like hitting a tree

He walked off

I chased him down the hill
and jumped in front and grabbed and hit
his glasses flew
then his arm came down, like you'd swat
a pesky fly

And I went down
(old Carl was strong and fast!)

From the gravel
I watched him stoop for the glasses
and put them on and look at me
sad faced and alone
and go on

in an afternoon
as hard as steel, I watched
and knew
who was ugly and who was good
old Carl

This year I've worked with some kids who were really scared of poetry in several middle schools in my system. The nice thing about the I Remember poem is that, if the kid will do the list, the repetitive statements themselves make a nice poem.

One Way to Grow a Poem

This is basically a prose-into-poetry exercise. It is a little artificial, but it works. Like the I Remember poem, it will also show your non-poets that they can write poetry. It's hard to fail with this one.

Begin with a free writing to music. Let your imagination go. Do several.

Read your free writing to a partner and with her advice pick the best writing. What sounds good? What's strange? Go with your hunches.

With your partner's help, divide the prose passage you have chosen into lines by using a slash (/) to separate phrases. Do not make all of your divisions at the end of sentences. Write it in lines. Divide stanzas where they feel right. **There are no rules.**

Now that it is in lines, cut it. Poetry usually needs less words than prose. Play around with the form and the lines. What is trying to emerge?

Proofread and do a clean draft. (Notice that proofreading comes almost last.)

Share your poem. And publish it in some way.

Teaching Journal

Grow a poem of your own or do an I Remember poem. Or try one of each, and teach the one you like best to your students.

Anatomy of a Poem

This poem starts with a jot list and makes the processes of writing visible to students. It is modeled after the Anatomy of a Memory which produces a prose narrative. It is closer to the way some poets work than dividing prose into lines. The steps also give you the opportunity to show students how by writing your own poem on the overhead or the blackboard. And I recommend you do just that kind of modeling after you try it out first.

Begin with a careful observation. A favorite spot on or near the campus, a field trip to a special or unusual place, or a favorite place in the neighborhood.

Observe your surroundings carefully and make a jot list of the things you see. Take your time and look closely. Be sensitive to the feel of the place. Include as many details as you can.

Look over your jot list to see what the experience is trying to tell you. Look for themes, vivid images, contrasts, original ways of saying things. What ideas are trying to emerge from the random words in front of you?

Now the work of the poet begins. Arrange your jottings into lines. **Do not rhyme them unless they make you.** Add lines as you feel them. If the poem takes off in a different direction, let it. This is your Zero Draft.

If the piece insists on being prose after you've given it a good try, that's OK, too.

Now look at your Zero Draft and your jot list. Have you left anything out that you want in there? Are there lines or parts of lines you want to add?

Rewrite the poem and do these things. Cut out anything you don't need or don't want in the poem. Check out your line length and see if any adjustments need to be made there. Sometimes I put two lines together that are too short or cut a line in two that is just too long. Do you want stanzas? Where? Let the form suggest itself.

Read the poem aloud to your partner. Listen carefully. With his help, make those fine adjustments it needs for now.

Read the poem to other friends and the class several more times. I need to hear a poem a lot before I'm through tinkering with it.

Publish it.

Magical Poems

What Melissa Moore calls Magical Poems are jotting poems, too. But quicker than Anatomy Poems. The idea is to fill a journal page with as many descriptive words and phrases about your subject as you can and then fashion the strongest ones quickly into lines, making the Zero Draft of the poem. Then you can switch things around and play with words and how they look on the page, and try it out on your partner.

A couple of examples will show you more than my explanation.

God's Seraphs

Innocent sincere naive
Enhancingly delicate
Angelically enchanting
Passionate soft tender golden beauties
Mystifying fragile mesmerizing oracular phenomenons
Selfless glistening gleaming magnificent lovely creatures
Graceful vigilant celestial spirits
Jubilant energetic adolescent decorum
Luminous covetable supernatural beings
Magically fluttering velvet wings
Immaculate One's children

(Sarita Kusuma, 8th grade, Merry Acres Middle)

The form of Sarita's poem turns out to be a simple catalog from her journal list. She arranges lines according to her whim. What rhyme she has is not deliberate. It just happens as she throws words together, but it does work. And her last line provides a kind of resolution.

I think Sarita's poem actually works better because she does not use punctuation. I read the words in a rush, tasting them together. Her classmate Leigh Ann's Magical Poem has a different shape, and she uses commas and periods to direct our reading.

The Magical Sea

Crystal, clear, blue, solemn sea.
Golden sand.
Sparkling, crashing waves.
Soft wind.
Romantic moonlit.
Passionate, heart-warming,
Magical, lovely, enhancing,
Life-long fantasy.

(Leigh Ann Huff, 8th grade, Merry Acres Middle)

Ugly Poems

At the opposite end of the taste spectrum, Ugly Poems are formula poems, but they give students a lot of freedom in subject and language. These are fun. Dan Kirby and Gale Hulme came up with the idea in their seventh grade textbook, *The Writing Process* (1982). The trick in writing a good Ugly Poem is to describe things without naming them in each line.

Line 1. Think of the ugliest animal in the world. Describe it without using its name.
Line 2. Describe how you feel inside when you are mad.
Line 3. Describe a color you hate.
Line 4. Describe the foulest smell you can think of. Do not name the source of the smell.
Line 5. Describe a garbage dump.
Line 6. Describe music that sets your teeth on edge.
Line 7. Describe the texture and taste of food you hate. Try using a simile.
Line 8. Describe a scene of violence—a fight, a riot, war.

Linda Darrah teaches with Melissa Moore at Merry Acres Middle. Her eighth graders are masters of the Ugly Poem.

Anger
Pinchers, legs, and big round eyes
Invincible, cruel; the world around me fries
Red is boring, uninteresting and dull
Like the smell of some nasty stuff in a bowl
Smelly, trashy, nasty, and gross
Wordless music which bores me the most
Leafy and round like a small rubber ball
War and hatred surrounds us all.
(Ashley Dorsey, 8th grade, Merry Acres Middle)

Anger
Roll after roll sagging over a baggy rear-end
Frightful, tense, steaming
Pale, grimy white like an old paint job
Pungent, steaming, unbearable
Saggy, smelly, lumpy
Slow, twangy, monstrous noise
Mushy, like fine-grained mud
Bloody corpse, shattered skull, dripping wounds.
(Mike Najjar, 8th grade, Merry Acres Middle)

Bio Poem

Melissa Moore and the rest of us got this formula poem from Rachelle Fowler who teaches in Lee County, Georgia. Rachelle adapted it from Anne Gere's *Roots in the Sawdust* (1985), her fine book that grew out of the Puget Sound Writing Program. The idea is to write a poem about a person following this loose pattern for each line.

First name
Adjective, or several
Family relationship (father of.../daughter of...)
Lover of...
Who feels... (several other Who-sayings, one for each line)
Who fears...
Resident of...
Last name

Give your students the basic formula, show them a Bio Poem you have written, and let them keep the formula loose.

Bio Poems are fun to write and can be published quickly. They are self-revealing in an easy sort of way, like this one by Jason in Miss Moore's class. In it I get a glimpse of an adolescent boy's love for a father who is a sea faring man.

BIO POEM:
DAD

John
Brave
Brother of Barbara Arnold
Father of Jason Hampton
Lover of the Marines, traveling, and Harley Davidsons.
Who feels he should be tough, that his Harley should sparkle, and that
  you should always wear a helmet when riding a motorcycle.
Who needs to spend more time with me, a new exhaust pipe on his
  motorcycle, and more letter writing time aboard his ship.
Who gives me a lot of money, good presents, and good information
  from overseas.
Who fears wrecking his motorcycle, the start of another war, me get-
  ting hurt.
Resident of the US Merchant Marine ship *Jack Lummus.*
Hampton.

(Jason Hampton, 7th grade, Merry Acres Middle)

Teaching Journal

OK, try them out. Write your own poem using the Anatomy technique. Try a Magical Poem, an Ugly Poem, and the Bio Poem.
Which ones work best for you? Show your students how to do them.

This Is My Poem to...

This is my favorite clustering and writing experience. It is adapted
from Gabriele Rico's *Writing the Natural Way* (1983), a book for college writers. It is guaranteed to show your non-poets that they really are
poets (everybody has a good poem in them.) The experience depends
entirely on your showing them how. So I am going to use a poem of mine,
not as a model for your students, but as one to show you how to write
one of your own. **Then use your poem as the model for your kids.**

Begin by thinking of a person close to you and whom you want to
write a poem to. Put the name in the center of your overhead or the
middle of your blackboard, and cluster impressionistic details about

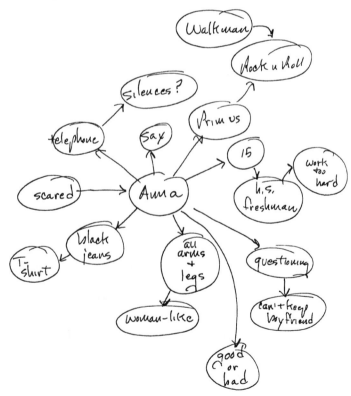

this person. (If writing in front of your students scares you, you can do the cluster and the poem in your journal the night before.) The notion of the cluster is to generate ideas for the poem, but also to get closer to the real experience of knowing this person.

I am going to write my poem to my daughter Anna who turned fifteen last month—and who I'm sure thinks she's the only female to go through the world-shaking experiences of trying to grow up. I continue adding details to the cluster until I am literally ready to write. If I start the poem and come up dry, I go back and add to the cluster until I'm ready to write again.

I talk the class through my cluster as I am putting it on the board or the overhead. Then they begin their own clusters. I give them a sample poem from an earlier lesson to show them the form I use, and we continue writing our poems together.

The form of the poem is simple, and that is really the secret to the whole thing. Any variation is OK, but suggest they begin the first line "This is my poem to…" or "This is a poem to…" and that one way to start the lines that follow are with **who** or **whose** or **and who**. The last line can be a conclusion or summary of the feelings in the poem. There is no way to do it wrong.

This is my poem to Anna, who is fifteen and not her daddy's girl anymore—and not a woman either
who is all arms and legs and dark hair and eyes and makeup and black jeans and t-shirts with funny pictures on them
who likes French and makes good grades and whose homework and stuff is an obstacle course through my house
who talks too long on the phone and can't keep a boyfriend but has lots of boy friends and always, always wants to know Why? in just that voice when I won't let her do whatever notion just ran through her head
who likes pizza and cats and MacDonalds and popcorn and sweet, sweet icetea and playing the sax and Heavy Metal rock and Monty Python
and who is too quiet sometimes and sometimes laughing and always outrageous and always arguing with her mom
who is too bad to be good and too good to be bad
who confuses my days, brightens my eyes, and brings wonder and chaos into my life
my daughter, Miss Anna, fifteen.

Give it a try. It works, and your kids may surprise you in their sharing.

And that, we think, is a good place to end this chapter on private writing and look ahead to the Public Self.

References

Brown, H.J. (1991). *Life's little instruction book*. Nashville, TN: Rutledge Hill Press.

Gere, A.R. (1985). *Roots in the sawdust*. Urbana, IL: NCTE.

Grossman, F. (1991). *Listening to the bells*. Portsmouth, NH: Heinemann.

Kirby, D., and G. Hulme. (1982). *The writing process 7*. Boston: Allyn and Bacon.

Kirby, D., and T. Liner. (1988). *Inside out*. Portsmouth, NH: Heinemann.

Leslie, C.W. (1987). *A naturalist's sketchbook*. New York: Dodd, Mead.

Rico, G.L. (1983). *Writing the natural way*. Boston: Houghton Mifflin.

Rief, L. (1992). *Seeking diversity*. Portsmouth, NH: Heinemann.

Romano, T. (1987). *Clearing the way*. Portsmouth, NH: Heinemann.

Sebranek, P., V. Meyer, and D. Kemper. 1992. *Write source 2000*. Burlington, WI: Write Source.

"I remember Carl" is reprinted from *Clay and Pine*, Georgia Southwestern College, Spring 1994.

Heather's Story

Summer of the Unicorns

Once upon at time in a magical world far, far away, the mares gather with their stallion before their departure to give birth. The stallion is happy and sad at the same time, happy to be a father and sad to see them go.

Two days later when the mares return, the young can walk. They look like their father with a silver mane, a nub for a horn, and a purple star on their head.

The next day the mares let the colts go frolicking through the lush green forest. They were fascinated by the butterflies and beautiful flowers.

But one day as they were grazing in the meadow, a troll from the Black Lake led one of the unicorns away. Luckily the stallion saw the troll and chased him through the enchanted forest all the way to the edge of the Black Forest where the troll was banished forever.

Just to be sure, the unicorns used their magic to put an invisible wall around the Black Forest and the Black Lake, so the Trolls couldn't get out, no matter how hard they tried.

(Heather Fletcher, 5th grade, Radium Springs Elementary)

8

Writing: The Public Self

More the Same than Different

Going down to the mentally disabled room, I expected to see people drooling and beating on their chests. I saw no physical disabilities. Not anything out of the normal. As a matter of fact, two of the boys in that class could beat me in running. The only reason they are in that room is they have to work individually with them. In some cases, it's like that in my class. All they need is a little extra help. From the smiling faces, and talking out of turn, I honestly thought I was in an ordinary classroom.

The students were asked to stand up and tell a little about themselves. The first student was a girl. She stated her name and said she liked football. Some of the guys laughed, but I know plenty of girls that like football. But there was one person who said he liked basketball and girls. Well, so do I. He like to run and do many of the things I liked to do also. Many of the people were just like me in their daily activities. I just wish people would realize that they are people, and have feelings just like me and you.

I used to joke about them and occasionally make fun of them. Going down there made me feel kind of stupid. Here I am thinking they were so retarded and everything, and they were just like you and me. They need no sympathy, just good friends. Once you talk to them, you will see. They are more the same than different.

(Ross Cook, 7th grade, Merry Acres Middle)

Ross wrote this piece for an essay contest on special education. A public exposition with a specified title and topic, restricted in form and length. Still the writing is all his because of the experience behind it. What he learned first hand is evident in his essay.

As she always does with essay contests, Melissa Moore at Merry Acres Middle made the assignment voluntary. Students like Ross who wanted to try it spent several class periods in small groups in one of the school's special ed classes, where the teacher Tina Williams put them to work with her kids on math problems. Coming back to English class, they talked about their experience, wrote the essays, edited them together, conferenced with Melissa and with each other, shared them with the class, and sent them to the judges.

Deborah and I think that is a good model for this kind of public writing.

Going public is what this chapter is about. Really, it continues the discussion in the last chapter because the processes and experiences with writing range from what might appear to be very private first thoughts in the journal to submitting a polished piece of writing to an unknown and distant audience. There are many kinds of public writing. Deb and I believe our job as writing teachers is to encourage students to risk themselves, first with their peers and us, then to seek audiences further and further away from the safe nest of the classroom. In one sense, to become public writers is to be real writers.

I like starting this chapter with Ross' essay because I know this young writer, and I watched him grow this year. I watched him share with his buddies in the safe environment Miss Moore had created. I remember when he lost his writing folder in the middle of the Journey. He is a real seventh grader! And I saw him do something one day I almost missed. He had a zero draft of the Journey and shared it with some others in a group. All of the stories were just starting and were pretty crude at that point. His was OK. When the reading and talking ended, Ross shook his head and said something to Bobby. He really liked Bobby's war story. "I don't like mine," he said. Just that simple. I thought he was just discouraged or didn't want to work on the piece maybe. You know how a kid will resist editing his work sometimes. I asked him if he were sure. He was. And he started over that class period and wrote a story that turned out to be much better than the first attempt. I think he grew in the process.

We don't define public writing too rigidly. Ross was becoming a writer among writers when his group shared zero drafts. That was the beginning of his public voice. And that sharing in his group helped him grow in the confidence I see in his essay for the contest.

In this chapter we will describe some writing experiences from outstanding teachers who encourage the public voice. And we will talk about publishing and practical matters related to getting your students into print.

Where I Stand

My goal with any class is to publish them right away. Beyond self-expression, there is only one reason to write—to be read by somebody else. Every writer needs the experience of seeing her words in print and knowing they are read by her peers. So I publish them in the classroom as soon as I can, in the first week if possible. The **Where I Stand** essay is fast, and it always produces good writing for me. Because the form is prescribed, it can be quickly edited and published. It is also personally revealing in a non-threatening sort of way, which makes it a good introductory piece to use.

Angela Moore at Georgia Southwestern College taught me how to write it. She got it from Lilly Bridwell at the University of Minnesota, who got the idea from a column by Robert Cromie in the *Chicago Tribune* (1969). So you see how these things work sometimes.

I use it to introduce myself to my students, and it gives them a model to follow at the same time. I change it slightly for each group, and it obviously is revised every time I use it. Here is mine, revised for you. You do your own for your kids.

Where I Stand
Tom Liner
June 5, 1993
Fair is fair. Because I ask you to write about yourself, I will share myself with you.

I am middle-aged, 49, a grandfather, and usually happy. I am something of a dreamer, a book reader, a writer, a thinker. And that's OK. I like me just fine. I live in Albany, Georgia—and that's in south, south Georgia! I have lived and worked in my home state almost all of my life. I am quiet most of the time, rather shy. I am a grateful Christian, and I hope it shows.

I like fly fishing, good books, cats, Saturday mornings, good coffee, kidding around with my daughter Anna, spending time with my wife Myrna, wool shirts, fire light, rivers, the deep woods. I don't watch much TV, but I like movies and like watching mysteries with the girls. The casual violence on prime time bothers me, and sometimes I get up and leave the room. We do watch *Doogie Howser* together just about every week. I like the Discovery Channel and a lot of the PBS shows. We just got a VCR, but I'm still leery of it. Some of my favorite musicians are Bob Dylan, Tim Hardin, Harry Chapin, John

Prine, Ralph Vaughn-Williams, Beethoven—many more. But I like church music best and sing joyfully off key. I like children of all ages. I like birds, especially the raptors, and all wild and free things.

I believe that peace is better than war, love better than hate, and that I need to leave this a better place than I found it. I believe in an earth ethic and a wilderness morality. I believe in a God of my understanding, and that you have a perfect right to your own. I believe in teachers and teaching and the public schools.

I do not care for book burners, land developers, Exxon Oil Company, bureaucrats or bureaucracies, cynical politicians, miners and loggers in national forests, bigots of any kind. I don't like red tape, traffic and concrete, cold weather, standardized tests, simple answers to complex questions, nuclear weapons, violence in any form, dumb commercials. I do not think big is better or that money is a measure of success, happiness, or right.

I am tired of hearing about how bad our schools are supposed to be and how white folks and black folks can't get along. I'm tired of pronouncements from the State Department of Education. I am sick nigh unto death of graft, greed, and corruption in high (and low) places. I am tired of ignorance clothed as authority. And I am tired of complaints general and specific.

I favor real reform in education, equal rights for everyone now, gun control, drug-free streets, protecting the environment from the greedy and the callous, and that somehow, with God's help, I have a small role in making all of this happen. I favor speaking the truth, with tolerance and acceptance, under any and all circumstances.

This list is incomplete. When you get to know me you can fill in the gaps.

Every time I use **Where I Stand,** I think of a joyful experience with some of the kids at the Alternative School in my school system. Deloris Spears is one of the best teachers I know. A saintly lady, she is patient and encouraging, loving and demanding. And she will not let a kid go. She has saved scores of them from the streets. She invited me to work with her with this particular class. I came, intending to spend a few mornings writing with them, and spent the school year learning from her and a bunch of tough, street wise and sometimes wonderful students, grades six through twelve!

We did **Where I Stand** in the first week, and she and I read ours to them first. I always make side comments and joke around a lot when

I read it. And the kids had some questions. Ms. Spears read hers and spoke seriously of her family and the experiences she had seen, and they really wanted to know about her. Then we told them to write the essay **just like we had done it**. The short introductory paragraph is optional, and so is the last one. Often students want to include them. But the important thing is to write the **"I am ..." "I like ..." "I believe that ..." "I do not care for ..." "I am tired of hearing about ..."** and **"I favor ..."** paragraphs just the way we did, starting each one with the exact phrase and writing the paragraphs in this order. Our instructions were rigid for this writing; and, after sharing and praising and editing conferences, we published every one of them. The class named the publication *The Life I Live Is My Life*, over my shrill objections. My friend Larry Aultman at the Learning Resources Center bound the booklets for us with a cover one of the students drew. Their faces when we put the publications in their hands—well, it was one of those shining moments you have every once in a while. You've seen it. You know what I mean.

Teaching Journal

As we suggested, write your own **Where I Stand** essay, just like I did mine, and share it with your students as a model for theirs.

The Anatomy of a Memory

This writing experience illustrates how private writing from the journal flows naturally into public writing shared and celebrated with classmates.

All writing has its beginning in narrative. This experience results in a personal narrative that we just call the Anatomy around here. Most good writing teachers I know use it in one form or another. I think Donald Graves taught it first. It always produces good writing for me, and it makes the processes of writing visible. It is a good piece to write early in the term, and it gives students techniques they can use in different ways with all of their writings.

Jay is another one of Melissa Moore's seventh graders. His journal illustrates one way to do the Anatomy.

Step 1: Priming the Pump

Jay's source for the writing is his **Life Map.** His directions are to choose a memory he would like to write about.

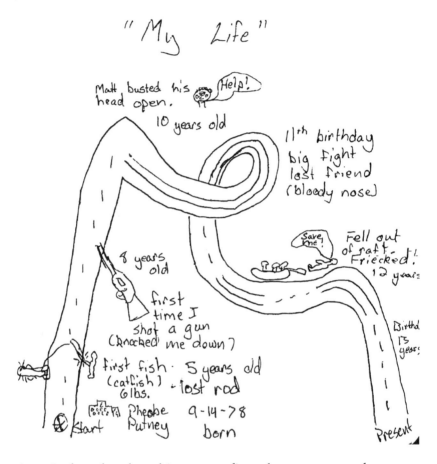

A typical restless boy, his map at first glance seems rather sparse. Contrast it with Misty's in Chapter 7 and you'll see there's not a lot on it. But look again. There are several clearly defined episodes with potential for good stories.

Jay is obviously quite an outdoorsman. He caught his first fish at five. A nice catfish, too, even if he did lose his rod in the process! And he's been hunting since he was eight. Matt, by the way, is his best friend. Jay had the experience most boys have of getting his nose bloodied when he was eleven. And I'm sure you notice the tiny raft from one of his whitewater experiences!

Another way to get them thinking is to ask your students to jot down quickly in brief note form three memories they may want to learn more about by writing. I ask students to try to limit each memory to a particular event that took place in one day in a place they can picture clearly. I find that helps get the details into the story later.

Step 2: Telling Tales

Jay looked over his Life Map and chose the incident when his friend Matt, who is in the same class, was injured on a rock slide on a stream in the mountains. The adventure resulted in 19 stitches for Matt! Then Jay told it to his partner.

Partners are encouraged to listen hard and ask questions to help the writer clarify details of the memory. This also is the first audience check.

Students who have jotted down three memories can tell all three, and their partners help them choose the best one for writing.

Do not skip this step. The talking and listening and responding are important. They are also a lot of fun.

Jay went ahead with what he called the "Head Rock" story and wrote a journal draft; but, hearing some of the narratives in process at his table, he was not satisfied. He went back to his Life Map and chose a white water rafting experience on the French Broad River when he was 12. As you will see, it is an exciting story! He checked it out with his partner and went ahead with it.

Step 3: Sensory Details

Other than the obvious enjoyment and motivation in telling the personal narrative to his peers, what determines if Jay's story will be really good is his selection of the right details to make it real to his reader. This is one place where the transfer from the telling to the page is critical, especially for young writers. And this is one place in the writing process where you can intervene. Miss Moore asked Jay at this point to make a jot list of sensory details, and to put down as many as he could think of. This is how he jotted them in his journal.

Detail List — Falling out of Raft

Sight	Sound	Touch	Taste	Smell
red huge	running	stiff	nasty	pine
raft	trickling	paddle	water	scent
flowing	water	very old	delicious	water-
green	excited	river	hotdog	like
brown	screams	warm	hot.	scent
rocks	cries for	embrace	fries	rubber
clear dirty	help	bouncy	sweet	burning
water	laughing	raft	coke	trash
black	voices	padded	gritty	barbecue
rubber	phrases	life-jacket	sand	cooking
bottom	rushing	coarse	warm	
white	hydrolic	branch	blood	
shoes	cracking	hard		
blue	branch	rocks		
bandana	splashes	jagged		
silver	thuds	undercut		
ring	rock			
painter rope				
blue				
paddle				
green				
shorts				
fear in				
eyes				
surprised				
faces				
swirling				
hydrolic				

Jay's list is substantial, of course; and that is what I'm looking for. If I look over his shoulder and see a very short list of general items, we need to talk about this thing some more. And he will need to stretch that list.

Another effective pre-writing technique I often use for getting the good details into the piece instead of jotting is **clustering**. It is the same technique from Gabriele Rico (1983) you saw illustrated with *This Is My Poem to* . . . in Chapter 7. You may use similar techniques like Turkey Tracking, Webbing, or Mapping. I like to teach jotting and clustering to young writers, so they have a choice of techniques. But I don't teach both at the same time.

Step 4: Zero Draft

This is not even a first draft. This is a discovery draft of the story written as fast as you can write it. If they get stuck, tell them to write around the hard parts. The Anatomy will probably be the longest piece of original prose many of your students will have written (I don't count dismal reports copied laboriously out of the encyclopedia). Encourage them to push on through and get the story told and to worry about spelling and punctuation and grammar and all that stuff later. Just get it done.

This is how Jay started his Zero Draft.

> Falling out of a raft into freezing cold water can really spook you.
> It doesn't happen to many people but it happen[ed] to me.
> The day started out as your typical day of rafting, cold, clear water, nice rapids, and beautiful scenery. Well, that was how it was for a while.

That is all he got done in one class period, and he wasn't satisfied with it. The next day he struck through the two short paragraphs and wrote "Too bland" in his journal, and started the Zero Draft over.

> I gazed ahead of the raft to see the biggest rapid, Frank Bell's, looming in the distance. I thought we were going to go down, have a great time, and take out. Boy!! Was I wrong.

Jay makes a note at this point that he needs a descriptive paragraph and drives on through the draft without stopping. And almost without indenting either. His Zero Draft is very rough. There is no conclusion and details are sketchy. It is two journal pages long in Jay's rather large blocky hand. It does not have the dialogue that will flavor the finished story. But he does get to the heart of the narrative.

Step 5: Audience Check—Partner Response

Jay reads the draft out loud to his partner. Hearing his story for the first time is really what is important. He also is instructed to tell his partner what help he needs with the story, what to listen for. **The writer always speaks first.** That's ownership. Your responsibility is to tell me what to respond to in your story. I don't just jump in and tell you to change things I don't like. The partner does, of course, ask questions.

Jay is still troubled by his lead. He and his partner talk about it, and he tries a new one.

> "Wow!" I said as I gazed ahead of the raft. I was looking at the huge, looming rapid ahead....

He has found his opening. But there is still a lot of work to do.

Step 6: Draft #1

Jay rewrites the story with the intention of fleshing out the skeleton he has formed. This is the first full draft of the piece. He needs to do three things with this draft, finish the story, add details of action and description to make the rafting adventure real, and add dialogue to bring to life the characters in the raft with him. Jay's story grows to over five pages in this draft.

As you work with your students, this is a good place to encourage them to do the same kinds of things Jay did with his story, fill out the details, work with the lead and conclusion, and get the dialogue in.

Step 7: Audience Check—Peer Editing

Now it's time to get down to the nitty gritty work of turning a good story into an excellent piece of writing. Miss Moore gives her students an editing check list at this point to help groups focus on specific things in the piece. Melissa likes to give students xeroxed lists they can keep in their journals and folders. The specific contents of the list will depend on the needs of the particular class. What do you see in their narratives they need to work on most? After hearing Jay read this version of his story, his editing group looked at these things.

Definite setting.
Chronological order, clear sequence of events.
Realistic dialogue.
Showing rather than telling.

Melissa also includes sentence structure variety and grammar errors and mechanics on the check list. I like to keep editing check lists simple, with no more than five items. Go with the most obvious needs and keep the focus on writers' concerns and not just a grammar and spelling check.

Step 8: Publishing

As soon as he can get on the schedule, Jay is off to Linda Clark's computer lab downstairs to type up his story. He will have a final conference with Miss Moore on the piece before it is finished, and his group will help him proofread. Finally he attaches the story to a colorful piece of construction paper with a photo of the raft on the French Broad River and puts it up on the classroom wall. The story will also appear in the class publication and be sent to the local newspaper for the regular youth column. It will also be chosen as a school winner and overall middle school winner for the county in the big writing contest promoted by the State Department of Education. From a personal memory in his journal, the piece has become a very public story indeed.

This is Jay's finished product. We include it because it is a good story—and a good illustration of the Anatomy—and so you can use it with your students if you are teaching the Anatomy for the first time. After that, you will have models of your own by people they know.

Drowning!

"Wow!" I said as I gazed ahead of the raft. I was looking at the huge, looming rapid ahead. "So this is why they call it a paddler's heaven." I was talking about Frank Bell's Rapid, the biggest rapid and hydraulic on the French Broad River, a truly beautiful and scenic river. However, it is not only known for its clear water and wonderous, green trees. In fact, it is probably better known for its totally awesome whitewater. That day in August I definitely noticed the whitewater more. I got plenty of it and then some.

The day had gone rather nicely, with a few minor rapids here and there. But when we stopped to scout Frank Bell's, I knew something was wrong.

"No way we're going to run that!" I cried nervously.

Our friend Tom Law, an experienced whitewater paddler, said, "Oh, come on, Jay, it's not that big."

"Bull!" I shouted.

"Don't be a woos, Jay!" said my good friend Brian Rooks.

"Shut-up! You're the one in the safest part of the raft!"

"Just because I'm in the middle doesn't mean I won't get thrown out."

"Maybe so, but being in the middle sure does make it a lot more unlikely."

My mom mentioned in a soft tone, "Now you two scaredy-cats come over and get in the raft. We're running it second."

"Uh-oh!"

"Oh-boy!"

Tom pushed the raft off shore and we started our descent towards the rapid. As we went over the first ledge everyone started screaming wildly. The first boat had turned over in the swirling, suction-filled hydraulic, sometimes called a hole.

About that time Tom yelled, "Hard right or we'll hit that rock!"

Everybody paddled their brains out and we just barely missed the rock, but there wasn't time to recover. We were headed straight for the hydraulic!

Tom frantically screamed, "Hard left! Hard lef..."

"Crrraaa...!" I screamed as the nose of the raft plopped down right in the middle of the hole. The nose dipped for a second and then came back up.

When we were about half way through it, I heard Tom cry, "Uh-oh! We're losing her!"

He was right. The raft sneaked up on its side and everybody's weight shifted away from my side. The boat acted like a catapult.

"Nnnooo!" I cried as I was shot out of the raft like a bullet. The boat righted itself, but I was sitting in the water with my paddle in my hands.

Soon as I had hit the water, which felt like hitting a brick wall, I had started to bob up and down from the pull of the hydraulic. My life jacket had been the only thing holding me up, until I hit the center.

About that time I got sucked under and held there. After what seemed like a year I was shot back up. But instead of breathing in the wonderous air, I hit something. I opened my eyes to see the black rubber bottom of my raft through the clear water. It was then that I went into shock. I thought I was going to die.

Just as I used up my last bit of oxygen, the raft passed over me and I came up gasping, my lungs yelling for oxygen.

Well, I caught up with the raft and was finally dragged back in. My mind was blurry and the only thing I could feel was my mom's warm embrace.

Tom joked, "Have fun, Jay? We saw you under the raft!"

"Uuhhh..." I mumbled as we beached the raft.

After the whole incident was over we went home to a warm blanket and a steaming cup of hot cocoa. Boy, what a day!

When I look back at it I laugh, but I wouldn't want that particular thing to happen again. In a way, though, it has made me want to conquer other rivers as well as that one. I still run rivers; in fact, I run even bigger ones. They're fun, too. Just as long as something like that doesn't happen again, I'll run as many rivers as I have the chance to.

(Jay McAfee, 7th grade, Merry Acres Middle)

Teaching Journal

You know what's coming, don't you. Now write your own **Anatomy of a Memory**. This is a major writing assignment, and you will need to give it some time. If you are very brave, do it with your students, demonstrating each step. Or write it on your own to share with them. Remember, the model of your writing—especially if you write with them—is more powerful than anything we can give you in this book.

Books for Little Kids

Linda Waters' seventh grade students at Radium Springs Middle School are making books to share with the little kids over at the elementary school. Linda is the kind of teacher who has so much energy and enthusiasm that you never see her still. And it's catching! She is also very, very proud of her kids, thinks they can do anything and tells them so, and shows them off every chance she gets.

Her students tell me about their work and walk me through the steps in the production. First she gives them an overview of the project. They will write and illustrate a book to share with little kids in kindergarten and the first two grades of the elementary school nearby. The story must be about a "human value" and teach a worthwhile lesson. Ms. Waters brings in a box full of children's books, and they read and talk about the values illustrated in each one. They brainstorm a list of things they want to teach the little kids.

> Honesty—not stealing, not lying, not cheating in school
> Tolerance for other races, accepting people who are different
> Saying no to drugs, the dangers of drug abuse
> Getting along with other people, not fighting
> Having a positive self-image, believing in yourself
> Being a friend
> Doing homework and school work, being responsible
> Child abuse
> Drinking
> Helping people who are less fortunate

Then they go to their journals to write exploratory drafts, frequently browsing the children's books for ideas. But they are not ready to make their books yet.

Ms. Waters has them take a sheet of notebook paper, fold it down the middle and fold it across two more times. That divides the page into eight even spaces on each side. They have just created a story board for planning the finished book, which will have 16 pages. Children's books have little print on a page, just a sentence or two with an illustration. They use the divided sheet to write the text of their book, seeing how the story will fit the pages. There is also room in the blocks to make notes about illustrations.

The planning sheet also gives Linda an opportunity to conference with each student on his story and a chance to make editing suggestions.

The books are put together simply by taking four sheets of legal sized paper (14 inches long), folding them together in the middle, and stapling them at the fold in three places.

Some of her students are anxious about illustrations because they don't think they can draw well enough for this project. Linda suggests three ways of doing the illustrations. First, those who want to can draw their own. She provides tracing paper so students can trace characters out of the children's books in the room and carefully cut them out and glue them in their creation. Or they can ask friends in the class to draw the character or scene on a separate sheet of paper, cut it out and carefully glue it into the book. The books encourage a lot of group work and a lot of cooperation among the class.

Finally the books are finished. The buses come and take the kids to Radium Springs Elementary School where the principal Jan Henningfeld and the primary grades teachers and classes of excited little kids are waiting on them. They have a wonderful time. Every class in kindergarten, first, and second grades gets to see and hear the seventh graders, including the special ed classes. For the little kids it's a real treat, and Linda's kids are heroes.

We will tell you more about making books later in this chapter.

Action Research

This research is not done in the library. Students have to go somewhere and make a contact and talk to somebody. Then they write a story about what they find out. So the minimum requirements are an interview and a narrative. Because they are interested in what they are doing, they often do much more. There is nothing new about Action Research. It's basic reporting. We just want a story instead of a news article.

This assignment is not one you want to use early in the year. It works better when your students are experienced and confident writers. We try to keep the steps simple.

Brainstorming. Using the board or the overhead projector, we lead the class in a brainstorming session about interesting people and events that are good prospects. The object, we remind them, will be an interesting true story about the person they choose. Many of the subjects are relatives, and that's OK.

The Interview. Students are briefed on how to do good interviews and etiquette. They are also asked to brainstorm a list of questions. We talk about open-ended questions, and sometimes we role-play interviews in class to sharpen our technique. Tape recording is optional, but students are told to **take notes even if you tape it.** Too many things can go wrong with a tape recorder. A week is a reasonable deadline for the interview to get done, by the way. Be patient. You will have to make allowances for missed appointments and scanty notes that have to be beefed up in a follow-up interview. Allow a second week for makeups.

The Writing. We always spend some time talking about what students learned in their interviews. The sharing sessions are fun, and they often direct students to the most interesting parts for their narratives. Help your students focus on only one event or interesting aspect of the person's life. That will help make their stories better.

Editing Groups. Ask your editing groups to help writers get some real dialogue (or monologue) into the stories. Where possible, we want to hear the voice of the person featured. And as usual, they need to help with getting in the good details. You will see other specific needs in your class.

Publishing. One reason why we like Action Research is the pieces are always good writings to publish in class. They are written to share.

Another approach to Action Research that works well is for it to be done by partners. This is a good project for students to collaborate on.

Melissa Moore at Merry Acres Middle has her seventh graders do a research project she calls a **Portrait.** As the name implies, her students' object is to write a profile of a person they know. They enjoy the experience. The interview with the subject is optional, but her students often interview friends and relatives of their subjects. Melissa stresses editing group work and includes student-student conferences and student-teacher conferences in the writing processes for the piece, as she often does with major writing assignments.

Pat Bradley at Albany Middle uses an interview with a family member part of the **Autobiographical Booklet** her kids do as a culminating project for the year. The object of the whole thing is "to learn more about yourself by learning about your family." The interviews are usually, but not always, with Mom or Dad; and they are relatively simple. Students have to write at least five questions for Pat's review before the interview, and the questions and answers are part of the project, along with a write up on what they learned from the interview. They also write a separate portrait piece about the relative they interviewed. The project itself, and especially the talking and writing they do about their relative, is always a special experience for Ms. Bradley's kids. We tell you more about Pat's project in the **Culminating Experiences** portrait after Chapter 11.

I-Search

Ken Macrorie is a particular hero of mine. I have read, enjoyed, and used his books for a long time. He developed the I-Search Paper as an answer to the dreary term papers college students are required to do, and his book by the same title (1988) will give you his techniques and a lot of student examples. That's one thing I always enjoy about Macrorie, he shows you how it's done.

I don't want to steal his thunder or try to repeat in a couple of paragraphs what he details in 350 pages. What I will do is sketch out for you very quickly how I've seen the I-Search used.

First and most importantly, **the topic finds you.** This is the heart of the research. The topic must be something the student really wants to know. No canned topics for this one. And you will need to take time with your kids to wean them away from choosing something to please the teacher.

I recently did an I-Search with a class of thirty-five students. The hardest, and most important, thing to do was convince them to choose something really important to them. Only two students failed the assignment. No, they didn't make F's. I don't remember their grades. They simply did not believe in the process and turned in dreary papers copied from encyclopedias.

Resource sessions are an important part of the process. Put all the students in a big circle that includes you. Each student in turn tells the class her topic, and all of you talk it over and suggest resources she might try. Most of your resources will be people.

You will be impressed as I was with how much the kids know. Together, they have a lot of information to share with each other. Their suggestions usually are genuinely helpful, and the resource sessions are fun. Keep them positive, and take lots of time for them and take time with them.

Tip: Once you start the resource sessions, keep an up-to-date list of all the research topics and who is doing what posted by the door of the classroom.

Keep requirements simple. Here are the requirements for the class I worked with as we did the I-Search together.

1. A real topic, important to you.

2. One printed source.

3. One live source.

4. A paper about your search at least one, but no more than five, computer-printed pages long, including a list of sources at the end.

No note cards, no footnotes, no outline, no complicated bibliography (keep the resource list as simple as possible.) Some students used their journals for notes. Some used big legal pads that were provided, which, as a matter of fact, is what I use when I research something.

Keep the paper simple. I suggest Macrorie's scheme for organizing the paper, but allow your students the freedom to write it any way they wish. Most will probably follow Macrorie's scheme. It is simple and makes plain good sense.

Write the paper in four basic parts. First, tell me what you knew and didn't know about your topic when you started. Secondly, tell me why you made this search. Third, tell the story of the search. Then tell what you learned—or didn't learn—in your search. Tell it like a story.

Thirty-three of the thirty-five students wrote exciting papers because they were excited about what they were learning. The one I remember best is Allison's. Her I-Search was on being a private investigator, and the best part was when a local detective let her handle his unloaded .357 magnum!

And remember. Unlike those boring term papers read only by the teacher, I-Searches are for sharing.

Teaching Journal

No, we are not going to ask you to do an I-Search or Action Research. This Teaching Journal is to push you to do some lesson planning for your classes. Outline a research project you want to use with them. You may want to try Action Research or a Portrait or the I-Search, or you may see other needs your students have or special opportunities in your local area. Get out your calendar and plan the steps they, and you, will follow with the Research Project and plan deadlines, resource sessions, conferences and editing sessions, and a time for sharing the finished products.

Getting It Ready for the Public

Writing Conferences

I do not consider myself good in writing conferences with students. Deb is much better at it than I; I've watched her do it. And Melissa Moore and Paul Gainer are wonderful. They seem always to know what to say and how to respond to push the student a little farther, to help him make just the right revisions or additions to really fix up the writing. They are warm and inviting and supportive and pushy and precise and demanding and—well, wonderful confidants and counselors and editors with their students. I'm not. I get tongue-tied. I think of the right thing to say, if at all, fifteen minutes later. Very often I enjoy the writing, but I come up blank. Very often I don't enjoy the writing, and I don't know what to suggest and how not to assume ownership and hurt the young writer's feelings. And sometimes I just don't know what to tell them to do.

If you sometimes feel the way I do in a conference with your student, take heart. This little section is for you.

I am still learning how to do it, but I have learned a few things about writing conferences through some trial and error and a whole lot of watching people whom I admire.

The writing belongs to the writer. I try to remember that. Have you ever taken the paper away from your student in a conference? I have. I have literally snatched it out of her hands and started marking it up before I could stop myself! Now I sit on my hands. It does not belong to me; I keep my hands to myself. And the apprentice writer gets to make all those decisions about what to fix—and what not to fix—in her writing. By the way, I have also learned from experience that it will be OK. She will learn, she will grow as a writer, the writing will get better. I can trust the process.

I am honest. Tactful, considerate, supportive—but I don't say, "That's nice"—when I should say, "It needs work." I do not embarrass students. I do not ridicule them. I try to know them as well as I can, and I tell them the truth.

The writer speaks first. In any conference about your writing, the first thing I need to know is what help you want before I jump into the middle of your work. I believe it is good for the young writer to be able to put into words what bothers him about his writing and what he wants to make better. That's part of the learning.

The writer reads the piece aloud. I need to hear it, and so does the writer. I always read a new piece of mine with a pen in my hand. And I encourage students to do that, by example first and by telling them to pick up the pencil literally when they start to read. I always make changes when I read my writing out loud. It doesn't matter how many times I've read it silently or how polished I think it is. As a writer, I must hear the piece.

And it helps me to hear it from the writer in the conference. I hear it whole. We are not distracted by glitches in spelling and form that will be fixed later in proofreading. More importantly, the rhythms of the writing are there, and the personality of its writer. It has a voice.

Be specific. "That's nice" or even "That's great!" do me little good unless you can tell me what parts are nice and what makes it great. Unless I answer a direct question from the writer, my first comment in a conference begins, "I like the part where you...." That gets us down to the nitty gritty immediately.

Reflective listening is the best response. I am not good at it at all, but I am practicing. I listen hard as the student reads, and I tell her what I just heard. And I tell her in as much detail as I can. Simple, but not easy for me. But it really does a lot for the apprentice writer. It literally gives her an audience's perspective on the piece. Try it. And don't be discouraged if it takes a little while to get the hang of it.

Conferences are brief. Five or six minutes. I try not to go over ten unless it's an unusual situation. I need to see everybody often, and we can continue our talk tomorrow. If I find I am staying too long in conferences, I time myself and break them off after ten minutes. I go to students usually instead of calling them up to me. It saves time, and I like to be among them.

Three kinds of teacher-student conferences. Deborah and I work with individual students and their writing in three basic ways.

There is the "How's it going?" conference done while the piece is being written or at any stage from journal to publishing. We just interrupt them and ask, "How's it going?" And get them to read what has been written to that point. Sometimes we stay and talk, if that seems appropriate or if the student wants help. Sometimes we point out something we like and move on.

We also conference with students over completed drafts, usually the first full version of a piece. This conference may take a little longer, but often it continues in a second class period. We talk about the whole piece and the writing. It is important in this conference for the student to tell me what she wants, looking toward revision. We try not to concern ourselves with mechanics in this session unless students ask.

The proofreading conference is for final cleanup for publishing. Frankly, if it looks like there are a lot of glitches in the draft, I assign the kid to his partner or his editing group to work the piece over again before he and I go over it. Even in this proofreading conference, by the way, we like students to read their writing aloud; and we want them to tell us what they want help with. It's still their writing, not ours.

Please note. I do not mean to imply we talk to the student only three times while the piece is written and revised. We will have several conferences on each writing from zero draft to published work.

Peer Conferences

Forgive me if I'm a little fancy with the terminology. What we're talking about is working with a partner on your writing. If real writing and sharing is going on in my class, this happens spontaneously anyway. Friends can and do get together about their writing at any time and at any phase of the writing. But I do nudge them to help each other in specific ways. That can be as simple as telling partners at large, "OK, partners, check out the dialogue on this draft"—or as detailed as an editing checklist or poster reviewed in a mini-lesson with the class.

Do not assume that because your students are reading papers to each other they know how to respond helpfully. They probably have little experience with this sort of thing, and you'll have to direct them, at least at first. I keep it simple. First, I insist that papers are read out loud to partners. None of this passing papers across the tables. As partners start working together on that first writing, I ask them to Listen, Praise (and this should be about something specific), Question, and Help. You may want them to take notes as they listen and talk, if you feel you need to check on them. Melissa Moore gives her students a half sheet of paper with the bold letters **P, Q, P** down the left side with space for notes by each letter. Her students are to Praise, Question, and Polish in conferences. They use the note sheets with partners and in editing groups and turn them in with the draft of the paper. She gives credit for them like any other assignment.

Keep this in mind. I teach a student to be a good responder to her partner every time I have a writing conference with her. I show her what to listen for and the kinds of things to say. This is the best way to teach the skill.

I also circle the whole class regularly for sharing sessions. We enjoy the readings very much, but I also use the sessions to model responses as each student reads. And I talk to them in these sessions about the kinds of things l listen for and why I say some of the things I do. I think it helps them when they are working together as partners and in the editing groups. **One caution:** My responses in the circle of the whole class are always positive. This is no setting for criticism of any kind. I am very careful about that, and I insist on it from them.

One more tip on this subject. I usually will not have a conference with a kid on a finished draft until he has read it to his partner and talked it over. "What did your partner say?" is my first question.

Editing Groups

I learned my craft sitting in small groups with other struggling writers, sharing with them, listening to them, arguing and laughing and crying with them. Editing groups grow writers. They will be some of the best cooperative learning experiences your students will have. They also take planning, and good groups have to be trained. Deb and I have used editing groups in the classroom for many years, sometimes more successfully than others. A few tips from our experiences may make your job with them easier.

I teach students how to respond by the way I respond. What I said about teaching partners to work together on writing is true of editing groups. Basically I show them how. I also participate in the groups as much as I can, rotating from group to group. I bring my writing to the group just like they do, but I've learned not to assume leadership in it. That's their job. And I'm learning to shut up and listen more than talking.

Papers are always read out loud. Yes, I've said that a lot in these two chapters. It's just that important.

The writer always speaks first and tells the group what help she needs with the piece. This will be awkward with inexperienced group members at first, but be patient and keep after them. It really does work.

Everybody in the group responds. No one can hang back and be silent. Insist on their participation in responding as well as reading. Everybody belongs. Everybody is a full member of the group.

Expectations of the group are clear. Kate Kirby in Gwinnett County near Atlanta taught me the simple notion of putting a poster up for editing groups each week. A typical poster while groups work on an Anatomy like Jay's might include a list like this one.

Show it, don't tell it.
Dialogue? Make sure it has some.
Strong lead.
Quotations and punctuation.
Verb tense consistent?

Five items or less on the check list, most of which deal with real writer concerns and a couple on mechanics and usage. The list is based on the perceived needs of the class and presented in a mini-lesson.

Other expectations of the group are also important. Deadlines need to be posted and explained. And groups need to know exactly how you expect them to function.

The circle within a circle for training works very well for me in showing students how an editing group should operate. Sandra Worsham from Milledgeville was Georgia's Teacher of the Year a few years ago, and she demonstrated how she trained rural and disadvantaged students to participate in a writing group. The circle within a circle is her technique, and it works.

As we get ready for our first editing sessions, I pull together a group of five writers, including myself, in the middle of the room. Pick four kids who have a lot of confidence for this, or borrow four of your kids from last year. I ask the rest of the class to circle closely around us. "Sit as close as you can so you can see what we are doing." Then I lead an editing session, being as careful as I can to explain things as we go along—reading the piece aloud, the writer's telling the group what help she needs, how we respond. I go deliberately around the group (I do read my writing first), showing that we all read and we all talk after each reading. I talk about the responsibility of the group leader to make sure everybody participates. Usually thirty minutes or less is enough time to demonstrate the group as it works and talk them through it.

All of us in the middle are self-conscious, of course; but we make it through OK and the demonstration really does help get the groups started well.

It's OK for kids to talk about experiences in editing groups. All writers do it. Most of us talk more about the experiences in the writing and the things that have happened to us the writing conjures up than we do about things like technique and form and character and plot and all that. The most commonly heard phrase is some variety of "That reminds me of the time . . ." Don't expect your students to be on-task and talking about making the writing itself better every minute they are in their groups.

Lighten up. They are on-task in the real sense anyway because there is a good bit of evidence such talk does help young writers improve. It may be the motivation in the fun of sharing that makes them want to write more so they can share it with their group. It may the a growing sense of audience. It may be that this kind of talking just fills up the well of ideas any writer needs. But the talk itself also helps students improve writing technique. Their writing gets better in groups where talk about their experiences as well as writing technique is tolerated and encouraged by your example.

Now I try to use a little common sense. If I pass by a group and they are talking about the dance after school or the fight in the cafeteria, I stop them and get them back to work.

Five is the right number in an editing group. James Moffett (1968) was right. I've learned from experience I want no less than four and no more than six kids in an editing group. No, I don't know why. Five is the magic number.

Going Public: Getting Them into Print

Publishing Do's and Don't's

Conferencing, editing groups, and publishing overlap in the working classroom. At the risk of saying things over, Deborah and I share a few things from our experience from those times when the piece is ready to be published.

1) *Never publish a student's work without her expressed permission.* We never assume she wants it on the bulletin board or in the weekly class publication. We've learned to ask. We are particularly careful about the student's journal. The rule here is ownership.

2) *Nobody is left out.* At the same time, we make sure every student is included in whatever publication effort is going on. Even when he turns us down about the poem we think is so special, we make sure something else by him is included.

3) *Publish often.* And publish in many ways. We have a read-around once a week. With some classes we try to have something from them in print for the class to read weekly. But every two weeks for run-it-off-and-hand-it-out publishing is reasonable. Some classes will require longer; and some writing experiences, like the Anatomy of a Memory or the Journey, will take several weeks before pieces are ready for print.

Culminating publications, like Melissa Moore's *The Young and the Writeous* anthology of student work or Deloris Spears' *The Life I Live is My Life,* are special to classes and will be remembered by young writers. We make sure we have those special publications.

4) *Keep production simple for most publications.* And let the kids do most of the work. That keeps publishing enjoyable for you and them.

Deb sets up a **Publishing Center** in one corner of her room with different kinds and colors of paper, wall paper samples and binding materials, rub-on letters, cardboard and poster board, scissors, glue, and at least one computer and printer—everything she can think of for the physical production of printed writing in the classroom. It saves her a lot of hassles.

5) *Protect students from public embarrassment.* Be honest with them about how their work will be perceived outside the classroom. My friend Willie in Ms. Spears' class at the Alternative School wrote well about getting into serious trouble. We enjoyed the sharing in class, but had to talk about how strangers would read the piece.

Print is powerful. You will have a student or two whom you have to advise to choose another writing to publish. Be frank about language and censorship.

6) *Seek wider and more distant audiences for your students.* We publish first in the classroom, then for the school and in our community. And then we try for distant audiences "out there." We are growing writers.

Do not overlook your local newspaper and cable TV company, and don't be shy about talking to them. Several years ago, several of us in my school system started a page just for kids' writing in our local newspaper so they can be read by everybody in town. It took some asking and talking and planning, and it takes a little work. Many newspapers have an education editor or reporter or friendly manager. Talk to them.

In our city the cable TV outfit started running high school news casts last year. No middle school programs yet, but they are possible. Don't be shy.

7) *When you push them out of the nest of your classroom, prepare them for rejection.* And rejection slips and turn-downs can be hard to take. Let them know how competitive it is to be published in a magazine, for example. Any magazine. But that, too, is part of the life of a writer.

8) *Keep in mind that writing, like any art, is a process and not a product.*

The Good Old In-Class Publication

This is the one I like best. For me it ranges from typing up and running off excerpts from student journals (with their permission) over the weekend and passing them out and reading them in class Monday to pieces that have been through the conferences and the editing group and crafted at the computer, like Jay's "Drowning" memory earlier in this chapter. The in-class publication is done often. It is usually xeroxed. But in the spring when the school is out of copying paper and you cannot afford to buy anymore yourself, it may be simply papers collected in a binder and kept in the room to pass around and read. However it is done, keep the production as simple as you can. The main object is for kids to see their words in print to be read in a community of writers. That's what makes it so special.

You will also want to make wall displays a part of your classroom routine. Danna Turner at Dougherty Middle has one wall covered with student poetry. In Melissa Moore's room writings go up as they are finished on a board strip that runs around the room. Jay displayed his story with a photograph, and he published it in the class book. Melissa keeps construction paper and colorful pens and markers and other materials on hand in her Publishing Center, and her students surround the class with clever illustrations and attractively displayed writings.

No matter how busy you are working on getting things ready to be printed, take time to circle the whole class for read-arounds. Reading in the big circle celebrates writing, and it brings everyone in the room together into a community of writers and learners. I suggest you make an opportunity for it once a week. And have big celebrations as you finish projects. Invite parents and your principal and the mayor and anybody else you want to show off your kids to.

If you are not used to doing read-arounds, keep a few things in mind. Allow no sarcasm, no ridicule, no negative comments in the big circle. I put up a **No Hunting** sign and enforce it. No cheap shots. Establish the ground rules simply and firmly. Respond to each reading with a specific, positive comment. You are modeling behavior for your young writers. This will take some concentration and cleverness in some classes, but you will get better with practice. Practice. Make sure everybody reads, and set the example.

Listening and sharing in the big circle with your kids will give you some of your best times in the classroom. Don't miss them.

Making Books

There are several practical ways your students can produce individual books in the classroom. Don Graves, in his well known text for elementary teachers, *Writing: Teachers and Children at Work* (1983), gives you step-by-step instructions for making books with wall paper and cardboard hard covers and floss-sewn spines. Finished, they are colorful and durable and can take their place on your classroom shelves or in the school library. They last for years. The materials to make the books are mostly free, as long as you know where to scrounge.

Regie Routman in *Transitions* (1988) also shows you how to make wallpaper books, but without the sewing. It is, by the way, a book written to elementary teachers that says a lot to me.

Becky Flanigan short cuts production by directing her students to use wall paper samples cut to size for soft covers, and she staples the spines like Linda Waters does. The books are still colorful, durable, and quickly put together. Other teaches use construction paper for their covers. It is not as durable as wall paper samples but can be decorated by each student.

Melissa Moore's culminating class project is a thick book including several pages by each student. The copies have a cover designed by students printed on heavy stock, and they are held together with rolled plastic binders on the spine. The local Learning Resources Center does the work, and you will want to check and see if you have such a supporting agency in your system or community. Still, Melissa's books do cost something for printing covers, sometimes for extra paper because of tight school budgets. You know how that goes. Her principal supports the effort, and sometimes she has to do some fund raising to get the books printed.

Don't be shy to go to your principal or the PTA about raising funds for book making by your students. Making books makes young authors.

Essay Contests

The Daughters of the American Revolution, MADD, the Farm Bureau, Civitan, the State Department of Education, the Bar Association, Kiwanis—and the list goes on. Organizations who send essay contests across the desk of your principal almost weekly. Each one is an opportunity for somebody in your classroom to be recognized, just like Ross' essay that starts this chapter. They are also opportunities for your students to write to those distant, faceless audiences and make their writing fit a particular mode and specific guidelines. The kind of task all writers learn to handle sooner or later. And the recognition when one of your students receives an award or a First Place certificate or a check makes the time and effort students put into these writings worth it.

We don't believe in asking every kid in the class to write to whatever essay contest has been announced. But you do want anybody to have a shot at it who wants to. Ask your principal or your department head to let you know about any writing contests that come across their desks. A lot of them go begging for entries. Post them in a prominent place and make sure your students know about them. It's helpful to keep a calendar of deadlines. Deb and I have found we have to nudge students to try them. No matter how accomplished the young writer, often he is shy about getting out of the nest. Talk about the contest with the class. See who might be interested and push him to try it. Don't insist if he just doesn't want to fool with it. Some writing contests obviously will be better opportunities than others or stir more interest than others, and you may have a group of students who want to write for these. The same processes and routines of conferencing and editing groups are used for this kind of writing where the rules allow, and most contests do not restrict how the piece is written as long as it is the student's work.

Be particularly aware of writing contests from your professional organizations, and especially those of the National Council of Teachers of English. Their eighth grade writing contest, for example, is well run, objectively judged, with high standards of excellence and reasonable writing tasks. NCTE's address is listed at the end of this chapter. Write them for deadlines and guidelines.

Literary Magazines

Frankly, I have mixed feelings about them. They can be elitist. Nobody but the Precious Few see their stuff in print, and the Precious Few are the ones who put the thing together. An unhealthy situation for any age, and certainly bad for middle school kids. And magazines can take a lot of work and money. So weigh your options carefully if you're thinking about starting a literary magazine at your school. It's a good thing to do, but you may want to do other things with your kids instead.

If your school already has a literary magazine and you don't have to sponsor it, enjoy it and help your kids get in it. My biggest thrill today is being read by my peers. If the magazine is too elitist, make noise about it and get the thing changed.

Deb and I started one at Model School in Kentucky because the kids wanted it, which is the best reason for doing one. And they were willing to work hard putting it together. We made sure everybody got a fair shot at being included in it. Basically that translated into whether a student was willing to work with us and her editing group to get a promising piece into shape, just like publishing in class but with a heavier emphasis on proofreading and looking good on the page. Copy had to be "camera ready," i.e. ready for the offset printer. We were doing the thing cheap! We all worked hard together. It was a good project and one the kids were justly proud of. I'd do it again like that anytime.

By the way, the time to stop a literary magazine is when the kids don't want to do it anymore or want you to do all the work.

Sources for Publishing Outside the Classroom

What we give you here is mostly a list of magazines your students can try. We tried to stick with sources that have a reputation and were likely to be around for a while. It is very frustrating to do all that work when there's nobody home anymore. Still, keep in mind that the list is not current as you receive it. We suggest you start your own file of good places for your students to send things.

Three tips that may save you and your students some grief. First, it is always a good idea to write to any publication and ask for editorial guidelines. Send them a SASE (self-addressed, stamped envelope) with your request. A lot of these folks are operating on a tight budget. Get the guidelines the first time one of your students sends something to the publication and keep a copy in your publishing file. Secondly, any submission to any publication should always include an SASE unless they tell you not to. You will not get a response without it. And all writing submitted needs to be typed or word processed. I put my name and address on every page.

We've tried to annotate the list where information was available. And some publications we chose just because they struck our fancy.

Two general sources first. Both of these are for professional free lance writers, so you will have to help students use them and glean their pages for appropriate publications.

The Writer's Handbook
The Writer, Inc.
8 Arlington St.
Boston, MA 02116.

The Writer's Market
Writer's Digest Books
9933 Alliance Rd.
Cincinnati, OH 45242.

Also, a tip of my hat to Nancie Atwell (1987), Candace Deal (1992), and Mildred Grenier (1987) for many of the titles you see here.

Action. 901 College Ave., Winona Lake, ID 46590.
For kids 9 through 11.

Bitterroot Poetry Magazine. P.O. Box 489, Spring Glen, NY 12483.
Submit three or four poems with SASE. $4 for a sample copy.

Boy's Life. 1325 W. Walnut Hillo Ln., P.O. Box 152079, Irving, TX.
This is the Boy Scout's magazine. First person adventure, fiction, poetry. Stories no longer than 400 words. Send submissions to Attention: Reader's Page Editor.

Caboodle: By Kids for Kids. P.O. Box 1049, Portland, IN 47371.
Stories, articles, poems, and puzzles. With each submission, send your name, address, age, grade, parent's name, school and address, teacher's name, and a statement signed by parent or student stating the material is original and the student's own work. This is a common requirement for student publications.

Child Life. 1100 Waterway Blvd. Box 567B, Indianapolis, IN 46206.
Science fiction and mystery magazine for kids to 14.

Children's Album. P.O. Box 6086, Concord, CA 94524.
Fiction and poetry by kids 8 to 14. Write for guidelines.

Children's Digest. 1100 Waterway Blvd., P.O. Box 567, Indianapolis, IN 46202.
Fiction, personal narratives, poetry, jokes, and riddles. Ages 8 to 13. Send SASE for guidelines for students. Sample copy 75 cents.

Children's Express. 245 Seventh Ave., New York, NY 10001.
Fiction, essays, interviews, a little poetry. Ages 6 to 16. Send full name, birth date, grade, and school.

Creative Kids. P.O. Box 6448, Mobile, AL 36660.
Stories, prose, poetry, plays, photography, games, and music. Ages 5 to 18. Send cover letter with name, address, birth date, school, school address, a statement signed by parent or teachers that the work is original, and a photo of the author. Send SASE for guidelines. Sample copy $3.

Cricket. P.O. Box 100, La Salle, IL 61301.
Poetry, stories, and drawings. Ages 6 through 13.

Dragonfly: East/West Haiku Quarterly. P.O. Box 11236, Salt Lake City, UT 84118.
Haiku only, as the name implies. Send SASE for guidelines and sample pages.

Ebony Jr! 820 South Michigan Ave., Chicago, IL 60605.
For kids 6 through 12.

Highlights for Children. 803 Church St., Honesdale, PA 18431.

One of the more popular magazines. Poems, stories, and drawings. Ages up to 15. Prose no longer than 250 words. Send name, age, and home address. They acknowledge submissions but do not return work. No SASE required.

Kids Magazine. P.O. Box 3041, Grand Central Station, New York, NY 10017.

Accepts all kinds of student work. Ages 5 through 15.

Merlyn's Pen. P.O. Box 1058, East Greenwich, RI 02818.

My personal favorite, a magazine made up of student writing. Short stories up to 3500 words, poetry to 100 lines, reviews, travel pieces, drawings. They answer each submission. Write for guidelines. Ask for a sample copy for your classroom. I think you'll want this one in your room.

National Council of Teachers of English. 1111 Kenyon Rd., Urbana, IL 61801.

Eighth grade writing contest. The *English Journal* at this address accepts teaching articles and poetry from teachers.

Poetry USA. Fort Mason Center, Building D, San Francisco, CA 94123.

Includes a section for writers 18 and under. Send to Young People's Editor, with name, age, grade, and address.

Scholastic Scope. 730 Broadway, New York, NY 10003.

The most popular classroom magazine in the country. Poems, stories, plays, mini-mysteries for Student Writing Page. Write for guidelines. Scholastic also publishes *Scholastic Voice*, which accepts student writing. And they sponsor the annual Scholastic Writing Awards Program for grades 7, 8, and 9.

Seventeen. 850 Third Ave., New York, NY 10022.

Girls 12 through 18. Hard to get into. Buys articles of 1,000 words and poetry up to 40 lines.

Spring Tides. 824 Stillwood Dr., Savannah, GA 31419.

Ages 5 to 12. Stories to 1200 words, poetry to 20 lines. Include name, birth date, grade, school, home and school address, and a signed statement by teacher or parent saying the work is original. Send SASE for guidelines.

Stone Soup. P.O. Box 83, Santa Cruz, CA 95063.

For kids under 15. All kinds of writing and art work. The whole magazine is student work. Nice.

Sunshine Magazine. P.O. Box 40, Sunshine Park, Litchfield, IL 62056.

Articles under 150 words and short poems. Send SASE for guidelines.

Young Author's Magazine. 3015 Woodsdale Blvd., Lincoln, NE 68502. Interested in a variety of material, including cartoons, prose, poetry. Ages 6 to 19. Write for guidelines.

Resources

Atwell, N. (1987). *In the middle.* Portsmouth, NH: Boynton/Cook.

Cromie, R. (1969). *Where I stand.* Chicago Tribune.

Deal, C. (1992). *Have your students' work published.* Connections. 29: 2-5.

Graves, D. (1983). *Writing: Teachers and children at work.* Portsmouth, NH: Heinemann.

Grenier, M. (1987). *The beginner's guide to writing for profit.* Babylon, NY: Pilot Books.

Macrorie, K. (1988). *The I-Search paper.* Portsmouth, NH: Boynton/Cook.

Moffett, J. (1968). *Teaching the universe of discourse.* New York: Houghton Mifflin.

Rico, G. (1983). *Writing the natural way.* Boston: Houghton Mifflin.

Routman, R. 1988. *Transitions.* Portsmouth, NH: Heinemann.

Melissa Moore and her Seventh Graders' Journey

Merry Acres Middle School, Albany, Georgia

> "You won't ever hear me say I gave up on anybody."
> —Miss Moore

> "You show me how, and then you walk in their midst."
> —Donald Graves

Melissa Moore's room is crowded. It's full of kids and interesting stuff. The phrase *print rich* is hardly adequate to describe it—*literature rich* and *writing rich* are closer to it. Everything in it reminds students that they are authors and readers, and everything in it gives them choices and responsibility for their choices. And everything in it affirms them.

On one wall "Blue Ribbon Writers" are attractively displayed with clever illustrations. There is a large "NO HUNTING" sign over the front board. By the classroom door is a display of "Publishing" with clippings of writings by students who have been printed in the local newspaper and other places. And there is a pocket for works to be submitted outside the school. Beside that is a "Due Dates" laminated notice board with dates for journals, including partner letters, teacher letter, vocabulary words (found by the students themselves in their reading), and "7 full pages" of their own writing. Journals are due every two weeks on a staggered schedule from different groups. Underneath the "Due Dates" poster are plastic stacked baskets labeled "Journals to be read" and "Journals returned to student."

One particularly crowded corner is a kind of writer-reader's resource center. There is an Apple IIe computer and printer on a small table. Behind it are boxes for journals. In the corner itself are three or four crammed bookcases. Over one full of young adult fiction is a "thumbs up" cutout drawing and a hand-lettered "Rule of Thumb" poster with these points on it.

1. Select a book.
2. Read the first page.
3. Count with your fingers the number of unfamiliar words.
4. If any fingers are not counted, then thumbs up to that book. Read and enjoy.
5. If all five fingers are counted, try another book.

The other bookshelves hold more books for reading, everything from Judy Blume to Mary Shelley, a set of dictionaries, several *Write Source 2000* handbooks, four class publications (named *The Young and the Writeous* by the kids!), the *Writer's Market*, a rhyming dictionary, a spelling dictionary, two almanacs, several illustrated book projects, thesauri, other resources.

On the other side of the room are filing cabinets holding student folders of finished work, more crammed bookshelves, a cabinet with different sizes and kinds of paper and wall paper samples for publishing and displaying writings, a large rough hewn lectern Miss Moore never uses except to put notices and papers on, containers with pencils and pens and markers in a variety of colors and paper clips and staplers, a boom box, and an overhead projector that somehow tilts slightly to one side.

Student work is displayed everywhere, in every available space around the sides and back of the room. Often the writings are illustrated. There are some cutout illustrations that are particularly eye catching. Some have photos with them. All are colorfully displayed in some way.

Students sit at small tables with a partner, but arranged so that three tables are pulled together in a rough U shape putting six kids close to each other. They arrange themselves around the tables according to their moods and the task at hand. The tables are loosely grouped all over the room. It looks random, but Melissa can be at the side of any student quickly.

During the 45 minute class period she will see and talk to each one at least once. How Melissa Moore feels about her kids is reflected in her room. So is her energy and her amazing ability to orchestrate the writing and reading and thinking and sharing and creating and growing of 34 seventh graders at one time.

It's 10:30, Tuesday morning, just a little past mid-year. Class routines are well established, and this group of seventh graders have an enthusiasm and confidence, a special something you sense just coming into the room. They like being here. It's fun. But it's more than that. In here they are challenged to grow. With each experience, they reach a little beyond themselves. Confidently and with a lot of support and encouragement, from each other and from Miss Moore. Like the Journey they are starting.

The Journey is a reading and writing experience developed by Angela Moore (no relation to Melissa) at Georgia Southwestern College. Co-director of the Southwest Georgia Writing Project, Dr. Moore is a writer of some note herself. Her journey activities were planned originally to teach students more realistically about literature by guiding them into writing literature themselves. Angela taught the technique to Melissa and other Writing Project teachers in the area.

The Journey is not something you can do in a class period. Like many good writing and literature experiences, this one takes several days. Normally Melissa will take two or three weeks of class time completing it. This one will take longer. First, her seventh graders are introduced to the idea of character building. They look at a variety of characters from their reading and how writers use details in making characters memorable. Students in this class have read widely in young adult fiction already, as the "Rate A Book" list on the wall indicates. They are not taught in a language arts block of time; but they are in this room two periods in the day, one in the morning for English and last period for Reading. They always choose the books they will read. But as they started new books this time, the class decided to read several titles in interest groups. Several of the girls are reading *The Hobbit*, a group of boys are reading *The Outsiders*, other groups are reading *Hatchet, A Swiftly Tilting Planet, Summer of My German Soldier*, and *The Contender*. As you will see, their choice of book and writing choices are related in sometimes obvious and sometimes subtle ways, but the connection is there. You cannot miss the observation that they are becoming better writers and more informed readers because they have real choices in both, first, and because they do the two things together. In any case, the discussion of character centers on examples from their reading and how the pros build character. Bilbo Baggins, Pony Boy and his buddies, Brian, Meg, Patty Bergen, Alfred Brooks, and the other characters from their reading will be their models.

"Now I want you to think of a character you want to take this journey." Out come the journals and the class freewrites for five minutes.

Then they share at their tables, beginning a portrait with words. Melissa puts 21 questions up on the overhead and gives them a sheet for individual responses. "Is your character male or female? . . . What is his name? (Give a first and last name.) . . . How old is this person? . . . What is the color of his eyes? . . . His hair? . . ." She wants them to focus on details, to see their character as more than a stereotype. More sharing with the whole class about their characters and how they answered these questions. At this point they have some details, a skeleton of a character. She's not ready for them to start the story yet.

The next morning they read Eudora Welty's "A Worn Path." It's not an easy story. As a matter of fact, it's often taught in college. Seventh graders and Eudora Welty? Well, why not? They read out loud. Ross reads a brief section, then calls a number at random between one and thirty-four. (Instead of calling on his buddy.) "Twenty-five" is Bobby, and he reads next. So it goes. At the end of the reading, Melissa tells them, "I want you to take about three minutes and write about that. . . . Just as though you were walking out of the movie theatre and had just seen a movie. What are your thoughts?" Out come the journals. She and the class write for a few minutes.

She reads what she has written about Phoenix Jackson and Phoenix's journey quickly and then calls for volunteers from the class to read their responses to the story. Because they have fresh thoughts down on paper, they have something to talk about. The discussion does not degenerate into a please-the-teacher guessing game students often play as they try to guess what you want them to say to your clever questions about literature. And everybody literally has something to contribute, although Melissa does not press them. Most of the talk about "A Worn Path" comes from them. She reinforces what each one contributes and asks questions to help them take their thinking further. There is a real feeling of sharing the story.

Ross reads his response first. He doesn't get it and asks about the title. She accepts his negative comments about the story and goes past them to the issues. The class talks about why Welty named the story "A Worn Path." Ross wants to know about the gun pointed at Phoenix and the dogs fighting. Melissa responds to something he says about the character's emotions by asking him if Phoenix seemed "emotionally strong." He nods. Ross and the others have gained a little insight into the main character and her journey.

Bobby reads his response. He does not understand what is wrong with the grandson in the story. More discussion. When someone says the story is hard to read, Melissa responds, "I wouldn't recommend it for fun reading either." And when Shawana says she thinks the main character is "out of it," Miss Moore asks her and the others, "Do you think Phoenix was helpless?"

Ross says, "She was real strong!" In the talking he has come from a rather negative attitude toward the story to admiration for the endurance of the main character. Partly because he was given a chance to respond naturally and share his response without having to please the teacher. And partly because he is able to hear the responses of his peers. Melissa accepts and respects students' comments, without trying to force her interpretation of the story. At the same time, she points out obstacles in Phoenix's journey and how the character is portrayed naturally—things they will have to grapple with writing their own Journeys.

Jason's response mentions the uneducated speech of the character, and the class talks about authentic speech in creating a character and what to watch for. Paul's response notices the name *Phoenix*, and Melissa asks him to tell the class the myth. And red-headed Julie's reading talks about the title and Phoenix's dignity and pride.

Reading, journal response, and discussion are all done within a 45 minute class period, and with time left to work with a partner mapping Phoenix's journey and the obstacles she faces and overcomes. "It doesn't matter to me how you organize it. Just do it. . . . Do it in your journal." And Melissa is among them as they work, looking over shoulders, talking quietly with them about different parts of the story they depict. The notion of being faced with obstacles will be important in their own stories in a couple of days.

The next morning her Character Development questions are back up on the overhead projector. She directs them back to their character descriptions. "Make it longer. . . . It's simply describing a person." Pencils are busy for ten or fifteen minutes until she stops them. "Put your pencils down and listen for concrete images."

The reading and responding are important, and she takes time for them. Jay, an athletic blonde with glasses and an Aztec t-shirt, reads first. Melissa points out his exaggerations in the character sketch and says, "I liked his description about the eyes. Read that again." In several of the stories they write, male characters will have interesting eyes, particularly in stories written by the boys! Tom is a tall, thin kid who sits in Jay's group. After he reads, Ross praises his character, "Kind of goofy. His hands are in his pockets."—and he hunches forward gesturing with his body to convey how he sees Tom's character. Melissa asks, "Tom, what do you think this guy does?" And she shares how she sees him. She always shares her visualizations when her students read their writing to her. she tells them what she sees, helping them add life to their characters bit by bit.

Paul is an intense writer and a voracious reader. Right now he is reading everything by S. E. Hinton he can get his hands on. Melissa praises his character, "I like that line—'His face was twisted into a grin.'" Bobby sits in Paul's group, and he likes violent stories. Melissa exclaims over the bloody knife his character holds. "Ooo! He's done something wrong!" And praises his description for having a character wearing "generic shoes." Erin is a cute, long haired blonde on the other side of the room. She is a prolific writer and, like Paul and several others, a hungry reader. As it turns out, the character she reads this morning she will not use for her story. This one is closely related to Phoenix in Welty's story, picking up on the detail of the untied shoes. Melissa's comments, as always, are specific and encouraging. "I loved that—the shoelaces that were 'dancing and whirling as she walked.' And I particularly liked the line, 'Nobody knew how old she was.'" She listens intently and highlights the significant detail. Erin smiles and blushes, beaming under her teacher's compliment.

Melissa takes time with the sharing. She knows it's important. She encourages them to comment before going on to the next reader. Their talk about the reading mirror hers. It is positive and specific.

She keeps the atmosphere as informal as she can with her active seventh graders. She circulates from group to group, kneeling beside a student, sitting on the edge of a table, listening in or adding her comments to theirs. Sometimes working through a particular writing problem with a student.

Toward the end of the period, she promises she will give all of them a chance to read their characters to the whole class. "Everyone wants to read theirs, so we'll read." But she postpones the other readings for the afternoon in order to push them to lengthen their character sketches. "Go back to the questions one more time. Write quickly as fast as you can. Write down everything you can think of." This is the third time they have written the character. She is pushing for good details like the ones they have been talking about in the sharing session. "Try to create the inside of the character through their physical description." And she talks about how Bobby describes his knife wielding character. "Show me the height of the person without just giving me numbers."

She pushes them. "I know what you are capable of" is a favorite statement. And she does not want a student to quit writing too soon or dare too little. "You go back and read it, and let the person with whom you share the table read it. And don't feel free to say, 'O yeah, that's good.' Ask them questions the way we do in class. . . . Keep working on it. You're not done yet."

The next morning Melissa's students are paired up for "psychotherapy" for their characters. One of the partners is the "psychiatrist" who interviews the character who will take the journey. The purpose of the exercise is to create a history for the character by answering questions about background posed by the partner. The exercise is fun—and funny sometimes—and the kids really get into it.

Melissa gives them the requirements for the Journey. It must take place within twenty-four hours. The character must face several obstacles in the journey—physical obstacles or conflicts with other characters or psychological difficulties. It must be a third person narrative. It must contain some dialogue.

They begin what Melissa calls their Zero Draft in their journal. They write in marbled composition books, very convenient for stacking in the classroom. This discovery draft is written very quickly. A few students get stuck, and she suggests they map the story, drawing in the obstacles along the way. Almost everyone writes to the end of the period without looking up, and they will write for another couple of class periods almost as hard.

Meanwhile, Melissa has put up on the board a list of over twenty titles of journeys written by previous students. These stories are in class publications on the bookshelves or on file in the room. They are encouraged to read some of them during the afternoon Reading class. Models from the professional young adult fiction writers and models from their peers—what Miss Moore creates among her students is a community of readers and writers. Each student is invited to become a part of this community. No one is excluded. They all are a part and *feel* that they belong. And they all know with absolute certainty that they can do anything she asks them to do.

During the second writing period Melissa kneels beside their tables to conference with kids as they write (she is young!) Now they have enough on paper to talk about. "How is it going?" She sees almost every student during the morning. Her conferences are very short, to the point, and always encouraging. Jessica is having trouble with her zero draft. She shows Melissa a map and her start. Melissa picks up a copy of Lypsite's *Contender* to show Jessica how he handles a similar situation.

She kneels beside Ross's table. She smiles and jokes with him. Ross is a wiggler, restless and rarely still. He quietly reads to her what he's written so far. She nods and asks questions and brags on the good stuff. His face lights up. So it goes around the room.

Toward the end of the second morning she interrupts them. "OK, I want to go around the room real quick and find out where you are with your story." But several students protest. "We *need to write*, Miss Moore!" She lets them continue.

The next morning several students are still working on their zero drafts, but some are ready to read. She calls for volunteers to share with the whole class. "Read either what you're having trouble with or what you like." Shawana, a pretty willowy black girl with dangly earrings and glasses reads. "I'm not having trouble with nothing," she declares with characteristic confidence. After the reading Melissa jokes with her about the handsome guy in the story and praises her characters' speech. She knows Shawana's style well. "Shawana always has that *language* in there." Paul reads the opening dialogue and the fight scene from his story. Melissa likes what she hears. "Wonderful! You can see the fight. It's real." And she talks with him about his characters and situation, and the characters and situations in the S. E. Hinton novels he's reading. Paul has finished *The Outsiders* for his group projects and has read *Tex* besides. He is looking for another Hinton book and is becoming quite an expert on her style and subjects.

The next step is trying out the piece with their partners. They are used to reading their writing out loud and do it unselfconsciously. They are also good listeners. "Comment. Be specific. Ask questions," Melissa reminds them. The room buzzes with reading and quiet talk.

The class will spend several days editing, rewriting, and more editing. They will be working individually and with partners and in groups to prepare their stories for publication and celebration. And during these days several things will happen in a kind of natural rhythm orchestrated by Miss Moore.

There will be a lot of reading out loud to the whole classes of pieces in process. This is always done by volunteers, but really these seventh graders are so comfortable and confident with Melissa and each other that all of them at one time or another will read their work in progress to the class. Melissa uses these readings to talk about technical aspects of story writing, dialogue, leads, plotting, character building. Her comments are always positive but specific. "I want them to do more than just say 'That's nice.'" And she asks questions about things that are puzzling or missing. She asks Paul about the setting of his story, which is nonexistent in the zero draft. Paul looks back in his journal to the list of questions she has given them to work up the character.

"It's a small town in Texas."—and they talk about how you describe a small town without being obvious. She knows he'll work that into his next draft. She asks a lot of questions about characters and how they are presented, how they talk, why they do what they do. Character is the heart of good story writing. She reminds them over and over again how the pros handle writers' problems in the books they are reading.

She always invites students to comment in these sessions. Her responses model theirs. They learn what to say by listening to her. As students are working through their next draft and then preparing the piece for publication, she reminds them often about what she calls PQP—praise, question, polish. This is her shorthand for their jobs as responders when they listen to a story or read it on the page. She gives them PQP note sheets to use as they listen to each other. That way, after the sharing and group response, the writer has something in front of her to work with as she revises.

During revision, rewriting, and editing, whole class sharing sessions are brief, no more than a few volunteers at a time. Most of the time is spent with partners in small response groups, and in reworking the drafts. Melissa will also have several technical discussions with the class. She puts up a chart on the Journey near the corner bookcases to help them work with each other revising drafts. It reminds writers and editors of these points.

1) Plot, character, setting fully developed.
2) Conflict established.
3) No more than a twenty-four hour journey with obstacles.
4) Dialogue included.
5) Evidence of at least one writing technique. [Such things as fore-shadowing, flashback, irony, local color, parallelism, sarcasm, satire, understatement.]
6) Story should represent plot line.
7) Theme must be developed.

Posted over the Journey chart is an attractive plot line diagram with exposition, rising action, climax, falling action, and resolution displayed in bold colors. The class has used it as a reference for fiction and drama, and they will use it in their book projects. Now it is a reminder for their own plotting.

Melissa's intent is for her students to revise their discovery drafts (zero drafts) paying attention to the aspects of the story, and to postpone grammar and mechanical concerns for later editing, and another draft. It is not that neat a process, and in fact they work on both pretty much at the same time. But she pushes them to see their stories as *writers* first, dealing with the kinds of concerns of character and plot that all writers struggle with.

At this point, about half of the class will type the revised draft of their stories, using the computers in Linda Clark's computer lab downstairs. Ms. Clark is the kind of friend and colleague every middle school language arts teacher needs. She works with up to ten of the young writers from Melissa's class at a time. She enjoys their writings, helps the new word processor-writers get started, consults with them over problems, and advises them on how to best show off their pieces. She has a thorough knowledge of writing theory and loves the energy and the antics of seventh graders. Typed drafts are not required, but the kids like working with the machines—and soon discover how word processing makes revision jobs easier. And they certainly like working in Ms. Clark's lab.

Another session with their editing partner, and Melissa edits each story for content. She does not red mark papers, but she does comment in the margins. Her "prompts," as she calls them, are positive, helpful, and personal. Her comments on Erin's story (printed at the end of the chapter) illustrate the kinds of things Miss Moore says.

She praises specific things in several places: "I like the details." "It's neat that he draws." "I like his thoughts and questions here." "I like the way Jim talks." "I like that!" (with a section bracketed.) She gives technical advice: "Avoid using a name so similar to *The Hobbit*." "A bit more here." "Rabbit—rabbit—rabbit" (at the end of a paragraph repeating the word three times). "Maybe build this up more." "Mention Bifor here at the end maybe." She asks questions: "Sold his works to whom? Where?" "Hopped where?" (about the rabbit) "Where did she go to get the food?" "I'm not sure I understand his fear?" "Why?" And she signs off with a personal note: "Erin, I love your story! Your word choices, sentence structure, everything reads so smoothly!"

The papers come back to students with her comments and their editing partner's comments on them. As far as the students are concerned, both are given equal weight. It is also obvious from Erin's revision that she felt free to take or ignore the advice. Melissa will edit these stories twice, have two editing conferences with each student, and talk to each of them almost daily about specifics in their papers, but she will not take ownership away from the young writer. Erin's writing is hers, and her decisions about particular things in that writing, finally, are hers, too.

Melissa asks for one more revision of the story, this time focusing on grammar and mechanics. She gives them a sheet she will use to grade the paper (they already have credit for their journals and the work they have done so far), and this time each student becomes an Editor for his partner and gets credit for his editing work. Melissa's second conference is with the writer and editor. Then some of the stories will go through one more draft, depending on how good the grade is. Melissa may ask for another draft if there are two many problems with style and grammar/mechanics in the paper. The student may decide to do another draft for a better grade, or just because the story will be published.

The final requirement for the Journey is that it be published in the classroom. Her students publish in two ways mainly. The finished story is displayed in the room, and later a class book of writings selected by each student will be printed (*The Young and the Writeous*, volume 3) In the cabinet in the back corner there are mounting supplies, brightly colored backing materials, paste and tape, colored markers, scissors. Displayed works around the room range from simply being a neat draft backed and hung with a photograph to elaborately illustrated and displayed writings. You can also see evidence of Ms. Clark's consulting in some of the fancy printing. The class book will be produced toward the end of the school year and will include writings by all of Miss Moore's students. Anticipating it, students are asked to put two copies of their finished stories in their writing folders. More conferencing, editing, and rewriting will be involved in that production.

And that's not all. Melissa gives several of her students the job of putting up a bulletin board in the main lobby of the school. It covers one large wall perhaps 50 feet long. She asked her principal for a small place to show off her students' work for the school. The next day he had this one put up. She advises, but the students are in charge of what writings to show off and how to display them. Her kids also seek wider audiences for their writing outside the school. Her kids always write for the essay contests that come through the school. This year they have written about oak trees, drunk driving, handicapped students, a variety of others. And Jay and a couple of the others have been published in the local paper in a column for young writers. Erin and Paul will both prepare pieces to submit to magazines with national circulations. They conference with friends and Miss Moore and re-type one more time.

These are busy days with students typing, reading and talking in small groups, partners editing drafts, conferences with Miss Moore, re-typing or re-writing, mounting and editing drafts for display, more sharing and talking. The room buzzes with action. Melissa makes sure nobody gets lost or ignored in the flurry of activity. She checks with each student starting the class, keeping up not only with the status of written drafts and editing work, but with the reading assignments and book projects students are starting on as they complete the Journey.

The Journey this time takes six full weeks of class time for the writing and the related reading in the morning English and afternoon Reading classes. The activities usually are completed in two or three weeks. This particular class obviously is very much into the experience; and because they are having such a good time with it, they work longer on their stories.

The last week two things come together, the groups' Book Skits and the Read-a-Round celebrating the completion of the Journeys. This is unplanned really; doing both in the same week has more to do with the fact it is the end of the six-week grading period than anything else. But the parallels between plotting, character building, fiction techniques, even details in such things as written description and dialogue and setting are obvious in the presentations of the novels and the students' reading of their own fiction.

Book skits are done early in the week. Bronwyn, Caty, Jenny, Jessica, Julie, and Erin present *The Hobbit* to the class. They have read the longest book, and their project is impressive—and hilarious! They are fully costumed as hobbits, elves, and a wizard wearing long bathrobes and beards cut from construction paper and held on by scotch tape. An elaborately staged video of the novel's highlights with homemade backdrops and their antics keep the class entertained. As required, they also chart and explain the Plot Line of the novel and describe Bilbo Baggins with a Character Cluster they have plotted.

The Read-a-Round is the grand celebration of weeks of hard work. Melissa makes a big deal out of it. The tables are placed in a big rectangle around the room so that students can see and hear each person read. Invitations are printed in Ms. Clark's room and sent to parents, administrators, and other friends of the class, like Ms. Clark herself. There is a party atmosphere with strawberry Cokes (!) and cookies and helium filled balloons and a big banner across one wall of the room proclaiming, "WE ARE PROUD OF OUR WRITERS!!!" Miss Moore arranges with other teachers in her team for the kids to be with her all morning so that every student can read.

After the initial excitement and hubub, they are in their seats and the room falls quiet—well, almost quiet. Melissa calls on each student by number. And they read, proudly, a little nervously at first but with expression so that you can hear the characters and see the scenes.

Greg reads first. "The Wild Journey" is wild enough! It is a nature adventure with a group of scouts stranded in the wilderness with a dead scout master, a red headed maniacal killer on the loose, bears and wolves, and a toxic waste dump. Matt is another of the outdoorsmen in the class. His story is about an ill fated wild boar hunting trip and a hero who suffers an injured leg, broken fingers, and an arrow through his hand, and who somehow manages to survive the ordeal. Jennifer's story is a psychological journey about a girl in a troubled family who finds out her parents are divorcing. It is sensitive and sad. Tom's story is about a character lost in the night woods. It has an eerie, dream-like quality, especially when you hear it read aloud. The obstacles in Christy's Journey are also psychological, involving a rather self-centered girl named Katrina who learns about appreciating others when her grandmother dies. Jason and Bobby both read war stories. Both are violent and bloody—and exciting! Desperate fighting, narrow escapes, high tech military hardware, super heroic American GI's and evil Iraqis—scenes to make Doc Savage proud. Red headed Julie's story is a melodramatic tear jerker about drinking and driving, and blonde Jessica's "A Day in the Life of a Blonde" is a funny satire of a well-to-do Valley Girl and a tragedy at the Mall. Jessica has suffered her own obstacles with the writing since her hand and forearm are in a cast. Shawana reads a very long story about best friends who have trouble over a handsome new guy at school; her dialogue is sharp and real sounding. Landon's main character is Joboo, a really strange street character who wears a flowered polyester suit and platform shoes, and who is pursued by a killer in a red Bronco? Jenny's character is a delightful four years old who does everything she can to frustrate her mother's attempts to take her to the doctor.

The reading continues. All final drafts are read. And they listen. They have heard every story in one draft or another read out loud to the whole class during the writing. They know the stories well. Because they work together in this community of writers and readers, they take ownership in all of the pieces. No one is bored hearing someone else's journey, even though they have spend hours and days together working on the pieces. They applaud and praise, sharing in the celebration with each writer, completing the Journey together.

Erin's Journey

Journeys

Boifur, being a regular dwarf, was only about up to the waist of you or I. He lived in an underground burrow, dug into the side of a hill that dwarves, elves, and hobbits from miles around named simply The Hill. Only it was not a dirty, smelly, sodden, below ground area as one might expect. This was a rather clean smelling and tidy burrow in which Boifur lived alone and happily with an occasional visit from his brother, a friend, or passerby in need of something or other (dwarf hospitality is very kind). A yellow, long-sleeved shirt hung loosely on his chubby body and was fastened with a wide red belt over a pair of brown pants that reached down to his knees. At the end of each pants' leg, a red string was tied around the width of Boifur's leg.

Boifur greatly enjoyed the outdoors. He could name every plant and animal within a thirty mile range of Wilderland, where he lived, and took pride in doing so. He also adored animals—so long as they were smaller than he was.

Boifur was also quite talented at whittling and made fine creations from cedar wood when it was available. Boifur occasionally sold his works at the street market for a small sum.

This story is about Boifur's start on adventures, for many others followed after he found out his love for them.

One sunny morning, Boifur was sitting outside his front door under an overhang protruding from The Hill. Wood chips scattered the slab of stone that served as a doorstep and Boifur silently carved away a small rabbit. He was chipping away the form of an ear when a shadow approached him. Looking up he saw Bifor.

"Hello, Brother," Boifur said cheerfully, looking up from his rabbit which was temporarily only a block of wood.

"Hi yourself. I have exciting news!" He obviously knew something he was dying to tell. "Randalf is back and is looking for dwarves willing to go on a journey. He asked me!"

Boifur looked at his brother's silvery eyes which were exactly the same as his. "You don't mean the famous wizard Randalf? The one who searches far and wide for gullible dwarves and elves willing to go on his silly adventures?" Boifur laughed. "Not that Randalf! Surely you mean another one! Right? And if he asked you one of those wild adventures, I sincerely hope you declined. You know how dangerous they are and that hardly anyone ever comes back with those luscious rewards he promises. Most of the time they receive their share of death! You should know that anyhow," Boifur finished and turned his attention back on his whittling.

Boifor looked thoughtful for a moment. "Well . . . actually," he started uncomfortably, "actually I said I would." Boifur's mouth nearly dropped below his long, grey beard. "Oh, come on! It'll be exciting! Those stories are just rumors. So far there are only thirteen of us. Everyone knows thirteen is an unlucky number. Randalf is looking for another dwarf. I told him I'd ask you, but you've made your answer quite clear. Good-bye, Brother."

"So long," Boifur returned.

About an hour later the rabbit had taken shape. Boifur put a few finishing touches on the wooden face and decided to keep this one for himself. He had always had a fondness for rabbits. He opened his dark blue door with its beautiful brass doorknob and knocker. Boifur walked down the long hallway and into the living room. Paintings of outdoor scenes hung on the dirt walls and in the back of the room was a fireplace with a forest of green and brown and yellow hung over the mantle. He walked over to the stone fireplace and set the wooden rabbit in the center.

You deserve the place of honor, he thought to himself. The forest paintings put him in the mood for a hike. He decided to take a different path this time than the one he usually walked. Boifur decided to walk through the Valley Woods. He had never been there but had heard the scenery was beautiful in May. Boifur briskly strolled into the kitchen and packed a loaf of bread and some cheese for his lunch into a leather pouch. He went back down the curving hallway and to the front door (not that there was a much better way out except for the windows). He stepped outside in the afternoon sunlight, took a deep breath, and the next thing he knew he was standing at the entrance to the Valley Woods. Fresh green trees towered over him on either side and a dirt path led into darkness. It was not an eerie darkness but more of a comforting darkness. Blooming flowers in the brightest of red, purple, and blue he had ever seen were all around and he was tempted to pluck a few and take them back to his mother on the other side of The Hill, but decided not to.

Boifur stepped onto the dusty path and began walking. At first he walked briskly, as the forest trees hovered far over his short body and frightened him, but after a few minutes he got used to it and slowed down his pace.

Boifur found a lot of interesting plants. Some were his favorite kind and he wished he had his sketch pad with him so that he could draw a few of them. Boifur made a mental note to bring it with him next time.

Walking deeper into the woods, Boifur came upon a strange plant. Probably the only one he would ever see because it was rare and grew only in specific parts of Wilderland. Boifur investigated closer. He was fascinated by the fan-shaped leaves and light blue berries that dangled from the limbs. All of a sudden, the branches shook, the berries danced, and a scurry of leaves was heard from below the bush. Boifur lifted the bottom most branches to reveal a small white rabbit. Boifur called to the rabbit. It did not respond in any way. This struck Boifur as odd because most animals were attracted to him. The ball of white fluff shifted and Boifur could now see the problem. A small twig was protruding from his back leg. As I have mentioned before, Boifur has a soft spot for those little twitching noses and crazy long ears and it worried him to see the stick in his leg.

"Come here," he whispered softly. "I won't hurt you at all. I just want to help." The rabbit turned its back on Boifur and hopped off into the forest on his three good legs.

Boifur was really concerned and followed the rabbit deeper into the woods. He was pushing aside limbs and twigs as he trailed him. Boifur thought he caught a glimpse of the white fur and followed it. He shoved aside a particularly stubborn branch that did not want to move. He stepped forward and scanned the trees for the white ball of fur.

The next thing he knew—Splash!—he was in the waters of a river. The water was freezing and stung him. Boifur struggled to keep his head over the powerful current. He occasionally bumped into a rock that blocked his path. He waved his arms frantically and screamed for help and prayed that someone was around to hear his pleas. The current carried him further and further downstream. He crashed into another boulder and had almost given up hope of a rescue when he heard a muffled "Hang on!" and felt himself being dragged in the direction of the shore. He looked up into the afternoon sun and felt himself go limp. He fainted.

"Is he alive?"

"What is he?"

"What happened?"

Boifur awoke to a commotion.

"Hey! His eyes are opening!"

Boifur saw an awkward creature. It had slick brown fur and a wide flat tail. Had he swallowed too much water? Was he dead? Was this heaven? Where was he? These thoughts ran through his head as he stared at the creature's huge, white buck teeth. He had to be dreaming. What manner of creature was this? Was he savage? Could he help Boifur in any way?

"What are you?" Boifur finally asked.

"Who am I? Who am I?!" the creature asked astonished at Boifur's incredible stupidity. "Why I am the swimming champ of Beaver Dam and you are lucky I was around or else you wouldn't be here!! Now maybe I should ask you the same thing. Who are you?"

Boifur paused as if he had forgotten his own name all of a sudden and again wondered if he was dreaming. "I—I'm Boifur," he stated.

"Yes, yes. Well, it's hard to determine exactly what you are but it appears you might be a dwarf." Boifur nodded. "I've had a few conversations with some dwarves and they seem to be peaceful. Is there anything you need?"

Boifur thought for a moment. A new body might be useful but he would settle for a towel. "Do you have a towel?"

"No, but we do have a substitute. Very much like one and very absorbant. Stanley, a cloth for the lad if you please!" the beaver ordered. He was obviously a powerful beaver. A small beaver tossed a green cloth-like thing towards the swimming champ. As the beaver had not stated his name, "The Swimming Champ" was all he had to go by. The swimmer took the cloth and handed it to Boifur. He immediately started to dry off.

"Wow! This is amazing! I'm dry already! What is it?"

"Grass and leaves with a few particles removed to make it absorbant. Wonderful isn't it? And so easy to make!" the beaver replied. Boifur felt his stomach rumble and realized he had not eaten since breakfast. He felt around for his pouch but could not find it anywhere.

"Uh, Mr.—whoever you are, would you happen to have any food

that I could digest? I seem to have lost my lunch."

"Of course! Susan, get the man some food! Oh, and pardon me for being so rude, they call me Jim Swimmer. Some say Jim, some say Swimmer. It doesn't really matter to me!"

Susan returned with a tray full of nuts and berries of all sizes and sorts and Boifur ate his fill. Boifur stayed a bit, then went on again. The beavers were kind enough to point him in the general direction of the path.

After walking a while, Boifur felt sure he was lost again. He sat down on a rotting log and set his head in his hands. Boifur looked around and realized that it was a whole lot darker in the depths of the forest instead of on the path. Boifur noticed that the forest was no longer friendly. The darkness was no longer comforting. It was a little past noon already and Boifur was ready for his afternoon nap. But he couldn't sleep in these woods. Too much could happen to him while he was off guard. Boifur heard a hoot and wondered if it was later than he thought since owls only came out at night. Boifur heard a rustle from some bushes beside him and hung his head again preparing for what was coming to him. He felt a nudge at his ear.

"Don't rest in these woods!" advised a soft voice. "Too many crazy things could happen. Goblins live nearby and trolls aren't that far either. Be careful." Boifur looked up to see a small doe standing over him. Her tan hair shone in the sunlight.

"Thanks for the advice. I didn't know," Boifur replied, truly thankful.

"What are you doing out here? I haven't seen you around. Are you new?"

"I guess you could say that. Actually, I've kind of lost my path. Would you know the way from here?"

"Well," the doe replied, "there are a lot of paths around here. But you probably want Hiker's Path. That's the main path that most of us try to stay away from. Some folks of your type come rambling through here and throw all kinds of things at us."

"Well, do you know how to get there?" Boifur asked, his face hopeful.

"Of course. I'll show you the way. I won't take you all the way there because that path frightens me a great deal but I will take you far enough so that you won't get lost again." And with that, the doe headed off into the forest and Boifur followed obediently.

After a while, Boifur recognized a twisted oak tree, and then a jagged rock, and then a short tree stump with a hole in the base of it.

"Just go right between those trees and then straight through the bush and you should be right on the path again." Boifur thanked her endlessly, said good-bye, and dashed through the trees. The branches whipped at his face but he didn't care; he was on the dirty, dusty path home again. From there Boifur ran all the way home. He flung open his beautiful blue door and tore into the living room. Boifur took a second to glance at the rabbit on his mantle and only wished he had been able to help the one in the forest. And with that thought he fell asleep. Why should he travel hundreds of miles for an adventure? He had one right at home.

(Erin Ritchey, 7th grade, Merry Acres Middle)

9

Talking It Out: Oral Language

"Listening skill is the foundation for reading skill at all ability levels of comprehension, just as talk skill is the foundation for writing skill at all levels of composition."

—James Moffett, 1983

Team Log, Team A
Grander Middle School

Dear Ms. Jacobs:

I know you're aware that as a team, we model keeping logs for our students by keeping a team log ourselves. I'm using it to respond to your questions from the other day. You asked me for my rationale when I told you during our pre-school workday the other day that this year the language arts classrooms would not be silent. I think you jumped when I said that, and I guess you would want to know what I meant by that since, as principal, you need to know what's going on.

I've been doing a lot of thinking, reading, attending workshops and talking to others in my department—and on my team—over the last year. I really thought about all the ways I might change my classroom so that the kids are more actively involved in learning. And, I guess I've become convinced that, for all of us, but especially for me as a language arts person, more productive talking and listening would have to be a very necessary part of the students' lives from now on.

Even before you asked, I wanted to share the reasons why we want to heighten the visibility of oral language in our classes, even in the whole curriculum eventually, and why I want to plan more systematic opportunities for all kinds of talking and listening to go on throughout the day and year.

As you are aware, I have been using reading and writing workshops for the last year, and in getting those started, I've tried to rely on a number of whole language principles. I'm convinced that natural talking and listening is essential to sustain those workshops. Talk about books, literature groups, peer revision groups, conferencing, sharing stories, recent readings, and learning logs, are at the heart of such a classroom. Meaningful talk makes them go. So that's definitely one of the main reasons.

A more general reason is that talking and listening together help develop thinking abilities. I'm convinced it's definitely a myth that "silence is golden." It's especially a dangerous myth in a language classroom where talking and listening are excellent prompts to writing and reading, better than the "seats and sheets" routines we sometimes get stuck in. By framing opportunities for students to do oral language with us teachers and among themselves, they can develop, at a critical time, better intellectual skills.

But those are not the only good reasons. Talking and listening can also promote social growth. Maybe that's what people worry about when they think about talking going on in the classroom. That it will be just socializing on school time. I guess some of that will happen no matter how relevant, orderly, and planned these oral situations are. After all, we know this is a time of life when students' social roles, as part of their beginning search for identity, are being redefined—so, sure, some of that will happen.

But it does anyway! How many times have any of us been talking to students, giving notes, directions, and we've had to shush people all around the room. The energy and the need is there— why not channel it productively to explore not only our language arts themes, but the relevant themes in their lives? When kids really have many issues to work out, they help each other to clarify and elaborate thoughts. They also hear each other's reasoning and points of view on social and moral issues in literature, society, nature, and in their own personal lives. They can reflect together on these.

A lot of consciousness-raising can occur when, as in our school, kids represent a wide multicultural background. If our diverse kids have opportunities to talk and listen to one another's unique perspectives developed within their own personal cultures, a great amount of cultural sharing can occur, not to mention the building of affective skills so necessary for our society today— like real empathy and tolerance for difference. I hate to sound so lofty, but if we are going to continue as a democracy, we better get less worried about having kids talk and listen to each other in class. Of course, I know we need to guide this so different kids join together as much as possible in different learning situations.

As kids think and grow in socially responsive ways, they're getting good, natural practice with language too: making meaning with new sentences, new words, new concepts, listening and decoding different dialects or translating their own, and understanding their ESL friends. Just as when they were little, they became more and more correct as adults modeled, coached, and let them explore language, so now they need this same treatment as they entertain new ideas with their new processing capacities, new social and personal roles and identities. New complexity in thinking should go hand in hand with a variety of language opportunities.

I guess I want to throw in at least one more "why" for you to think about. It goes back a bit to the myth of "silence is golden." It's another reason why it's not. From a gender and multicultural standpoint, I think we need to be sure our teaching does not contribute to girls "going silent" at adolescence or any other person to whom our society might have sent messages of marginality. We need fewer people whose relationship to self, voice, and knowledge is grounded in silence and disbelief in oneself. We need to think consciously of ways talking and listening can maintain every person's positive sense of self. We need to watch how we as teachers talk and listen so our own biases, be they about gender, racial, ethnic, class, or ability level, don't appear as the real message behind our oral ones. We have to hear the different voices ourselves if we expect them to.

Well, those were the basic reasons we discussed for wanting to balance our curriculum with oral language infused more openly and informally, yet systematically. I think in most classrooms, there is a tendency for speaking and listening to mirror a traditional teacher/student dichotomy. We speak and they listen—if we're lucky. We need to reverse that in a natural language classroom, reverse it consciously along with offering good guidance to kids.

So, we're meeting to discuss ways to include all kinds of talking and listening opportunities in our rooms later this week—department first, then team. Please sit in on either one; we'd welcome you there. I hope now these rationale statements help explain my remarks earlier!

Sincerely,

David Bland
Team Chair, Team A
Language Arts Department Head

Frames for Speaking and Listening

David Bland's positive vision of oral language promises an exciting year's worth of learning experiences for everyone involved, including the principal. For all of us thinking about the issues as he has, knowing about more helpful oral language experiences and contexts might provide us an increasingly better framework for including many diverse strategies. I agree with Stephen Tchudi (1989) that the spoken language cannot really be taught, but what the teacher can do is create as many varied opportunities for oral language to occur as possible.

A Speaking Frame

One of the earliest looks at the place of speaking and listening in the language arts was James Moffett's curriculum. In both his *Teaching the Universe of Discourse* (1983), and *A Student-Centered Language Arts and Reading*, K-13 (1983), he stressed that speaking and listening were the true basics rather than reading and writing. More fundamental than any of them was thinking itself. Thinking involved composing and comprehending, orally and in writing. The more sophisticated thought was in various oral contexts, the more fluent in the print contexts.

Brian Cambourne (1988) is also convinced of the strong relationship between oral language and written language, especially the learning processes involved for both. In Cambourne's mind, two assumptions about language learning ring true: (1) the oral and written forms of language are only superficially different, and (2) learning to talk is a profound intellectual achievement (pp. 29-30).

Learning oral language as a child occurs without any formal instruction, but certain conditions must occur. To Cambourne, it follows that our classrooms should offer similar conditions for learning reading and writing. Tom has already discussed Cambourne's conditions for the natural learning of reading and writing, but it's important to remember that those are grounded in the natural conditions for developing oral abilities. To us it follows that maintaining these conditions in the classroom can only enhance further growth in talking and listening.

The importance of oral language in developing thought and communication brought forward a new definition of and use of dramatics and speechmaking in the classroom for James Moffett. They weren't just frills; they were at the heart of learning to communicate, be they done informally (improvisations, dialogues or small groups), or formally (rehearsed plays or speeches). They were integrated with composition and literature; they were not separate subjects. Drama, something we usually think about as scripts and acting and full-blown plays, was not only that, but everyday action, life itself, the here and now. Rather than a fringe unit or exploratory course, drama in this broad sense was all of classroom learning (Moffett, 1967).

Thinking of oral language activities as a range of informal to formal talking and listening gives us a helpful framework for thinking about how to plan chances to challenge oral skills to grow. Moffett actually placed this informal/formal dimension on the communication triad of speaker-subject-audience, and on the abstraction level between speaker-subject or the distance between speaker-listener. These were the expandable parts in almost any possible combination. For example, the most intimate oral communication was with oneself, thought itself in other words, something he called reflection. Imagine musing on a topic, anything from ephemeral to sophisticated. You're the sender and the receiver, internally the speaker and the listener. I do that all the time. We all do.

Or the speaker could dialogue intimately with another person on any subject from casual talk to philosophically abstract ideas. Or she could have a conversation with a small group of people, with topics ranging from mundane to meaty. At the most distance between herself and listeners, the speaker could give a formal speech, or read or act out a formal part in a play in front of a large anonymous audience. Needless to say, the ways listeners listen shift as each part of the triad expands or contracts.

Marvin Klein (1977) also had a helpful framework for helping us cover all the possible talking and listening contexts with kids. Proposing that speaking could be internal dialogues or monologues with the self or external, Klein then divided external talk into types: proposing, describing, explaining, inquiring, or exploring. Each type changed depending on speaker abilities and attitudes as well as whether the context was intimate, informal, formal, or even ceremonial (p. 35). Claire Staab's (1992) categories are similar: talk is asserting, controlling, informing, forecasting, or projecting (pp. 73-74). The assumption is that students need chances to talk in all these ways, in many different contexts.

Regardless of which kind of framework you select to help think about speaking possibilities in the classroom, the point is that kids ought to be engaged in all these kinds of oral contexts pretty often. These kinds of frameworks provide a fertile matrix for many types of activities kids could be involved in. A quick list of opportunities might include:

—time in the day for quiet reflection, perhaps right after reading, writing or viewing something;

—paired, informal conversations about any topic of interest, perhaps about something just watched or studied; explaining a new concept to each other; describing to another directions for doing something;

—small group conversations, primarily "how to get this done" talk, or discussions elaborating and refining ideas and opinions;

—role-plays, improvisations, pantomimes;

—reader's theater, chamber theater, or story theater productions with the whole class;

—videotape productions or talk shows for the whole class;

—speech-making for the whole class, school, or part of the community;

—formal dramatic scenes or plays produced for larger audiences.

Teaching Journal

Take out your journal again. Think over your classroom activities. Jot down all the activities that give kids chances to speak meaningfully in your class. All kids, not just a few. How often do all students engage in speaking? Try to place your activities on a continuum of speaker-audience opportunities and speaker-subject ones. Are there opportunities that your kids should have that they don't? Wind this entry up by making a list of missing possibilities that you can try out with your classes.

A Frame for Listening

Other language arts people have focused on listening as a key comprehension activity. Listening may seem simple and automatic enough, but it's not. It's linked to its comprehension companion, reading. We won't go into all the physiology of hearing and the psychology of it (paying attention, motivation, concentration), but people have written on that in detail (Lundsteen, 1979).

Types and levels of listening seem to be the most beneficial aspect of the listening literature if you need a framework for planning. Experts point out that we listen at different levels of complexity (Quandt, 1983). Usually, schemes go something like this:

—*literal levels*—listening just for surface value, receiving information and remembering the facts;

—*interpretive or critical listening*—listening for the underlying meanings;

—*evaluative listening*—listening to assess the oral product against a set of criteria, comparing and making judgments about it.

Each level in this scheme calls for more sophisticated thinking on the part of our kids. They are cognitive kinds of listening.

There are two kinds of listening that speaks directly to the affect, too—*appreciative listening* and *aesthetic listening*. Sometimes our kids need to just listen to enjoy, not for information or to figure out meaning or to judge the worth of something. Sometimes they should listen to appreciate the beauty and skill of well-crafted words. When we take the time to read aloud entertaining stories or poems or anything beyond the daily announcements, we give kids these kinds of listening. It models for them important "language is fun" and "language is beautiful" attitudes.

Another quick, focused list of strategies relying on a range of listening levels might include:

—any of the list for speaking could use a listener (drama needs an audience; small groups need each other);

—oral readings (teacher to students, students to each other);

—listening to storytellers;

—listening to controversial topics discussed in small or large groups and testing our opinions against others';

—reflective listening in dialogue;

—listening to recordings of literature, to others' 'rehearsal' reading;

—listening with a purpose to poetry readings, enjoyment or for meter, lyrical styles, or personal interpretations;

—listening to debates or speeches to help evaluate the best productions;

—watching and listening to speeches, debates, or plays for enjoyment or critical evaluation.

Teaching Journal

I hope you kept your journal out. Now just add to your last list the activities you do that ask students to listen for different purposes. Are there gaps in kinds of listening that your students could be doing? List these as potential activities.

Keeping Track: Assessments

There are ways to assess kids' speaking and listening, too:

—*self assessment checklists*—Use journals or other open-ended reaction forms, or rating scales and checklists which ask students to reflect on their own involvement in listening and speaking;

—*peer responses*—Use rating scales and checklists made up with student help and ask kids to react to each other's involvement. These are especially useful for small group assessments;

—*teacher charts of students*—Moffett's (1983) are really good, or use a variation of the clipboard that Melissa uses for reading and writing workshops;

—*teacher curriculum/instruction responses*—We can monitor our daily classroom activities to see if we are using the spectrum of discourse (Moffett, 1983), creating a range of oral language contexts for kids to experience their voices in our rooms.

—*audiotape or videotape recordings*—These tools can help us see ourselves from the outside, and we can take our time and focus on any aspect we want to or need to.

The Whole of Oral Language

Pushing speaking and listening into the limelight helps us remember that these skills are primary. And they give us a map for using the whole range of oral language possibilities. Good natural language teachers do this with reading and writing. Like Deborah Bova does with reading and writing workshops, you take time to teach kids how to function in such an open, natural environment. You build trust early, help kids gain confidence as writers, and create that base to work from. With oral language, it's the same. Get students talking naturally and purposefully. Then go to more formal talking and listening.

But like anything else in language arts ecologies, oral language strategies should have real purpose as part of the whole. They don't need to become isolated drill and practices for their own sakes. The more naturally integrated speaking and listening are into the learning, the better. There's a balance between their visibility for their own sakes and as a means towards an end in reading and writing. This kind of task and topic talk will happen naturally if you're allowing reading and writing to grow in the kind of workshop Tom's talked about in chapters 5-8.

Two other important dimensions cut across speaking and listening, aspects that Mr. Bland and his colleagues might also want to think about. I'm thinking about teacher/student talk and student/student talk.

Teachers Talk and Students Listen

They sure do. All the time. As David Bland's memo says, teachers can do almost all the talking, and we just hope they're listening. No matter how student-centered your classroom gets though, you'll always be talking to students. Natural language teachers realize this but want to spread the language around. We want students to continue to grow their own language with use.

Joan Tough's book *Talk for Teaching and Learning* (1985) has some interesting things to say about this inevitable teacher talk. Like everybody else, she sees this relationship on a continuum of personal, informal one-to-one talking to more formal and large group discussions. This captures the distance between speaker and listener. The complexity of the subject can vary in all situations though, and will call for different listening levels. Bottom line, though, for any of it to be good, teachers have to be genuinely interested in the kids, and the kids have to know it.

Tough sees dialogue as a method for communicating genuine interest and for fostering kids' thinking especially in tutorial or teacher-led small groups (pp. 89-90). Good dialogue on any subject sounds like this:

—*orienting strategies*—questions or comments that ask the student to think about the topic more;

—*enabling strategies*—teacher comments that push the student more than the first response to the orienting question; they suggest follow-though, more focus, or clarification;

—*informing strategies*—comments that give more information to the student, so she can push on with her thinking;

—*sustaining strategies*—supportive comments;

—*concluding strategies*—ones that signal a switch of topics or that the teacher is leaving the student alone to work and think more.

(pp. 91-92)

Many of these sound like they could have come from the suggestions on conferencing with kids offered by Donald Graves (1983) and Lucy Calkins (1986), two of the best people on conferencing I know of. The real key to effective conferencing we learn from Graves is really listening. We need to listen well enough to be led by children to making helpful comments. We need to listen to our writers' needs at that moment in the process, and be willing to listen longer so that kids may talk and take more responsibility for their own composing process. And the key to this kind of listening and responding, Calkins reminds us, is to forget about ourselves.

It's the quality of these exchanges that's critical—genuine warmth, care, and investment is the invisible language behind the words. We'd add a couple of our own thoughts about oral languages that keeps the class natural:

—We can remember to acclaim kids' uses of language. Note what's interesting, unique, a risk taken, whether failed or fulfilled. Note it, then say it;

—We can remember that our own talking and listening models language within any context, too.

All of these kinds of talking and listening suggestions fit more into a tutoring, conferencing, or small group context. Tough implies (and we agree) that whole class teacher talk ought to be used sparingly to:

—stimulate interest in something;

—frame a starting point for an investigation;

—summarize a project, a lesson;

—give information everyone needs efficiently and quickly.

(pp. 123)

We communicate messages to kids through other kinds of oral channels: one to one, small groups, or with our whole classes. We should be more cognizant of the ways we say things. In talking about unconscious verbal and non-verbal messages in the pluralistic classroom, Ricardo Garcia (1991) notes several problematic situations:

—*Sometimes we don't mean what we say*—All of us have done this. This is when we keep saying "fine," or "great job," as an automatic response to kids who seek our attention. We don't mean to put them off, but eventually middle school kids will label this as insincerity.

—*Sometimes our body movements may offend others*—Garcia gives the example of female teachers sitting on desks, a practice many of us have done, especially reading a story aloud. But in some cultures like the Latino culture, this behavior denigrates women. Or when kids don't look at you directly when answering, as in some Native American cultures, they might have been taught that a direct look is disrespectful. Just be aware of how your students might perceive your actions.

—*Sometimes we don't think about the messages behind spatial arrangements*—Are the genders separated on two sides of the room? Is there racial separation in seating, in our small groups? We need to help all people work together.

—*Sometimes we need to think about physical contact between teachers and students*—Garcia calls this "haptics" and reminds us that, particularly with adolescents, even young adolescents, touching may be culturally labeled as OK or not-OK. We need to know who we should pat on the back, give a quick hug to, and who really won't appreciate it.

(pp. 198—199)

More Keeping Track: Assessments

We need to monitor our own talk with our students. Here are some ideas:

—Ask a team member or a department colleague to come in and do some recording of your talk in some of these ways that Tough mentions. But this can be touchy! Prepare yourself well for this.

—Videotape a lesson or a series. You can then watch the tape yourself later and reflect on what you see in your teaching journal. Review it and be tough on yourself!

—Some colleagues could observe with some more formal instruments. The Flanders Interaction Analysis form (1970) helps us see who is dominating the classroom conversation, and forms based on Galloway's (1968) ideas of non-verbal messages can show more about patterns of verbal and non-verbal interaction.

—Myra Sadker (1973) developed ways to assess teachers for gender bias in their classroom communication as well as self-assessment questionnaires. You might use one of those questionnaires to get a sense of your own biases.

—Audiotape yourself and then listen to it critically. (Tom says to be careful and prepare yourself for this too. It freezes him up to think about this. If you're not comfortable, find another way.)

—Take a piece of the class that's audiotaped and transcribe it. Give it to the kids and ask for honest feedback.

—Invite your kids to send feedback letters on this to you. They can be anonymous if they or you want.

—Simply use your teaching journal periodically to self-reflect on your talking and listening. It's a good consciousness raiser, if a little more subjective than the other ideas.

Teaching Journal

Select one of the ways of keeping track of your own talk and listening interactions. Try keeping a record for about a week. Keep the notes in your journal. At the end of the week, sit back and reread your notes. Write a reflective journal entry assessing your oral interactions. Don't be shy. Acknowledge what you think you do well. Point out for yourself ways you can improve your own communication. Set it as a goal for yourself.

Students Talk and Listen to Each Other

Using Groups

This is where we want to go—meaningful oral language among our students, spontaneous or planned, all types, all levels. Kids who are practicing the spectrum of discourse live in our rooms. Natural teachers want themselves out of the center of the classroom and kids empowered and responsible for their own learning.

We can structure in a range of speaking and listening opportunities just by using a plentiful variety of small group strategies as a staple in our language arts classrooms. Like teachers and students, kids can pair up and conference, assess each other's work, brainstorm ideas for a project or paper, plan for future language activities. They can do these things—and more, too—in slightly larger small groups.

About the most thorough description of small group work and explanation of "how to's" and "when's" before the cooperative learning folk emerged was Gary Gerbrandt's *An Idea Book for Acting Out and Writing Language, K-8* (1974). It's still a useful book. It's almost a blueprint for putting meaningful class time into kids' hands. What was helpful to me about it was Gerbrandt's identification of types of groups and tasks and the movement toward flexibility and choice in group composition.

He started out with types of groups demanding simple talking and listening skills:

—*research and reporting small groups*—Kids gather information on a topic and report back to a large group;
—*debating small groups*—Kids debate about ideas among themselves within the small group;

Then the groups became more demanding of social and intellectual skills, sometimes prompted and modeled by the teacher:
—*specific task small groups*—Students solve a problem which will take some planning on their parts and a longer period of time to sustain gathering information;
—*instructive small groups*—This is a special intervention group in which the teacher teaches a specific topic encouraging lots of student interaction with him; this helps in the learning process for using groups;
—*interrogative small groups*—Another teacher intervention group, the teacher playing the Socratic gadfly in order to challenge the group

to generate better talk. She should distance herself as her objective is accomplished.

And the most liberal and most demanding of groups:
—*sequential thinking small groups*—Kids have a lot of freedom to operate, but roughly they follow the steps in true discovery or inquiry;
—*digressive small groups*—A long term and sophisticated brainstorming group, like a think-tank on real issues of concern;
—*evaluation small groups*—Actually an extension of the one above, these groups now assess the ideas of the former group;
—*teacher-like small groups*—This is almost a form of cooperative learning with teaching of content objectives in heterogeneous groups occurring.

(pp. 5-7)

Tom and I would only add one more to Gerbrandt's groups:

—*the editing group*—A response group focused on one another's writing. Tom has talked a lot about various kinds of these in the writing chapters.

A couple of specific group strategies come to mind as examples of some of Gerbrandt's group types. I think many of us naturally use research and reporting along with debating small groups. For example, simply have kids read and share their own composed scripts in parts in small groups. Or if you are doing drama as literature, kids can read plays in small groups, taking characters' parts in each scene. The groups don't have to dramatize the same play. I've done this with a play as complicated for eighth graders as Shakespeare's *Romeo and Juliet*. Students became characters, did dramatic readings of scenes, and I moved around to listen, then intervened and probed and answered student questions, working quickly from group to group. It combines debating and interrogative groups.

As kids develop more group skills, Gerbrandt sees the control of the grouping process moving from teacher to students, from required grouping and restructured groupings, to preferred and interest groups (pp. 10-14). These types of groups and control over grouping made the immersion of students in small group learning a mirror of their developmental processes, a movement within groups toward increasingly more abstract tasks, thus from simple to complex cognition, from forced to open choice of working groups. If the teacher has been modeling a dialogue that assists thinking, students can be coached and encouraged to follow that model in helping each other think through tasks.

Gerbrandt's small group plan is comprehensive overall, but Jo Anne Reid's (1989) suggestions are even more helpful for guiding the internal group processes during group meetings. Reid, along with co-authors Peter Foresstal and Jonathan Cook, envisions five stages a group's work profits from:

—*engagement*—This is when students prepare by participating in a shared experience that gets them ready for groupwork;

—*exploration*—Reid describes this as an unstructured time during which students process new information in their own particular ways;

—*transformation*—During this phase, the students use the new information to begin to accomplish the group goals;

—*presentation*—The students share their findings in different small groups as a way of getting feedback on their work so far;

—*reflection*—All students look back at the information learned and the process used and hopefully gain a better understanding about learning and the new ideas.

(pp. 28-31)

These stages make groupwork more thoughtful, more productive, less ineffective. And they are stages that teachers model for students as they help structure groups and that students can internalize and monitor themselves as they grow toward more autonomous group work.

I've watched Pat Stull work with her fifth graders on dialogue poetry using a similar group process. The kids would select a poem from Paul Fleischman's *Joyful Noise: Poems for Two Voices* (1988). They pair up and read aloud, practicing the music. When they perform this mini-drama in front of the class, their voices blend in unison, then separate suddenly as the poem's duality takes them apart. The music is enjoyable. Poetry is not a dirty word to her fifth graders, and in part, the group structure helps ease the tension of performing in front of a big group.

Another small group activity I've tried is with literature which poses moral dilemmas for one of the characters. When my students were dramatizing *Romeo and Juliet* in small groups, we balanced that with some interesting class discussions on problems relevant to their lives, too. I remember one occurring at the point where Romeo and Juliet are married by Friar Lawrence. The question posed was "Should Romeo and Juliet defy their social and cultural backgrounds as well as parental authority in order to marry for love?" We used the moral dilemma discussion strategy (Galbraith & Jones, 1976) popular then: everyone answered individually on paper first, then they divided into small groups to discuss their reasons for their positions. The whole class then discussed all the reasons they came up with for either position. The class discussion ended up with the kids writing brief reflections on their opinions after hearing everyone else's reasons. It made a great, if lengthy, pre-reading phase before the rest of the play and set us up for more discussion later. And it was the guided sequencing that helped make it productive discussion.

A lot of adolescent literature is full of moral dilemma discussion points. Here are a few:

—Robert Lipsyte's *The Contender* (1967): Should Alfred reveal the gang's plans about the break-in or go along with them?

—S.E. Hinton's *That Was Then, This is Now* (1971): Should Bryon turn Mark in for his drug dealing?

—Paul Zindel's *The Pigman* (1968): Should John and Lorraine use the Pigman's house for a party while the man is in the hospital?

—Walter Dean Myers' *Hoops* (1981): Should Lonnie throw the game or break with his friends and play his best?

—Gary Paulsen's *Dogsong* (1985): Should Russell leave Dograh on the ice alone to die?

—Paula Fox's *The Slave Dancer* (1973): Should Jessie jump ship and try to gain his freedom or continue to play his fiddle on the ship?

—Elizabeth Speare's *The Sign of the Beaver* (1983): Should Matt go with Attean and his grandfather or not?

—Hal Borland's *When the Legends Die* (1963): Should Bear's Brother (Thomas Black Bull) return to the settlement after both his parents are dead, or should he remain true to his isolated life in nature?

A few of the oral assessments mentioned before can be adapted and developed to help keep track of oral language development, like specially tailored rating scales or checklists, completed by teachers or students themselves. If you're really interested in tracking oral language, notes in each student's anecdotal logs or charts will help keep track of how that student uses language aloud. The clipboards that Tom has talked about in the writing chapters make a quick way for you to keep a running log of comments and to assess group participation. This could be part of a week's work overall:

	J's	Books	Folders	Group Part	Pre-wr
Sandra	x	x	x	x	
George		x	x	x	x
Betty	x	x		x	
Thomas	0	x	x	abs	x

Or there could be a separate clipboard for group work altogether.

Many people formalize group evaluation so that students reflect and share immediate feedback. Reid (1989) suggests teachers prepare a group "dichotomous" checklist with questions the students answer such as "Did everyone participate?" and "Was there any argument?" A "yes" or "no" column beside the questions is big enough for a check and a larger column next to those is for narrative comments (p. 89). These instruments help formalize a reflection stage for all groupwork and they're easy to design and to tailor to the specific tasks.

Cooperative Learning: A Special Case of Talking and Listening

I've already mentioned cooperative learning. These are special kinds of groups that can empower students to teach and learn with each other. They work a little like Peter Elbow's (1973) teacherless writing class. I think they call for more sophisticated kinds of interaction skills than some of Gerbrandt's groups. But just like kids can develop interactive work abilities with those, so too can they here.

Of all of them, I like the Jigsaw (Slavin, 1987) version best. It's a good way to get kids to learn about one thing well, become the expert, then teach that to everyone else along with learning the other group members' areas. I routinely do this in one of my methods classes which includes my language arts folks, so I'll explain the process through my own lessons.

To learn the basics about role play, small groups, or inquiry approaches, I divide up the class into groups who research the pedagogy on each method. They're assigned to gather all the information on one approach (purpose, rationale, "how to do it", some variations, etc.). They return to class where they meet with others who researched the same approach. Together they fill in each other's missing information. They increase their expertness.

Phase two begins then. They re-mix into groups of three, each representing a different approach. They have previously planned how to teach these strategies to the others, so that they can thoroughly understand them. They're encouraged to do this interactively. As the teachers, they can't just lecture or give out notes. The listeners are asked to interrupt, to ask questions, to probe. Final evaluations are individual quizzes, but also each group's scores are compiled for a group grade. So, the more points peers can earn, the better. This second part of the evaluation is reward only though. If the whole group does better on their individual quizzes than each did on the quiz before, then the whole group gets bonus points recorded that they may use anywhere in the course on any one other grade except the final average. Helpfulness and understanding has been critical—so has listening and speaking clearly.

There are other group types, like Student Teams Achievement Division (STAD) or Teams-Game-Tournament (TGT) (Slavin, 1987), that can serve as structures to engage students in purposeful speaking and listening. And the cooperative learning folk are pretty structured about evaluation, too. There is always an assessment phase so the group can see how well it functioned, and generally the results of the group work are evaluated. I like the one we used with the bonus feature for the whole group. The students enjoyed the fact that a group grade was not mandated but a reward. They actually seemed to work harder to help each other learn.

Communication Among Different Kids

Of course, one of the main tenets of cooperative learning is its suitability for classrooms of diverse kids. The groups are supposed to be stocked with kids of differing abilities, differing genders, and differing cultural or racial backgrounds. Ricardo Garcia (1992) applauds cooperative learning as a good structure for multicultural concerns, but I think he adds another dimension to it.

Putting our diverse young adolescents in learning groups may help with cognitive growth and social growth, but it can also help with empathic growth and the growth of values. This is the kind of social and emotional growth that includes developing qualities of tolerance for others, for ambiguity, respect for differences, and pride in oneself. The kind that promotes positive identity-seeking where no one loses voice or goes silent. Garcia bases these interactions in the "contact thesis." The contact thesis includes all group differences: gender, racial, ethnic, class, exceptionalities. It's really when people who work together over a period of time get to like, know, and trust each other as equals (p. 178). Cooperative learning is only one way to make this contact possible, but a powerful way if different students work on common tasks for a sustained time with a teacher who stresses equity (p. 18). If you're teaching thematically, whether on a team or not, and if your kids are empowered by writing and reading workshops, chances are better that appropriate relationships can grow into existence.

The teacher is an important key to building successful exchanges student to student. Just mere contact without heightened consciousness doesn't do it. In fact, Garcia goes further to suggest that a teacher should provide study opportunities promoting not only our core similarities, but differences as well: study on minority/majority group communities, gender-role stereotyping, in-group/out-group processes, studies of handicapping conditions, prejudice, stereotyping (pp. 182-184). All these issues that normally divide us and that we cover up should become topics of study. As language arts teachers, we can certainly address these issues in our literature and writing opportunities (choices in a wide variety of multicultural literature, and a wide range of personal writing and research options, for example). Our oral language opportunities can support intergroup contact through planned student to student talk. Social issues like prejudice or stereotyping or historical incidents of these, can be the focus of paired, small group, or cooperative learning strategies, the focus for group research, interviews of others, reporting, and discussing issues in class. These ideas are great for interdisciplinary team units, too. Already, a lot of middle grades language arts teachers integrate language around themes like "The Holocaust," a unit which hardly avoids a significant 20th century event.

The short list of possible discussions above suggest other rich ideas too. You could use the moral dilemma discussion strategy mentioned before as a way to study problems. Powerful too is the idea of telling stories. Peter Frederick reintroduced me to this idea at a faculty workshop and with his wonderful article "The Power of Story" (1990) about telling stories of our own teaching. I had thought sharing stories of experiences was over with "show and tell" but the oral narrative holds us in its grip all our lives. For Peter, storytelling as teaching tool is powerful because inviting stories is "particularly important for women and racial and cultural minorities who . . . have had their stories silenced . . . by academic rationality and objectivism" (p. 7). Stories help us center our classrooms squarely on the affect of each individual, help us connect language and kids and our rooms.

Keeping Track

Again, self-assessment tools that work with other oral language activities might certainly work here, too, especially just focusing your teaching journal for a week, or a unit, on these kinds of communication issues.

Other assessments might include:

—*taping*—Audio or videotaping could help us see not only how much our classrooms allow for talk, but we can gauge the sensitivities in the patterns of talking and listening to our students.

—*asking kids for feedback*—A technique I learned to use with my classes several summers ago at a Great Lakes College Association workshop involves just simply asking students periodically three questions: What's going well? Not so well? and What suggestions do you have? It strikes me that those three questions, somewhat modified to ask about your oral response and interactions, could bring you honest feedback from individual students. They can be anonymous, or if the trust and openness is there, then ask each student to write you.

—*keeping your teaching journal with a focus*—Use your teaching journal daily to help heighten your consciousness of oral interactions. Or make it a team effort. Watch each other and talk about *talk* at team meetings.

Teaching Journal

Do this by yourself, or if you can, with your team. Sit down and think back over the last unit or two that you have taught. What small group approaches did you use? Make a list of them. Are there other group strategies you could have used, or that students could benefit from? Target a part of your next unit for group work, perhaps a kind of group, or a way of helping guide it that you have not tried. Plan it out roughly. If you are working alone, share your plan with the team or with a friend. Don't forget when you try the strategy, use your teaching journal to keep track of how it goes.

Drama and Speech

Tom and I felt we needed to add a final footnote on the subjects of drama and speech. We've already talked about the fact that speaking and listening, in small groups on tasks/topics, as well as role plays, improvisations, reader's theater, a play or scene acting, or videotapes of productions, can all describe doing drama and speech in our classes. We've got these ideas listed as possibilities that weave through a natural language curriculum.

But sometimes we may want to treat drama and speech as something unto themselves. This is fine, with one caveat—that if you are going to do drama as literature, you should not start out by assigning plays for silent reading unless kids have a lot of experiences with drama orally, including some acting. Do the other informal dramatic activities first. Do them before you ask students to put on the school play.

The same with speeches. Give a lot of experience talking first with groups or pairs. Get the comfortableness there before creating speeches and studying how best to sway your listeners with your speech. While some of this is OK, to my mind, the middle school language user ought to be immersed in all the other oral language ideas. Formality can come later. There's plenty of time. After all, there's still high school and college. Maybe we can just concentrate on building confidence as oral language users.

Pat Stull and her fifth graders do a good job of marrying these two notions of more formal drama and speech. But their project remains more pleasurable than threatening. They do a regular project in class called "The Newscast." It's a complicated individual group project requiring lots of levels of talk and listening for both reporters and audiences.

Each fifth grader applies for a job as an anchorperson, a newsperson handling state or local news, a feature reporter, a weather reporter, or a sportscaster. The anchor handles national and international news. She is also responsible for coordinating topics among all the rest of the news team.

When kids apply for the news jobs, they give first, second, and third choices. They make choices every six weeks and their new roles are dependent on what experiences they had before. So each new six weeks, there are three new news teams. Each reports once a week, so overall, each student is speaking formally (while others listen for information) at least once a week.

Stories must all meet two selection criteria: they must be newsworthy or of interest to the class, and they should in some way be related to the sub-theme of the curriculum for that six weeks. Everybody uses a lot of different resources: National Public Radio, *Newsweek*, different local news and newspapers. Everyone does research on his own and writes up a report. On the day of the newscast, the team practices together briefly in the morning. Their targeted time is 10 minutes. One commercial may appear (usually hilarious), but most of the time remains focused on news.

The Newscast contains a unique twist, another integration point. It's tied to a mini-economy game. If the kids don't come within plus or minus 30 seconds of the 10 minutes, the pay each earns as part of the news team (and as part of a related class simulation) is docked.

And they all evaluate each other, using a form that Pat and they put together earlier in the year. Here's a possible form based on what they developed.

NEWSCAST EVALUATIONS

Newscaster _____

Date_____ Evaluator _____

Preparation:	Well prepared
	Obvious practice
	Interesting information
	Knowledgeable about subject matter
	In presenter's own words
	(5) _____
Speech:	Fluid, flowing
	Not too fast/too slow
	Clear, distinct
	No inappropriate gaps
	Correct punctuation
	Not too loud/too soft
	(5) _____
Delivery:	Good eye contact
	No distractions
	Good "connectors"
	Pleasant appearance
	(5) _____
Team member:	Listens while others present
	Appears interested
	No distractions
	(5) _____
Comments:	Total _____

For every news team member, there is a peer evaluator who is a listener and not a member of that team. News team members recommend the evaluator, but this may be overridden by Pat. There's also a timekeeper who tries to help the anchor pace the show. Once a week, when you're not on a team, you're an evaluator. And once a week, you're simply the audience. Even the audience, though, writes down three important facts they learned which they share with Pat. This way she can assess listening as well as receive fuller information for her own evaluation.

Excitement tends to run high when formal Newscasts appear after lunch hour. The class assembles quickly and everyone bustles around setting up furniture properly. Evaluators and timekeepers are chosen and set. On the day I watch, John leads as anchor, sharing news on the latest shuttle mission and on the word that U.S. troops may go to Somalia soon.

"Now to Bradley with state news." He passes along the focus to the state newscaster on his right who covers a story on an Indianapolis pit bull attack. Aron follows with local news on the town library as well as advice on alleviating stress for pets during the Christmas holidays.

"Now back to John," Aron ends. John pauses for a short commercial.

Commercials are the few seconds the group gets to be creative and silly. Today's sponsor is Unlucky Charms and the whole team takes part in a very physical, funny push for their cereal product. The whole thing eats up 24 seconds though.

Soon Brian is on with features followed by Abigail with the weather. Megan ends with sports news on the Wabash basketball win, Purdue's game, and Hose's upcoming competition.

John signs them off with nearly a minute left, well under what would yield the best pay! There's some consternation, but quickly Pat steers the whole group toward discussion.

The discussion over what has just occurred is really what spurs this oral event into thoughtful speaking and listening. While kids obviously listened attentively during the Newscast, it's equally obvious that now they listen critically and speak opinions, advice, and evaluative comments.

Pat in particular wants the listeners to share general comments on the presentation. It's not a one-way exchange. The listeners point out what would make the Newscast smoother (longer stories, someone says, and not overusing certain words, someone else contributes). Newscast team members seek input. Brian, for instance, asked for feedback on their commercial, while Steve simply commented on how hard it was to present while seeing people writing. "There's so little eye contact," he noted.

Pat lets them move to discussing the news itself, keeping it focused on the national and international news. In fact, they get carried away for 10 minutes talking about Somalia, arguing the pros and cons of U.S. involvement, exclaiming over the pictures of starving people they've seen, comparing this disaster with Hurricane Andrew. They pose questions about whether it's right to send anyone over to interfere. Often, various members imagine the Somali view. Pablo says, "If I were in Somalia, I'd be frightened of foreign troops. I might not know why they're there." Amidst the rising bubble of talk, Pat settles it down by asking for evaluations to be completed and feedback to be given to each member of the group. Gradually the hum dies as talk becomes writing in the usual way of the school day.

If talking and listening goes well in the class, as it does here with a more formal situation, then one thing is very noticeable—it's energizing, and it flows easily in and out of reading and writing as does reading and writing out of oral language on any level.

Special Problems with Talking and Listening

Off-task talk—Generally, if your groups are organized, with a specific task, time limits are clear, what's due is obvious, and students know the group membership, a lot of this will be minimized. Listen, and if most of the talk and listening is on focus, don't worry about it. Tom says to be careful about squelching off-task talk too soon, though, especially in writing groups. Experience sharing in this case is really vital and very much on-task. But if off-task talk is clearly hindering group progress, there may be several things you can do:

　　—re-structure the groups;
　　—conference one-to-one with the students having problems;
　　—build in concrete ways to give feedback on group effectiveness, so learners can themselves see the patterns discouraging learning.

—*Silent, disengaged kids*—Usually small groups invite quiet students of either gender or any cultural background to open up when they won't do it in larger group exchanges. In fact, breaking into small groups before large group discussion is a good strategy for getting these kids involved, "loosened up," and ready to participate. If nothing else, the silent kids can be the group spokespersons, reporting out, listing, and summarizing for the class. They need to hear their voices to grow the confidence needed to use them freely.

Sometimes in small groups, though, kids remain silent. Assign roles and rotate them, so there's a balance between leaders of the conversation and listeners in the group. Above all, if the silence continues, find out more about why. There could be more than just a little reticence here, or discomfort with one's "new" voice as a young adolescent. Severe self confidence issues could lie behind this behavior, something both you and the student may need good sensitive outside help with. Sometimes it's culture. You need to know that too.

—*Speaking anxiety*—There is such a thing. When I began to explore writing anxiety in the late 1970's, I quickly learned that the research on this problem had grown out of earlier research on speaking anxiety (Daly & Miller, 1975). Some people have a real reticence about themselves as oral language users. Some things that might build confidence are: (1) sharing personal experiences in small groups; (2) sharing book talks in small groups; (3) small group brainstorming; or (4) small group project planning (Quandt, 1983). Ultimately, keep the class flexible and remember different learning styles abound.

—*Gender issues, or helping voices remain loud and clear*—We've said it before; silence is not golden. While Gilligan (1990) and Hancock (1989) find that young adolescent girls' voices disappear or become distorted just at this critical time for identity formation, Belenky and her colleagues (1986) find a great deal of silence still existing in older women. Something happens, or doesn't happen in the years between 12 and 20 for girls. We expect boys to be bad; we expect good girls to be quiet. As I've argued elsewhere, part of the problem may lie in teaching a gendered curriculum itself (Butler & Sperry, 1991). Or as the Sadkers (1982) have found out, it could be a problem with teacher-student communication. Or a problem with the socialized and limiting sex role definitions our society places on its young. Or all three and more.

*—Dialect issues, or honoring all voices in class—*It's simple. You let them have their voices, let them use them without discrimination. Oral language always works to communicate messages. Holding any standard above another is a prejudice. If they weren't getting messages across, then kids would change their own language. There would be a reason to change. Just because we think they should change isn't good enough. If you are worried that you'll be unfair to your kid's futures, you can tell them about the realities and expectations in the world. You'll find Tom and I disagree a little on this point. Tom, for example, says those realities just don't exist. If you think they do, let them know, but don't denigrate, push, and drive kids into silence and away from the delight and power of a diversity of language.

Teaching Journal

You might want to write this entry with a friend or with your team. Think of an issue or problem relating to students talking in class, something that might even make you hesitate to plan more chances for talking and listening. Reflect on what might be at the root of this problem. Then brainstorm some possible solutions you could try next time the problem arises.

Connections: Speaking and Listening Extensions with Writing and Reading

If we look back over some of the various strategies already mentioned in this chapter, I think we can see that many are already integrated naturally with reading and writing. Of course, if the language arts environment is whole and natural, that rhythmic shift from oral-to-written-to-oral, or oral-to-reading-to-oral will occur naturally, too. This movement is really what Peter Frederick (1985) called using "energy shifts" in the classroom. Energy shifts are conscious movements from one structure for learning to another during class—a sound way to run any class given learning style preferences, attention spans, and all that.

Yet, these are strategies that enhance the oral component visibly so that teachers and students can evaluate oral language growth. There are other core strategies in the heart of the language arts ecology where oral language is even more naturally a part of reading and writing.

Other Oral Language Connections with Reading

—*book talks*—Sometimes you can just talk or ask more formal questions about the books being read.

—*oral reading*—Teachers to students, students to each other—any audiences for oral reading will do.

—*shared readings of drafts, finished products*—Any writing workshop time in the day will provide such exchange.

—*oral brainstorming, clustering, mapping*—This is excellent for pre-reading, post-reading wind-ups, before writing a piece or reading a piece, for project planning.

—*dramatic reading groups*—You might do just as I did in class when teaching *Romeo and Juliet* and with literature in general. Many teachers choose to have a reader's theater from time to time in class.

—*choral reading*—There are neat poems that are meant for two voices just like music is, and many plays or pieces of them provide for this activity.

—*radio plays*—These are somewhat time-consuming if students compose and stage their own. But a lot of learning goes on when you take the time for this—and a lot of enjoyment and careful listening as students present to and entertain one another.

Other Oral Language Connections with Writing

—*writing feedback groups*—What we mean here is response groups, based on Peter Elbow's teacherless writing concept.

—*student-to-student conferences*—These are student partners sharing drafts, giving feedback.

—*editing groups*—Most of us use this more formal and more focused talking among students as they near the ends of their drafts.

—*read arounds, or reading celebrations*—Students may read drafts or finished products. This event is a whole class sharing, not for feedback for revision, but just to honor each other's voices.

Teaching Journal

Go back to a unit you recently taught and revise it, planning in more opportunities for speaking and listening for students. Remember to keep it natural. The purposes for speaking and listening should be authentic, not drills or just games played at half past the hour, nor two days worth of speeches assigned out of the blue.

A Glimpse: Bringing It All Together

Oral language and print might be woven naturally throughout instruction in something like the following way. What follows is simply a short unit based around a piece of literature, a novel, that I taught with some of my seventh and eighth graders.

The Pigman's Legacy

It was 1982. This is my second year as a laboratory school demonstration teacher and as the language arts teacher on our team. It was spring, and for the first time in two years, I had a student teacher, another Deborah.

The team wasn't engaged in an interdisciplinary project when Deb and I sat down to look at our program goals and where to go with our language arts students. It was a chance to focus on writing, reading literature together, and on having kids talk to us and each other about books.

They had been selecting and reading literature all through the year and individually talking about their books with me. But we wanted to read a book with the whole class and make the form of the novel a bit more visible in our conversations. After a number of talks and observations, we selected *The Pigman's Legacy* (1980) by Paul Zindel and decided to focus about two weeks on it. We came to this decision for a number of reasons. We watched what the kids were reading and liked, and Zindel was surely one of them. And the book seemed to us to deal with a number of relevant issues in our students' lives, both male and female: underlying themes of human guilt and innocence, responsibility and maturity, the change from childhood to adulthood, parent and youth relationships, and indeed, friendships between and among the young and the old. Lots of things we knew from them and the themes in their journals and writing folders that they thought about.

We based our reading process squarely on small group/large group discussions. Of course, a focused journal-writing was the final cornerstone of the experience. In fact, we invented what we thought was an appropriately developmental form of journal-keeping, which we even labeled an *empathic journal*. This is a specially focused journal topic based on drawing the reader's feelings into the literature by having them imagine being in a situation like the characters are in. Usually we discussed their feelings. This is done before reading so that identification is heightened as they begin to read.

I think three lessons during the unit show the natural engagement of these 7th and 8th graders with reading, writing, and oral languages:

> Day 1: Student reading from journals
> Teacher oral reading to class

On the first day, Deb and I set up an opening journal writing which highlighted the core theme of the book. "Write about a time in your life in which you learned something about yourself or about how human beings act." After writing, some students shared. Of course, Deb and I read ours, too. We used their voices as a springboard to introduce the novel.

After I gave a 10 minute overview of the book, Deb began reading the first chapter. Everyone had her book, and was eagerly following along while Deb modeled a lively, engaged, inflected reading tone, dramatically portraying dialogue and scenes.

> Day 6: Students read silently
> Student conference with instructors one to one

This day was a Uninterrupted Sustained Silent Reading day for reading Chapters 9 and 10. The brief discussion of chapter 8 served as a way to focus on 9 and 10. While kids read, we chatted with each student briefly about his or her opinions, feelings, and personal perspectives on the book—a one-to-one conversation mode.

> Day 8: Student small group and large group discussions

Everyone had read the book by this time, and had been prepped ahead for reading silently at home as they were every day. (We took very seriously the notion of "pre-reading" anticipations and probably spent from 10-15 minutes at the end of each class leading into the night's reading.) Upon returning to class this day, we opened with two possible journal-writes: "Write about the way that the relationship between Dolly and the Colonel parallels the relationship between John and Lorraine" and "Describe how the setting of this last chapter is appropriate to the game theme that seems to pop up through the book. Is the book saying something about the relationship between real life and games?"

In small groups kids shared their answers for each focus, reading from their journals, or just telling the basics of what they had written. A simple "research and report" group of sorts. A pre-selected group leader kept everyone contributing and made sure responses to both questions were shared. A group recorder jotted interesting ideas. The small group interaction involved everyone and was essentially a warm-up, a loosening up so more kids shared the group ideas within a large group discussion that followed, one where kids continued to listen, talk, and build on other's ideas.

Oral language happened naturally in this unit. Students talked— all of them at one time or another. And it was unobstrusive, yet thoughtful talking and listening. We think there were a couple of reasons why:

—the relevance of the book and its key themes in our students' lives sparked sharing and debate;

—no discussion questions were factual or had right answers. The best questions are real inquiry ones, the ones that have no correct answer but which have answers that can be correctly defended when grounded in the text and in democratic human rights and values. If a question already has an answer, why bother to ask it? "Why do you think this?" and "How did you feel when . . .?" along with "What made you feel that way?" probe thinking and feeling and relating to books a lot better than "What color was . . .?"

—the deliberate availability of modes of talk and listening allowed students a range of comfortable entry points into the class dialogue. One on one, in small groups, as a whole group—all contexts rhythmically wove through the unit, a full scale of opportunities.

Tom and I don't know how David Bland's principal will respond to the team log. We hope she nods and agrees and comes to see, to talk, and listen herself to the richness and diversity of middle schoolers' own unique voices. If they are reading and writing in a workshop classroom, there surely will be the continual and natural hum of young voices.

References

Belenky, M., Clinchy, B., Goldberger, N. & Tarule, J. (1986). *Women's ways of knowing*. New York: Basic Books.

Borland, H. (1963). *When the legends die.* New York: Harper and Row.

Butler, D., & Sperry, S. (1991). Gender issues and the middle school curriculum. *Middle School Journal,* 23(2), 18-23.

Calkins, L. (1986). *The art of teaching writing.* Portsmouth, NH: Heinemann.

Cambourne, B. (1988). *The whole story: Natural learning and the acquisition of literacy in the classroom.* Auckland, NZ: Ashton Scholastic.

Daly, J., & Miller, M. (1975). The empirical development of an instrument to measure writing apprehension. *Research in the Teaching of English,* 9, 242-248.

Elbow, P. (1973). *Writing without teachers.* New York: Oxford University Press.

Flanders, N. (1970). *Analyzing teaching behavior.* Reading, MA: Addison-Wesley.

Fleischman, P. (1988). *Joyful noise: Poems for two voices.* New York: Harper and Row.

Fox, P. (1973). *The slave dancer.* New York: Bradbury Press.

Frazier, N., & Sadker, M. (1979). *Sexism in school and society.* New York: Harper and Row.

Frederick, P. (1986). The lively lecture. *College Teaching* 34(2), 43-50.

Frederick, P. (1990). The power of story. *AAHE Bulletin.*

Galbraith, R., & Jones, T. (1976). *Moral reasoning: A teaching handbook for adapting Kohlberg to the classroom.* Anoka, MN: Greenhaven Press.

Galloway, C. (1968). Nonverbal communication. *Theory into Practice* 7, 172-175.

Garcia, R. (1991). *Teaching in a pluralistic society* (2nd ed.). New York: Harper Collins.

Gerbrandt, G. (1974). *An idea book for acting out and writing language, K-8.* Urbana, IL: National Council of Teachers of English.

Gilligan, C. (1990). Teaching Shakespeare's sister: Notes from the underground of female adolescence. In C. Gilligan, N. Lyons, and T. Hamner (Eds.), *Making connections: The relational worlds of adolescents girls at Emma Willard School* (pp. 6-29). Cambridge, MA: Harvard University Press.

Graves, D. (1983). *Writing: Teachers and children at work.* Portsmouth, NH: Heinemann.

Hancock, E. (1989). *The girl within.* New York: Faucett Columbine.

Hinton, S. E. (1971). *That was then. This is now.* New York: Viking Press.

Klein, M. (1977). *Talk in the language arts classroom* . Urbana, IL: ERIC Clearinghouse on Reading and Communication Skills and the National Council of Teachers of English.

Lipsyte, R. (1967). *The contender.* New York: Harper and Row.

Lundsteen, S. (1979). *Listening* (2nd ed.). Urbana, IL: ERIC Clearinghouse of Reading and Communication Skills, National Institute of Education, and National Council of Teachers of English.

Moffett, J. (1967). *Drama: What is happening.* Urbana, IL: National Council of Teachers of English.

Moffett, J. (1983). *Teaching the universe of discourse* (2nd ed.). Boston: Houghton Mifflin.

Moffett, J., & Wagner, B. (1983). *A student-centered language arts and reading, K-13.* Boston: Houghton Mifflin.

Myers, W. D. (1981). *Hoops.* New York: Delacorte Press.

Paulsen, G. (1985). *Dogsong.* New York: Scholastic.

Quandt, R. (1983). *Language arts for the child.* Englewood Cliffs, NJ: Prentice-Hall.

Reid, J., Forrestal, P., & Cook, J. (1989). *Small group learning in the classroom.* Portsmouth, NH: Heinemann.

Sadker, D., & Sadker, M. (1982). *Sex equity handbook for schools.* New York: Longman.

Slavin, R. (1987). *Cooperative learning* (2nd ed.). Washington, DC: National Education Association.

Speare, E. (1983). *The sign of the beaver.* Boston: Houghton Mifflin.

Staab, C. (1992). *Oral language for today's classroom*. Markham, Ontario: Pippin.

Tchudi, S., & Mitchell, D. (1989). *Explorations in the teaching of English* (3rd ed.). New York: Harper and Row.

Tough, J. (1985). *Talk for teaching and learning*. London: Schools Council Publications.

Zindel, P. (1968). *The pigman*. New York: Harper and Row.

Zindel, P. (1980). *The pigman's legacy*. New York: Harper and Row.

10

Messing Around with Media

"One experiment was conducted in Germany, where 184 volunteer television viewers were paid to give up TV for one year. At first the volunteers reported that they spent more time with their children, went to movies more frequently, read and played more games, and visited friends and relatives more....But within a few weeks things began to change. Even though the people were paid not to watch, one man dropped out after only three weeks. No one lasted more than five months. Why? Tension, fighting, and quarreling increased among families without television. When the experiment was over and the sets were back on, these effects disappeared."

—Jeffrey Schrank (1975)

"If you have what's out there, you're already behind."

—Johnny Palmer, assistant principal

"It takes longer than it takes."

—Lewis Miller, media specialist

Perhaps you share my experience. I used to be fully confident about this media stuff. I loved cameras and films and rock-n-roll. Most of all, I loved gadgets. I still do. My room was the one with the reel-to-reel tape recorder playing in the corner, usually a 16 mm projector loaded with Learning Corporation's latest film, and somebody running around snapping photographs to be developed in the darkroom we had made out of an old storeroom my principal let us use. Then personal computers came along. For a while there was one bulky TRS 80 in the math chairman's classroom, and the next thing I knew there were Apples and IBM's and Tandys and Lasers multiplying like lemmings all over the school! Video tapes got smaller and easy to use and pretty cheap. Now everybody has a VCR, and school libraries have dozens of tapes on the shelves. I hear a lot about CD's and video laserdiscs and networking and digitized images and laptops and desktop publishing and multimedia systems and all kinds of strange and wonderful things. Most of the time I don't think I know enough to even ask questions that make sense.

We know any discussion of media can be bewildering, and Deborah and I will try to be as clear and practical as we can. Most of the jargon is from computer technology, a field growing faster than anything else in our schools. It can sound like another language—Martian maybe, or at least Star Trekian. We'll avoid jargon as much as possible, and try to explain it clearly when we have to use it. We are not computer wizards, although Deb and I both use them. But we know some teachers who really do weave their magic with the machines, and we rely on their knowledge and advice heavily in this chapter. We want to share with you what these teachers are doing with media, give you some suggestions about things you may want to do with your students, and point out some of the better resources. Where we think it helpful, we will tell you what kind of equipment you'll need. Guessing at costs is risky because there are so many changes in technology coming so fast, and there are people in your school system and in your community who can give you better and more current information than we can. The good news is prices are likely to come down on most gadgets when they are no longer new. At any rate, take any estimates of cost we give you with a grain of salt.

I've noticed that English teachers often don't like computers very much. Maybe we're a little afraid of them? Machines in the classroom when you are trying to manage thirty middle schoolers can be a hassle anyway. It doesn't take too many bad experiences to send me back to paper and pencil and the textbook. Who needs it?

Well, the kids do, actually, in this Communication Age in which we find ourselves. Except for talking face-to-face, most of the language they will experience by a vast margin will involve the electronic media. To ignore all other media except print leaves a very big gap in their language arts education.

Teaching Journal

Get a cup of coffee and a few minutes of quiet and do a free writing on your relationship with media in your classroom. Films, video, tape recorders, computers, all that stuff. What are your triumphs? Your tragedies? What machines are you confident with, and which ones scare you? What do you want to learn to do you've never done with your kids before?

Share your reflections with a buddy.

Media Literacy

Part of being educated is learning **about** things. How is that done and why does it affect me that way? And you don't have to watch very much M-TV or scan the marquee of too many movie houses or spend any time at all with prime time television, not to mention the cable channels, to know your students need guidance, real information, and knowledge about the visual media. I sought Jeff Fletcher's advice on what should be included in this chapter at a recent NMSA meeting. You've seen Jeff's fine photographs on the cover of the *Middle School Journal*. He teaches at Appalachian State University in North Carolina. Without hesitation, he suggested first we talk about visual literacy. "Anyone can view a picture, but we need to learn to see it critically." I was interested that this man who spends so much of his time with the still images of photographs talked mostly about his concern for students' watching the moving images on the TV screen.

TV: Great American Waste Land or Our Greatest Resource?

Probably both. No doubt your students watch a lot of wretched stuff. But don't we all? They also have access to some wonderful things they cannot see anywhere else. And TV itself and video taped segments from it are teaching tools waiting to be used.

Note: Please be aware of the copyright laws when video taping anything from TV to use in your classroom. *CNN Newsroom, A&E, The Discovery Channel,* many of the shows on your local Public Broadcasting channel, and some others are liberal in the use they allow educators. But do not assume that you can use everything in your classroom you tape on your VCR at home. I don't bring video tapes rented for home use into the classroom either. It's neither legal nor ethical. Remember the example you set for your kids.

With that awareness, I do encourage you to use TV programming in your classroom wherever it fits the needs of your students and whenever it meshes with the themes and content of your classes. If you have not done so, survey your students about their TV watching. You may want to prepare a sheet for them to fill out as you do with the Reading Survey at the beginning of the year, or you may want to do this informally in class discussion.

TV Survey

1) How many TV's are there in your home? Do you have a TV of your own?

2) Do you have cable service at home? Which add-on channels do you get (e.g. HBO, Home Box Office, the Disney Channel, the Sports Channel)? Do you have more than one add-on channel? More than two?

3) How many hours a day do you watch TV?

4) List your favorite shows. Which ones do you never miss?

5) Do you have a VCR at home? How many videos do you watch in a normal week?

6) What are your favorite videos? What are they rated?

You will want to participate in the discussion with them. And you will find it lively.

Several years ago in a popular writing series my friend Dan Kirby included a section on journal writing he called "Talking Back to the Tube." Planning time and a method for students to become more aware of their TV viewing was a good idea then, and it's still a good idea. Besides, I like his title. The idea is to raise students' consciousness about what they are watching and to encourage critical viewing without being too heavy handed about it. For no more than a few weeks (a month is too long!) have students log their TV viewing, list the day, time, and types of shows, and respond to what they see in no more than a page. You can let them react to whatever they want to talk about or guide them with questions or a specific focus you want to give the response journal during any given week. The TV Response Journal also lends itself to group work.

Tube Talk

TV Journal for Week 2: Murder and Mayhem

Your team has been assigned one TV channel to monitor during one hour of prime time (8:00 -11:00 p.m.) viewing this week. Each of you will probably want to watch a different show on this channel each evening to see more programs, but this is not a requirement. During the hour your task will be to record all acts of violence on the screen, record the time as closely as you can, and very briefly describe the kind of violence seen. After the hour, write your personal response to the show and its violence.

Channel _____ Day of Week _____

Name of Program _____

	Time	Violent Action	Why?	Weapon(s)
1.				
2.				
3.				
4.				
5.				
6.				
7.				
8.				
9.				
10.				

Response:

Take several days or a whole week and respond to nothing but commercials. Before they begin watching, spend some time getting them ready for what they will see. Talk about the language of advertising (e.g. weasel words, testimonials, vague claims, statistics). Look at how emotional appeal is used to sell things, the use of celebrities, and how commercials are filmed. As your students watch commercials, have them record the channel, program, and time for each (as they do in the example with violence above) and ask them to identify the product and kind of appeal the commercial makes to viewers. After several days they share their observations in a general class discussion.

Analyze news programs with your students and their favorite prime time shows. Help them to see how characters are created, especially watching for stereotyping and how film techniques are used. You may want to teach some of the basics of the film maker's craft, lighting, camera angles, different kinds of shots, fades and cuts, and editing if you are comfortable with them, and if your students' interest remains high.

But you don't really have to get that technical to have a lot of fun and learn a lot about television and how we respond to it. Culminate the viewing journal by asking them to describe themselves as TV consumers.

Teaching Journal

Keep a Tube Talk journal yourself as your students watch and write and discuss their TV viewing during these activities. Save room in your weekly TV journal for reflections on which activities and discussions were particularly lively and insightful, and which ones fell flat.

Cable in the Classroom

In most communities, the local TV cable company will provide free cable hook up to your school. Several channels are available for video taping, *Arts and Entertainment, C-Span, The Learning Channel, Nickelodeon, USA Network,* and several others. An attractive and useful program guide, *Cable in the Classroom* magazine, is available and is published monthly except for July and August. It contains a lot of information about what's on the tube for the month, including a detailed listing by subject from 30 channels, 19 of them Cable in the Classroom members promising commercial-free programming, support materials upon request, and liberal video taping permissions for teachers. A convenient list of all the programmers, their addresses, and some toll-free phone numbers are included in each issue. The centerfold is a taping calendar for you to post in your room with highlights of the most interesting programs. There is a "Sourcebook" column with information about study guides, videos, and other support materials, and even a "Parents' Page" to photocopy and send home each month. There is a lot of material available to help you use cable TV for any theme, unit, or subject you want to teach. A year's subscription is $18.00, but our local cable outfit gives us several subscriptions we share through the media centers of our schools.

Cable in the Classroom Magazine
80 Elm St.
Peterborough, NH 03458
1-800-343-0728

Computers and the Language Arts

You see that I'm already talking about computers, even when I try to talk about using TV in your classroom. You can't get away from them. They are related in one way or another to just about every use of the media, or they can be. For most of us, computers are at once fascinating and aggravating gadgets. They are wonderful tools, especially for writing. The kids love them. They make my job and yours easier, when they are working properly and I understand how to use them. But when all I get on the screen is "Input Error" or the thing beeps at me or it won't save my writing or my hard work disappears without a trace—Grrrrrr!

Don't be discouraged. And don't be afraid of the machine. It's just a tool, like a typewriter or a calculator or a telephone, only just a little more complicated. I am not a computer whiz by any stretch of the imagination. I am learning a little, and I do a lot of word processing because I write. Frankly, my first experiences with the machine were frustrating, and the thing intimidated me. I had been teaching a long time. I was doing just fine, thank you; and I didn't want to fool with it. But I am a writer, and a writing teacher. Within a couple of years it was clear I needed to know how to do basic word processing at least, and my students surely needed the experience. So I got a buddy to teach me. Fred Lamb, a music teacher, interestingly enough, got me started on an Apple IIe and a simple word processing program. By making a lot of mistakes and asking Fred a lot of questions, I was writing a little bit on the machine by the end of the day. I've been making mistakes and asking questions ever since. Somewhere around your school is a teacher who loves computers and can help you. If you somehow have escaped the computer so far, get yourself a buddy and start writing with it so you can help your kids.

I personally am not comfortable with the suggestion you hear a lot—just get one of the students to show me and the other kids how to use the computer. Sure, some of them have a lot more time at the screen than I do, and there are some students who really are computer buffs. But any program I want them to use, I need to know how to use first.

Teaching Journal

Your job for this Teaching Journal is to survey the computers in your school. Specifically, find out how many computers are, or may be, available to your students. What kinds are they? Which ones are hooked up to printers so they can easily be used for writing? What word processing programs are available for your students to use? If your school has a computer lab, when is it available and how many machines can your students use during particular periods or times of the day?

Write down the numbers and the brand names and the writing programs. The survey will give you an overall look at technology at your school, for use now and also for planning with your colleagues. And if you have to scrounge like many of the teachers I know, you will know where equipment is available for your students.

Word Processing

I am not a computer teacher; I am a writing teacher who uses the computer. The distinction is worth making. I teach students the rudiments of word processing because that is how I write. As a craftsman, I teach them to write by showing them how I do it. It's just that simple. I write with them, so we do word processing together, too, as often as we can get to the machines.

But word processing also does a lot more for me as a writing teacher because it makes publishing easy and almost instantaneous, and attractive. It makes editing and proofreading a lot easier than all that re-writing, and students really like to work on their writing on the screen. Because the writing appears on a screen where we both can see it easily, conferencing is easier between me and a student and among students. And most students just like to write with the computer. It is very motivating.

I have some experience doing this, so I know the particular word processing program students use is not terribly important—as long as it is one that is not more of a hindrance than a help. They, and I, can learn to use other, perhaps more sophisticated word processing programs easily once they are comfortable with the first one. Use what is available in your school and don't worry about it. If you have several to choose from, start with the one you use, or get the advice of your media specialist or computer lab teacher. Students who have a computer at home (I do not; I cannot afford it yet) tell me they have no problem writing with a different program and different equipment at home. Switching back and forth does not bother them, as soon as they realize two different machines, even some made by the same company, are not compatible.

I have not found it necessary to buy any of those programs with canned writing lessons. Frankly, I've yet to see one I liked. I want the kids to choose what to write. My job is to show them how to write and how to make it better. All I want is a word processing program that gets the words on the screen and on paper, lets us make whatever changes we need to make in editing quickly and easily, and will save our work so we can get it back up on the screen when we want to.

Keyboarding instruction is handy for middle school students, but it is not necessary for them to start writing with the machines. There is a useful keyboard chart to help them with finger positions in the back of *Write Source 2000* (1992), and I encourage students to get comfortable with the fingerings because it makes writing easier. There are also simple keyboarding programs like *Touch Typing for Beginners* that will teach your students quickly how to get around a keyboard. Whatever you do, don't stop them from writing because they haven't been taught to type. They do just fine hunting and pecking. The research indicates it will not hurt their writing; nor will hunting and pecking hurt their typing, when they finally do learn to type.

I feel like I need to say a word to two about equipment and word processing. The range of sophistication with computers is so broad from one school to another and there are so many different choices to make with hardware and software with the limited funds you have, it can all be rather bewildering. But don't be discouraged. We hope the experience Deb and I have had with word processing and other applications of computers in language arts and some of the things we have seen in other classrooms and schools will be helpful to you whether your school is high tech with all kinds of fancy and expensive equipment or if you teach in a school where you're struggling to buy a few machines for your students.

Situations and resources can be very different. You will see a portrait of Mike Barton and his colleagues at Tuttle Middle School right after this chapter, and wouldn't it really be neat to work in a school equipped like Tuttle Middle and have Mike work with your kids! He works in a school with a fully equipped and networked computer lab with IBM computers and lots of fancy software. The media center has a CD ROM tower, *New Grolier Electronic Encyclopedia* and *World Book Information Finder* and National Geographic's *Mammals* and Software Toolworks' *World Atlas* networked to the classrooms, and a multimedia set up for student projects. He even has a large screen projector to show off all of this wonderful stuff for a group or entire class. Tuttle's students can also communicate with other students, schools, colleges, and even agencies like NASA using the computers, software, and modems available in the school. At the other end of the spectrum are teachers with one computer in their rooms, or none at all, who have to scrounge any way they can to get their students access to the machines. Still, it can be done with understanding and cooperative colleagues.

My personal opinion is that you need two to five computers and a printer in your classroom and a computer lab in your school where you can schedule your whole class or groups. If a middle school can afford a lab, it should be open to students and teachers who need to use it, and not scheduled all day for computer literacy exploratories. I've seen too many situations where teachers are scrounging to find machines for their students to use and the school has a nice lab essentially closed to them. Ideally, the computer lab teacher is available to team with the other teachers in the building, the way Linda Clark and Melissa Moore work together at Merry Acres Middle.

A writing lab with either IBM or Macintosh computers can cost well over $50,000; but you can put an IBM clone and printer in your classroom for about $800. So you can see the range of choices you and your school have to make as you get into word processing, or when you start to upgrade or add to your equipment. That is, if you are asked at all. Most language arts teachers use what we are given and have no voice in the choices of equipment or the program to run on it. With more and more word processing going on in our middle schools, however, that is changing. Be prepared and ask for what you want. I've done a lot of talking to computer people these few weeks as I wrote this, and I want to comment on some of the kinds of choices we are looking at in my school system that may be helpful to you.

Should I buy an IBM or Macintosh or some other computer for word processing?

I use an IBM clone. I use *Windows 95* with Microsoft *Office*, which includes *Word*, a very good writing program that I enjoy and find easy to use; but I am used to it and have been using it for some years now in different versions. Deborah uses a Power Macintosh 6500/250 computer, which has *Word* and some other things we'll talk about. She also uses *WordPerfect*, version 3.5. I have some experience with that program as well. Deb also still has a *Claris Works* word processing program, and she tells me a lot of the Mac people like it. The choice of the hardware seems to be no big deal. Devotees of IBMs and Macs do tend to be strong in their preferences, but it is not unusual now for a teacher to use one kind of machine at school and another at home. As you can tell, you'll see much of the same software on each.

What software is best for teaching writing?

Deb uses *Word* (a part of the Microsoft *Office* software package), and so do I. She also uses Corel *WordPerfect*, and she likes both programs. Today (1998) they are the two best choices. Tomorrow that could change. I really like *Word,* but I use it every day. That is what makes the difference. Teachers tell me it is a good writing program for middle school students. The point is, you and your students will do just fine with either one, once you're used to it. I have also used *Works*, which I think of as a simpler version of *Word*, and that program is also serviceable. Don't be bewildered by all the brand names. They all work just about the same. The choice of a particular one is not all that important.

What printer do I want?

The simple answer is the best one you can afford. Cost is the biggest factor when you choose the printer for word processing. Your school can buy a relatively cheap dot matrix printer for around $200, and even less if your buying several pieces of equipment at one time. Dot matrix printers are the ones with the funny looking square letters, but you can buy different fonts or styles of lettering for these machines also. On the other hand, a letter quality printer can run $1,000 and more. A versatile and reasonably priced printer we use a lot around here is the *Image Writer II* (about $400). Color ribbons and a variety of fonts are available for it, and I'm told it works just fine for desk top publishing.

So, after I see how much I can spend for one, my next question is what do I want it for? If all you are interested in is getting your students' writings into print in any form, then a cheap dot matrix printer will do just fine. There is no reason to spend money on a machine with all the fancy bells and whistles. But if you want to do desk top publishing, where you can change the size of the print, write fancy titles, arrange the writing into columns on the page, produce a newspaper or some other professional looking publication, then you will need a more expensive printer, perhaps a laser printer. Think through what kind of text is needed, get the best advice you can find—and the best price—and select the printer or printers to fit your needs.

Keep in mind that one printer will serve several computers, so the cost may not be as ghastly as it sounds at first blush. In planning a writing lab for one of our local schools recently, I was advised by the experts to use one fancy, and expensive, printer in the lab for final published text and three other dot matrix printers for all the writing getting to that finished draft. There is no problem hooking all thirty machines up to the printers so the students can use both as they need to.

Ink jet printers are talked about a good bit around here. They are not as expensive as laser printers, and I am impressed with what you can do with them. They have three disadvantages. Their ink cartridges have to be replaced often, and maintenance is a little more expensive than replacing ribbons or toner cartridges on other machines. Some feed single sheets of paper. And the ink has to have a little time to dry, which can result in smeared writings if students aren't careful. Minor things to me, except for the expense. But you make your own decisions. By the way, I read a comparative review of ink jet printers by Lanny Hertzberg in *Electronic Learning* (April 1993). I recommend his article to you. Price range? Around $200 to over $2,000!

Most desk top publishing is done with more powerful machines (i.e. ones with a lot of memory) like the Macintosh or IBM, and special software. But as Janie Martin at Highland Middle has shown me, you can do some pretty impressive things with an Apple IIe and the Image Writer II set up.

What software do I need for desk top publishing?

Which brings up the question of the program to make this kind of publishing work. Remember this: **For desk top publishing, be sure your computer, printer, and software are compatible.** That is the way to avoid frustrations for you and your students. Both Linda Clark at Merry Acres Middle and Mike Barton at Tuttle Middle use *Express Publisher.* Mike has it on the network in the computer lab. Ms. Clark's lab is not networked. A few teachers in my system use *PageMaker.* They tell me it takes a little time to learn, but they and their students like it. Janie Martin at Highland Middle caught me in the hall at her school the other day and practically hauled me into her room to play with *The Children's Writing and Publishing Center.* It is a simple desk top publishing program, easy to learn and easy to use. Mrs. Martin tells me she got hers from the Learning Company. The program is less sophisticated than *PageMaker* and similar programs.

What about networking?

Networking is expensive. That alone may make you skip to the next section, so I wanted to say it first. Because of the expense, it is not usually done in regular classrooms, but it is what your school will eventually want in a computer lab and the media center. What the network does is link all of the computers together to a central "server" where the software is available (or most of them, perhaps leaving one or two as "stand alones"). That way, you don't have to load each machine with a disk before you can use whatever program you want. And the network puts the teacher in instant touch with each student's screen. The advantages for the writing teacher are obvious.

Typically, a network contains several different programs, and students may work with different ones all over the room at the same time. The network at Tuttle Middle School includes thirty machines in the computer lab and nine computers on the same network in the media center. The network software includes Microsoft *Works, Linkway, Excelsior Gradebook, Express Publisher,* and *Touch Typing for Beginners.* In addition, there are six different programs on "stand alones." And there is some additional equipment to use with the *LinkWay* multimedia program. (More on Multimedia later.) So you can see the kinds of choices Mike Barton, the media specialist, Brad Mullendore, the lab teacher, and their colleagues at Tuttle Middle had to think through, talk through, and plan for. This is an IBM lab, but you will have comparable choices to make with a Macintosh lab. Even more than putting one or two or five computers in your classroom, **networking takes careful planning.**

How expensive is it? I've done a lot of talking to experts about a writing lab for one of the schools in my system; and, as I told you, the basic lab with 30 student machines will probably cost more than $50,000 by the time we finish planning. And that is only for word processing. Tuttle Middle spent $130,000.

Are laptop computers practical?

Yes.

A good laptop will do anything a good PC will do. Deb uses a Power

Macintosh and really likes it. Melissa Moore at Merry Acres Middle uses an IBM version, and she is rarely without it.

Some schools without computer labs use a bunch of laptops with a printer as a portable writing lab. Many schools check out laptops to students. Some even check them out to teachers. There is even a laptop for students that you can spill your soft drink on without hurting it!

Some laptops cost more than PCs, so check around and do some comparative shopping. I do not have one yet, but I am saving my pennies.

Good Sources of Information

By the way, you will find *Electronic Learning* magazine by Scholastic informative and unintimidating. Written for teachers, it is one of the best media mags I know. Make sure the media center at your school gets it.

Electronic Learning
Scholastic, Inc.
P.O. Box 53796
Boulder, CO 80323-3796

Media and Methods has been around a little longer. It is written for your school's media specialist. It gets too technical for me but is still a good reference. Both magazines have blurbs on a wealth of new gadgets and software you can find out more about by simply marking a postage free card and dropping it in the mail.

Media and Methods
1429 Walnut St.
Philadelphia, PA 19102

T.H.E. Journal is free for the asking to any educator. Just write them and tell them where you work and that you want their magazine. It is rather technical for the hard core computer buffs.

T.H.E. Journal
Circulation Department
150 El Camino Real, Suite 112
Tustin, CA 92680-9833

Curriculum Product News is a magazine for district level administrators that carries descriptions of a lot of new products. It is another magazine you want in your school's library. Unlike the other magazines, you'll have to put a stamp on the product service card in this one before you drop it in the mailbox.

Curriculum Product News
Educational Media, Inc.
992 High Ridge Rd.
Stamford, CT 06905

Teaching Journal

This Journal is for those of you who have not done word processing or have not done any writing with a computer in a long time. Go to your school's computer lab or media center or to the teacher's room down the hall where there is a computer, a word processing program, and a printer and **write something on the machine.**

In your journal—or on the screen—write about this experience with the computer and share it with someone.

The point, of course, is to find out how to use the word processing program available to you so you can use it with your students.

Multimedia

"Multimedia computing is not just some small niche area of computing. Pretty soon it will *be* computing. Multimedia communication skills will be necessary for the *minimum level* of business and professional communication."

—Fred D'Ignazio

Deborah has Microsoft *PowerPoint* on her computer, and she likes it. My friends Thomas Searles and Minnie Suttles team teach ninth graders in a Title I class at Albany High. They tell me their students regularly use the program and really like it. They also tell me it is easy to use. Barbara Ham is the math supervisor where I work, and she tells me another packaged program she has seen is *Hyperstudio*. These are packaged programs that may even come installed in computers in your school. You no longer have to put a collection of media together the way Mike Barton at Tuttle Middle School did in the classroom portrait that follows this chapter. They allow you and your students to use sound, pictures from the Internet or CDs or that you scan into the machine, even videos you find on the Net or bring to class, and put them all together in projects.

Don't be overwhelmed by the strange names. Get some help from your media specialist or computer lab teacher and plunge in. Remember, if you are adding multimedia software to your computer, make sure you have enough capacity to run it without glitches. That is the same caution we give you for any new bells and whistles you add to a machine. Of course, if you add things like scanners or video recording devices, make sure they are compatible with your equipment and that you have what you need to hook them up.

Digital cameras can be used with most modern computers. You can print out the pictures and store them on discs. All of this stuff, of course, costs money. It is worth the extra expense if your computers do not already come equipped with something like *PowerPoint?* You'll have to decide. But Mike Barton and Brad Mullindore and their colleagues at Tuttle Middle School certainly think so. Brad says their students' favorite part of the *Link Way* software they use is the paint program "where they do their own creations." The students' projects are impressive. They have trouble getting kids out of there at the end of the day, and students are waiting on them first thing in the morning and at lunch to get into the media center. However, multimedia at Tuttle Middle School are parts of well planned team teaching where technology is used to enhance learning across the disciplines.

More Sources of Information

Mike Barton at Tuttle Middle says these are his favorite sources of information about computers and software.

Creative Computer Visions
P.O. Box 6724
Charleston, WV 25362-0724

Learning Services
P.O. Box 10636
Eugene, OR 97440-2636

National School Products
101 East Broadway
Maryville, TN 37801-2498

Power Up!
P.O. Box 7600
San Manteo, CA 94403-7600

Barbara Ham suggests you check out ISTE (International Society for Technology in Education) and the SAS Institute, both of which help teachers with the exploding world of technology.

On the Internet, you can reach ISTE at http://www.iste.org.

The SAS Institute is at www.sas.com/nec98 or:

SAS Institute, Inc.
SAS Campus Dr.
Cary, NC 27513
(919) 677-8000

Videodiscs and CD ROMs

Videodiscs look like shiny l.p. records, and CDs look like little records. They are both produced and read with laser technology, and their great advantage is they hold a lot of information. (One CD holds what 14 average hard drives or 3,928 floppy disks will hold!) You will find whole encyclopedias, atlases, indexes with texts and visuals on CD's. There is a set of videodiscs with every major news reel and TV news story of the twentieth century included! Whole art museums are on videodiscs. Wonderful resources for your students and you.

A CD ROM (Compact Disk—Read Only Memory) is hooked up to a computer to access its information. And several can be "stacked" in a CD ROM "tower" and networked. Videodiscs are usually viewed with a player and a TV monitor, but some of them can be hooked up to a computer also. Be careful about this. Remember to check the compatibility of the equipment with the computer you intend to use. Also, there are three kinds of videodiscs. Level 1 disks you merely load and play. You can access different parts of Level 2 disks with a bar code and a light pen. A disk you cannot access has no advantage over video tape except it is virtually indestructible, and it may be a good master source for making copies on video tape. Level 3 disks also give you access to any part of the disk through a bar code and light pen or with an easily accessed menu or index. But the main thing about Level 3 disks is that they are "interactive," i.e. they are the ones you hook up to your computer. But you can use them with a player and TV monitor as well. Level 3 videodiscs cost more than Level 2 disks, which cost more than Level 1, sometimes a lot more.

The main disadvantage to CDs and videodiscs is they are relatively expensive, but prices are becoming more reasonable. You do have to have special equipment to run them. Except for networking towers, however, the machines are not very complex nor hard to use. You can run CD ROMs on some videodisc players.

Along with computer technology, this stuff is the new wave in education. **Be careful what you choose.** As with all media products, you can spend a lot of money for a real dog. Beware of videodiscs that are merely slide shows in a fancy format and of either kind of disks you cannot access or that are awkward to use. So far, except for massive library collections like the complete unabridged text of 950 books and collections of every poet you've ever heard of, the really good CDs and videodiscs I've seen have been in social studies and science. Wonderful material for interdisciplinary units and projects. I am looking for some good collections of film versions of short stories, perhaps some interviews with living authors (e.g. people like Walter Dean Myers and S.E. Hinton); and what I really look forward to is a good film study collection. Think what the possibilities for drama are. For example, if you have the money, you can already get all of Shakespeare's plays in print, instantly accessible by act and scene. Now how about seeing them on the stage? See what I mean?

Some of the textbook publishers are already coming out with videodiscs to accompany their new series. Evaluate them carefully.

Take a look at the "Good Sources of Information" above for magazines that will make your job of choosing videodiscs and CD ROMs easier.

Teaching Journal

If your school has CD ROM or videodisc players, view some of the available CDs or videodiscs and make notes about each title. Don't worry that they are not language arts materials, because they probably won't be. But see which ones you want to use with your kids for particular units, projects, or research.

Keep your notes in some form (an annotated list of titles on a word processing file would be handy!) and use them as the beginning of a resource file for your classes.

Internet

We are sure you and your students have access to the Internet at your school. Perhaps in your classroom, certainly in your media center or computer lab. So you literally have all the information in the world at your fingertips. Zillions of websites! All of them with strange names and stranger addresses. That's what it feels like, and that is the problem. We have the greatest learning tool since moveable type in our classrooms, but how do we sort through all this stuff? Where do we start?

The short answer is anywhere you like. Ask your friends and spend time browsing, surfing the Net, and enjoy yourself.

To help you with your exploring, check out the sites John Byrne reviews in the Software column of the **English Journal** (April, 1998). His "Super Sites for Teachers of English" is the best concise guide I have seen.

To begin where Byrne ends his column, be aware of the search engines he recommends: The All-in-One Search Page (http://www. albany.net/ alliance); Meta Crawler (http://www.metacrawler.com); Search Com (http://www.search. com); Mamma (http://www.mamma. com); The Best Search Engine (http:// www.wp.com/resch). These **meta** searchers give you many more sites than the usual search engines, so you can find more things, and quicker and easier.

We will not give you a pale copy of Byrne's excellent review here, but list some of the more interesting sites to help you get started. Keep in mind that the more useful sites on the Internet will give you links to still more related sites.

The United States Department of Education (http://www.ed.gov)

ERIC (http://www.ericir.syr.edu) Byrne describes it as "the king of the educational world wide web." He likes the Q & A Service especially, the Virtual Library, and the ERIC Toolbox.

KIDLINK (http://www.kidlink.org) This is a good resource for "kids of any age." Your students can communicate with young people in 87 countries through this site.

World Art Resources (http://www.wwar.com) 3,000 categories of art world wide can be found here.

Mammoth Music Meta-List: (http://www.vibe.com) The "giant" of music sites," featuring all kinds of music from opera to rap.

Project Gutenberg (http://www.promo.net/pg) This is the best of many sites for books on-line. Thousands of books are distributed free to teachers. Titles are posted in chapters for downloading.

R.L. Stine's Home Page (http://www.scholastic.com/goosebumps/ index) Byrne reminds us that many authors have home pages. You can find them easily with the search engines he recommends.

Bridge (http://www.bri_dge.com) A favorite site for publishing on-line, it will publish "any humble short story, poem, or book review."

Inkspot (http://www.inkspot.com) Good how-to information and resources of all kinds for writers.)

School Sucks (http://www.schoolsucks.com) This one is not a recommendation, but Byrne reminds us of this notorious site where students can download book reports.

These ten are only a taste of the sites Byrne covers, but enough to take you and your students places you have not been. In addition, my friend Thomas Searles recommends another site for your students.

The Alphabet Superhighway (http://www.ash.udel.edu) Here students have an opportunity to display their work. There are resources for young writers and their teachers and parents. Whole classes can create and submit "Exhibits." There is a dictionary and thesaurus on line, and even a "Grammar Doctor."

Finally, here are two of my favorites, I'm sure you'll recognize.

CNN Interactive (http://www.cnn.com) For daily news events, sports, and much more.

Discovery Channel OnLine (http://www.discovery.com) This one links with **Discovery Channel School**, and there are always exciting things to see.

But How Do You Pay for All This Computer Stuff?

First, plan carefully. We've said that a lot in this chapter in different contexts, and it really is a main ingredient in schools as successful as Tuttle Middle. This is not something you can do in your classroom by yourself with only your kids. It takes the school working together, choosing equipment and software, deciding how the machines will be shared and what kinds of programs all of you want for your students. And where the money will come from. Take the time. It's worth it.

A good place to start grappling with the problem of paying for what you want to do may be the February, 1993, special edition of *Electronic Learning* that deals with finding the money for technology for your school. There are articles on grants, fund raising, and partnerships. There is even an article on making your limited resources stretch as far as they can. Check it out.

One more tip about money. Check with the computer experts at your school or in your school district about software available through *Shareware* or similar resources. Jerry Holmes tells me there is a lot of good stuff out there that is free.

More about Computers

No, we're not through with computers yet. Before we talk about photography and video tape, we want to mention a couple of things you may be interested in. And we want to remind you of one problem with computers in your school.

Accelerated Reader

Paul Gainer and his students at Dougherty Middle like *Accelerated Reader,* and so do other teachers and students at his school. It is a reading management program. Students select books from a reading list with 125 titles (and many more titles can be added), read them, and use the computer program to take a brief comprehension quiz over them. Based on the number of questions they answer correctly, and the length and reading level of each book, they get points. The program keeps up with each student, what she has read, and the points received.

The kids like *Accelerated Reader.* They are very competitive and really get into this business of who has the most points and who has read what. As a matter of fact, I was surprised at their enthusiasm. When Donna Thomas, Media Specialist at Dougherty Middle, gave me the demo to preview, I saw nothing wrong with it as long as the kids have the choice of what to read and the activities with reading didn't stop with reading the book and taking the little test and getting their points. The book list is a good one, based on Newbery and other award winners, with a wide range of titles. All it does really is put kids in touch with books and gives them a way to keep records on their individual reading. Paul was interested in it, so why not? Why not indeed. I was by Paul's room yesterday after school. There were three kids waiting to use the program, including Frank, who is a whole story himself. He is the only kid I know Paul has thrown out of class for doing absolutely nothing! Yet there he was with the others, grinning and pestering Paul for his turn to be checked out on his book.

There is a demonstration disk Advantage Learning Systems will send you for a modest, refundable fee so you can check out *Accelerated Reader* for yourself. The program runs on IBMs and Macs. Software for the basic book list cost about $500, Ms. Thomas tells me. And she said the books themselves cost her media center about $1,000. Want to add a favorite book not on their list? No problem. There are clear instructions for making your own tests and weighting the points.

Disadvantages? There is no attempt to relate writing to reading in any way. This is strictly multiple choice stuff. But most of the canned writing assignments I've seen on computer screens are far inferior to what you want your students to do with writing and literature anyway. And of course there is the cost. A lot of schools keep the program in the media center for all the students to use. It's not the kind of thing your students will use every class period anyway. Here is the address for more information.

Advantage Learning Systems, Inc.
P.O. Box 95
Port Edwards, WI 54469-0095
1-800-338-4204

Gradebooks

There are many gradebook programs on the market. Barbara Ham reminds me that they are nice, but you can tailor your own with a good spreadsheet program like Microsoft *Excel* (part of the *Office* software package) or something comparable. I do my grades that way, and, if I can do it, with a little instruction from Barbara, so can you.

Warning! Beware of the R-bbit!

"Meet the enemy, as I met it at the 1983 convention of the International Reading Association...Its name was R-bbit (which I pronounce 'are-bit')....

"I encountered the r-bbit when I investigated why crowds of teachers were consistently gathering in one area of the exhibition hall. The teachers were, I found, observing a demonstration of a reading lesson. They were gazing at a cartoon representation of a desert scene on the screen of a small desktop computer. There was a bright blue sky above, a yellow landscape below, a few cacti, and in the center of it all a rabbit with large floppy ears and a mischievous look. In large print on the side of the screen were the letters r-bbit. A flashing message at the bottom of the screen was appealing: 'Please tell

me your name.'...Eventually a teacher typed 'Cynthia' on the keyboard, and the computer immediately responded, 'Can you fill in
the missing letter in r-bbit, Cynthia?'"
—Frank Smith (1986)

That was fifteen years ago, but it might as well have been yesterday.
The software is seductive with pretty graphics, vivid colors, cute characters. If you pay enough, it will call you by name and keep up with
all of your scores and the scores of every student in the room all day
long and print out individual and class reports at will. It will generate
pie graphs and bar graphs in three colors—if you pay enough. And all
of the teaching is still the tired old fill-in-the-blank-and-see-if-you're-
right-or-wrong drill, what Frank Smith calls "drill and kill." Make no
mistake, a lot of educational software on the market—and most of it
in language arts—is just that deadly, however flashy it may appear and
however glossy the packaging and high powered the sales pitch.

One questions will help you evaluate any piece of software: What
will the student do? If it is fill in the blank (or a cloze exercise) or
respond with a yes-no answer or choose a multiple choice answer, then
why do you need an expensive machine to run it in the first place? All
you're looking at is an electronic work sheet. Your kids will be much
better off if you spend those hundreds of dollars, maybe thousands,
on good books to read. Middle school students need to be actively
involved in their learning and active in making meaning. See if the
program you are thinking of buying helps them do that.

By the way, the R-bitt is just one of the sacred cows in language arts
teaching Frank Smith takes on in *Insult to Intelligence* (1986). This
is a book you want on your desk.

Shooting It: Video and Still Photography

This is not a technical discussion, merely a few pointers about making video productions and photography projects in your classroom
that we hope will save you some frustration. The great appeal of the
camera is that we all like to see ourselves through the camera's eye, in
photographs or on the screen. That is a powerful motivator to use
with your students.

There is a very simple and joyous thing I like to do with kids. I bring
my camera to school as we are working in the spring or toward the
end of the term. And I shoot slides of them as they work, especially
if we get to go outside on pretty days because the light is better. It never

takes them long to get used to the camera. I always have it slung over my shoulder or around my neck, and I bring it every day so they won't be camera shy. Slides are cheap, and I shoot a lot of them. I make sure I have several shots of every student. Nobody is left out. The best slides are loaded into a carousel projector tray. I like the 80-slot trays because they are not bad to jam, and 80 photos are a lot. I preview them carefully (I'm bad to get them in the tray upside down and backwards!); and a couple of students, working in sworn secrecy, pick out some background music. On the last day of the term, we set up the slide projector and the cassette recorder and have an informal show. We are the stars, it is a showing just for us. It is always a grand celebration. After we've looked at the pictures until we are sick of them, I give away most slides to the students in them. A few I keep just for me.

I use an old single lens reflex camera for several reasons. It's the only adjustable camera I have; and I teach interested students a little bit about light, shutter speeds, and lens openings (f-stops). Nothing complicated, just what works and what doesn't and why. A SLR camera has the unique feature of letting you look through the lens itself to focus and shoot. I like that when I work with brand new photographers. The camera does not have a flash, so we learn to shoot with available light. I do that out of necessity, but I also don't like the distraction of a flash in the classroom. I want candid shots most of the time. The camera has no real monetary value, so when a kid finally does drop it, I won't be out any real money. But I tell you, I doubt my camera will die that way. Kids are always very careful with it. I'll probably be the one to do it in.

I recommend this kind of class project to you. If you don't want to fool with an adjustable camera, cheap 35mm range finder cameras with built in flash are available at many discount stores for around $30. If you want to learn more about photography and have students who really get into it, the best book for the student photographer, or the experienced photographer who just wants to know more about how cameras work, is Mark Jacobs and Ken Kokrda's *Photography in Focus* (1990). And the Eastman Kodak Company has a lot of pamphlets and books about taking better pictures. You can find them at any good camera store or your public library.

The best place I've found for developing my 35mm slides is Clark Color Labs. Their rates are reasonable, and their work is usually good.

Clark Color Laboratories
P.O. Box 96300
Washington, DC 20090

Because it is a mail order outfit, film processing takes about two weeks. For class projects, remember to give yourself plenty of time. But that is true of your local drug store's film developing service, too.

Although I have not used it myself, I want to mention the *Polaroid Education Program.* In exchange for film purchases, the company will give you one of their instant cameras for your classroom. They also have workshops available for teachers and an attractive Activity Book. However, the cost of their film is certainly more expensive than shooting 35mm slides.

Polaroid Education Program
28 Osborn St.
Cambridge, MA 02139
1-617-577-5090

Dos and Don'ts of Photography Projects

1) Still photography makes for wonderful group projects especially; but, with groups or individual students, the key to quality is in the planning. There is nothing wrong with teaching kids to use the camera and just letting them shoot a little. That's a good thing to do, and it teaches a lot about seeing and what the pros do with the photographic image (and how things that look easy can really be hard to accomplish). But if you want projects the kids can really be proud of, you'll have to insist that they plan them.

The best tool for planning visual productions is the **Story Board.** Xerox the example on the opposite page, make lots of copies, and give them to your kids to sketch their shots and the dialogue or music they want to go with each. It is a simple idea that will save you and them a lot of frustration. You can also use the same story board sheet for planning video projects.

2) Remember the 15 second/minute rule for slide-tape presentations. No slide should be on the screen for more than 15 seconds, and that's the longest time for a very special one. And no slide-tape should run longer than 15 minutes.

3) What is true for slides is also true for video shots. Encourage students to use a lot of very short shots rather than an aimless and con-

Sample Picture/Sound Story Board

Picture   Sound

tinuous running of the camera. A video editor helps, if your school has one. Ask your media specialist or technology teacher to help you.

4) Instrumental music is always better for slide-tape projects, unless the song has a special meaning for its audience.

5) In costuming and background, pay attention to contrasting colors. Better contrasts will add a lot to the visual appeal of the production.

6) Sound can be your biggest headache. Help your students with audio taping and using microphones. Modern video cameras are wonderful machines, but their built-in mikes rarely do a good job. If your school can purchase or borrow a remote mike, it is well worth the trouble to use. Insist that students make test shots just to see if the sound is OK. Most of us don't realize what that truck rumbling by outside the window or restless foot scraping during a crucial shot can do.

Help students tape record their favorite music for slide productions through jack wires and not with a microphone. Show them how to set up the equipment and how to read a VU meter so they won't wind up with an annoying electric buzz.

7) The rule in people photos is to shoot from the chest up whenever possible. The great photographer Robert Capa said, "If your pictures aren't good enough, you weren't close enough." He was right. Get closer is also good advice for most video camera work.

8) Remember: It takes longer than it takes. Allow a lot of time for any kind of media project.

9) Also remember: The reason for the whole thing is the process, not the product.

Cameras are fun. Enjoy them.

References

D'Ignazio, F. (1992). Getting a jump on the future: Everything you'll ever need to know about multimedia authoring tools. *Electronic Learning.* 12, 28-31.

Electronic Learning. Feb. (1993). Special Edition: How to find the money for technology.

Hertzberg, L. (1993). Jet set printing: Ink jets offer cost-effective alternatives to laser printing. *Electronic Learning.* 12, 36-39.

Jacobs, M., and K. Kokrda. (1990). *Photography in focus.* Chicago, IL: National Texbook Co.

Kehoe, B.P. (1993). *Zen and the art of the internet.* Englewood Cliffs, NJ: Prentice Hall.

Schrank, J. (1975). *Understanding mass media.* Skokie, IL: National Textbook Co.

Sebranek, P., M. Meyer, D. Kemper. (1992). *Write source 2000.* Burlington, WI: Write Source.

Smith, F. (1986). *Insult to intelligence: The bureaucratic invasion of our classrooms.* Portsmouth, NH: Heinemann.

Hey, Mr. Barton, look what we found!

In the Media Center, Tuttle Middle School, Crawfordsville, Indiana

The sign says

Library

Mr. Barton

The library, in a way, is Mike Barton. He shapes it to fit what he sees as the growing availability of technology for kids and teachers. It is his place, his concept, his plan. On the other hand, the library is less his and belongs more to the teachers and students of Tuttle Middle. Clearly, when they are there, they own it.

Tuttle's media center is quiet for the moment. You come in through wooden double doors at the main hub of the school near the office and the cafeteria. The school's design is convenient, functional. Inside there are the usual walls of books and a wall of windows showing the playing field and trees outside, still green in September. Nice. Functional. A pleasant place to work. You don't really notice the machines at first.

Mike Barton is busy moving things around. He has eight computers in the center's mini-lab now. But the high school is moving, and he is expecting nineteen more. Right now he is carrying books out and down to storage while he waits for Gary Linn to bring a social studies group in. This class is working on an interdisciplinary unit on Our Changing World, using multimedia for their research and projects.

Mr. Barton goes out the door with an arm load of books as a few students trickle in quietly and head for the computers. Boys and girls, they sit down immediately and tap into the networked system. They are comfortable; they know what they are doing. Others come in and start to work. The place is a bit noisier. Soon the whole group of about twenty students and Mr. Linn are here. The kids spread out around the library tables to work on their projects. Mr. Barton is still gone. The place is theirs.

The kids group up. "Two's and three's," Mr. Linn reminds them. The kids continue to work; and Mr. Barton is back, looking over a shoulder, answering a question, talking and smiling, sometimes leaning down to tap a key when a kid is stuck on something. He helps. You see and feel the presence of this tall man with greying hair. He makes it look easy. When he is helping, it is easy.

The students at the computers are searching information from CD ROM's on the cold war. Their main sources are World Book and Grolier's. Mr. Linn reminds them to print their article once they find what they are looking for and come back to their tables to work with their partner or group. Mike, a student at one of the screens, is having a problem. Mr. Barton quietly troubleshoots with him. "Let it come all the way out"—he is talking about the printer. They watch the colored bands on the screen and the paper feed out of the machine. The boy looks up and smiles. It worked.

Mr. Barton roams, leans over a girl's shoulder, taps keys. They watch together the screen turn the right colors, the right piece of information appearing, the right thing to print. He moves on, stops to talk to three boys at one of the tables, studying several printouts with them. "Hey, Mr. Barton, look at what we found!" So it goes.

This is a big project. Twenty more kids are upstairs now with Mr. Ervin working on maps and timelines of important events. All levels are mixed, and it is impossible to tell which ability group the students used to be in. This is the Social Studies part. English and Science and Math work on other focuses, Soviet life, Chernobyl, travel. In a few days, the students will start jigsawing together all of their information, reading, graphics, written descriptions. Each group will make a display and teach about the changes in a particular country they have chosen to research. In essence, they will have an exhibition.

Right now Mr. Barton watches quietly. The computer area is emptying out. A few more kids come back to the machines to type in more indicators and get a little more information. Two boys sit together and talk through the CD ROM procedure. They read important parts together.

Mike indicates another pair of students, a boy from an "Accelerated and Enriched" ability group sitting next to a blonde girl slouched down in front of a screen, but who nevertheless is busy with the computer. Last year she was the school's troublemaker, her academic future dubious at best. This year she's at the door in the morning waiting for Mike Barton to open the media center so she can get at the computers, and she's there after school working—and learning. Watching the pair work now, you can't tell any difference between them. She and her partner sort through their printouts. Do they have them all? Mr. Barton moves in to help. "Mr Linn, what are the three things you want turned in?" The two men move around the room, talking, joking, moving kids along, answering questions.

In a few minutes the class leaves, the girl and her partner the last ones out the door. Mike Barton expects another group in a few minutes.

Summer at Tuttle Middle

"Link"ing Kids with Writing, Reading, Social Studies, and Computers

Summer is not usually the time for school. But what Mike Barton, Gary Linn, Brad Mullendore, and a group of eighteen or so Tuttle Middle kids did with social studies and computers last summer kept them in school for four weeks—and they liked it! In spite of the fact it wasn't for credit. In fact, it was hard to get everyone out of the building at the end of the program.

I sit one afternoon this winter with Gary Linn. We pull around desks to talk in his room while the kids are gone for a period. I want to hear about last summer.

"This was a computer-social studies enriched class. We got a grant, state funds to cover an experimental course for four weeks, two hours a day—a course open to any Tuttle student." Gary wants kids to study other cultures and ways of life; he's trying to teach them awareness, appreciation, and understanding of how other people live, the way, he believes, to combat stereotyping and ethnocentrism. It's easy for kids to develop these attitudes. After all, we're land-locked, right in the middle of the country in a small town which is pretty homogeneous racially and ethnically. Gary cares deeply about these goals. He wants to see real changes in his students.

The summer added a new twist—using the computer to research, compose, and publish a unique form of composition, a multimedia presentation with upscale technology. This was definitely not the traditional read-the-text-write-a-paper approach.

"The basic thrust," he continues, "was kids taking a culture, singly or in groups, and exploring it thoroughly. But before they chose one for in depth work with computers, we all experienced many cultures through class field trips and class talks by outside experts."

I recognize some of these outsiders. They're folks from my college, from around town. A lot of Crawfordsville is well-traveled. Gary is able to get people to describe being in Haiti, England, Mexico, Israel—there are others.

"For other countries there were no speakers. We went on field trips to restaurants and ate Greek, Italian, and Jewish cuisine. There's an Asian market in Lafayette, too. We went to a Jewish temple in Lafayette, an Islamic mosque in Plainfield, and to the Indianapolis Walker Theatre, and African American theatre. Only after all this did the kids select a culture to explore and present."

Gary tells me how he helped the kids shape their research focus. "Each project had to touch seven to ten cultural aspects: history, clothing, rituals, religions, holidays, things like that." And how he helped shape the publication. "If they focused on a country, they picked a historical, scientific, recreational, or cultural site and created a travel log, as if they had toured the country this summer. Using the computers, they presented their trip to the rest of us, just as if they had really come back home and were eager to share every experience with their friends. I told them to make the sharing festive, to bring in that country's food, music, whatever."

I nod, thinking that there was not only extensive reading for a purpose, composing in a unique form, but lots of oral interactions too.

"To get this done, the kids were in the library for their two hours most days, working on collecting data, reading, writing, talking over information, and keying it into computer programs."

Somewhere in all this Mike and Brad joined Gary and his kids. They took over teaching the kids, and often themselves, how to use the CD ROM programs and the Linkway program to create a multimedia composition.

*   *   *

Mike and I sit near the small computer lab in the library. "Basically the kids used the computers two ways: for researching and reading research, and for composing their findings. Brad and I took the group to the computer laboratory and taught them the *Linkway Live* program. Most kids knew how to use the computers to access CD ROM material. They do this all the time during the year for Language Arts, Science, and Social Studies. They can access encyclopedias and other databases for background materials.

"What I have them do is find the materials on the databases, print it out, then sit down and read it with highlighters so they are reading selectively, reading for what they need. They're not copying whole pre-prepared reports to hand in." I see that even now he has a box of high-lighters near the printer ready to go. "Ninety percent of this research was done here, the rest at the town or college library.

"Brad and I were here during the two hour class every day. It took us two hours to teach all the Linkway programs and another three hours of letting kids experiment and practice to get it down." This meant learning Linkway's word processing program, its paint program, and how to feed outside information into the program's folders.

All this was whole class teaching, he tells me; but soon enough the kids were involved with their own small group or individual research and composing. "We moved from whole class teaching toward assisting, to being resource people."

The kids looked for verbal information, and they collected pictures. "Brad and I set up the *Xapshot* camera and let the kids take pictures they found for their computer compositions. We converted them to computer disks so they could be fed into the writing. Some days we spent all afternoon shooting pictures the kids found and helping them put them on their disks. Later they moved these to the appropriate point in their texts. All this information was kept in Linkway Folders on the computer disks until time to really compose. We were all right there together and we told the kids, "We don't know any more than you some days!"

"As far as their composing process goes, we had the kids take all the CD ROM information they'd read and wanted to use, along with their pictures, charts of data, all that stuff, and before inputting any text into Linkway, they storyboarded everything. It was sort of like doing a rough draft. They had to think it through, talk it through with each other."

How they collaborated, how the process really worked and felt is what Leslie, Emily, and Hope tell me about.

* * *

The three girls sit at the library table during their advisory periods, a little nervously. They are wondering what they did to get in trouble. That has to be why they're here! I try to smile brightly and set them at ease. I tell them I just want to know how their summer program with Linkway worked. They giggle. They're relieved, maybe pleased.

Hope is a seventh grader. She and Emily and Leslie, both eighth graders now, chose to work together on the reading/writing/social studies project. They pretty much take turns telling me about how it worked, what they learned.

"We could have done it by ourselves," they explain, "but we learned more together because we could do a lot of talking and explaining things to each other. We weren't as confused this way. But we did have a lot of questions in the beginning for Mr. Barton, Mr. Mullendore, and Mr. Linn."

I ask why they wanted to come back to school for four weeks of their summer. They think a minute. "Well, we like social studies, and it seemed a good way to learn to use the computer. We didn't have to have any computer experience, so it was OK."

I want to hear more about how the process worked for them. "What did you pick to work on? How did you start and agree to get it all done together?" My own students are always suspicious of such group projects, thinking one person will have to do all the work. I'm sure this didn't happen here.

In fact, what they say echoes Gary Linn and Mike Barton. "Well, we picked Greece. Mr. Linn had ten things we needed to find out about the culture, so the three of us split up the ten and used the Grolier's and the World Book CD ROM's to find the information. We read and highlighted the important stuff for notes to use later." And they learned how Linkway worked.

Once they shared their sections, Leslie composed them into whole sentences and paragraphs. "I typed it into the computer," Hope smiles. "I even tried to add voice—you know, real sound. But I used up more bytes than I had—just with one sentence! We had to delete it. We didn't use the sound of the country's anthem either. Sound just takes too much space." That's interesting.

Leslie took the lead to check the text again. "I used the editing guide to help me focus on it."

After storyboarding, Emily put most of the pictures into the composition with the scanner. "We all found pictures to use—maps, too."

"Everyone else saw the final composition when it was our turn to present." It was piped to every other group's PC, and the kids watched and listened as Emily and Leslie read the piece orally. Hope liked the food. "We had gone earlier to the Parthenon Restaurant for Greek food, but we served Greek food we made that day anyway."

The girls' smiles tell me how they feel about their work. "Altogether, we composed forty pages or so—text, pictures, maps, graphs. Of course, it didn't take that long to read and share it."

I ask them what they've learned with the summer project. They are quiet only a minute, and Leslie says, "It was a lot more fun than composing a paper." Hope and Emily nod. "And we all learned about all the information on Greece because we went through everything together."

Advising is over, and we hear the soft double tones Tuttle Middle uses instead of bells marking the end of the period. The girls head off to class. I watch them, thinking of the computer's potential enrichment of reading and writing in classes.

But only if it is done right. And it's right when it integrates reading, writing, the subjects for real learning—and people.

11

Assessment and Evaluation

"To reclaim their classrooms as places where genuine learning and teaching can take place, teachers must reclaim assessment and accountability."

—Frank Smith, 1988

When many of us think about assessment and evaluation, we imagine gradebooks, white and green sheets with little bubbles on them, and number two pencils. For a long time, testing, either standardized or our own homemade varieties, have dominated our imagery. That's probably because these tests have dominated our classrooms and our curriculum.

I recently read a very good comprehensive list of reasons why standardized tests in the language arts (most disciplines for that matter) just don't do anything for students. Constance Weaver (1990) argued forcefully why these tests harm kids. Clearly, the tests and their usage angered her. By the time I finished reading, I was angry too. You can read them yourself, but I think a few of them are so close to the heart of teaching middle level kids that they need to be flagged right here. Middle level teachers need to realize:

—**that standardized tests are anti-developmental**—Weaver reminds us that our students do not develop in the same ways and not at the same times. But standardized tests assume that there is "a" model of growth that students should follow month by month, year by year.

—**that they are anti-diversity in other ways, too**—She also reminds us that many of these tests continue to be biased against culturally different children, as well as students who have different learning styles.

—**that they are anti-whole, real, and naturally meaningful learning environments**—What these tests support is part-to-whole teaching.

They reinforce the use of basals, of drills and worksheets, in short, of artificial "dummy runs" which survive in the name of getting kids ready for the test.

—that they are anti-authentic or engaged learning (which ought to bother any teacher)—Since we fear that our students won't pass these tests if we don't teach part-to-whole, our classrooms become dominated by these basals and drills, and they become boring.

(Weaver, 1990, pp. 185—197)

I would add one more based on these last two insights of Weaver's:

—that they are anti-interdisciplinary curriculum—If I am always worried about the final number on a score sheet, then I will probably concentrate on my students' scores and on my class numbers, not on our instruction and how our students learn from day to day.

Look closely. These tests nullify almost all our principles for natural language learning that we pointed out way back in chapter 1, not to mention that they are out of line with the middle level concepts mentioned in chapter 4. Chris Stevenson (1992) tells us that one of the major goals in middle level education is helping young adolescents learn to be "accountable for themselves as learners" (p. 247). They need to learn this through guided self-evaluations, by being asked on a regular basis to think about what they are learning and what they still need to learn. That is the only way anyone takes responsibility and ownership for her own development. Not by coloring in bubbles over a span of two days following weeks of exercises, fill in the blank practices, and teacher led drills.

So what is there to reclaim? Just standardized tests? No way. Most evaluation systems reduce assessment to periodic grades on a lot of artificially chopped up parts of a subject. And that's another thing teachers are doing their best to reclaim. But assessment is so much richer than that, and evaluation need not be the part we all hate to confront—students and teachers alike. Not if it's natural and a natural part of life in classrooms.

Maybe a good way to start thinking about "reclaiming" is just to get these two ideas straight—assessment and evaluation. It is said that assessment is a seamless part of class. It's so seamless to me that I have trouble separating assessment from evaluation, sometimes even from activity or method. But we need to try.

According to both Weaver (1990) and Stevenson (1992), assessment is the gathering of information and evaluation is judging it. The best acts of assessment are done not just through one means, like testing, or even just a couple, like tests and a few papers, but involve lots of ways to gather the information:

—collecting multiple work samples (possibly in portfolios);
—recording observations;
—having conferences with students;
—using interviews;
—keeping and reviewing journals and logs;
—student writing of self-evaluations;
—keeping "clipboard" notes or anecdotal records;
—using surveys and/or interviews.

Evaluating each student's growth in learning involves using this gathered data to make a judgment about the learning that's gone on. Evaluations occur informally when we look at the kid's work and say to ourselves: "I think Rose needs more work with nonfiction prose;" or "Roger needs to read more poetry; he's an avid fiction reader, but needs to branch out."

Of course, evaluations can be set up more formally, too, like when we devise a rating scale to record and reflect our evaluations of a piece of writing a kid has submitted. And, tests and quizzes still are evaluation instruments allowing us to make what can be a little bit more of an objective evaluation of someone's understanding, appreciation, or skill. The easiest way for me to make some distinction between the two is to imagine assessment as a line, something smooth and continuous and never-ending, and evaluation as a point on the line, something finite and contained—for a while. But the point is part of the line, too, and ultimately, each evaluation becomes part of continuing assessment.

Grading is a third part to all this in my mind. While assessment and evaluation are natural parts of growth, grading is an arbitrary thing. It's just the use of a code we've agreed on to stand for our evaluations. Let's not get this mixed up with the other two. I wish students wouldn't.

Teaching Journal

Think back over your own teaching. Are there times when you felt frustrated by "teaching to the test?" By having the tests drive your curriculum? It might help to free-write your own stories about standardized testing and teaching. What other ways have you found to collect information about your kids? Make a list of all the ways you use to find out about how they're doing. Add to the list the ways you evaluate without testing, even your own tests and quizzes.

My examples of assessment and evaluation are all homemade. They are ways teachers are "reclaiming" this usually foreign and painful part of instruction. They show that assessment is becoming for lots of people that "seamless" part of instruction natural teachers imagine. That's why in all the strategy chapters in this book you'll find suggested ways to assess and evaluate, sometimes suggested tools for both; we wanted to be seamless too. Instead of repeating any of that, what I want to do is give you portraits of total management systems, some alternative ways of managing assessments and evaluation in more natural middle grades classrooms. In each of these portraits, teachers balance keeping their assessments and evaluations authentic with the need to comply with synthesizing evaluations into a grade.

Portrait #1—Pat Stull, 5th Grade, Hose Elementary School

A lot of assessment and evaluation goes on in Pat Stull's classroom as you have probably seen from other parts of this book. Like many other teachers Tom and I have seen, Pat keeps several running records on various activities the kids are engaged in across the day. These "clipboards" are handy ways to keep running notes (somewhat like anecdotal records) on all kinds of things. Some are used to keep points, like Melissa's; Pat's are often notes. She kept one for part of a writing workshop where kids were just getting started on drafts. It is reproduced at the top of the next page.

It seems that a big part of the overall scheme for evaluation relies on just these sorts of teacher-made, informal instruments—these and the kind Pat uses for the "Newscast" as well as others—checklists and rating scales, for example. The documentation is there when you're ready for evaluations—or ready for grading.

In her self-contained classroom, Pat ultimately has to grade learning according to traditional separate subjects. She has to put a grade down every six weeks on things like social studies, science, or math. In her case, language arts is defined from the grading standpoint as four separate subjects. Pat smiles a little as she tells me what they are: English, spelling, reading, and handwriting.

CHECKLIST

Name	#			Jopic		Start 1-5	
~~Bradley B.~~	1			after hours			
	2			adventure in school			
~~Alan~~	3						
	4						
Steve / Aaron	5			Classroom			
	6			objects alive @ midnight			
~~John~~	7						
	8						
Ashley H./Christy	9			Cardinal			
	10			family			
Melissa	11						
	12						
Brandon / Alan	13			Human turns			
	14			into inanimate object			
Christy	15						
	16						
Pablo / Brian	17			Joke chapter			
	18						
Sheila /Melissa	19			mouse family			
	20						
Aaron	21						
	22						
~~Brad S.~~	23						
	24						
~~Megan~~	25						
	26						
Cameron / John	27			Pencil comes			
	28			alive			
Ashley W. / Meg	29			S-alliteration			
	30			Sister - snake			
Abigail - alone	31			Caterpillar			
	32						
~~Brian~~	33						

Those are the school-mandated definitions of language arts. Pat is required to give a grade in each of the four areas every six weeks after assessing and evaluating the kids for that time.

To look at her classroom, though, you would seldom see any of those arbitrary lines of separation. One morning, I came in while her students were beginning an exploration of a new kind of literature which they would later read more of and which they would also write themselves. Kids grouped or paired themselves to read orally. The room was noisy with enjoyment of the piece, with natural questioning, with stopping and explaining the story, and wondering curiously about unfamiliar words. As I watched, I saw Pat quietly beckon to a group, then another group, and each would come at their turns to a clear table to the side of the room. There, through a combination of pre-testing and looking at personal word lists, students came away with a list of words to learn for the week. They would partner-check them at the end of the week with a post-test. The oral reading groups were not random at all; they were also spelling groups whose word lists were primarily words they used everyday, or could use, but did not know how to spell correctly yet. Their flow back and forth, in and out of their reading, was as seamless as the acts of assessment I see in many natural language rooms.

While the spelling time blended naturally and effortlessly into the room, this spelling grade is actually a little more than a spontaneous part of language growth in the classroom. Pat explained to me the planning behind what I saw: "The kids work with 25 words per week from various sources: some from sources covering the 'most frequently used words in writing,' some from words missed in their writing during the week, some from whatever they're reading. One group uses words from 'vocabulary stretching' lists. Each person decides on 10 words she doesn't know well and they challenge each other to learn them. At the end of the week, they mix groups and give each other quick check-up quizzes. That's graded for the spelling grade. Handwriting gets graded once a week, and its grade comes from that spelling post-test. There's no direct class time spent drilling. Kids needing help get it individually—as they need it."

English, too, is graded, and Pat evaluates the kids using two kinds of assessment and evaluation opportunities. One part of the "English" grade comes from the journal-keeping kids do. They leave their journals for her on Thursdays. She looks to see if the entries are there or not in her assessment, and evaluates accordingly. There's still some, but very little, mandatory skills work. She takes a grade on these exercises from a workbook; no more than 20 minutes a week is spent on very basic skills. Of course, most of the skills teaching goes on within and across the day, embedded in the reading, writing, and sharing and what kids need for their writing.

Like Linda Rief (1992) with her graded writing, Pat learned to accommodate to the imposed structure and still leave room for authentic assessments, for teacher-student meaningful evaluation. She blended in the forced separations as naturally as possible. English, spelling, and handwriting were all parts of a continual flow of reading/writing activity. Real language dominated the room. It was easy to see this when I saw the time spent on project learning logs, reading for enjoyment, or for learning about something you were going to do (like taking a class camping trip!). Or a student could spend his time writing poetry, stories or even letters he was going to share with a real audience (like the Santa letters at Christmas sent to first graders who wrote their Christmas lists and expected answers!).

And **reading** gets a grade, too—but this is even less separated from the flow of the classroom than anything else. There is no basal text here, nor teacher materials from a series. But the kids read all the time, whole class things together as well as their own separate choices. Real books like Tom talks about in chapter 6 (in fact, he's listed some of the 5th grader's favorites), and other things in all the other subjects. All of it is meaningful reading. Sometimes they take short tests over what they read, but a great deal of assessment and evaluation is based on written response papers on literature and topics in literature as well as on discussions of the reading. Pat assesses reading by oral discussion using checklists, a simple "check plus" or "check" or "check minus" system. She makes sure she notes everyone. When the kids read *A Christmas Carol,* they each brought a question that had no right answer. Pat looked at their questions, guided the discussion, assessing and then evaluating. Questions like "Why is this story written 150 years ago still produced? Why is it still popular today?" engage students in real inquiries.

And so, at the end of six weeks, an overall evaluation is made and a grade gets put down, always a reductionist version of the rich interactions that pass each day.

You'll notice that Pat doesn't have to give a grade for something called **writing**. Language arts is defined by the school as everything but writing. She's lucky. But there are ways to do that without interfering with the learning—just look back at Nancie Atwell's system or Linda Rief's. But the assessment and the evaluation is there with all Pat's kids' writings anyway—just not the grade. Pat says, "I use my assessments to evaluate and then to plan what I need to teach and how to help the kids improve. It helps me know when to stop and do mini-lessons, what short lessons to do."

The stress on writing development and the importance of assessment in that growth is featured prominently in the whole writing program at Hose Elementary. Bound by a teacher-created comprehensive portfolio assessment system (which really is the evaluation system rather than a means to get a grade), continuous writing workshops (which mix classes), and a thriving parent-supported publishing center, writing growth is shaped all the way from first through fifth grade. Ongoing writing of all kinds is developed in classrooms or in labs, where peer editing and conferencing occur spontaneously. The fifth graders are old hands at this, even enough to determine what they like about writing. I took this list from a longer list on posterpaper on the wall outside Pat's class door. The kids had said they like writing when:

—we can choose what we write about
—we have an interesting topic
—we have adventures to write about
—we're in writing lab
—we can illustrate our stories
—we can think up a story ahead of time
—we can write poetry

At 10 or 11 years of age, they still like writing. I wonder if it has a little something to do with its freedom from grades, and the teacher's freedom to create a suitable writing framework.

A little later in this chapter, I describe some portfolio systems and publishing as a form of assessment, both of which teachers are using, too. They are evaluation systems that do not require grading; they're too authentic for that. But a quick glimpse of the writing workshop structure right now puts Pat's assessment and evaluation in context a bit more.

The Hose Writing Program is described and compiled within a school handbook by teacher Margie Zimmerman:

> Any reader interested in implementing a writing lab in the classroom would profit from reading *The Art of Teaching Writing* by Lucy McCormick Calkins {1989}. . . . While Hose School teachers have adapted Ms. Calkin's recommendations to fit their classroom schedules, we agree that a student benefits from time set aside to concentrate on writing and the opportunity to write from personal experiences and interests. . . . In general, time set aside is spent on 'creative writing' as opposed to writing in one of the content areas. Thus, it obviously does not constitute the total amount of time a student spends writing. Sometimes students work on teacher-directed activities. At other times they are able to work on self-directed writing. . . . Maybe the most compelling case for a writing lab format is the psychology it sets up in a child. 'Getting finished' is no longer the paramount idea for a piece of writing. . . .
>
> (Zimmerman, 1992)

Pat explains to me exactly how this works for her group. "The two fifth grade classes here meet, usually apart in their two rooms. But at least once a week, one writing lab occurs together. Shelley (the other fifth grade teacher) and I mix the two groups, half and half in each of our rooms. Other lab times occur during the week but we don't always mix classes. This cross-grouping helps kids in different rooms know each other and provides everybody with different experiences and perspectives."

"The two halves," she continues, "regroup somewhat each semester. Usually Shelley and I meet and agree on language development instruction to focus on with the groups; most often that's just done class by class, or even one on one since our different writing directions often turn up different skill needs. Sometimes the kids will work on an in-common activity (the Santa letters were an example), sometimes not."

"There isn't any requirement that one project must be finished before another is begun. Students may have several pieces of work 'in progress' at various stages of completion. Shelley and I will share the conferencing, and peer conferencing is really automatic."

These are real assessments of writing. Scenes like these don't need "reclaiming." They already are in the realm of the possible, the real, the natural, and the effective contexts for growth.

Portrait #2: Melissa Moore, 7th Grade, Merry Acres Middle School

Like Pat, Melissa must give kids a grade for English and for Reading once each six weeks. Other teachers on the team give the other subject grades. Melissa's system of assessment, evaluation, and grading for English and Reading mirror what she thinks the kids need to get out of these classes. Melissa speaks better for herself than I do. She tells me:

"I guess the purpose of my language arts program is to help students develop individual appreciation and understanding for reading and writing as tools for communication. I want the students to find purpose, enjoyment, and reward in reading and writing. I want them to become a part of their writing and to become a part of the books they read."

"In writing I work on process and mostly revision techniques. We talk a lot about writing honestly, allowing your own personality to be in every piece, about images, and writing so that the reader is there with you. I focus on getting thoughts down on paper and making them your own. Not much editing. I get them going on writing workshops and stressing revision; eighth grade will stress more editing."

"In reading class, we simply read. I teach them reading workshop. No child will finish seventh grade without reading several books. I also focus on vocabulary. We try to use these words in our oral and written communication."

And so Melissa's scheme for assessing and evaluating in each of these classes reflects her beliefs, what she and the kids spend the most time on together. In English, Melissa, again like Pat, likes to emphasize the writing going on; journal pages or rough draft pages, and finished writing pieces count a lot. The other part of it is objective tests and practice skills work on relevant mechanics and usage. Her "clipboard" points help her assess, evaluate, and ultimately "get a grade" for English.

The Reading grade is book and writing-based. Again, there's a lot of similarity here to Pat's reading program. There aren't any basals. Real literature, real books kids like, share, write about, and talk about make the program. These acts of reading, writing, and sharing are what is assessed, evaluated, then graded. Bringing your book to class earns "clipboard" points, selecting and writing Book Quotations (BQ's) counts, as do writing literary letters and making creative book reports each week. (See Carla's Book Quotation example on the next page.)

And, of course, the vocabulary component is there. But like Pat's spelling component, vocabulary learning and growth is a natural extension of the language activity in Reading class. Melissa explains how this natural flow occurs.

"We spend one day a week having each student teach a new word that she discovered through reading. We vote on five words to use and study all week and then test on Friday. So, each student adds thirty five words (based on the number of kids per class) to his vocabulary notebook per week, but is tested on only five."

So the final grades each six weeks? English comes from averages of:
—tests (which count twice);
—completed writings (which also count twice);
—journal (graded every other week at first, stretching to every third week);
—clipboard points (tallied every couple of weeks and divided by possible points for a grade for those weeks);
—some daily grades.

✓   2/20 (100)

Carla Brandon   17 de Marzo
Reading-BQ

"Everything was green, so green
it went into him."   wow!
The Hatchet by Gary Paulsen

The other night my sis-
ter and I were star gazing
on the trampoline. The tree
was about 7 ft from us but
as I looked up into it it
just took me. It was
lush but that didn't work
because it was a pine
tree. It was just full and oh
I don't know. Anyway,
I read this quotation the
next day and it explained
my feelings perfectly! I
admire Gary Paulsen so
much for this because
when I feel something,
I can never just write
in one short sentence and
tell the reader what I am
trying to say. Paulsen did
just that. It amazed me.
I envy this author so
much. I don't know how
he just does it. I love
that quotation. ☺ Continue to open your
mind! Continue to read & write and you will do the
same. What about that 3rd avenue poem?

Reading comes from averages of:
—clipboard points for the week (one grade weekly for bringing a
book to read, the possible 20 points for BQ's, and literary letters);
—one creative book report each six weeks;
—vocabulary grades weekly.

Real Assessments and Evaluation: Clipboards and Conferences

That's how Melissa systematizes her assessments and evaluation to end up with grades for each class. But both the kids and she realize the grade is just, as she says, the "tool for quickly communicating the assessment and evaluation of each student. It's really a way to tell parents the standing of their child and it's a concrete reminder to students about their efforts."

But the heart of language growth, what she and her kids experience each day is very different, just as Pat's is. Melissa gives few daily grades. So, the kids and she get a better sense of where they are and where they need to head just by consulting her "clipboard." "Assessment is the clipboard," insists Melissa.

Pat uses a chart form clipboard to jot notes and running records on. Melissa may do that, but also uses points. Clipboard points are given on an assignment which is usually very subjective, those kinds of activities with no right or wrong answers, those that are hard to put a letter grade on. The assignment might be worth 10 clipboard points and students could gain anywhere from 0-10 points on it. Melissa's got lots of concrete examples.

"Students might be asked to revise a paragraph by using more specific verbs. If the task is completed and done well, then maybe 10 clipboard points would be awarded. Publishing, handing in PQP (praise, question, polish) slips after response groups, writing a silly story with new vocabulary words, reading in a read-around, homework, bringing books to reading and then reading the entire time, BQ's, and literary letters all are examples of activities that receive clipboard points as a way of assessing students' work."

"I like the clipboard point system," she reflects. "I can assess and evaluate without making the grade the reward. I can reward the students for effort, remove the threat of failure so they're more comfortable expressing themselves and taking risks."

Maybe you're ready for a concrete example. There is an example of one of Melissa's clipboards on the next page.

The clipboard, a running record of how students are doing, is one way to give feedback to kids, one way to keep track of data for making evaluations. It is also a reference for setting future reading and writing goals. Melissa uses others, too, others which involve her kids in self-evaluation and in reflecting on their own growth.

She continues: "Students have a writing folder for finished pieces

Name *Homeroom 25 Yellow*   Open management chart

English

1-28 Bookshow / 1-29 Corrections		2-2-93	P. 98-99	2-15 P.81	Mylove J Stuart	C. 12	2-26	3-3 Paragraph	3-10	anecdotes	
10	10	10	15	10	20	10		10			95
10	10	10	20	10	20	10		10+	10		100
	10	10		10			9	10			49
10	10	10	20	10	0	10					20
10	10	10	15	10	20	10		10	10	10	100
10	10	10	Ab.	10		10		10	10	10	80
10	10	10	20	10		10	7	10			80
	10	10			20	10		10			60
10	10					10					30
10	10			10		10			10		40
10	10	10	20	10		10		10		10	90
10	10	10	20	10		10	10	10	10	10	100
10	10	10	20	10	20	10	10	10	10	10	100
10	10	10	20	10	20	10	10	10	10	10	100
10	10	10	20		18	10		10			88
	10			10		10					30
10	10	10		10		10					50
	X		20	10	20	10	10	10	7	10	100
10	10	10	20	10	20	10	10	10	10	10	100
10		10	20	10		10	7	10		10	77
10	10	10	20	10	20	10	10	10			100
	10		20	10	20	10	10		10	10	100
10	10	10	20		20	10					70
10	10	10	20	10		10		10		10	90
10	10	10	20	10		10	10	10	10	10	100
10	10	10	20	10	20	10	10		10	10	100
10	10		20	7	20	10	10	10		10	97
10	10	10	20	10		10	10	10+	10	10	100
10	10	10	20	10	20	10	10		10	10	100
10	10		20	10	20	10				10	90
10	10	10	20	10	20	10	10		10	10	100
10	10	10	20	10		10	10	10+	10	10	100
10	10			10	20	10		7			67

of writing. Their own writings show connections students have made from books they're reading."

She gives Carla as an example. Carla said, "Miss Moore, I've noticed in my book that Brancato uses very few tags with her dialogue. Instead, she has the characters doing something after they say something."

Melissa continues. "And then in Carla's writing I see a definite change in her dialogue. She has fewer tags and more actions of her characters. She's more satisfied when she brags about the improvement to me."

Melissa mentions a few other ways the kids can evaluate themselves. They keep daily progress forms in their notebooks so they can make goals and assess their progress; they record and write letters to her, to each other, and use the journal to identify their own areas of growth; they have a log sheet to record each book they read and movement from one type of book to another is easily seen and also shows growth!

And Melissa conferences with them. Each time she returns finished writings, she talks with students. They individually bring writing folders up to her desk, they both review the writing, read the student's response to it, and then Melissa's own list of strengths and weaknesses. "After the conference, I feel the students have a truer understanding of accomplishment and a goal for the next piece of writing."

"The conferences are better than any grade given." She gives Jane's case as an example. "Jane's grade was lower than she thought it should have been. Through the conference she discovered that she received high scores in the area of content and style; she knew she would. She's a good writer. Her low scores were in the area of usage and mechanics. Her writing was full of misspelled words and incorrect punctuation marks. Although editing counts less than content and style, Jane is in the gifted class and quite capable of editing. Jane was reminded of the process of writing and that getting the good story is where she works the hardest, but that it doesn't stop there. She takes the time to edit her pieces now so that the reader can enjoy the writing without being interrupted by obvious mistakes."

Like Pat's class, Melissa's is filled with chances for real interaction, for real growth in reading and writing. The grades are there, but they don't get in the way of meaningful assessment and evaluation, of keeping the classroom "reclaimed."

Teaching Journal

If you haven't already, start thinking about what you really want your kids to get out of your language arts classes. Brainstorm that for a while. Make a jot list now, let it sit, and come back to the rest of this later.

If you can clarify those goals, or if you already have, then think about how you might take your current system, especially if you find that everything gets a grade, and try to move it more to a clipboard or point system. What kinds of things could you do in class under this system that encourage process, growth and progress rather than product? Try to do a "clipboard" draft which allows you to evaluate kids more on growth and progress than on just tests or quizzes, finished papers, or workbook exercises.

Portfolios and Exhibitions—More Alternatives to Traditional Forms of Assessment and Evaluation

Like cooperative learning a few years ago, portfolio assessment, especially for reading and writing, is all the rage. And like cooperative learning, the reasons are good. Linda Rief (1992) points out some important effects the portfolio has on kids, classrooms, and teachers. The best one is that it makes learning and evaluation the responsibility of the student as much (or more) than the teacher. They get to see in this collection of writings a picture of who they are now as language users and a map of where they're going. And they can say in conferences where they think they need to go. They become their own best evaluators—whether it shows up in the grades or not!

Portrait #3—Tambra Cambron, Sixth Grade, Tuttle Middle School

There are all kinds of ways to keep portfolios and do portfolio assessment in various classes. One really interesting system exists in Tambra Cambron's class. Tambra is a sixth grade Learning Resources Teacher at Tuttle Middle School, but she's also a language arts teacher who knows a lot about early literacy and whole language. Tambra tells me she seized a rather unique opportunity this year to develop writing and reading workshops and a portfolio system with one of her sixth grade groups.

At Tuttle, sixth graders return to their homebase teacher for 25 minutes at the end of each day where they generally work on academic assignments. One group of sixth graders could not return to homebase because their teacher had to cover a seventh grade section of Math. Tambra jumped in and took the 22 sixth graders under her wing—as long as she could develop reading/writing workshops and portfolios with them. That was fine with everyone.

Tambra's sixth graders come from low socio-economic to middle class homes in Crawfordsville. Some are already "at risk"; others are eager to make the shift from elementary schools to middle schools go well. They are a very mixed group, with a whole variety of language development issues, abilities, and needs. When they moved into Tambra's room, they all began what's turned out for most a long, but wonderful journey.

Tambra's class is unique for another reason—the careful education and involvement of parents all along the way as the portfolios developed. That's right. The parents get educated, too. If you've been wondering about parent issues with portfolio assessment, especially communication about what you're doing, maybe Tambra's system will help.

At the beginning of her year with these 6th graders, Tambra gave a parent workshop on her new class. She sent out letters. "I had a fairly good turn-out," she beams. Each parent had a folder which was designed to take them through the orientation, workshop-style. The folder had articles on portfolios, hand-outs on the writing process and on comparing traditional approaches to process approaches, as well as several blank response and webbing sheets. Several blank journal entry pages completed the packages. All of these were used or referred to as the workshop orientation went along. The parents not only heard what a whole or natural language class was all about, they experienced it!

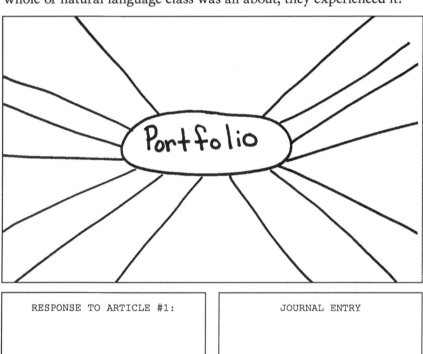

| RESPONSE TO ARTICLE #1: | JOURNAL ENTRY |

AS A PARENT WHAT CAN I DO TO HELP?

1. Provide lots of reading material for your child. This could be anything from newspapers to comic books. Surround your child with print.

2. <u>Take time</u> to ask your child about information he/she has read. What does your child think about this topic? Encourage your child to keep a journal of topics that come up in your discussions.

3. Share a book with your child.

4. Let your child help with cooking. Students learn to follow directions and read cookbooks when they get to cook.

5. When you read your child's writing samples, do not criticize everything you see that needs fixing. First, look at the positive parts of the writing piece. Example: I really like the way you started the first sentence, because it made me want to read more.

6. Encourage your child by giving sincere compliments.

"I wish I could have done a videotape of the workshop and of what we did that evening for the parents that weren't able to come," she says. "But maybe next time. And the communication kept on as you'll see."

Right at the year's start, she had similar discussions with the kids. "I wanted them to know what to expect from me, what the purposes for writing and reading were, and that this class might be different."

On the very first day, the kids started writing their journals. That, and much of the other writing they did the first semester (they moved from personal narratives to persuasive, research, stories, poetry, and more) she modeled for them with an overhead and her own writing since many had not written whole pieces before. The writing all went into a portfolio, physically a big notebook with sections in it for all response sheets, evaluations, skills work, work in progress ("sloppy copies"), and finished pieces ("neat sheets").

Slowly trust was built up and students, shy at first about sharing, clamored to read aloud. "By Christmas," Tambra remembers, "they were not writing for the same purposes anymore. They were choosing their own writing topics. I had modeled a lot the first semester; now I conference most of the time." And literature, explored often using reader's theater, continued to balance the workshop.

Somewhere during that first six weeks of the semester, Tambra started bringing in various assessment tools, several self, peer, and parent evaluation forms which were very response-oriented. "At this point, confidence was more important than anything," she says.

```
Writing
Self-Assessment

Name:_____

Title of Piece:_____

Why did you select this piece of writing?



What do you see as the strengths?



What was especially important to you when you were writing
this piece?



What things did you wrestle with?



If you could work on this further, what would you do?



What were some of the reactions you received?



How is this the same as or different from your other pieces?



Other Comments:
```

PARENT FOLDER REVIEW AND REFLECTION

Student:_____Reader:_____ Date:_____

   Your child has chosen one or more samples of his/her writing for you to evaluate. The best assessment of student writing begins with the students themselves, but must be broadened to include the widest possible audience. I encourage you to become part of the audience.

   After you have read your child's selections of his/her work, please talk to your child about the writing selections. In addition, please take a few minutes to respond to these questions.

Which piece tells you most about your child's writing?

What does it tell you?

What do you see as the strengths in your child's writing?

What do you see as the needs to be addressed in your child's growth and development as a writer?

Other comments, suggestions?

Thank you so much for investing this time in your child's writing.

Mrs. Cambron

                    Listener's Compliments
1. I like the part where
_____

2.I'd like to know more about
_____

3. I think your main idea is
_____

4.You used some powerful words like
_____

5.I like the way you described
_____

6.I like the way you explained
_____

7.I like the way you wrote
_____

8.Your writing made me feel
_____

9.I like the order you used in your writing because
_____

10.I think your dialogue was realistic, the way the character said.
_____

11.Your writing reminded me of
_____

Listeners' Comments and Suggestions

1. What is your favorite part?

_____

2. What part are you having trouble with?

_____

3. Could you write a lead sentence to "grab" your readers?

_____

4. Do you need a closing?

_____

5. I got confused in the part about

_____

6. Could you add more to this part because

_____

7. Could you leave this part out because

_____

8. Could you use a different word for _____ because

_____

9. Is this paragraph on one topic?

_____

10. Do your paragraphs seem to be in the right order?

_____

11. Could you combine some sentences?

_____

Still at that point, the parents were still tied into the process. Tambra's sixth graders would take home their portfolios for parents to read and respond to, which after reading their letter, they knew how to treat (see letter to parents on the next page).

"At the end of the six weeks, the students and I chose two samples of personal narratives and we sent them home, with all evaluations, for the first six weeks. These were the products of our efforts."

Although the administration, parents, other teachers, everybody, in fact, was happy at the end of the first six weeks, her principal suggested that she make these response and evaluation sheets a little more quantifiable. "So I constructed this second sheet," she says, "as a way to pull together everyone's evaluation for that six weeks. Before this goes home, everyone—me, the writer, and the parent and peer—would have done an evaluation and contributed it, but this composite just puts the whole picture together."

The rating scale/checklist format (see examples on the following pages) allows Tambra to take the step toward a grade a little more easily, but the point is still assessing and evaluating. "The responses help me see what to watch for, what to assist with as the writer enters a new six weeks. They can focus the conferences I have with each student."

Conferences are what she mainly does now, here in the spring of the year. Those and mini-lessons. Like anyone teaching language naturally, talking about the writers, sharing perspectives, giving shape and focus to words, is all part of the working ecology of language growth.

"I read their pieces with them many times," she says. "My conferencing always depends on where the writer and the piece are. If it's a very rough draft and parts are still unclear, I ask: 'What do you mean here?' 'Is there another way to say this?' or even, 'If another person were reading this now, would they know what you mean?' These questions always lead to expansion—more details, clarity, that kind of revision. Only after this will I engage in an editing conference. We never do less than two conferences per piece."

In the editing conference, Tambra points out places where spelling, grammar, or punctuation is a problem. She tries first to help the writer see the error. "Do you need anything right here?" she'll start.

"I do many mini-lessons on grammar, spelling, or punctuation at this stage," she confides, "because many of them just don't already have the knowledge base to see what they need. But I don't teach these lessons in the abstract, in a set part of the week or day, nor would I

Dear Parent,

Today your child is bringing home his or her portfolio. On the left side of the portfolio are the "sloppy copies" or "rough draft" samples that your child has been working on this six weeks. The left side of the portfolio contains selections of your child's best work. Below is a description of the use of portfolios and the process for choosing what goes in the portfolios.

A portfolio can be a collection of one's best work. It can also be a collection of work in progress. The purpose of a portfolio is to showcase work. In this class, the students keep portfolios to show their writing progress over time. In addition, the work in the portfolios helps give a better picture of the student's achievements.

Your child is encouraged to choose work that his is his or her best work. Your child must ask himself questions about meaning and grammar to decide what characterizes "best work." This means that the students are evaluating their own work, as well as each others' work. This helps students to feel ownership of their work and to be aware of how they are progressing.

Today, your child will share his or her portfolio with you and will also ask you to evaluate one piece from the portfolios. A sheet is provided for you to make your comments. Please be aware that this is your time to make positive comments, because this is a sample of your child's best work. There will be many more evaluations throughout the year. You will want to notice any positive changes in your child's writing.

Thank you for taking time to sit down with your child and talk about the portfolio. I think that the portfolio will give you a better idea of your child's progress than a letter grade. Please make sure that the portfolio is returned by Monday.

Sincerely,

Tambra Cambron
English Teacher

The following is a combination checklist of writing skills and parent, teacher, and student evaluations of a specific writing piece. This checklist is used as a way to grade the student's progress for the six weeks.

Student's Name _____

Key: 1 = Mastered   2 = Needs Practice   3 = No Evidence Of Improvement

Name of writing piece: 1)
                         2)
                         3)

Parent Evaluation	Date	Date	Date
	Piece #1	Piece #2	Piece #3
1. Used a good topic sentence	___	___	___
2. Used details to support topic	___	___	___
3. Used descriptive vocabulary words	___	___	___
4. Showed knowledge of paragraph development	___	___	___
5. Sequenced ideas well	___	___	___
6. Used capitalization	___	___	___
7. Used complete sentences	___	___	___
8. Used correct punctuation	___	___	___
9. Showed neatness in handwriting or typing	___	___	___
10. Portfolio copy was free of errors	___	___	___
Total	___	___	___

Peer Evaluation	Date	Date	Date
Name of Peer Evaluator 1) _____	___	___	___
2) _____	Piece #1	Piece #2	Piece #3
3) _____			
1. Ideas were easy to understand	___	___	___
2. Interesting piece of writing	___	___	___
3. Had a good beginning	___	___	___
4. Had a good ending	___	___	___
5. Used correct capitalization	___	___	___
6. Used correct end punctuation	___	___	___
7. Had complete sentences	___	___	___
8. Used commas in the right places	___	___	___
Total	___	___	___

Key: 1 = Yes 2 = No Self-Evaluation	Date —— Piece #1	Date —— Piece #2	Date —— Piece #3
1. I have a good beginning.	——	——	——
2. I have details that relate to my topic.	——	——	——
3. All my sentences begin with capital letters.	——	——	——
4. My sentences have end punctuation.	——	——	——
5. I have corrected misspelled words.	——	——	——
6. I have good sequence of sentences and ideas.	——	——	——
7. I used new vocabulary words.	——	——	——
8. All my sentences contain subjects and verbs.	——	——	——
Total	——	——	——

Teacher Evaluation Teacher's Name _____ 1 = Mastered 2 = Needs Practice 3 = No Improvement	Date —— Piece #1	Date —— Piece #2	Date —— Piece #3
1. Used good topic sentences	——	——	——
2. Used details about topic sentences	——	——	——
3. Developed ideas well	——	——	——
4. Used expansive vocabulary	——	——	——
5. Wrote for a purpose or an audience	——	——	——
6. Had complete sentences	——	——	——
7. Had complex sentences	——	——	——
8. Sequenced ideas well	——	——	——
9. Used paragraph formation	——	——	——
10. In stories, used story elements	——	——	——
11. Used correct end punctuation	——	——	——
12. Used commas to combine sentences	——	——	——
13. Used correct capitalization	——	——	——
14. Spelled words correctly	——	——	——
15. Showed self-directedness with writing topics	——	——	——
16. Organized ideas well	——	——	——
17. Understood the writing process	——	——	——
18. Shared writing with others	——	——	——
Total	——	——	——
Composite Total	——		

teach the same lesson to everybody. The lessons are very contextual. They meet a need. They have a point."

It's near the end of the second semester now. Parents are still complimentary. "Sometimes when they note what their kids need, they criticize before I would. Some would like me to move too quickly toward correctness. I just keep up the communication and tell them again what this is all about. I've really wanted the year's reading and writing to encourage thinking, the development of ideas, and the exploration of thought in writing. I've wanted the kids to develop fluency, and the ability to question themselves and their own work—to develop some metacognition, I guess."

And has it worked? I look through many portfolios. I stop and spend some time with Rochelle's, looking at her first journals and her recent pieces. Rochelle is a twelve year old sixth grader, an eager writer. Her writing over the year looks like this:

```
                                       August  31;
        Dear journal

               Today i went to all of my
        classes. witch are Mathamatics ,Spcial
        Studies ,Science , Reading and English.
        all I have done all day is reading. I
        read math problems , and many more things
        too.

               Today I am riding the bus with
        my Best Friend. Her name is Michell
        Grater.
               Thats all Iam wrighting for
        today.

        BY: ROCHELLE DOUGLAS
```

```
                      Bill Clinton will be a good
    president    by: Rochelle Douglas.


             He will lower taxes for middle class
    people, and higher them for higher class peo-
    ple.
    This is a good thing because he is helping the
    environment. He is puting restrictions on fac-
    tories so they can't pollute the air.


             Ithink he is a good man because he
    is healping us people.


             BY: ROCHELLE DOUGLAS
```

All the kids, like Rochelle, are readying their portfolios with both developing and finished recent work. Most are like Rochelle's: they show a writing and reading metamorphosis over time.

Tambra rounds out each child's writing and reading profile. Not only the writing appears along with lists of books each one read, but a student's reading and writing attitude surveys, evaluations and response sheets throughout the year along with Tambra's own summative "clipboard" and a yearly narrative evaluation. Even a casual glance at these big portfolios shows change over time, like Rochelle's, what I would call healthy growth.

"I hope next year someone will look at these portfolios instead of just reading and writing test scores. This way, they'll know my kids as real readers and writers." I hope so, too. Smiling, I push the spectre of standardized test scores to the back of reality.

Portrait #4—Pat Stull's Fifth Grade Class Revisited

Portfolios in Pat's fifth grade classroom embrace one of the more complex systems I've seen. Every writer in Pat's class has three port-

MARTIN L. KING J.R.

M.L helped make whites and black people equal. He helped support it. Where colored and white children could go to school together. He helped pass a law that stated," Whites and colored people should have equal rights.

Martin L Kings famous words " I have a dream means something to me. If you have a dream to do something you can accomplish it. But first you must set goals, and put your mind to it. It also states that in the future he wants white and colored children to play together. So there will not be a lot of racism in America. We should treat them like us whites. We should not judge them by there color of skin. When they were brought to America they became American citizens. They could give us useful information on there black African heritage.

BY: Rochelle Douglas

folios at all times during the year and for all years, grades one through five. One, the yellow, holds the kid's "writing life," as Pat terms it. This is the writing that's come with her from first grade to fifth year. It's what each year's teacher and the student think are the best works, the ones most representative of her writing development. Each year, the yellow folder and its "showcase" pieces travel with the student to the new teacher who can get a sense of the young writer coming into his room for the next year. The yellow folder is there forever—or at least until the end of the fifth grade.

Each year, each writer has a blue and a red portfolio, too. The blue and red folders are in a large crate on a shelf in the room. The blues are this year's permanent works, those finished pieces selected for preservation as examples of works finished that the writer is proud of, the ones they offer for evaluation, perhaps for publication, or perhaps for the yellow folder. The red folder is on-going portfolio work. There are lots of unfinished pieces there, bits and pieces of drafts and half stories; they're drafts to pull out and work on—maybe, maybe not.

I look in some red folders, the working ones. Pablo's is filled with a variety of on-going projects:

—a clustering for a "choose your own adventure" story, some opening lines, and different versions;

—an unfinished short story, and a second, a sci-fi one, with dialogue;

—a goodly collection of cinquains, haiku, limericks.

If anything, John's has more in progress. He likes stories:

—a five page unfinished story;

—five stories called "Zapp," "The Roach Hotel," "Vice Versa," "Castaways," and another on camping;

—a partly finished "create your own adventure" piece;

—lots of haiku.

Sheila's seems to lean to poetry:

—lots of haiku;

—a free-verse poem;

—a lengthy story and a camping narrative.

And Christy is still thinking:

—lots of clustering, some of it linked to her haiku;

—limericks;

—a camping narrative.

Some pieces have been completed and selected out, but these are all still there for further work, or just waiting for new pieces to join them.

And that happens. When I see the red working portfolios two months later, Sheila's and Christy's are the most transformed. Sheila's poetry drafts are still there, but now she leans to stories. There is a long, new one in there and even a letter. Christy's "thinking" on paper has moved into poetry. In fact, her final writing project for the year will be an anthology of her poetry—and a lot of the samples are already kept in the red folder.

Pat and I sit and talk about how the portfolio assessment system is really more than a repository for writing. It's more than a place to collect the writing.

When the three-part portfolio system comes to Pat for each student, the yellow folder contains samples the previous teacher and the writer selected as samples to pass along. But the teacher's writing evaluations are there, too. Pat doesn't like to look at those at the beginning of the year. She likes to have the students write in her class, and she assesses and evaluates the work herself before looking at comments passed along from the year before. Then she can compare, and see growth and change, having formed her own impressions. She can pass along her thoughts on the evaluation forms and with brief conferences.

Conferences are as varied and occur as often as writing. In fact, conferences are not usually a separate part of the schedule. They're part of that seamless web of the class, too. Having seen student writing needs, she can focus on them in the current writing and offer suggestions as she moves around the room.

At least once a six weeks, the students or she, or both, select a piece from the red folder, and shape it up for the blue folder. What the students place there, Pat evaluates using a structured form (see next page) to focus her responses. Kids have access to it and take the initiative to follow up with her about her more formal response.

It's toward the end of the year that kids are asked to engage in significant self-evaluation of the year's worth of writing. They look back through all their writings to do an across-the-board evaluation of how they've grown as writers. Pat gives them a self-evaluation questionnaire to help them out.

The kids do learn from their own thoughts. Not that long ago, I sat with four of Pat's fifth graders, Sheila, Christy, Cameron, and Brian, talking about their portfolios. We sat as a small group right outside Pat's door, and they clustered around a table with me, clutching their yellow portfolios in front of them. They'd just gotten those put together that morning after deciding for the last few days what to place in them.

"Every six weeks," Sheila said, "Mrs. Stull asked us to select a finished writing from our red working portfolio to go into the blue one." As Pat said, it would be evaluated so that everyone had feedback on growth, on needs. "For our yellow one, the one we've collected our best and most important pieces from year to year, Mrs. Stull asked us to put things in from this year's blue folder, to add these to the pieces from grades 1-4. We put in our element report from science, one poem of our own choice, and two other pieces that we thought were our best."

They didn't just want to tell me how they evaluated their growth as writers this year. They were already writing a self-evaluation for

---

FIFTH GRADE CREATIVE WRITING
Upper Elementary Student Evaluation Form

Date Evaluated

IDEAS AND CONTENT
1. The writing is clear, focused, and interesting.
2. The writer has a theme but the reader must second-guess main points.
3. Information is limited or unclear.
Comments:

ORGANIZATION
1. Organization flows smoothly.
2. Despite problems the organization does not get in the way.
3. The reader is confused.
Comments:

WORD CHOICE
1. The writing conveys the message using rich language.
2. The language is ordinary, but functional.
3. The vocabulary is limited.
Comments:

SENTENCE FLUENCY
1. Variation in sentence structure makes the writing interesting.
2. Sentences tend to be short, choppy, and monotonous.
Comments:

CONVENTIONS
Key: 1 = Always 2 = Usually 3 = Seldom
Writes in sentences.
Uses correct capitalization.
Uses correct punctuation.
Spells correctly.
Paragraphs correctly.

Mrs. Stull. They wanted to talk about what the yellow portfolio showed them about their growth over the grades, growth they had a complete picture of now.

"My portfolio shows me that I can really write poetry," Christy says. "I used to think that I could never start a poem and finish it. Now I see I can write all kinds of poetry with confidence." She's just finished her Young Authors project, which turns out to be an anthology of her own poetry.

"I learned that poems don't rhyme," Brian says, flipping through his portfolio. He also just completed a book of poems. "Hey, I've become a better speller over time," he adds. "But really, I see I've gotten better as a writer. I used to think I couldn't write anything but adventure stories. Now I'm writing a lot of things; I've got more confidence to do it."

Christy agrees. "I've moved from fantasy things to poetry and even adventure stories. I know I can write more things now."

Sheila agrees, too. "I thought I could only write poems, but my portfolio has lots of things in it I've written. Looking at it makes me feel like I can write a lot more. Plus, I know I'm a better speller, too, now." She's just completed a 31 page novel.

"Looking at this (the portfolio) makes me think hard and remember," Cameron adds. He remembers his past and present as a writer. He's surprised to see the growth in his thoughts from third to fifth grade. "I noticed a major contrast in my thinking. I'm a lot more able to write about a lot of things now."

"And," he continues thoughtfully, "looking back allows you to plan for the future. You can see how you've changed and where to go now."

The portfolio assessment works for these kids. In Pat's class at Hose Elementary, it takes the place of a grade for writing. And, its legacy is that the kids still like to write, and they still do write. And perhaps that's the best assessment we could get of any writing program.

Reflections on Portfolios

From watching Pat and Tambra handle their classroom portfolio systems, we realized that there are several key points to keep in mind, points that seem to make keeping portfolios go well from start to finish:

(1) **Involve parents**—Communicate what you're doing with everybody, and where possible, bring them in on it. Tambra tells me she has parent volunteers in to help with workshops. Talk to your team, the

other English teachers, too. Tell your administrators. And let everybody know why portfolios work.

(2) **Let kids know what's going on**—Tell students about writing and reading naturally. They need to know what they're doing and why, too. They buy into an ecology of language growth better if they have a stake in where they are going.

(3) **Be systematic and organized**—Develop a management system for using portfolios, for keeping papers, for responding and evaluating them. Plan in-class time for using the portfolio for self-assessment and other assessments of growth periodically. Find a place to keep the portfolios. Teach the set-up to the kids, and stick with it.

(4) **If you've got large numbers, don't let that frighten you away from portfolios**—Remember that if you are doing whole language, the portfolio is not that much extra effort. Giving students choices about evaluation, just like you do about what they write or read is really less work, not more.

(5) **Know why you're doing this**—If you've clarified your goals for language growth already, you've got a start. You'll get a lot of questions. It helps to know what you're about.

In our resource chapter, chapter 13, Tom and I suggest entire texts devoted to portfolios. You might want to check them out. They'll give you more advice about other details you might want to know about before starting.

Teaching Journal

Begin to plan for establishing a portfolio system in your classroom. Separate a page of your journal in half and label one side "reading" and the other "writing." Jot down in each column the kinds of workshop experiences that could be accumulated and held in the portfolio.

Since the portfolio is not just a repository, begin to plan: (1) how you might use it to help assess students' reading and writing, and (2) how you might use it to help students begin to evaluate their own reading and writing. Jot your ideas for each focus, and then write out some tentative plans. If you work on a team, you might try out your ideas with team mates, perhaps for a team portfolio.

A Final Note: Exhibitions—Reclaiming the Audience for Writing and Reading

I read Ted Sizer's book, *Horace's School* (1992) three summers ago while preparing for classes. His idea for evaluation, called "exhibitions," rang a bell for me. Basically, it is authentic assessment or actually having students produce what they have been developing the skills and knowledge for. It means having them apply problem-solving abilities to real situations, developing and showing their values and sensitivities as they create an artifact that demonstrates clearly that the desired learning has occurred. Panels of judges decide if the learning has occurred. In each chapter, there were sample exhibition topics; I liked them all because kids could show what they learned meaningfully.

I realized sometime later while thinking about this chapter why I liked his idea. If you believed in writing real pieces for real audiences, in reading for real purposes, in talking for a reason, which means you believed in publishing students' works as well as in permitting a buzzing classroom, then you were already a believer in assessment of accomplishment by "Exhibitions." But Exhibitions with a capital "E" because in these cases, you are carrying the idea one step further. Rather than presenting work to a panel of academic judges, students present work to real audiences. These are, after all, settings for ultimate assessments and evaluations.

Sometimes we can do "exhibitions' to show the complex synthesis of difficult tasks as Sizer advocates. Sometimes we can do "Exhibitions" just to celebrate our students' accomplishments, just to savor them, just to let the real world share and react to them. There are lots of ways to Exhibit kids' work and learning. Among these below, you'll recognize a lot of ways to exhibit that you've already done:

(1) Writing Magazines—

I won't say much about these here except to remind you that Tom has already talked about lots of good sources for these back in chapter 8. If you don't believe in commercial publishing for kids, then try your own. Tom and I put together a combined middle school and high school publication, complete with editing crew and typist and covers and school art—and all back when we were at the EKU laboratory school. It was a lot of work, but a lot of fun for my seventh and eighth graders. The most fun was watching the faces of the kids who never dreamed that they would write something, much less see it in print. Talk about pride—in a really good sense!

(2) Around the Classroom or the School—

The ways of publishing informally are myriad. In fact, I don't think there's a teacher in the world who doesn't do this. You can always hang kids' posters on the wall, hang papers—stories, poems, biographies, whatever, even create thematic bulletin boards to exhibit certain kinds of writing kids are doing. Pat did a neat one just this year when she had the kids illustrate a word they'd created, and they hung them on the room's coat closets. They're called "sniglets" and are a lot of fun. Reading them reminded me just how much pleasure fifth graders still take in the word itself. Anybody who can creatively make up new words for humorous and even pretty complicated modern emotions, deserves an audience for it. I had to smile when I read Steve's sniglet, illustrated by Pablo:

"shraid" (shrad) adj—being afraid of turning your back in the water, sure that a shark will sneak up and eat you.

And I chuckled when I read "CMP"'s:

"microace" (mi kro ace) verb—the act of pushing the button to open the microwave and the door slamming in your face.

Oral language too can get evaluated, or just celebrated this way; we do it every time we set up a reader's theater, or plan and deliver a class play to the whole school. Or when we have kids "present" whatever they've found out in their explorations to the rest of the group.

(3) Community Projects—

We probably don't do enough of this. Maybe it just takes too much time or maybe too much energy. But synthesizing what kids know, produce, and learn for our community builds some kinds of connections that are really important. Better than Parent's Night, better than PTA. Chances are probably out there, or we can make them easily enough. I've been lucky enough this year to watch two examples of this kind of Exhibition in the community by kids, both with writing.

One of them is a sorority project (Tri Kappa) called "Dial-a-Tale." You have already read about Aaron's and Steven's submission. This is the background to that production. The project is handled through the town library, and local students write stories for telephone audiences kindergarten through third grade. The stories produced by young

writers are submitted to local raters who select the best ones to be programmed for use in the Dial-a-Tale bank of stories. Younger kids
call the right phone number and can select a story to listen to over the
phone, a story produced by other young writers who shaped the narrative for an even younger audience. If you skipped Steve's and Aaron's
piece in our section called "Reading and Writing Our Way to a Story,"
you should go back and read an example of the work young writers
do for young readers.

Another project that turns into a community project or fair is called
the Young Authors Project. This was the project that Christy, Cameron,
Sheila, and Brian (in Pat's fifth grade) had just gotten ready for. In
Crawfordsville, this is a springtime annual event that runs across all
grades and levels of the language arts curriculum. For Pat and her fifth
graders, it is a culminating event, a chance to synthesize all that the
writing curriculum has tried to do. Pat tells me that it's a real opportunity for the kids to go back into their portfolios and develop something still there, or to come up with a brand new idea. You already
heard what Christy, Brian, and Sheila created.

Regardless of what writing idea they go with, a considerable amount
of time is spent drafting, illustrating, and peer editing, a lot more time
at the computer lab for many. Take Cameron, for instance. For his
Young Authors Project, he wrote a story, a piece of fiction about the
adventures of a sixth grader. He had started the story much earlier in
the year and it sat in his red folder for a long time. Every now and
then he added to it. He kept thinking of ideas. Finally, he added a pro-
logue. "I would write on it," he said, "then have people read it—sometimes Brian, sometimes my friend John." Within two weeks of Young
Authors night, he worked every day on it, and took the manuscript
home to work on illustrations. "I must have revised it two or three
times," he said. Sometimes Mrs. Stull read the draft and gave suggestions. "For editing, we mainly had people read the draft, telling
us what to look for. The spell-checker on the computer helped, too.
Maybe the writing took a little less than a month," he reflects.

A lot of Hose students will use the Publishing Center now if they
haven't before, the Center staffed by volunteer parent help where final
copy might be typed and books can be covered and bound together.
Pat's group decided to bind their own books they proudly tell me.

But the end purpose, the final Exhibition, is the Young Authors
Display. One evening is set aside for a reception for various classes; it
might take about a week to schedule in all the classes of young writ-

ers with produced works into the small spaces in the town library. Each author shows her book and everyone browses and reads the published writing that kids have taken so much time to compose, revise, and edit—just for these audiences. It's a real celebration of reading and writing.

Sometimes each school does its own celebration for the young authors, too. I was invited to see one evening's display at Tuttle Middle School. Housed in the gymnasium, it seemed truly a community event as I threaded my way through the crowds of teachers, parents, siblings, and curious people like me.

Young Authors Night at Tuttle always boasts a room crowded with display and products from all kids, grades 6-8. Half the gym is already overwarm this particular evening, and lots of long cafeteria tables hold books, posters, prints, and murals. "It's really become a Young Artists Fair," I'm told by Susan Streetman who teaches language arts on the seventh grade team. "The books really dominate grades 1-6. By the time kids move to the middle, the medium switches, at least by seventh grade, and we encourage artistry. This project cuts across all grades in this system, and all media in 7th and 8th grades."

Teachers lean against the stagefront behind the tables of punch and pastries. They're practically invisible watching the kids, parents, and visitors like me take it in. Visitors carry cameras; the kids play music and sing. Their talent verifies what Susan says.

At one side of the gym sits Susan's seventh graders' displays of their work. I move closer and see that the kids have become the authors they researched. Susan stands nearby. She tells me that the students (mainly from one class, but some from all her classes) spent the whole year writing and getting feedback on creative writing. This writing, though, was expository and about writers that they now wanted to know more about. The group brainstormed authors in class and at home with their parents. They made choices, and researched them. The public and college library books, articles, and CD Rom material—all were resources.

"The whole class is a workshop. They helped review each other's writing for revision, and for editing. I gave mini-lessons on simple documentation so they could learn the principle of handling borrowed information. Finished products were not papers really, but oral talks by the student as the author."

"We ended with an author's convention in the library, where everyone came in costume as the authors and gave their talks introducing themselves as that person. As each one talked, Mike Barton took a picture with the Xapshot camera and using Linkway, we captured a picture of the real author, the costumed seventh grader, and a slice of the author's life composed by the young writers. One screen per person."

Two computers sit on her tables. By simply tapping a command, the kids and their authors flash by. Mike has worked his computer magic again. I watch Shakespeare, Mary Shelley, V. C. Andrews, and lots of others go by.

I wander on—past class bulletin boards of ballads, poetry, Sally's classes' Family books, Tambra's 6th graders' portfolios, showing it all from "sloppy copies" to "neat sheets."

I pass Sheridan Hadley, Tuttle's assistant principal. She's ladling out punch. I mention that this project reminds me a little of Sizer's exhibition concept. I know that the school is an Essential Coalition School and teachers, administrators, and parents are reading and discussing *Horace's School*.

"Well, it's not quite that concept," she refers to the evening's displays, "but it is a public sharing."

It is not an exhibition in his sense, but I think it is even better. It is a celebration that offers not only the opportunity for a real public evaluation, but real enjoyment too. And maybe enjoyment is the real purpose of creation anyway, and the purpose we most often forget about in school.

References

Rief, L. (1992). *Seeking diversity: Language arts with adolescents.* Portsmouth, NH: Heinemann.

Sizer, T. (1992). *Horace's school.* Boston: Houghton Mifflin.

Smith, F. (1988). *Insult to intelligence: The bureaucratic invasion of our classrooms.* New York: Arbor House.

Stevenson, C. (1992). *Teaching ten to fourteen year olds.* New York: Longman.

Weaver, C. (1990). *Understanding whole language.* Portsmouth, NH: Heinemann.

Zimmerman, M. (Comp.). (1992). *Writing instruction and portfolio development.* Crawfordsville, IN: Hose Elementary School.

Culminating Experiences

Pat Bradley's Autobiographical Booklet
7th Grade, Albany Middle School, Albany, Georgia

> "I learned this about my family. I look like them, act like them. I guess that makes me one of them. Everyone else has their own family who is special to them, but not as much special as my family is to me."
>
> —Rebekah Clower, 7th grade, Albany Middle

I was with them the whole six weeks, fifth period, seventh grade, in the spring. It was not dull. For a lot of reasons, the energy and movement and noise and silliness and eagerness and intensity and fun and even just plain hard work of 27 seventh graders, for one thing. Add to that the energy and intensity and laughter of Pat Bradley, their teacher—and you know you're going to learn some neat stuff and have a good time in the process.

This is about Ms. Bradley's culminating project for her seventh graders, what she calls the Autobiographical Booklet. Deborah and I tell you about it to encourage you to think about culminating experiences for your kids. Experiences for the spring, to end the year with, and memories to carry with them into the next grade or, if you teach eighth graders in most places, into high school. And if you are working in a school where there is not very much interdisciplinary teaching going on, then it is a way to put some things together, to make connections. We only have two criteria for culminating experiences. You want them to be intensely and personally interesting to all of your students, and you want them to be failure proof. The first criteria generally takes care of the second one. Besides, by now you already teach in a failure proof classroom anyway. By the way, you don't really have to teach it in the spring either. You can do it any time you want to, or you can make it the culmination of a theme you explore with your kids all year. That's what Sally Remaklus does with her eighth graders at Tuttle Middle School. Deborah sketches the outline of Sally's Family Album project after I describe Pat's Autobiographical Booklet.

Culminating projects of various kinds are the bread and butter of middle school language arts classes (or maybe I should say the dessert.) Linda Rief (1992) describes the Reader's-Writer's Project her eighth graders do during the last six weeks of the school year. They choose an author, genre, or theme "they want to know more about;" and they study it in depth. They research the project in three different ways, do three different kinds of writings on it. Then they write a process paper telling what they did and how they did it, and they do an oral presentation on their topic to the class.

Another culminating experience I've heard described is the Magazine that Ross Burkhardt's students do in April and May each year. Ross teaches eighth graders at Shoreham-Wading River Middle in Shoreham, New York. The Magazine produced by each kid is the product of a personal inquiry project that will involve math, science, English, social studies, and computers before it is finished. They begin with a subject they want to know about, and they ask themselves at least ten questions about their subjects in their journals. That gets them started. They do a lot of journal writing and pondering about their subjects as they begin. Ross prompts them with questions about how their work is going from time to time, and he sits down with each student in conferences about the work with the journal between them. Group work and peer editing are very much a part of the projects; and each Magazine must contain at least twelve items, including the write up of an interview on the subject. Because students are personally involved in their topics, most Magazines are much longer. Each student makes 20 copies of her Magazine and makes a list of who gets a coveted copy. Ross also winds up the project with oral reports as Magazines are finished.

Ross Burkhardt also does something else at the end of the year I want to share with you before getting back to Ms. Bradley's project. His eighth graders write "Letters to Myself," which he does not read but puts in a large envelope and files by class and year, to be opened when the present eighth grader comes back for it when he is ready to graduate from high school. I like that!

Pat Bradley's Autobiographical Booklet also involves a general outline of requirements, but a lot of personal choices within these parameters. What I want to do here is give you her outline and some student examples of each of the activities within the booklet. In case you are wondering, no, her students do not write an autobiography.

The Autobiographical Booklet has one objective and one purpose, as Pat describes it to her students. The objective is "to find out more about yourself by finding out more about your family." The purpose is her motive behind it: "The whole purpose of this project is for you to talk to your parents and your grandparents." She reminds them of these two things they are about often during the six weeks they work on the project.

Mary Barton, 7th grade, Albany Middle — photograph by Helen McCorvey

Forrest Leffer, 7th grade, Albany Middle — photograph by Helen McCorvey

They get ready for the project the six weeks before they start it by reading novels with strong family themes, some positive, some negative—*Dicey's Song, A Day No Pigs Would Die, The Island, Old Yeller, Tex, Where the Red Fern Grows, The Red Pony, The Hiding Place*. They choose their own novels, with Pat's approval, and with the understanding they will read each novel with at least one other person in the class. The reading and journaling and sharing in the groups and the class is interesting and instructive, and is a natural lead-in for her kids to look at their own families in the Autobigraphical Booklet.

On the first day of the project, Pat previews assignments and deadlines on the overhead. She gives them the contents of the booklet. This is the order she wants for the assignments in the book, with my comments and some examples of her kids' work.

Autobiographical Booklet

1. The Cover: Collage

As you can see from the photograph of Mary's collage, some of these are quite elaborate.

All of them reveal the personality and interests of their creators.

Although you don't see it in Forrest or Mary's collages, most of the class is into sports, and I see a lot of baseball, basketball, hunting and fishing on the covers. As I read the Autobiographical Booklets later, one of the things I see over and over again is how athletic this bunch of kids are. Forrest himself is a snow skier (unusual in South Georgia!), baseball player, and wrestler. He is the smallest kid in the class by far, but it hasn't slowed him down any. Like several of the girls, Mary is a young ballerina; she also is an outdoorperson. Many of the girls play basketball; and baseball is a major sport among the boys, two playing on a national championship little league team. They are a physical bunch!

However, with the collages some instructions are in order. When Ms. Bradley tells the class about the collage, somebody asks, "What's a collage?" To which one of the girls responds, "It's one of those flowers that go on your wrist."

"No, that's a corsage!" Pat is incredulous, and the class breaks up.

2. Family Tree

As you can see on the next page, they are required to include parents and grandparents on the Family Tree. Steffani's is even in the shape of an oak tree with flowers at the roots and birds in the branches. And Katie includes her cat on hers. "The whole purpose of this project is for you to talk to your parents and your grandparents," Pat reminds them. And she tells them, "If your parents are divorced, you choose which ones to include. I don't care." She is matter-of-fact about it. There is no problem.

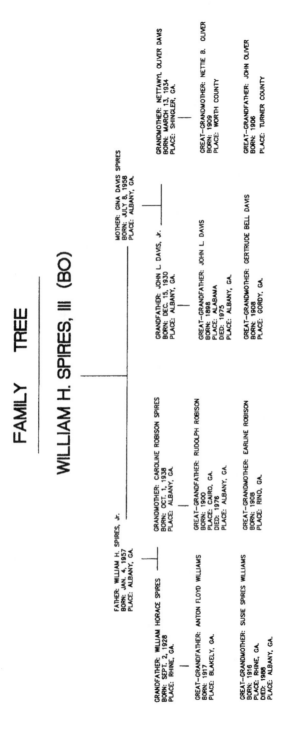

FAMILY TREE

WILLIAM H. SPIRES, III (BO)

FATHER: WILLIAM H. SPIRES, Jr.
BORN: JAN. 4, 1957
PLACE: ALBANY, GA.

MOTHER: GINA DAVIS SPIRES
BORN: JULY 8, 1958
PLACE: ALBANY, GA.

GRANDFATHER: WILLIAM HORACE SPIRES
BORN: SEPT. 2, 1928
PLACE: RHINE, GA.

GRANDMOTHER: CAROLINE ROBISON SPIRES
BORN: OCT. 1, 1938
PLACE: ALBANY, GA.

GRANDFATHER: JOHN L. DAVIS, Jr.
BORN: DEC. 15, 1930
PLACE: ALBANY, GA.

GRANDMOTHER: NETTAWYL OLIVER DAVIS
BORN: MARCH 13, 1934
PLACE: SHINGLER, GA.

GREAT-GRANDFATHER: ANTON FLOYD WILLIAMS
BORN: 1917
PLACE: BLAKELY, GA.

GREAT-GRANDFATHER: RUDOLPH ROBISON
BORN: 1900
PLACE: CAIRO, GA.
DIED: 1976
PLACE: ALBANY, GA.

GREAT-GRANDFATHER: JOHN L. DAVIS
BORN: 1898
PLACE: ALABAMA
DIED: 1975
PLACE: ALBANY, GA.

GREAT-GRANDMOTHER: NETTIE B. OLIVER
BORN: 1909
PLACE: WORTH COUNTY

GREAT-GRANDMOTHER: SUSIE SPIRES WILLIAMS
BORN: 1916
PLACE: RHINE, GA.
DIED: 1988
PLACE: ALBANY, GA.

GREAT-GRANDMOTHER: EARLINE ROBISON
BORN: 1908
PLACE: RINO, GA.

GREAT-GRANDMOTHER: GERTRUDE BELL DAVIS
BORN: 1908
PLACE: GORDY, GA.

GREAT-GRANDFATHER: JOHN OLIVER
BORN: 1906
PLACE: TURNER COUNTY

Bo Spires, 7th grade, Albany Middle

3. Pictorial Time Line

I like this part best, and we cannot show you the photos of themselves and their families they include because color is too expensive to print in a book like this. (I don't think their parents would part with prized family shapshots either.) "You must have at least one photograph of yourself for each year of your life," Pat tells them. That causes quite a commotion. "Oooo! Do I have to use pictures when I was little and looked funny!" The photos really are fun. Especially since there are five pairs of twins in the seventh grade this year at Albany Middle, and Pat teaches them all!

You've seen Mary's collage. Her entire book is a montage of photographs and her skillful artwork with her words woven among her images. It is clever and funny and full of color and Mary's zany creativity. Forrest's Autobiographical Booklet is just as much fun in a different way. I am intrigued by a photo of him with his older brother taken in 1990 at the site of the Woodstock Music and Arts Fair. But my favorite picture captures him on snow skis in a spectacular jump, snow flying, poles flung back for balance, the background blurred with his speed.

I choose Katie and Bob's books as fairly typical of the class' projects, as typical as you can get with something as deliberately individual as this. Bob is a blonde, blue-eyed sportsman, even his one-year-old and two-year-old photos are action shots, one on a scooter and one on a rocking horse. There is a football picture and several baseball photos in his Time Line, including a district tournament and a little league World Series. Bob is always in motion. In Katie's Time Line you see a pretty petite girl with glasses and long blonde hair. There are smiling and serious photos of her in ballet tights at dance recitals and on the boards, a funny picture of a nine-year-old angel with furry wings and halo with her older brother in black Ninja garb for Halloween, a rather shy Pippi Longstockings with exaggerated freckles and pigtails standing out from her head!

The photographs of all the kids are a lot of fun, and of course they tell me a lot about them I didn't know. There is Forrest behind a drum set in a rock-n-roll combo, Phillip water skiing, Mary Ann and Sherry and Tiffany with their horses, Eric singing in front of the Union Baptist Church Choir, Beth and Evie with their animals, Ben with an impressive string of catfish, Zack with his first deer, big Kedrion in football uniform, Felisha roller skating, Trish and Erin in Albany Middle basketball uniforms, Mary Ann playing league softball, Tiffany shooting pool, and Michelle modelling. Glimpses of them outside of the classroom doing the things they really like.

By the way, they laugh a lot at their kiddie pictures, but I sense no real embarrassment since everybody is involved. And they enjoy sharing the photos as much as we do. Ms. Bradley does give them the option of bringing a note from Mom excusing them from including photographs. The rare parent can be sensitive about it, and there are students who come from homes where there are no photos to bring.

4. Interview

The interview is brief, only five questions and answers, and a write-up about what they learned doing it. Still Ms. Bradley walks them through it. She is patient to be sure they know whom to choose to interview and what to do. The interview is related to one of the compositions they will write for the book, either about a person who has influenced them or their most famous (or favorite) relative or someone related to their goals. Pat is not surprised when most of them interview their mom or dad. She is specific in her instructions. "When you turn this in, I want a list of your questions. I want your questions and notes on their answers. And I want your write up on what you learned about them."

Looking back at Bob and Katie's Autobiographical Booklet, I see that both of them interviewed their mothers. I like one of Bob's questions especially.

> Question: How would you want your kids to grow up?
>
> Answer: Independent and strong willed, but I would like them to have a good sence of humor. If they can learn to laugh at themselves, then they can teach others to laugh with you & not against you.

And Bob's write up of the interview is typically middle school male.

> The reason I picked my mom is because she will give me good answers. She gave me strait answers and she didn't lie. She told me who influenced her to make good grades and other important things like to help the environment and to love animals. She is very nice and cares about Candice and I.
>
> Bob Aman, 7th grade, Albany Middle

As you might expect, Katie's write up is longer; and she gives us the dialogue between them. I particularly like the way she starts the essay and her reason for choosing her mom in the first place.

Interview Write-Up

I interviewed my mother since one of my goals is to be a successful mother. First, I asked her, "When you were young, did you think you wanted children when you were old enough?"

She replied, "I didn't want children in high school because I wanted to be a scientist, I couldn't be both. In college, I changed my mind."

Next, I asked her, "Are you a happy and satisfied mother?"

She answered, "Yes, I'm glad to have children. I think they enriched my life and made me a whole person."

Then, I asked, "What do you find most difficult with motherhood?"

She said, "Keeping your patience when children tease and don't understand serious moods. Also, allowing children their own individuality. It's hard to 'let go'."

I then asked, "What do you find most pleasant with motherhood?"

She answered, "Sharing memories, watching children learn and experience new things, and I enjoy the challenge of figuring out how to best guide and teach for the future."

Last, I asked her, "What are some of the things you do with your children, and do you enjoy them?"

She replied, she deals with conflicts with us, and does outdoor activities, like picnics, games, etc. She said, "I love traveling and experiencing new places and meeting new things together. I love all times I spend with you."

Katie Rodman, 7th grade, Albany Middle

But Eric surprised me. He interviewed Pat Bradley. I've known Pat for a number of years, and it is interesting to read how Eric sees her.

Interview Summary

I interviewed Mrs. Bradley. She told me it took her 5 years to become a teacher. She has her Master's Degree so it took her a little longer. She said the reason why she became a teacher is because she has always enjoyed working with children. She helped with Sunday School and Vacation Bible School when she was a teenager. Also she was a counseler at a summer camp. In the interview she told me that sometime when I have had a bad day, students have been really bad or there's just too much paper work, if I am frustrated—then she wished she had picked another career. I asked her how long do a teacher have to teach before they can retire? She said they have to teach 30 years before they can retire. She told me the best way to learn a student's name at the beginning is to put them in alphabetical order.

Eric Raines, 7th grade, Albany Middle

5. Almanac

The Almanac assignment is a list of "ten events that happened the year you were born, from at least three different topics, like sports, entertainments, inventions, disasters." Pat has a stack of almanacs in the front of the room. She tells them to share, and gives them a tip. "The almanac you need is the year after you were born." They talk a little about how almanacs are written, what they have in them, and how you use one. And the kids are quickly into the stack of books.

I don't think the lists reflect the fun the kids had sharing this mini-research task. As you might expect, Bob's list for 1979 has a lot of sports in it. I was interested to learn that "Ken Fraser caught a 1,496 lb. Blue fin tuna in Aulds Cove on Oct. 26." That is some fish! Bob was probably more interested that Montreal won the Stanley Cup and that Moses Malone was the MVP of the National Basketball Association. He also noted that Tom Watson made more money than anyone else on the PGA tour. Bob is also a golfer.

Katie's list for 1980 has a lot of disasters in it, a tornado, fire, and the Mt. St. Helens eruption. She starts it with the chilling statistics that 53,172 people died in car wrecks and that 7,257 died by drowning that year. She does note that Ronald Reagan was elected 40th president. And I note that the kids are careful not to put the same things on their lists. Rarely is an item repeated.

6. 5 Compositions

Pat gives them five writing tasks to fill out their books. "I'll give you the topic. It'll be about yourself." She usually begins each writing on Monday. There is no length requirement, but she is specific about what she wants in the process of writing each one—a jot list or cluster, a fast draft of the piece, response from a partner or group, and an edited and proofread copy for the book. There will be at least one editing conference with her before it is finished. This is routine for these kids; they've been with her all year. Although she only has two Apple IIe computers in her room and one printer, every student has at least a couple of writings typed and checked out on the computer. Her students slip into other rooms up and down the hall to borrow computers to write, and four at a time go to the media center where Merlene

Jones makes room for them to work. I get to help the library crew with their writing and editing, since I'm available. It is not an ideal situation, but the students adapt easily. They manage nicely.

I am impressed, as I always am when students write about themselves for publication, with their willingness to work over a piece several times without getting bored and with how much fun they have writing and talking about what they are writing.

The first writing is about *My Pet*. Pat really enjoys talking with her kids, sharing with them and listening to them, as they begin working on an assignment. "I am going to go around the room before the bell rings. I want you to tell me one thing about your pet." I think it is one of the things that make her such an outstanding teacher. She listens with her eyes, smiles often, and it's real. She likes their company and likes being among them. "Alright, whose got the most unusual pet?" There is a lot of talk about rabbits and ferrets and finches and turtles and horses and colts and ducks, and a lot of laughter.

Once the pieces are finished and in the books, I think my favorite is Forrest's.

DANCE

The pet I'm writing about is my dog, Dance. He is a black Great Dane that stands about 6 feet on his hind legs. Dance has a kink in his ear and tail, they both got caught in a door, and the only white spot on him is on his upper chest. He was born about 5 years ago. Dance was the only male in a litter of 13 puppies. He had a former owner that had a female Great Dane that was bred to my stepdad Van's male Great Dane, Hawk. The former owner knew almost nothing about raising Great Danes so 3 of them died. Van took the remaining puppies and revived them back to good health.

Dance leans up against people he likes. He thinks he is a little puppy still, so he tries to sit in your lap (he is very heavy, unfortunately). He does a lot of other goofy things too. He, sometimes, lies on his back, sticks his legs into the air and lets his lips flop over his face. Another thing he does is that when he sleeps he moves his legs up and down as if he is chasing something. Dance really likes Van, my cat, many people, and me.

Before we had Dance, thieves stole 2 lawn mowers and 3 bicycles from us, but after we got Dance only 1 bicycle and 1 VCR was stolen because Dance was locked up in the front of the house, and couldn't get to the thief. We didn't know it was gone until that night.

Forrest Leffer, 7th grade, Albany Middle

"How long is it supposed to be?" someone asks the standard question as they are writing.

"We'll see after we read it." Pat smiles.

"We've got to read it?" from a chorus of voices.

Yep, it sounds like middle school alright. Even though these kids share their stuff all the time.

The second writing is about *A Person Who Has Influenced Me.* "Think," Pat says. "Your parents have influenced you. Who else?" James wrote about his grandfather and their special relationship.

The Person Who Has Influenced My Life the Most

The person I feel that has had the most influence on my life is my Grandfather E.W. Tolbert. My grandfather has been my "Bud" since I was 2 years old I have always called him "Bud". From the time I was 3 years old I spent almost every Friday night with Bud. We would have long talks about all sorts of things. We can talk politics, religion, sports, current events, anything and everything is what we discuss. We have watched just about every John Wayne Movie ever made three or four times.

Bud grew up in Columbus, Georgia and went to old Industrial High School where he made pretty good grades. He always told me about a man named Bob Eubanks who was a very big influence in his life. He got Bud a membership at the YMCA and got him interested in basketball and taught him alot about life.

Bud was in the Army during World War II. He says the Army taught him leadership and self confidence. He says the experience for the most part was pretty enjoyable.

Bud also has given me my great love for sports. He always comes and watches me play ball and gives me pointers. We have spent many quarters at the batting cages.

Bud has influenced my thinking in many different areas of my life. He has helped me to be able to know right from wrong. He is always there encouraging me to be the best I can be and to never give up on anything.

James Tolbert, 7th grade, Albany Middle

Bob talks about a favorite uncle who taught him to shoot and hunt, and who is instructing him as a tournament archer! I wonder if there is any sport Bob hasn't excelled in? And Katie talks about the influence of her third grade teacher, Mrs. Malcom.

The third writing is on *My Goals.* "You know I want more than one paragraph," Pat tells them. "You are going to give me some detail, aren't you?" They talk about short term and long range goals—"for this six weeks or for your life."

Bob's goals are just what you might expect. Here is an excerpt from his first paragraph.

> My goals in life are to finish high school and go to Georgia Institute of Technology (Georgia Tech). When I grow up I want to be a famous baseball player. I would like to play for the Atlanta Braves, but I wouldn't be upset if I was on another team. I would sign a contract for million dollars . . . .
>
> Bob Aman, 7th grade, Albany Middle

His friend Ben has more immediate concerns, but he is also a sportsman.

> My goals are short term. I really want to make the honor roll bad. My dad would be very happy. Another goal is to hit a home run this season or the next. I also want to steal a lot of bases. Another goal is to take care of myself and that means no smoking, no drinking, and especially NO DRUGS. Another goal is to become a better sports player. My most favorite sports include golf, baseball, football, basketball, and water skiing. I want to shoot a better score in golf, hit a homerun in baseball, slam dunk 10 feet in basketball, and learn more and harder tricks in skiing.
>
> Ben Thompson, 7th grade, Albany Middle

Katie is precise, to the point, and determined. This is part of one of her paragraphs.

> Once I've grown up, I plan to be three things. First, I want to be a happy and successful wife. Next, I want to be a successful mother. I plan to have one or two children. Last, I plan to be a successful school teacher. I want to help kids learn to be as successful as I plan to be. I will teach them that, in order to be something in life, you have to go all the way through school. . . .
>
> Katie Rodman, 7th grade, Albany Middle

Next they are to write on their *Most Famous Relative*. If they don't know a famous one, Pat tells them they can write about their favorite relative. Bob writes about his mother. "She is crazy but she taught me my manners and all that other stuff." Katie writes about her three girl cousins from different parts of the country and whom she sees when her mother's family gets together in the summer.

Mary Ann wrote about three of her relatives.

My Most Famous Relatives

I suppose my granddad is the most famous person in my family because he has won the National Championship for horseshoe pitching several years in a row. He was at one time the best horseshoe pitcher in the United States!

Next I would say my Greatgrandfather Redfearn. He was one of the best lefthanded pitchers that played at the University of Georgia. I never knew him or saw him play but I'm sure he was a wonderful pitcher.

The next famous person in my family is my great uncle. He played in the movie "The Mighty Ducks" as a hockey coach and is also in alot of Nordic Track commercials. I don't know him either so there's not much more to tell.

Mary Ann Portt, 7th grade, Albany Middle

The fifth writing and last piece in the Autobiographical Booklet is about *Four Favorite Things*. Pat tells them to pick four different categories (e.g. foods, animals, sports, hobbies, music, people) and write about them. Bob writes his favorites in reverse order, and all of them are related to his love of sports of all kinds.

4 Favorites

My fourth favorite thing is kneeboarding [a form of water skiing]. Ben taught me how to do it a couple of years ago. It is very fun and challenging. I am fairly good at it, but Ben is better. I can do a 180 [degree turn], 360, side slide, and I can stand up on it.

My third favorite thing is swimming. I go swimming at my grandparents mostley, but I do go with my friends too. I love to swim for hours and get a sun tan. I like to do all kinds of dives off the slide into the pool.

My second favorite thing is my favorite food, "deer meat." My favorite part is the backstrap. It is very good when you chop it up in little squares and rap bacon around it and cook it on the grill. I like the other meat on a deer but the backstrap is better.

Now. my favorite thing is sports. My favorite is baseball. I made all stars five years in a row. I have won seven tournaments out of ten. Last year I hit a home run to win the state tournament. I started playing golf about five and a half years ago. . . . My best score on 18 holes is 84. . . . I am not the best in basketball but I am allright. . . . Now you know what my four favorite things are.

Bob Aman, 7th grade, Albany Middle

Well, Bob didn't exactly follow Ms. Bradley's directions, but I see his energy and openness in this piece. Katie's fifth essay is also typical of her straightforward approach to any writing task.

My Favorites

My favorite animal is a cat. I love cats. I have a cat myself. Anyone can have one. I like them because they're loving, cuddly, playful, and cute. I'm planning to have alot of cats when I grow up.

My favorite sport is swimming. I wait for summer so I'll be able to swim. I get my swimsuits ahead of time so I'll be ready. I only like to swim for fun, though. I don't like to race swim.

My favorite drink is Cherry Coke. Everytime we get fast food or go to a resturant, I get Cherry Coke if they have it. Whenever we go to the store, I try to talk my parents into getting it. There's one problem I run into, though. My brother likes it too. He'll sneak two a day. I try to hide it from him, but my parents get mad and say, "It's as much his as it is yours."

My favorite hobby is babysitting. Of course, it's a job too. But I love little kids. Plus I get paid and help out the parents. The worst part is diaper changing. Other than that, I love it.

Katie Rodman, 7th grade, Albany Middle

After the last writing is printed, the last conference held, the last editing and proofreading taken care of, the photographs pasted in the book and the family tree drawn and the collage made, after all the Autobiographical Booklets are put together, Pat and her kids have a grand celebration. It is like a read-a-round with pictures. Every kid shows off her book, talks about her family and her goals and her pets and answers a lot of questions from her friends. The books are passed around. There is a lot of laughter over the photos, and all of them learn some things they didn't know about these people they go to school with every day. After the racket dies down, Pat gets them all together and asks them what they learned from the project. Forrest learned his great-grandfather came from Sweden. Zack learned his last name is German. Ben learned that his great-great-grandfather invented the garbage truck! Ashley learned that her great-great-grandmother was a full blooded Cherokee. Jesse learned that Bob is his cousin. Evelyn learned that she is related to the founder of her home town. And the discussion continues, each one surprised and delighted by something learned about family. Like Rebekah says, "Everyone else has their own family who is special to them, but not as much special as my family is to me."

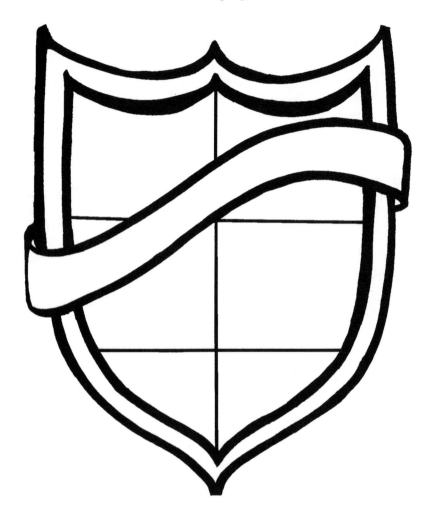

Sally Remaklus' Year-Long Family Album Project

8th Grade, Tuttle Middle, Crawfordsville, Indiana

Sally's classroom is at the end of the hall on the second floor of Tuttle Middle. It's light and airy, full of kids' projects. 9:00 a.m. is team planning time usually, but not today. Sally is busy helping her eighth graders in all her classes put together their Family Albums, full of a lot of the year's writing.

All of the eighth grade year, much of Sally's reading and writing program relates to Self and Family. It's not the only focus; there are still chances to choose your own topics for writing, your own reading, and there are other class reading and writing projects. But the kids understand that, as part of the whole year, they are building a portrait, a book, about who they are for themselves, their families, friends.

The final books being finished now are bound by huge three-ring binders. Everyone has the same three sections: the Past, the Present, the Future. The kids create the past section, called "Roots," during the early part of the year, sometime from the first week in class to the Christmas break. The Past develops two ways, as a family genealogy study and as a personal past. It is very much an integration of social studies and language arts, a kind of "team is me" thread starting early and running through the whole year.

Even on the first day of school, they're writing poetry that many will feed into the book; short Name Poems or Color Poems are popular choices. The focus on names continues as kids explore the origin of their names, researching the meanings and using parent interviews and resources from the libraries. Some of Sally's important yearly goals deal with descriptive writing and research, so this gets them started.

While this exploration continues, kids also begin to develop their own Crests. Eventually, the crest will serve as the cover of the book. Individually designed, it is illustrated slowly over the year as the reading and writing focuses move from past to present to future. The banner across the six illustrated spaces is for a motto or appropriate title like "A True Friend." And the edges are also decorated.

Even the Crest serves as another writing focus at times. Sally uses it to help students develop another writing goal, how to organize spatially. "I want anyone to be able to 'see' your Crest without looking at the design itself," she tells them as they work on descriptions of it.

By Thanksgiving, she and the kids have moved into a full fledged genealogy study, focusing on family roots. "This phase helps teach kids the uses of primary research," she says. Kids use the phone to interview distant relatives. They write letters for family information. And they interview and record data for later development. Once they've done the research, they represent their genealogy with charts (family trees) and maps showing where their families came from. They bring in lots of artifacts, especially old pictures and letters, which join their own compositions in the book.

Sometimes her students do different options with this family past part. Some research the history of their houses; and these stories, drafted and redrafted, find their way into their books. One year Sally and her kids read historical novels. They studied the elements of this kind of literature, created time-lines of events in the stories, then applied those time lines to their own families, tracing the historical events in fiction with those in the histories of their families. Sometimes they write their own autobiographies. They build them from short self-anecdotes, learning to use flashbacks to recapture birth and childhood, building eventually the story of their lives. Sometimes they have taken an historical figure, studied the history of her time, gathered a lot of details about her, and written their own historical fiction about the character.

There are lots of other times that literature ties in with their family writings. One experience Sally particularly likes she calls Snapshot Writing. She adapted the assignment from her professional reading, and it is a kind of descriptive writing where they work on imagery and descriptive verbs especially. To prepare for the writing, they read a chapter or section of a book full of imagery, like *Ragtime*. (Sally does caution that this whole book is not for eighth grade.) They all listen to the reading first, listing the images they hear in five sensory columns. In groups they put their images up on a big poster, making a word-mural of the scene. "Generally, we have a really good follow-up discussion on imagery and perspective," she says. This leads into brainstorming for, and writing imaginatively and sensuously about, their own descriptions of family scenes.

The section of the Family Album called Present includes descriptions of themselves as eighth graders or more poetry. Again, Sally uses literature to focus the writing. Often the whole group will read the play based on *The Diary of Anne Frank*. They talk about Anne's "two sides." A lot of writing exploring their own two sides occurs, some of it winding up in the Album.

The Future section, completed toward the end of the year, is usually a little shorter. After talking about what Anne Frank took into hiding and talking about what they value, her students write their own Last Wills and Testaments. They interview a partner and talk about their Future Goals and write humorous Obituaries. In the process, Sally has an opportunity to talk about hyperbole and other language concepts.

"They are always feeding things into the book; it's always in transition." The room is often full of kids composing, sharing, or getting feedback from other readers. But by the end of the year, all final drafts are in the book, to be shared at the Young Authors' Fair and then taken home, a repository for the eighth grade self.

Compositions in the FamilyAlbum

Past	Present	Future
Name Origin	Physical Description	Want Ads
Crest	Interviews	Wills
Crest Descriptions	Things I Like	Humorous
Family Group Sheets	Friends	Obituaries
Pedigree Charts	Neighborhood	
Maps	If I Were a Color	
Family Anecdotes	Being Fourteen	
Character Sketches		
Historical Fiction		
—Timelines		
—Stories		
—Author's Note		
Autobiography		

Reference

Rief, L. (1992). *Seeking diversity. Portsmouth*, NH: Heinemann.

12

Dealing with the Nasty Realities: Barriers to Natural Learning and What You Can Do about Them

"Having people care about you was probably the only thing that made any of it right. Having them not care made your whole life wrong."

—Walter Dean Myers (1988)

"Giving up the familiar is never easy, but doing so can be one way to make teaching the kind of rewarding and challenging business it can be."

—John Mayher (1990)

Do what you can. We know it is not always easy, and in some places just plain hard, to teach your students in appropriate ways. Your principal doesn't understand, your school board doesn't understand, the kids parents don't understand, and neither do the teachers on your hall. The schedule is rigid, and there are five ability groups in the school hierarchy. You have to teach the basal. You have to teach traditional grammar. You have to teach the stuff on the latest idiot test from the state department of education. Besides, your kids have real problems. The list goes on and on. It's a tough job, sometimes tougher than it should be. You are a professional and you love kids and you know a better way to teach them—you do the best you can with what you have to work with. We all do.

This is our "yeah, but . . ." chapter. "Yeah, Deb and Tom, I really would like to teach that way, but there is this problem." And our intention is to bring comfort to the weary, the discouraged, the frustrated. We figure you agreed with something we said, or you would have thrown the book down a long time ago. You are a Natural Learning teacher, or want to be one. But it's rough out there. Our hope is to offer you support in the face of real difficulties. You may have a shorter or longer list of serious problems for the Natural Learning teacher, but these are the ones we think of immediately, with suggestions and reflections we hope are helpful.

1) Traditional Grammar, Spelling, Vocabulary Requirements

We are constantly amazed and appalled at well meaning teachers who suck the marrow, the very life itself, out of language with useless and near meaningless drills, exercises, diagrams, lists, and monotonous definitions. And all for students in the middle grades who are endlessly fascinated with language itself. The possibilities are wonderful, and the practice can be so wretched.

OK, we'll get off our soap box and try to be a little more practical about what you can do when you are required by an unenlightened department head or badly written curriculum guide—or the pressure of the expectations of other teachers in your school—to teach formal grammar from the Warriner's book or one of its clones. Or if you are required or pressured to teach vocabulary or spelling lists.

First, **do teach language.** Teach language at every opportunity. That does not mean you have to bore your students into a catatonic state with the Parts of Speech. There are many, many other ways to teach the wonder of the language we speak and write; and there are certainly much better ways to teach "correct" usage and mechanics than by a list of rules based on how Latin works. Most of the time, documenting the usage and mechanics you do teach in the course of teaching writing is enough to satisfy administrators and parents and maybe your colleagues, especially when they see what your kids can do.

Secondly, in most cases we do this to ourselves. Rarely today is formal traditional grammar teaching required in any curriculum guide, although it certainly is taught. We are merely uncomfortable because Miss Cumquat, who will be teaching them next year, always starts the year with the Parts of Speech and marches grimly through the Warriner's book during the year. She has taught here for years and is the arbiter of what should and should not go on in English class, and she makes sarcastic comments in the lounge about what they didn't learn last year. Face it, Miss Cumquat will make those same sarcastic comments whether you knuckle under to her idea of grammar teaching or not. You simply do not have to do it.

A practical middle ground on the grammar issue is to get a good handbook like *Write Source 2,000* and use it for direct teaching when you see things the class needs. Teach students to use it in response groups and in conferences during revision and proofing. If you are afraid of what they will face with Miss Cumquat next year, frankly review them in the spring on all that stuff. They won't remember it (they wouldn't if you bored them silly with it all year either), but you will feel better.

A reasonable middle ground on vocabulary and spelling is to let the kids make up the lists the way Melissa Moore does at Merry Acres Middle. Using the vocabulary words is a big deal with her young writers when they check each other's stories. It rarely happens any more, but you may work in a school where a prescribed spelling list is issued by the language arts department or even by the principal. We have had that experience. If you cannot talk them out of it or if they won't let you teach vocabulary in more relevant ways, then you just do the best you can with a bad deal and pray for change. Try not to let it consume a lot of your or your students' time, and help your students find some context for the words on the list.

Always, always communicate with your principal about what your are teaching, how your are teaching it, and the wonderful results you are getting in your students' writing and reading. Show off your kids and your kids' work. It's good for them, and it really goes a long way toward acceptance of your program in your school.

2) Labels, Tracking, Ability Grouping

Most of the middle schools in the school systems where we work are ability grouped. The issue has been around some time now, and we believe most informed educators know the practice is particularly bad for young adolescents. Still, the schools are slow to change. Probably, your school separates students into high, middle, and low groups, too. If not, count your blessings, praise your administrators, and find something more interesting to read.

There are three things you can do in a tracked school. First, let people know it's bad for kids and you don't like it. Secondly, do whatever you can to prove to the low and average groups (whatever euphemistic names your school gives them) that they excel just like the kids in the prestige track. That's quite a job, but it is vital. Linda Darrah at Merry Acres Middle did a simple but profound thing a few years ago. She issued her low level classes the same "difficult" textbook the other English classes had, instead of the low level text adopted by the school system. She saw an instant change in her kids. Avoid the stigma of different books and different assignments whenever you can.

Also, look for ways to get the groups together for meaningful assignments and projects. This will take the cooperation of your colleagues and careful planning. Be careful not to make it the kind of experience where the smart kids are helping the dumb kids. Rather look for real cooperative learning situations where all students can share in the experience and the learning. Good integrated studies across the disciplines are your best bet, the kinds of things Deborah talks about in Chapter 4.

Labelling raises the issue of Gifted programs. And these may be mandated by law, as they are where we work. It is a very touchy issue besides. But the Gifted label can be just as isolating and just as damaging as the Dummy label. Your school may have choices about how gifted education funds are administered and how gifted programs are implemented. Study those choices carefully. Talk about them with your principal and your colleagues. We think the answer for mandated programs is basically the same as when you have ability groups you cannot get rid of—mix the kids up as much as possible at every opportunity. Do whatever you can to end their isolation.

If you and your colleagues are convinced changes need to be made in your school, Anne Wheelock's *Crossing the Tracks* (1992) will tell you how other schools have untracked and what you need to do to be successful in getting rid of the labels at your school. If you feel isolated yourself, read her book and share it with your principal. Make a beginning.

3) At-Risk Kids

About seven percent of the students in Tom's school system from grades eight to twelve drop out during the school year. That is according to the last figures from the state department of education. Statistics are hard to keep with a mobile student population. But nationally we don't seem to being doing very well with the dropout problem either, probably somewhere from a fourth to a third of our students don't make it to graduation. We all know what that means for their future, and for the future of our society. Where we lose them is middle school. Sometimes the body is still there, but the kid is waiting for the legal age and he's gone.

There are a lot of reasons for these troubled students, only some of which you have any control over in the classroom and the school. We don't want to get into finger pointing at legislators indifferent to overcrowded classes and inadequate budgets, state departments of education with politically motivated requirements and tests that seem designed to drive kids out of school, ineffective juvenile justice systems, dull textbooks and duller curriculums, overworked single parents or indifferent parents or hostile parents, or the teachers they had last year. The question for most of us is, now that we've got them, how do we help them right now, right here?

First, let's deal with the criminal element and get it out of the way. **A message for administrators:** Set up the best alternative education program you can with the very best dedicated teachers you can find. Then tolerate no violence in any form toward students or teachers. There is no reason for it and no reason to allow it in any middle school. The same should be true of any larcenous activity, including illegal drugs and drinking.

Secondly, as we discussed, if your school is still ability grouped, untrack it. That change may not be easy, but it will save some of your kids.

The issue is self-esteem and knowing I can learn and I can do well. You and your fellow teachers and administrators must convince every student in your care of this truth. And it must be genuine. A start for the language arts teacher is doing the kinds of things we've talked about in this book. Things like real choices in what to write and what to read, frequent publishing of student writing and other work, cooperative learning and interdisciplinary teams. Still, with some students it will be a hard sell at first because they've failed so much before you got them. Failure is so painful it is much easier for me not to try than face the possibility of failing again. But once you are able to show a kid what he can do, and that it is genuinely good, you've got him and he will open to learning in beautiful ways. Don't let him go without showing him that he is a learner.

One of the things we have done to students to drive them out of school is bore them to death. The simple answer is quit boring them. With your fellow teachers, closely examine what you are teaching. Be ruthlessly critical. Learning is not dull; challenge is exciting when it is attainable. Seatwork and worksheets and isolated skills are **BORING.** Throw out the worksheets. Do something real.

And there are things you have to do we can only tell you about that are up to you: You have to believe that every kid can learn. And you have to care about them, all of them, and let them know you care.

4) Kids Who Can't Read

What do you do about the ones who just can't read? Go back and take another look at Chapters 5 and 6, to start with. Then do what Paul Gainer does at the start of each school year. Expect every student to choose a book, sit with the book, and turn pages during the class time assigned for reading. And to do nothing else but "read" during that time.

They read. Nobody finishes a year with Paul without reading a book. And when you've done it and you know you can do it, just like everybody else, you're on your way. The books in Paul's room cover a wide range of difficulty without being elementary. That helps, but it is not really why they work. They are interesting to the kids. The other kids in the room like them and talk about them and do things with them. Choice. Peer response. Interest. You want to read the thing, too.

There are other things you can do that help. Read to your students every day. Share your excitement and love of books with them. Work head to head with the students who are not too self-conscious to let you tutor them. Show students how you read different kinds of texts, as much as you are able. Do as much real talking about reading and books as the school routine will allow. Make it impossible to fail.

And there are some things not to do. Don't do things instead of reading. Don't put the kid in an SRA kit instead of giving him a book. Don't try to teach phonics to a young adolescent. Don't bury them in worksheets on vocabulary or comprehension. Don't make students struggling with reading read out loud to the class. Don't give up on anybody.

5) Kids Who Can't Write

It's really the other side of the same coin. We've already talked about motivating writing in real ways a lot, but keep these things in mind. Any child who is not severely brain damaged can learn to write, and about ninety percent of it is showing him he can do it. Real choices, genuine positive response from you and especially from the other kids, and time in class to write and work on writing are essential. But your expectations that they will write every day, and will write well, are what make it happen. That and your example. I would not be taught by a carpenter who did not have a hammer and saw in his hands often. Writing is a craft. Like all crafts, you teach it by showing them how.

6) My Principal Doesn't Understand!

Well, sometimes she just won't. Our friend Angela Moore is fond of saying "there are the informed and the uninformed" when it comes to language arts teaching, or natural teaching and learning in any discipline. Your job is to inform your principal, if necessary, by showing her what your kids are learning and what they can do when they are taught humanely. Invite her into your room and into your activities before she comes in with the annual evaluation form, and invite her in often.

We have been particularly blessed with liberal principals who trusted us and really let us do what we thought best for our kids, **if we sat down with them and talked about it before we did it.** Communication and planning ahead of time, taking the time to talk and being open, really can win you a lot of support. Our principals also trusted us because we pitched in and worked for the good of the school and didn't just do our own thing. And that's important to keep in mind, too.

We have seen principals interested in good language arts programs because the teachers where good and the kids were happy and enthusiastic about learning. And we have also seen principals become real fans and supporters of programs because parents started showing up at the school for read-a-rounds and projects and response groups and special publications. Is your principal indifferent? Get your parents involved in your program.

Don't fight unless you have to. Chances are, you won't win. And even if you do, the kids lose.

If you are convinced you work for a bad principal (and those cases really are rare in our experience), then get a job in another school as soon as you can. Meanwhile, go in your room and shut the door and teach your kids.

7) Teaching a Junior High Schedule

So what do you do if you are teaching in a school that looks and feels like a little high school, six class periods a day, no block scheduling time, no advisory time, no team planning time, that kind of thing? In the short run, you do the best you can with what you have to work with. In the long run, you argue for change to a schedule more appropriate for middle school kids and their needs.

You may have a fifty-five minute class period, but you know your kids cannot sit still nor concentrate that long. Middle school kids are just not made that way. So you will have to provide them not only opportunities for variety within the arbitrarily long class period, but a chance for physical movement as well. It's not immaturity really; it's a physical thing. Let them move around.

Put an aquarium or hamster cage in your room, if you like those kinds of things. That will give the kid some place to go by on the way to and from the pencil sharpener. Move them in and out of groups during the period. Move them to and from the computers for editing and publishing. Plan for movement.

Just because you don't have an easy schedule for a team, doesn't mean you and your colleagues cannot work as a team. Take a look at the suggestions in Chapter 4. Get a buddy in social studies or math and do things together with the kids. Relate your teaching so they may relate their learning. Teach projects and inquiry and live research with people in the community. Look beyond the walls of your classroom for possibilities. Don't let an inappropriate schedule make you teach in inappropriate ways.

A related problem is a schedule that separates the language arts themselves. You may have a reading class and an English class, or you may teach one and your neighbor down the hall the other in the school's schedule. We've talked some about this common, if outmoded, practice in the chapters on reading and writing. And you have some examples there of how other teachers handle it. The answer is basically the same—put them together. If your fellow teacher across the hall will work and plan with you, good. If not, teach them both in your classroom the way they should be taught, really related, unseparated, whatever the class is called.

8) Teaching the Required Basal

It may be rare, but it still happens that some school districts and school principals require that a particular reading basal be taught. Well, be honest with yourself first and see if this is something you're doing to yourself. Expectations are not necessarily regulations. Just because reading at your school has always been taught out of the county's adopted basal does not mean you have to teach it that way. If that is the case, first try to negotiate with your principal, or county office supervisor, if you need to. Give him some articles to read. Tell him why you want to teach a reading workshop in your room. Ask for his support.

If basal teaching has been the tradition at your school, you will have to educate parents to what you are doing and why. That goes with the territory anyway. Always keep parents informed about expectations in your classes. That is only fair.

If you cannot get out of using the basal, supplement it with as many paperbacks and interesting activities as you can. There are no reading basals on the market today that do not have related reading lists for students. These books are part of the basal program. Get them and use them. And add books of your own related to the themes or "skills" taught. We know of no current basal program where reading paperbacks is not encouraged in the teaching guides.

9) Teaching Students with "Substandard" Dialects

We want to say this clearly. **There is no such thing as a substandard dialect.** Who do you think you are, putting kids down for the way they talk? We are language-making beings. Our language **is** who we are. Think about that.

Tom works in a school system where most of the students are black. He grew up in Northwest Georgia at the southern tip of Appalachia. If you ever talk to him on the phone, you will know immediately he's from the hills. His dialect and the dialect of the students he works with have several things in common. Both are consistent in their grammar but change in lexicon. Grammar describes the dynamics of language. We are not talking here about usage exercises. The lexicon is our vocabulary. Both dialects are vital, alive, interesting, and very creative. Both work very well where they are used. They work in all situations among the dialect group, including professional ones. If you go trout fishing in the hills of North Georgia and you want to ask the locals about the fishing, take Tom with you. He talks their language. It has been well established that black students are not unsuccessful in job interviews because they speak a dialect. They sometimes do not get those jobs because their skin is black and they're talking to a white guy. Both dialects are looked down upon. Anybody ever call you a "cracker"?

You really don't have to worry about them. Teach them the best you know how with a variety of language experiences, lots of reading, lots of writing, talking, listening, researching, working together, and they will do just fine when the time comes for that interview.

Naturally, we do not imply that you must accept cursing or put-downs or racial slurs or sexual references. We don't accept bad manners either.

And one more point about those two dialects. Both dialects are beautiful. Just as your students are beautiful. Honor their language.

10) Students Who Don't Speak English at Home

First, honor their language. That answer is the same. In most, but not all, situations in the United States, the home language of these students will be Spanish. You may have a student or several students or most of the kids in a class who speak very little English, in the case of migrant workers' children in rural South Georgia, for instance. Bilingual kids, of course, are no real problem in this regard, and will enrich the experiences of the other students in the classroom, and your own for that matter. With large numbers of students who speak little English, you will have to get some help. Don't try to handle it on your own.

Get your counselors or principal or district office specialist to get in touch with the ESL (English as a Second Language) staff in your State Department of Education and find our about materials and other assistance. In many cases there are federal funds available.

If you live in an area where you can expect large numbers of Spanish speaking students, you will also want to pick up as much Spanish as you can just to relate to your kids. They are not the only ones who get to learn, you know. Don't be shy about asking for classes in conversational Spanish for teachers. You are not the only one with the need. And don't be shy about asking your district to pay for it.

We find the professional reading in this area rather slim. Unless we overlooked them, there were no titles in the NCTE catalog on ESL teaching. Heinemann has four, aimed at teaching adults and college students to write. Frankly, we have not read them; but Marie Wilson Nelson's *At the Point of Need* (1991) and Llona Leki's *Understanding ESL Writers* (1992) look helpful. We do know that both of these writers have a lot of experience teaching ESL students.

In Tom's school system, most situations involve one or two families' relationships with a school. The principal and the district office find tutors for these kids to help them get started. It is a reasonable request for you to make in similar situations.

Try not to get frustrated. Be as flexible as you can be. And as positive with students having a difficult time of it. They will learn fast. Expect them to. Also, expect them to behave. Don't let them hide behind the language barrier. Respect their language, their culture, their experiences.

Keep these two things in mind. These students can succeed, and excel. They are not second class citizens, not curiosities. They are middle school kids for us to teach.

11) Abused Kids

What do you do when you suspect child abuse? **Report it immediately.** And pray. And maybe cry.

Don't mess around with this one. Just tell your principal, right then. We are talking here about physical abuse and sexual abuse, not verbal abuse, bad though it is. There are only two times when we break the confidence of a student, including revealing the contents of her journal. When we suspect abuse and when there is a hint of suicide.

We talk a little about suicide next. But with abuse, the word is **suspect,** however small the clue. Just report it.

Be aware that abuse happens in every neighborhood in your community. Every neighborhood. You will have to deal with it sooner or later. Probably sooner because abuse cases are increasing in our country at an alarming rate. Crack cocaine has a lot to do with it, but so do the stresses on parents. Sexual abuse does not happen as often as physical abuse, and it is harder to detect. But it happens to boys as well as girls. Family members, friends, and neighbors don't want to see or report abuse. Denial is one of the problems with this horror. Children protect their abusers.

Be aware of the signs of abuse. Our friend Anthony Wright is a counselor at the Bridge, a shelter for abused and neglected children in Albany, Georgia. He says teachers should watch out for these danger signs of physical abuse.

1) Extreme depression, periods when the kid is really down for no reason.

2) Deviant behavior to get your attention. "Keep in mind," Anthony says, "these are extremes."

3) Tenderness to the touch. If you pat the kid on the back and he winces, check for unusual bruises. Especially bruises where he wouldn't get them in youthful horseplay.

4) Extreme introversion. The kid who is just abnormally shy and alone.

5) Extreme restlessness.

6) An unwillingness to go home. This is the kid who hangs around school and you know she just doesn't want to go home.

7) Exaggerated reactions to reprimands. If he acts like he's afraid of being hit, he probably has been.

Tony tells us that in cases of sexual abuse, some of the same symptoms apply, introversion, depression, restlessness, not wanting to go home. And the kid will be a lot more intense emotionally. It's the kind of situation where you know something is badly wrong with the kid. You may not know or suspect the cause, but you know when something is wrong with one of your students. Report it.

12) Suicide

This is serious. At the first hint of a possible suicide, **report it.** All kinds of kids try it, girls and boys, good kids and bad kids, rich ones and poor ones, in about equal proportions. Assume nothing. Listen to the kids and watch what they are doing, knowing it is possible.

Listen for cries of help. "I can't take it any more." "I'm no good to anybody." "Nobody will miss me." Watch for unusual behavior. When a kid neglects her appearance or health. Unusual tiredness, isolating, sudden changes in school performance or attendance, angry outbursts, restlessness and irritability, running away from home, cutting or burning herself, being preoccupied with death. Often your first clue will be in her journal. We know, a lot of weird behavior kind of goes with middle school, doesn't it? But watch for extremes. And if a kid says or hints she might kill herself, believe her.

We heard Dr. Harry Finlayson, principal of Newtown Junior High in Newtown, Pennsylvania, speak at NMSA a few years ago. His school, like every school, has had tragic experiences with suicide. He recommends your school do two basic things—have a plan to make teachers and administrators aware of the danger signs, with an assessment team to determine the seriousness of the threat when reports are made and clear procedures for getting kids help, and have a school-wide plan for responding to a suicide when it does happen. Certainly we can do no less than try to help a suicidal student. At the same time, we need ways of helping the survivors, students and teachers, work through their shock, grief, guilt, and fear when a suicide happens in our school. And a prompt, thoughtful school-wide response can stop other suicides from happening. One of the terrifying things about suicide in adolescents is that one can trigger others. The school's response is important.

You may want to contact Dr. Finlayson directly for more detailed suggestions on what your school can do.

Dr. Harry J. Finlayson
Newtown Junior High School
116 Richboro Rd.
Newtown, PA 18940
1-215-968-7200

13) Standardized Tests

Sometimes the tail really does wag the dog. Frank Smith (1986) refers to the "tyranny of testing" in our country's educational life; and we agree there really does seem to be no relief from externally imposed, inappropriate, threatening, mindless tests. They take up hours and hours of precious class time. They scare everybody in their sphere of influence from superintendents who don't want their school systems to look bad in the paper to principals under the gun to improve test scores to parents concerned about how Johnny is ever going to make it into college (or out of elementary school) to teachers bewildered by ranks of scores and a blizzard of jargon to the kids who spend the hours and hours bubbling in bubbles or writing uninteresting drivel on demand. Why so much testing? "There is one reason only for the insistent control of programmatic instruction and tests in classrooms. The reason is **lack of trust.** Teachers impose programs and tests when they do not trust children to learn, and politicians and administrators impose programs and tests when they do not trust teachers to teach." Frank Smith again. And we need to think about that as teachers, too, not just when we are irritated by the latest basic skills test or curriculum test or graduation test or promotion test imposed on our kids and us. Do you trust them to learn or not? Think about it.

Nevertheless, standardized tests are a fact of life, as our administrators and the testing directors in our local school systems tell us. As long as they go with the territory, how can we best deal with them? First, **don't be afraid of them.** If your kids are reading a lot and writing a lot and enthusiastic about learning, they will do just fine. We make you this promise about standardized tests and natural language arts learning: Students taught this way will do at least as well as traditional, skills-based classes taught to the tests. In other words, they will do no worse than they have been doing anyway. Cold comfort perhaps. We all want our kids to shine every time with every experience, even tests foreign to the way we teach and how we know kids learn. Finally, these tests are only a small part of school life. They are not the be-all and end-all of your teaching career.

Secondly, **learn all you can about the tests.** Go to the workshops. Read the material from the publishers of the tests. In Tom's state, the testing authorities provide manuals on various tests' objectives with full explanations of how the tests work. Copies of raters manuals for the writing tests have even been provided. A lot of teachers worry themselves and their kids sick over the tests, but don't do their homework. Read the stuff. Study whatever material is available on a particular test that will help you put your kids at ease with it. And make sure they know what the test is testing and the kinds of things they'll have to do on it. Volunteer to rate or score tests or review test items where such help is requested. Learn all you can about standardized tests so you can help your kids do their best on them. **Then get your students ready to deal with the practical problems of the paperwork of tests.** Don't scare them to death. Just tell them how to take a long and boring test and show off best what they know. Test anxiety is the middle school kid's worst enemy in these situations. Have number two pencils on hand and other materials that may be called for. Work with your principal to have the best setting for the test, hopefully in your room where students are comfortable, and with a reasonable schedule and plenty of breaks. We know one school that improved their scores twenty percent on the state mandated writing tests by having juice and cookie breaks at appropriate times. The worst situations we've seen are students crowded into the auditorium, cafeteria, even the gym to take a big test monitored by strangers. Our job is to help students be as confident and comfortable as they can be in the testing situation.

Use the information tests give you. After all, you and your kids spend a lot of time getting that information. We don't suggest you take the test makers' descriptions too literally. A "composition" score on a test with no writing, for example, should be immediately suspect. But look closer and see what is really being compared among groups of students. Is this information about your classes you can use in your teaching?

But remember. **Teaching is always more important than testing.**

Middle school language arts teaching is an exciting, challenging, wonderful job—but it's not easy. In some schools—and in all schools at some times—it can feel like missionary work. It's not a job to do alone. If you are new at it, or an old pro trying to do it by yourself, get yourself a buddy. We may or may not agree philosophically or in methodology, but we need each other's support. And remember.

Don't be discouraged.

Don't give up.

Don't lose your sense of humor.

Be good to yourself.

References

Leki, L. (1992). *Understanding ESL writers.* Portsmouth, NH: Heinemann.

Mayher, J.S. (1990). *Uncommon sense.* Portsmouth, NH: Heinemann.

Myers, W.D. (1988). *Fallen angels.* New York: Scholastic.

Nelson, M.W. (1991). *At the point of need.* Portsmouth, NH: Heinemann.

Smith, F. (1986). *Insult to intelligence.* Portsmouth, NH: Heinemann.

Wheelock, A. (1992). *Crossing the tracks.* New York: The New Press.

13

Extensions: Sources and Resources

"Tis the reader that makes the book good."
—Ralph Waldo Emerson

Tom and I knew there would be some readers who would want to read more. So this chapter includes all those sources we promised in earlier chapters that we would refer to later. And it includes some resources we thought would help you explore more ways to create meaningful language experiences in the middle grades.

I've organized this as an annotated bibliography, chapter by chapter, with anywhere from 5–15 sources per chapter. Each section lists sources in an order corresponding to the order those topics are discussed in the chapter. Unless I've said otherwise, the books are in paperback. We hope you'll pick up further resource suggestions from the bibliographies by the writers and authors we mention here as well as some additional ideas for your classrooms.

Chapter 1—A Language Arts Ecology: Natural Language in the Middle

The resources I'm going to mention here focus on natural learning, too, and they talk more about how to foster such learning in language arts, how to create and sustain an effective ecology. There are very few books out on language arts and middle grades exclusively, and some may not be about doing language naturally. The best books, as we've said, ones you want if you don't already have them are:

Atwell, N. (1987). *In the middle: Writing, reading, and learning with adolescents.* Upper Montclair, NJ: Boynton/Cook. 295 pp.

This book broke open and made wonderfully visible the world of middle graders learning language. Coming from the reading and writing traditions of Donald Graves and Lucy Calkins, Nancie Atwell brought alive for eighth graders the concepts of writing process, writing and reading workshops, and mini-lessons. Her book is really a very graphic story of how she turned her eighth grade English class in Boothbay Harbor, Maine, into a natural place to read literature, write, revise, conference, keep learning logs, and publish works. Her book will show you one way to set up your classroom as a workshop and how to keep track of student programs and growth in such an environment. The book is full of usable ideas and formats for transforming your own curriculum if you're ready for a metamorphosis of your own.

Atwell, N. (1997). *In the middle: New understandings about writing, reading, and learning (2nd ed.)*.

In this very updated version of *In the Middle*, Atwell shares her insights on writing and reading which she gained while working with middle schoolers since the first edition. Refined versions of reading and writing workshops along with an extensive set of materials in the appendices offer much assistance to the teacher who wishes to create, or recreate, the language arts classroom.

You might also be interested in checking out Nancie Atwell's sequel to *In the Middle*. This book of essays is entitled *Side by Side* (1991, by Heinemann, 184), and she shares more ideas for classroom teaching in it.

Rief, L. (1992). *Seeking diversity: Language arts with adolescents*. Portsmouth, NH: Heinemann. 299 pp. Hardback.

Linda Rief is also an eighth grade English teacher. She's also teaching in New England, in fact, in a junior high in New Hampshire. Well-written, entertaining, and very informative, Rief's book on her classroom gives us another set of pictures, another story of a language arts environment where eighth graders and she read, write, and learn naturally. Like Atwell's book, Rief's shows us one way to create reading and writing workshops, how she handles mini-lessons, and how she keeps track of student work and evaluates it. Rief's book includes also some projects she and her students do together: integrated units, art integrated with language, and the reading of whole class books meaningfully. Her chapters on portfolios are very helpful. Like Atwell's approach, Rief's is helpful for getting ideas if you're a teacher willing to learn with your students.

What makes both these books so unique is not only the approach used for learning language, but the clear message that the heart of success in growth and learning lies in the teacher's interactions with his students. Other books we'll mention will tell you this; these two books **show** you this inescapable part of teaching naturally. The middle grades teacher teaching language naturally is a special kind of person.

It seems that when practicing teachers write about the whole language movement, the piece appears more in the form of an article, a column, or a chapter in a book. Here's a good example:

Jones, J. (1992). Whole language across the curriculum: Every
 child's success story. *Middle School Journal*, 23(3), 44-48.

Jeanneine very competently describes whole language, but the article's uniqueness lies in the arguments for the appropriateness of whole language for middle level students. Jeanneine reminds us of the need for, and the ability of, kids to see connections and relationships, along with their need for attention to real and relevant issues. Then, pushing further, she argues for extending meaningful communication across the entire curriculum. What's always so good about Jeanneine's columns is true about this one too—it's full of cross-disciplinary whole language examples.

Although not a middle level teacher right now, Tom Liner works almost everyday in classrooms, and his short history and definition of current middle level teaching and whole language will give you a quick view of our roots:

Liner, T. (1992). Curriculum or curricula? Language arts and crafts
 in middle schools. *Midpoints*, 3 (2). 12 pp.

Tom wrote a piece for NMSA's *Midpoints* series a couple of years ago in which he assessed where language arts in the middle grades stands today. It's an occasional paper chronicling the growth of English as a subject through this century until the present rise of whole language, where he then takes on the issues surrounding whole language teaching in the middle: testing, teaming, training teachers, and meeting student needs today. It's also got its own comprehensive bibliography. Tom leaves us feeling that we are making some strides.

There are several texts, not written by the practicing teacher, which are appearing now and which deal with whole language, either K-8 or middle grades alone. The latter is very rare. The one I know is:

Manning, G., Manning, M., & Long, R. (1990). *Reading and writing in the middle grades: A whole language view.* Washington, DC: National Educational Association. 64 pp.

This is a short monograph overviewing the foundation of whole language in learning theory followed by many ideas and suggestions congruent with whole language principles appropriate to middle grades. In its brief 64 pages, the authors cover writing and reading workshops, and a section on trouble-shooting concludes the text.

Some of the K-8 whole language books might still be helpful to a middle grades teacher. Most ideas are adaptable, so don't let that scare you off. If this doesn't bother you, and you're one of those people who doesn't have a lot of time, then just go straight for one of the classics on this philosophy of teaching language:

Goodman, K. (1986). *What's whole in whole language.* Portsmouth, NH: Heinemann. 79 pp.

Laid out in a relatively brief, easy to read format, Goodman's book tells us how whole language helps kids grow healthy language abilities. He covers some language theory, the reality and promise of school as a setting for learning language, the definition of whole language, and most important, who the teacher is, or needs to be, in this kind of classroom.

Some others you might check out are:

Cambourne, B. (1988). *The whole story: Natural learning and the acquisition of literacy in the classroom.* Auckland, New Zealand: Ashton Scholastic. 207 pp.

One of the earlier books on teaching and learning language naturally. Tom Liner swears by this one. It's easily readable and a very good balance between theories of learning, reading, and writing and practical suggestions on getting started transforming your classroom, your curriculum, yourself, and ultimately, your students. The examples are elementary grades, but the message is for every level, including the middle.

Manning, G., & Manning, M., (Eds.). (1989). *Whole language: Beliefs and practice, K-8.* Washington, DC: National Education Association. 242 pp.

This book really does focus on the early years of literacy development, but, if you've got the time for it, it might be interesting to explore your middle graders' literacy development as a child: the negative effects of phonics instruction; the positive effects of using invented spelling; why reading comprehension is stressed, and not reading skills. Other authors write on literature, journals, what whole language is, even about the educational needs of such teachers. This tends to be more discussion and theory rather than a sharing of ideas and active experiences.

Routman, R. (1991). *Invitations: Changing as teachers and learners, K-12.* Portsmouth, NH: Heinemann. 502 pp.

While Routman's first book, *Transitions* (1988), focused on defining whole language in the context of the early grades, in this book, she shares how the focus on whole language at all levels (including middle) empowers both teachers and students to learn. Routman's underlying focus lies on "change." So she talks about the stages of becoming a whole language teacher, and often stops and gives step by step procedures for how you might get started using literature discussion groups, how you might create an encouraging environment for writers, and how you might schedule and manage journal-writing. Important to the middle grades teacher is her section on "Integration" (chapter 12). Welcome to anyone will be the chapter on whole language and the learning disabled student (chapter 14).

Weaver, C. (1990). *Understanding whole language: From principles to practice.* Portsmouth, NH: Heinemann. 309 pp.

Weaver's book could fall squarely into the K-12 category. It's a highly theoretical perspective on whole language rather than an activity-rich book. It's for those of you who really want to understand not only the idea of whole language better, but its placement inside a tradition of pedagogy in American schools. It's for those of you who would like to read more about the research basis for both whole-to-part teaching as well as about part-to-whole approaches (phonics as an example). Phonics, comprehension, and evaluation get the same scholarly, theoretical review. There are portraits of whole language teachers scattered throughout the book.

To see exactly how whole language looks in the middle in classrooms other than Atwell's or Rief's, take a look at this text:

Mills, H., & Clyde, O., (Eds.). (1990). *Portraits of whole language classrooms: Learning for all ages.* Portsmouth, NH: Heineman. 307 pp.

Of the 16 chapters in the book, four deal directly with 5-8th grades, while two, the "portraits" of the resource room and an ESL classroom, contain examples of middle grades learners working within a whole language framework. One of the other portraits (Betty Slesinger's piece) explains how a whole language approach works in the middle grades remedial classroom. Although one portrait contains a classroom of mixed 4th and 5th graders, the teacher, Thom Wendt of Grove City, Ohio, details a very usable integrated unit resting on whole reading and writing principles. For a fully student choice driven whole language classroom, check out Eric Stone's description of his fifth grade in Owen County, Indiana.

Yatvin, J. (1994). *Developing a whole language program for a whole school*. Newark, DE: International Reading Association.

Yatvin shares her thinking on constructing a whole language curriculum and how to prepare an entire school environment for a successful implementation of such a program. Although the experiences on which she bases her ideas are not just middle school based, suggestions and guidelines apply well to that level.

Heinemann has published several other good texts on whole language (K-12 or elementary) which seem very good but that I'm less familiar with. A couple of additional helpful texts would be:

Edelsky, C., Altwerger, B., & Flores, B. (1990). *Whole language: What's the difference?* Portsmouth, NH: Heinemann. 120 pp.

Goodman, Y., Hood, W., & Goodman, K. (1991). *Organizing for whole language*. Portsmouth, NH: Heinemann. 408 pp.

You've probably noticed that nearly everyone who's had anything to say about whole language has said it with Heinemann's blessing. Heinemann is a publisher that has promoted the notion and philosophy of whole language a great deal, but there are others. This is another title that I am less familiar with, but which looks helpful and worth learning from:

Hydrick, J. (1991). *Whole language: Empowerment at the chalk face*. New York: Scholastic. 224 pp.

NCTE is another leading publisher of materials on whole language teaching. They often publish collections of articles from its various journals, including affiliate journals, which deal with the topic.

From the New York State English Council:

Blake, R. (Ed.). (1990). *Whole language.* Urbana, IL: National Council of Teachers of English. 160 pp.

From Oregon state's *Oregon English*:

Hardt, U. (Ed.). (1988). *Whole language.* Urbana, IL: National Council of Teachers of English. 77pp.

From the *Virginia English Bulletin*:

Kelly, P., and Self, W. (Eds.). (1991). *Whole language in the English classroom.* Urbana, IL: National Council of Teachers of English. 146 pp.

And finally,

Barbieri, M., & Rief, L. (eds.). *Voices from the middle.* Urbana, IL: National Council of Teachers of English.

This latter title is a new journal published by NCTE specifically focused on middle level language arts. It is a quarterly journal, and the first volume appeared in the 1994–95 year. Should provide excellent coverage and focus on topical middle level issues in English teaching.

Chapter 2—The Middle Schooler

The sources cited at the end of the chapter offer extensive information on the young adolescent, but if you are even more interested in finding out about what young adolescents are going through, or what adolescents in minority groups experience, then here's a few more resources:

Ames, L. B., Ilg, F. L., & Baker, S. M. (1988). *Your ten to fourteen year old.* New York: Delacorte. 346 pp.

The second of this book's three parts covers the development of young adolescents each year from 10 to 14 years old. For each age, the researchers share characteristics of ethical, emotional, social, and identity development. Each year's activities in school are covered too. Part three shares signs of growth in the maturing young adolescent.

Manning, M.L. (1993). Cultural and gender differences in young adolescents. *Middle School Journal, 25* (1), 13–17.

Manning gives us a picture of development and diversity with respect to both gender and culture. A lot of good recent data on the interaction of these factors and the impact on self-esteem, identity, achievement, and self-concept. He ends with some directions for all educators.

Czikszentmihalyi, M., & Larson, R. (1984). *Being adolescent: Conflict and growth in the teenage years.* New York: Basic Books. 322 pp. Hardback.

The authors have put together a comprehensive look at the adolescent's life—from environment, internal feelings, interactions, to change and the move toward adulthood. Many good case examples and crammed full of information to help us understand the modern teen.

Scales, P. (1991). *A portrait of young adolescents in the 1990's.* Chapel Hill, NC: Center for Early Adolescence. 91 pp.

Focused solely on the young adolescent, Scales' book first refreshes us on the developmental characteristics and needs of young adolescents, then the bulk of the book shares the trends and issues shaping young adolescent life currently. Scales covers it all—homelessness, health, mortality, family, and education. A book you can't miss if you teach young adolescents.

Takanashi, R. (Ed.). (1993). *Adolescence in the 1990's: Risk and opportunity.* NY: Teachers College Press.

Takanashi's book offers at least a dozen well-known writers' perspectives on issues of adolescence and schooling. While some of the book does relate more to older adolescence, a number of chapters reference specifically the early adolescence tasks, opportunities and problems generally encountered in the middle grades—key developmental tasks, school-community issues, and models for parent involvement in adolescent education.

There are also a few good sources that just focus on at-risk issues for younger and older adolescents:

AAUW Educational Foundation and National Education Association. (1992). *How schools shortchange girls.* Washington, DC: Author. 116 pp.

While not specifically keyed to development or middle level adolescents, the report nevertheless heightens consciousness about trends and issues in gender equity and schooling. What's also interesting and informative in the report is the breakdown around racial groups and socio-economic class.

AAUW Educational Foundation. (1994) *Hostile hallways.* Washington, DC: Author.

Again, this is not specific to the middle level, but harassment is no stranger to the middle. A potential risk to development that both males and females may experience.

Dryfoos, J. (1990). *Adolescents at risk.* New York: Oxford University Press. 280 pp. Hardback.

This book is about those 10-17 year olds who have a limited chance to grow up as productive adults. Dryfoos studies four high risk categories: delinquency, substance abuse, pregnancy, and school dropouts. She also tells us what works to prevent these risks and what doesn't, ending with some strategies for preventing such adolescent behaviors.

Hechinger, F. (1992). *Fateful choices.* New York: Carnegie Corporation of New York. 255 pp.

What *Turning Points* was to the educational ideas appropriate for young adolescents, *Fateful Choices* is for the health professions. Hechinger defines the at-risk population of 10–15 years olds right away and what conditions make many kids "at risk." The book isn't just a report of how bad it is, however. Its focus is really on prevention of further at-risk situations for adolescents. Hechinger describes existing programs working to alleviate problems and gives us some thoughtful and sound suggestions.

Occasionally, we find an article here or there which relates handling a particular subject to the developmental characteristics of students, 10-14. Often, they **show** us middle graders' growth; they tell the story of growing up in school, and share scenes of that growth with us. *Middle School Journal* authors do really well at this in all curriculum areas. Sometimes, the *English Journal,* too, will focus on real developmental pictures. Some fairly recent pictures from these resources are:

Dickinson, T. (1992). Sitting in Karen's room. *Middle School Journal,* 23(4), 47.

In this brief piece, Tom Dickinson watches a fifth grade classroom, seeking to understand the development of fifth graders and where that fits into middle level teaching. Good classroom dialogue and discussion help make the case that fifth graders are in many ways moving into early adolescence.

Hudson, T. (1987). Odyssey in the middle grades. *English Journal*, 76 (5), 91-92.

A nice piece reminding us that the cognitive development of our middle schoolers affects what we do with literature. Hudson suggests a few ways we can deal with reading in order to maximize enjoyment and understanding. It helps to have a good memory of Homer's *Odyssey* while reading the article, as Hudson compares the teachers' year and experiences with middle schoolers with Odysseus' journeys and trials. Fun to read.

Milgram, J. (1986). The inner world of the sixth grader. *Middle School Journal*, 18 (2), 12-13.

This piece imaginatively enters the private thoughts of nine sixth graders seated in a social studies lesson at school. Milgram makes his point dramatically with realistic pictures of physical, emotional, and social concerns and the impact of these concerns on middle schoolers' abilities and their willingness to participate academically.

Chapter 3—The Middle School Language Arts Teacher

A list of additional resources that discuss good teachers, or good language arts teachers at the middle level would probably double the size of the book. I'm offering you only a few of our favorites in this section. One I mentioned at the end of chapter two is one that talks about the whole language teacher. While it's not specifically on the middle grades teacher, what Sharon Rich describes is perfectly pertinent for teachers at this level:

Rich, S. (1989). Restoring power to teachers: The impact of 'whole language.' In G. Manning, & M. Manning (Eds.), *Whole language: Beliefs and practices, K-8* (pp. 220-228). Washington, DC: National Education Association.

"The true whole language teacher demonstrates that the answers to theory-to-practice questions do not reside in a text but within the self." Rich lays it on the line immediately. Whole language teachers must be strong; they are knowledgeable, independent, and caring. They reject pre-planned curricula, and together with kids, they develop their own. They're often swimming against the traditional school currents so they need their strengths to continue traveling upstream. Rich is blunt, too, about the challenges, but makes the job of the whole language teacher so appealing and heroic, it's hard to resist making the transition.

Like some of the best material on student development, some of the best profiles of middle grades teachers are just that—portraits that really show us a good middle grades teacher or middle grades language arts teacher interacting with students and materials, sustaining all the while a good learning ecology. In chapter 3, Tom described many of these teachers from his experiences. Others are to be found in some series in *Middle School Journal* or *English Journal*.

Liner, T. (1990-91). Being among them. Column in *Middle School Journal,* 21 (5). And 22 (1, 3, and 5).

The four articles include one written by Tom Liner in volume 21 before the column was actually created for volume 22. Tom profiles a science teacher, a math teacher, a principal, and a language arts teacher. He spends time with them all in these four articles, and his stories capture the excellence of the contemporary middle level educator. Even though not all of these are language arts teachers, fundamental qualities of good middle level teaching—their enthusiasm, love for students and deep appreciation of the age group, their knowledge, flexibility, humor—come through on each piece, outlining the characteristics that make teaching in the middle successful.

And Tom's portraits were followed by more from Terry Martin the next year:

Martin, T. (1991–92). Being among them. Column in *Middle School Journal,* 23 (1, 3, and 5).

Of Terry's three columns, two describe middle grades language arts and reading teachers. They are energy-filled women who know how to work with students, their teams, and integration of subjects into meaningful active-learning experiences for students. Again, great pictures of the kinds of courage, spontaneity, and sound practice that realize Sharon Rich's image of the whole language teacher.

And, finally from *Middle School Journal's* third columnist on middle level teachers:

Mason, D. Being among them. Column in *Middle School Journal,* 24 (1, 3, and 5).

Teachers with a difference—DeWayne Mason's middle level teachers show us other ways of working effectively with young adolescents in ESL classrooms and with at-risk populations. Yet the same teaching themes are there for the middle grades language arts teacher to learn from—the organization, the sensitivity to kids' needs, and relevant learning topics in classrooms.

Middle School Journal has long had a column written by middle level teachers for other middle level teachers. For two years, since its revival in the fall of 1990, readers have been lucky enough to read:

Jones, J. (1990-92). Teacher to teacher. Column in *Middle School Journal*, 22-23 (1-5).

Jeanneine Jones was a language arts/social studies team teacher at Western Middle School for years. Many of her columns are "think-pieces" about issues common to all middle level teachers, but some are about language education and its importance in the total curriculum. At any rate just reading her column opens for us a view of the way sensitive, excellent middle grades teachers think and act.

Other language arts teacher-columnists have written about what it's like to teach middle level students in language arts rooms, too. A good recent column in *English Journal* is:

Nelms, E. (1990-). The middle view. Column in *English Journal*, 79-.

This occasional column probably grew out of the late 1980's "Junior High/Middle School Workshop." Since 1990, it was written by Elizabeth Nelms, a teacher at the P. K. Yonge Laboratory School at the University of Florida. Like Jeanneine, Elizabeth Nelms takes on a number of topics (research in the classroom, literature and themes, testing, responding to writing) and through her perspectives, we see an indirect portrait of another creative, knowledgeable, and sensitive language arts teacher working with middle graders.

And finally, a recent portrait:

Halle, R., & VanAllen, L. (1994). Middle school teachers ARE different. Middle ground. Column in *English Journal*, 83 (5), 85.

If you would rather rely on lists, characteristics and standards describing good middle level teachers, try to get hold of the National Board's *Standards for the Preparation of Early Adolescence English/Language Arts* (1993).

Chapter 4—Building Blocks: Exploring, Interdisciplinary Teaming, and Integrating Curriculum

Most of the sources in the bibliography at the end of Chapter 4 really deserve a look if you're serious about integrated curriculum, interdisciplinary work, teaming, and how the language arts fits into this. A few are repeated here, but most of these are truly just extensions.

George, P., & Lawrence, G. (1982). *Handbook for middle school teaching.* Glenview, IL: Scott Foresman. 360 pp.

I know this may look dated, but this was a book I cut my teeth on as a beginning middle level team teacher and teacher educator. The parts on team teaching are still interesting and good for the emphasis on bonding together as a group. What I was really alluding to in chapter 4 was the chapter on teaming in this book, specifically to the page that outlines a continuum of team types from fairly traditional discipline teams to the most flexible options of interdisciplinary teams integrating all their academic work with themes, problems, or questions. An interesting portrait of possibilities, it's not related specifically to the language arts, but if you're part of a team, or planning to be, it's a clear guide that helps. The text may be out of print, but you can still obtain it from many libraries.

Erb, T., & Doda, N. (1989). *Team organization: Promise-practices and possibilities.* Washington, DC: National Education Association. 128 pp.

While George and Lawrence's little overview gives you a list of possibilities for forming teams, Erb and Doda tell you how to do it, what you need to think about, who to include, and how. The book is full of sample forms to help organize and keep a team on track and full of sound advice on common issues that arise with teaming: reluctant team teachers, staying on task, and working with students.

Dickinson, T., & Erb, T. (Eds.). (1997). *We gain more than we give: Teaching in middle schools.* Columbus, OH: NMSA.

The entire book offers a definitive casebook of articles exploring many facets of teaming at the middle grades. For a glimpse of teachers implementing "whole language across the team," check out the

Butler and Liner article of the same title. The chapter shares the work of several teams as they developed methods for integrating the language arts throughout the interdisciplinary team's curriculum.

Although the following items are theoretical also, and none directly deals with Language Arts and the middle level, they're still good background pieces on the latest ideas in curriculum development at the middle level:

Dickinson, T. (1993). *Readings in middle level curriculum: A continuing conversation.* Columbus, OH: National Middle School Association.

This book was originally based on two back-to-back theme issues focusing on middle level curriculum which the *Middle School Journal* editor pulled together over two years ago. Twenty-one chapters on current curriculum issues at the middle level dominate the text. Reading them will give anyone a good general sense of where middle level curriculum is now and is headed, especially with curriculum integration, or as it's referred to earlier, the "second path." Several pieces on the "don't miss" list include:

Arnold, J. Towards a middle level curriculum rich in meaning, 63-72.

Arnold argues that methodology and process are important in teaching, but they are inextricably bound to content. Arnold advocates a curriculum "rich in meaning" which means dealing with what's worth knowing (knowledge relevant to the needs and interests of young adolescents) and with values. A nice set-up for integration and whole language.

Stevenson, C. You gotta see the game to see the game, 73-82.

"How should the middle level curriculum be?" Stevenson asks, and asserts this is the real question. For him, conditions for a good middle level curriculum begin with "engagement," the heart of authentic learning, or personal investment in intellectual pursuits. Rather than prescribe curricula, Stevenson helps us realize what **needs** middle schoolers have. Responding to these will lead to an appropriate curriculum, and an appropriate natural language classroom.

Brazee, E. and Capelluti, J. Middle level curriculum: Making sense, 143-51.

Both authors embrace the ideas behind Beane's notion of appropriate curriculum for the middle grades, and describe ways to make the transition from traditional curricula to this new paradigm. A good blueprint for a whole school, or for individual change.

Both Brazee and Capelluti have gone on to write even more extensively in integrated curriculum. A recent source I've not read, but which should prove to be cutting edge is:

Capelluti, J. & Brazee, E. (1995). *Dissolving boundaries: Toward an integrative middle school curriculum*. Columbus, OH: National Middle School Association.

And a companion edition of *MSJ* may be the March, 1994 one which contained a new focus section on integrated and interdisciplinary instruction:

Erb, T. (Ed.). (1994). Focus section on interdisciplinary instruction. *Middle School Journal, 25* (4), 3–41.

At least eight pieces detail projects with interdisciplinary work. At least three emphasize language arts, but most to some extent deal with developing language and literacy through thematic or integrated instruction.

Again, I like pictures of the things that are natural learning, the events that should go on in classroom. Just such a series of portraits, even action plans, can be found in:

Arnold, J. (1990). *Visions of teaching and learning: 80 exemplary middle level projects*. Columbus, OH: National Middle School Association. 150 pp.

The subtitle to this tells us just how many projects we'll experience, but probably half of these are integrated or interdisciplinary, too. Thirteen projects are in language arts, twelve under the heading of multidisciplinary or interdisciplinary teaching. They cover computers and language arts, team approaches to reading, desktop publishing, mythology, and more. One of the best interdisciplinary sections is language arts/social studies team teacher Ross Burkhardt's "Interdisciplinary Multi-Media Projects," a unit integrating writing and technology with small group collaboration around a theme chosen by teachers and students together. Many of the 80 portraits are as informative as this one.

Beane, J. (1997). *Curriculum integration: Designing the core of democratic education*. NY: Teachers College Press.

A more updated rendering of Beane's ideas on an integrated curriculum for young adolescent education. Beane explains history and current issues, and chapters four and five offer examples of collaboratively planned questions for curriculum organization and instruction as well as discussion of underlying necessities for integration (building relationships and classroom communities, etc.). Final chapters explore the future for integrated curricula.

Lounsbury, J. (Ed.). (1992). *Connecting the curriculum through interdisciplinary instruction.* Columbus, OH: National Middle School Association. 162 pp.

As John Lounsbury says in the beginning, many of the articles in his book were in *Middle School Journal,* so they comprise a lot of good thinking on teaming and interdisciplinary instruction. He organizes the book around a rationale for interdisciplinary work, planning for it, and portraits of it in action. These profiles contain language arts teachers working with other disciplines. The collection concludes with advice on how to keep the team going.

Pate, E., Homestead, E., & McGinnis, K. (Eds.). (1997). *Making integrated curriculum work: Teachers, students, and the quest for coherent curriculum.* NY: Teachers College Press.

This book is an excellent piece which chronicles the journey of its editors toward a more integrated curriculum over the years they have worked together. It offers a glimpse of the processes behind making theory come alive in practice, and also profiles many strategies for teaching a middle level integrated curriculum.

Stevenson, C., & Carr, J. (Eds.). (1993). *Integrated studies in the middle grades: Dancing through walls.* New York: Teachers College Press. 211 pp.

Chris and Judy open this newest book with a couple of good overview chapters which include a short, concise, very usable rationale for integrated studies and appropriate goals for integrated learning, plus a blueprint for planning. This is helpful, but the best parts are yet to come. Over a dozen existing integrated study units, written and taught by middle grades teachers and teams, follow, and they represent more plans for action. Several are grounded in language arts, but all integrate communication processes meaningfully—through journals, research, poetry, polished written pieces, interviewing, group work, and reading—non-fiction, fiction, and poetry.

And continuing the move toward a truly integrated instruction are those authors in a recent *MSJ* focus section:

Erb, T. (Ed.). (1994). Focus section on teachers' roles in curricular change. *Middle School Journal*, 26 (2).

If you do want to focus on integration and the language arts specifically, although not necessarily just middle level:

Moffett, J. (1992). *Harmonic learning: Keynoting school reform.* Upper Montclair, NJ: Boynton/Cook. 136 pp.

Without really being a direct part of middle level curriculum reform, Moffett's thought and vision, as always, are congruent with many of the same reform themes. This book, too, like his earlier *Teaching the universe of discourse* and *A student-centered language arts and reading, K-13* (with B. Wagner), pushes the necessity of integration—not only of the language arts, but of all the subjects.

Chapter 5—Reading and Writing Connections

Tom has already referred extensively to a very good source for reading and writing connections when he talked about Jane Hansen's *When Writers Read* (1987). There's more to her book than what he says, but he still gives you the heart of it. And that book should give you many ideas for doing reading workshops where reading and writing make sense together. If you're still working with basals but are convinced you should make your move, there is a recent short piece in *Middle School Journal* that can help you think about how to do more of what Hansen advocates:

Barclay, K., & Lane, J. (1993). Reading, writing, thinking, and change. *Middle School Journal*, 24 (5), 37-43.

Both these educators describe the shift from a basal text and separate skills teaching approaches to a whole language environment where writing and reading workshops exist. What is really interesting is not only the transformation of the curriculum, but the positive reaction of the students to the changes.

You might want to know more about another source Tom mentions, especially if you're on your way to change, or even if you already have metamorphosed:

Gere, Anne Ruggles (Ed.). (1985). *Roots in the sawdust.* Urbana, IL: National Council of Teachers of English. 238 pp.

I use this one a lot in my content area reading and writing class at Wabash College. It makes a good case for how "writing to learn" can help learning in all subjects, but examples from all kinds of disciplines (science, math, philosophy) make perfectly clear how you might incorporate the book's ideas across the team's work. Gere's got favorite techniques that differ a little from Tom's in Chapter 5 and that will add to the ones he's taught you: dialectics, unsent letters, scenarios, and admit slips are some of them.

There are a number of content area reading and writing books out there, even some for just middle, or middle and secondary, that will give you more ideas on writing and thinking about a topic before you read about it. They're usually called "pre-reading" or "anticipation" techniques. Of course, as Tom says, a lot of the ideas he mentions (webbing or semantic mapping, for instance) can be used in the middle or at the end of an activity as a kind of post-reading response. Here's a few others that may help you add to your bank of ideas:

Duffy, G. (Ed.). (1990). *Reading in the middle school* (2nd ed.).
Newark, DE: International Reading Association. 235 pp.

Duffy's authors hone in on the middle level; in fact, the first four chapters lay out middle level education foundations (development, management, and organization). Then we get to reading and writing suggestions in subsequent chapters where you'll find not only classroom ideas, but broader team, school, and staff change suggestions.

Ruddell, M. (1993). *Teaching content reading and writing.* Boston: Allyn and Bacon. 419 pp. Hardback.

This is one of the best reading/writing content area books I've seen ever. It's very much an integrated reading/writing strategy book, and as such, Ruddell covers a lot of good "how to's": double entry journals in all content areas, journals, learning logs, group reading and mapping, reading response groups, portfolios, and other authentic assessments. Good sections on middle schools and interdisciplinary teaming along with sections on literacy and gender, multicultural, bilingual, and exceptionalities ensure the book's usefulness.

Several other resources offer some suggestions for melding reading and writing which would help your reading workshops run smoothly:

Brown, J., Quirk, B., & Stephens, E. (Eds). (1988). *A two-way street: Integrating reading and writing, middle school edition.* Urbana, IL: National Council of Teachers of English. 93 pp.

A large sized paperback filled with book descriptions which are followed by possible discussion or pre-writing questions, recommendations for handling the text, and other suggested writing projects for each book. Plot summaries accompanying each book are helpful for the teacher, too.

Dyson, A. (1989). *Collaboration through writing and reading.*
Urbana, IL: National Council of Teachers of English. 284 pp.

This is a collection of seven lengthy chapters, all the result of the meeting of an interdisciplinary group of experts on reading and writing. The group explored the relationship between the processes. The aim was to point the way toward the integration of language arts. Many chapters are theoretical; the Moffett piece suggests activities which combine reading and writing.

Hart-Hewers, L., & Well, J. (1990). *Read it in the classroom!*
Portsmouth, NH: Heinemann. 126 pp.

A practical "how to" book which lays out clear examples and suggestions for basing classroom reading on real books, and the role of writing in response to literature. A large part of the book deals with integrating all the subjects around themes, and yearly plans founded on such broad integration fill the last part of the text.

Parsons, L. (1989). *Response Journals.* Portsmouth, NH: Heinemann. 96 pp.

Don't skip Parson's first chapter on what the response journal is. It's not the tired old diary form of journal-keeping at all, and he is very clear about when, where, and how to use this kind of journal. In fact, these questions are answered throughout the rest of the book in relation to both reading and responding to books and media particularly. Parsons populates the text with a variety of samples and formats easily adaptable. Equally usable are his chapters on leading conferences and evaluating the response journal without making it a turn-off. A very handy book for planning your reading workshop.

Chapter 6: Book Stuff: The Ins and Outs of Outside Reading and Reading Inside

Tom tells you in this chapter about all the ways to get interesting literature for kids to choose from for their own reading goals. And that's the way it should be—a room (or rooms if you're a team integrating curriculum) full of books from YA literature to classics. Here's a few more sources to help your collection grow:

Nilson, Eileen Pace. (1991). *Booklist for junior high and middle school students* (8th ed.). Urbana, IL: National Council of Teachers of English. 342 pp.

Tom mentions this one in particular when he's giving you the address to NCTE in chapter 6. It's a good recent resource handbook superior to the booklists in most catalogues because it's annotated. Without necessarily seeing the book itself, you can usually tell from reading Nilson's annotations if the book will fill a gap by being on the shelves in your room. The book is sectioned by genre or topic categories for ease of use. Another edition exists now besides the one that Tom talks about:

Webb, C.A. (1993). *Your reading: A booklist for junior high and middle schools* (9th ed.). Urbana, IL: NCTE. 250 pp.

Two more sources of lists that I have not used but which are recommended by Karen Wood are:

Reed, A. (1988). *Comics to classics: A parent's guide to books for teens and preteens.* Newark, DE: International Reading Association.

Teen's favorite books: Young adult choices, 1987-1992. (1992). Newark, DE: International Reading Association.

And there are some more annotated lists, with even more focused listings:

Stenslund, A. (1979). *Literature by and about the American Indian.* Urbana, IL: National Council of Teachers of English. 382 pp.

This annotated bibliography is still a useful resource. The bibliography sections cover myth and legend, fiction, biography and autobiography, music and art, as well as traditional and contemporary life and customs. For each section, Stenslund prepared a separate middle/junior high section.

Bishop, R.S. (Ed.). (1994). *Kaleidoscope: A multicultural booklet for grades K–8.* Urbana, IL; National Council of Teachers of English.

A very recent release which I've not had a chance to see but every preview description sounds as if the resource will be extremely helpful even if there will be a great deal focused on younger children.

You might ask your librarian for several of these sources below although the first two are easily seen by reading **English Journal** fairly frequently:

"Booksearch" column in *English Journal*;
The ALAN Review;
Hornbook;
Children's Literature in Education;
The Wilson Library Bulletin;
School Library Bulletin.

Any of the companies that Tom mentions in chapter 6 will list many of the books he mentions, or that Nilson and Davis do, on their booklists. One other word here about the *Write Source* catalogue that Tom talks about: they have a good multicultural literature section.

Don't forget when you are looking for both ideas for teaching literature and titles to check some of the texts for adolescent literature, such as:

Monseau, V., & Salver, G. (Eds.). (1992). *Reading their world: The young adult novel in the classroom.* Upper Montclair, NJ: Boynton/Cook. 200 pp.

A special section on "Teaching the Young Adult Novel" offers a good set of suggestions and essays on thought-provoking issues; cultural diversity, gender, and censorship are among them. The other two sections include articles discussing the legitimate rationale for reading YA literature, and several YA writers describe their processes of writing novels for young people.

Stover, L. (1992). Must boys be boys and girls be girls? Exploring gender through reading young adult literature. In N. McCracken & B. Appleby (Eds.). *Gender issues in the teaching of English* (pp. 93-110). Portsmouth, NH: Heinemann.

This is an excellent piece to help guide you to select gender-fair YA literature for use in your classroom. Stover analyzes a number of recent books and gives suggestions for guiding discussions on gender issues.

Tom mentions a couple of books that would help you on censorship issues as you continue to fill your room with books.

Davis, J. (Ed.). (1979). *Dealing with censorship.* Urbana, IL: National Council of Teachers of English. 228 pp.

These essays cover various types of censorship cases and give advice for, and excellent models of, ways to prepare for challenges to your and your students' rights to read.

Moffett, J. (1988). *Storm in the mountains: A case study of censorship, conflict, and consciousness.* Carbondale, IL: Southern Illinois University Press.

In this book, Moffett returns to Kanawha County many years after the censorship issues surrounding the use of his *Interaction* series about 20 years before. The book is an attempt to come to grips with the psychology behind the book censors as well as the politics that allow such occurrences. An interesting concept he introduced for most readers was "agnosis," or the "not-wanting-to-know" (p. 167) reasoning behind some censorship problems.

Reichman, H. (1990). *Censorship and selection.* Chicago: American Library Association. 140 pp.

Reichmann's book updates us on the recent target areas for censorship: global education, witchcraft, creationism, and secular humanism join with traditional targets like sex, profanity, politics, racism, and sexism. Good sections on getting prepared for attacks on students' rights to read and teachers' academic freedom, plus some helpful warnings against self-censorship.

Still, no matter how many books support your reading workshop, or how wisely you select, you'll be glad to know there are other resources that have good suggestions for teacher-student interactions with books. Tom mentions collages in chapter 6. There's an older book, but a favorite of mine, that's a great resource for ideas for relating reading and visual material:

Hawley, R., & Hawley, I. (1974). *Writing for the fun of it.* Amherst, MA: ERA Press. 107 pp.

This book was an early attempt to link the values exploration movement with early writing process approaches. Full of creative ideas for gathering and organizing materials for writing and reading, it contains a very pertinent section for this chapter. Chapter 5, "Scissors and Glue Activities," outlines ideas for creating "self collages," "clipped poems," "theme collages," "literature collages," "story collages," "picture theater," and the really involving and interesting "fantasy wall." I'm sure it's out of print by now, but again, a good library would have it.

Roser, N. & Martinez, M. (Eds.). (1995). *Book talk and beyond: Children and teachers respond to literature*. Newark, DE: International Reading Association.

While this book's chapters (written by other authors) offer discussions about teaching a variety of children, sometimes including those bordering on becoming young adolescents, the ideas presented here are perfectly applicable in middle grades language arts. The book abounds with examples of structuring and running literature circles, book clubs, and helping students work with story talk, or meaningful conversations about real literature.

Wilhelm, J. (1997). *"You Gotta BE the Book": Teaching engaged and reflective reading with adolescents*. NY: Teachers College Press.

Through observing the reading interactions and engagement of several of his good middle level readers with books over time, Wilhelm develops theory for teaching literature out of his intellectual engagement with his students' experiences. Part of the book details his own early questions about student readers and non-readers; for example, what makes a good reader read, and can those attitudes and conditions be fostered for more reluctant readers. In the latter half of the text, Wilhelm shares his ideas for actively involving all students more in reading literature: emphasizing visualization (art); using drama in various ways; and using various types of reflective responses. The text is an excellent resource as well as a powerful model for pursuing meaningful classroom research with students.

Some other good ideas could come from journals and books devoted just to literature. As you read them, keep in mind that nothing should go on that does not help kids naturally learn:

Carter, C., and the Committee on Classroom Practice. (1985). *Literature—news that stays news: Fresh approaches to the classics*. Urbana, IL: National Council of Teachers of English. 120 pp.

A collection of brief essays describing unique approaches to teaching classical literature in K-college classrooms. At least three interesting units affect middle level learning: one on the *Odyssey,* another on *Romeo and Juliet,* and a final one on teaching *Animal Farm.*

Davis, J., & Davis, H. (1989). *Books for the junior high years*. Urbana, IL: National Council of Teachers of English. 115 pp.

One of those rare focuses on just the middle, this is a publication of Southeastern Ohio Council of Teachers of English and NCTE. The book is an accumulated wealth of articles (24) discussing issues and ideas in teaching many books that are popular with young adolescents.

English Journal (1991). 80 (1). Focus section on literature in the
   middle.

Six pieces especially for the middle grades teacher try to deal with the teaching of classics all the way to enticing reluctant readers to read. A good piece on nonfiction in the middle rounds out the group.

Schullstrom, F. (1990). *Expanding the canon.* Urbana, IL: National
   Council of Teachers of English. 77 pp.

These are articles from the *English Journal* in the late 1980's, all focusing on the use of multicultural and ethnic literature. Many sample lesson narratives here are high school, but two on teaching Native American tales and on teaching from an Afrocentric perspective apply to the middle level.

Finally, all of us are concerned about our reluctant readers. The beauty of integrated and natural learning is that it can be so appealing to these readers you want especially to reach. One old source, that luckily gets constantly revised and reprinted, shares a unique plan for encouraging hostile readers:

Fader, D., with Duggins, J., Finn, T., & McNeil, E. (1976). *The new
   hooked on books* (2nd ed.). New York: Berkeley Books. 294 pp.

I'll never forget Fader's twin assumptions for enticing reluctant readers—"saturation" and "diffusion." And that's what you do, although Fader does give us guidelines for setting up such a flexible reading program. One of the best parts, too, is the booklist at the end, yet another source for book orders for relevant reading.

Related, but shorter, is:

Wood, K. (1993). Promoting lifelong readers across the curriculum.
   Middle School Journal, 24(5), 63-66.

Karen Wood has long written a column for *Middle School Journal* called "Out of Research—Into Practice." In this column she writes about proven principles for encouraging all middle grades readers' positive attitudes toward reading. Briefly she gives us pointers to encourage student reading, then shares ideas for integration and for keeping track of selected reading. By the way, this piece is another good source for middle grades literature titles from sources like NCTE, IRA, and other major publishers.

Chapter 7—Writing: The Private Self

It's a little hard to separate these two chapters on writing, but anything I've found useful or think will be helpful to you for "expressive" writing, for "getting it down," for the kind of writing that's very personal, like poetry, or journals, and for sensitively responding to those writings, will be in this section. There's a lot out there on writing. We won't come anywhere close to covering it all, so again these are just our favorites, the ones that have helped us and the teachers and students we've worked with.

One of Tom's favorites on writing and the writer is really a must for young writers to read and savor:

Bradbury, R. (1990). *Zen in the art of writing*. New York: Bantam. 150 pp.

In a wonderfully readable book, Bradbury describes his growth as a writer—his apprenticeship and his slow path to his own originality. Best of all, he shares a wealth of his own personal strategies that worked to free the original writer inside. An entertaining and teachable life story for any young aspiring writer.

Tom talks a lot about journals in the early part of the chapter. One of the best books I know of about journals is:

Fulwiler, T. (1987). *The Journal Book*. Upper Montclair, NJ: Boynton/Cook. 416 pp.

While this is not a book about keeping journals at the middle grades per se, there are many suggestions and models any teacher could adapt to the classroom. What's really enlightening are the examples of how journals are used in other disciplines. Like Gere's book *Roots in the Sawdust*, Fulwiler offers all kinds of suggestions teams could benefit from.

Fulwiler, T. (1967). *Teaching with writing*. Upper Montclair, NJ: Boynton/Cook. 158 pp.

Strong on journals and writing to learn. Although aimed at high school or college, it's got some ideas for all teachers. Fulwiler not only talks about journals, but each chapter on the writing process models the journal as a teaching tool.

One of Tom's favorites, focused on journals, is:

Goldberg, R. (1986). *Writing down the bones.* Boston: Shambala.
    171 pp.

An enjoyable book for journal writers. The subtitle is "Freeing the Writer Within", and for the teacher using journals, it's not only full of potential topics and directions to go in to begin that process of freeing, but it's full of writing wisdom. Goldberg coaches you in each chapter to think, feel, and write out the hidden words and images of your own experiences.

Several general purpose writing process texts have especially good ideas for personal writing of all kinds;

Kirby, D., & Liner, T., with Vinz, R. (1988). *Inside out: Developmental strategies for teaching writing* (2nd ed.). Upper Montclair, NJ: Boynton/Cook, 271 pp.

Although this book covers the bases on the writing process, I have always found it especially helpful for ideas for building confidence in writing, for dealing with journals, and for enticing kids to write poetry. The authors treat these topics very sensitively. Supposed to cover middle and high school, and, for once, that advertisement is perfectly true; it really is appropriate for the middle grades.

Romano, T. (1982). *Clearing the way.* Portsmouth, NH: Heineman.
    191 pp.

Another book that's very good on handling the process approach to writing, although it is mainly focused on high schools. Romano is easy to read and his ideas are adaptable, as are Liner's and Kirby's, to the middle level. Tom Liner says this is very strong on journals and especially how not to get trapped by problems grading them.

Before I move on to some extensions for poetry ideas, let me mention another very good text that fits well with another role of journal-keeping, and that's the role of writing for learning. Both Fulwiler's and Gere's books are considered "writing to learn" books. Writing for learning can be and is used often in all disciplines which makes writing a natural connector within teams. A pertinent resource is:

Atwell, N. (Ed.). (1990). *Coming to know: Writing to learn in the intermediate grades.* Portsmouth, NH: Heinemann. 233 pp.

This is not a middle level book dealing exclusively with grades 5-8. But it does deal with many examples of teachers working with journals and learning logs in all subjects in the 5th and 6th grades. At least one 6th grade teacher talks about a personalized writing and research focus; a fifth grade teacher talks about learning logs in mathematics. Some teachers in the text already work in team situations; others integrated their academic studies using logs and journals, a kind of "team is me" approach.

And when we're talking about "writing to learn," we're one step away from writing in the content areas, or writing across the curriculum, and there are books that teams can learn from. I'm thinking particularly of:

Tchudi, S., & Huerta, M. (1983). *Teaching writing in the content areas: Middle school/junior high.* Washington, DC: National Education Association. 64 pp.

The authors cover how to develop writing lessons in content areas for middle level classrooms. Then much of the book offers sample lessons and topics to develop into lessons across a variety of subject areas. Evaluation of content area curriculum is also done. A good handbook for your team.

Wilde, J. (1993). *A door opens: Writing in the fifth grade.* Portsmouth, NH: Heinemann. 125 pp.

Portraits of lots of fifth grade writing going on in one New Hampshire teacher's classroom. Should be helpful to those teaching the very young younger adolescent and dealing with a variety of content areas, too.

And now for poetry. It's really not as tough as we remember it. There's a lot of good teaching texts for poetry and young adolescents now. Most connect poetry reading with poetry writing. None of these give poetry a bad name with kids:

Koch, K. (1974). *Rose, where did you get that red?* New York: Vintage Books. 361 pp.

This was one of my favorites as a middle grades teacher because it was so empowering to my seventh and eighth graders as both poetry readers and writers. They could really read John Donne or Shakespeare, hash out their feelings and the poems' meanings for themselves, and write poetry loosely modeled after these great authors. Koch's notion of the "poetry idea" and using it to teach is crystal clear from his essay on the subject in the book. Other Koch titles exist, which are adaptable, too, like *Wishes, Lies, and Dreams,* or *Sleeping on the Wing.*

Grossman, F. (1991). *Listening to the bells: Learning to read poetry by writing poetry.* Portsmouth, NH: Heinemann. 151 pp.

A fine book for growing young poets, Tom says. The author's a poet and lessons and examples are from her work with student poets, mainly in middle school. Chapter by chapter, Grossman leads us through poems composed out of experiences from childhood, personal hopes for the future, poems of the self and of aloneness. In between composed pieces, she asks us to reflect, to write, and to share our own creations on these everyday experiences made rich with the power of poetry.

And handling appropriately the personal writing in the journal, or poetry writing, or just zero-draft or one-time only "writing for learning" pieces is always a question on our minds. For some more ideas, check out:

English Journal. (1990). 79 (5). Focus section on responding to writing.

This is a theme issue devoted primarily to "personal writing" and responding to it appropriately. Nine articles (the ninth is a column, "The Middle View") cover many aspects of response: teachers writing students back, peer readers, self-editing, and shared readings. Articles outline in detail how teachers work with these kinds of approaches. Two of the pieces deal directly with the middle level.

Chapter 8—Writing: The Public Self

Public writing is the writing you want to share with others, especially after it's been drafted, revised, and edited. Tom does a good job of taking us through strategies for doing the writing process in a writing workshop in chapter 8. In addition to the good sources he's already mentioned in the chapter, and in addition to sources like Romano's *Clearing the Way,* Kirby, Liner, and Vinz's *Inside Out,* mentioned in the resources for chapter 7, here's a few more that will help build a writing workshop:

Calkins, L. (1986). *The art of teaching writing.* Portsmouth, NH: Heinemann. 347 pp.

This is still a wonderful book on process, one of the best. I find it especially good on conferencing with student writers. Some vignettes do include middle school/junior high examples; in fact, a good section exists on young adolescents and their writing.

Elbow, P. (1973). *Writing without teachers*. New York: Oxford University Press. 196 pp.

I can't resist placing this one here. Although I read this originally as an "adult and older adolescent" book, I found it immensely adaptable to the middle grades classes I taught. With some adaptations of structure, and with some good modeling of appropriate comments for responding to writing, the kids could listen, react, and talk about writing in very helpful ways. It's simply a sound guide for group work and writing, and full of useful ideas.

Farnan, N., & Fearn, L. (1993). Writer's Workshops: Middle school writers and readers collaborating. *Middle School Journal, 24*(4), 61–65.

This piece is another "picture" of a classroom in operation. The authors give guidelines for response groups which have been adapted to middle level learners. The kids' reactions to doing workshops are interesting and informative. A good chart sets off some helpful types of feedback the authors use in responding to writing.

Frank, M. (1979). *If you're trying to teach kids to write, you've gotta to have this book*. Nashville, IN: Incentive. 218 pp.

An early book on the writing process and letting kids write in a supportive and encouraging climate for writing. Frank deals with all the fears: How do I start? Where do I get writing ideas for my kids? Will I ever run out and what do I do then? What about evaluating all that writing? And what about those kids who hate to write? Her book is filled with good ideas for developing a writing workshop tailored to handle some of these questions and issues.

Macrorie, K. (1985). *Telling writing* (4th ed.) Portsmouth, NH: Heinemann. 312 pp.

Tom says this has always been one of the best books out there on the writing process. It's in the fourth edition now, so that says a lot. What I like is the wealth of good student models throughout the chapters on journals, developing form, sharpening writing, and using conventions. A lot of practical, natural advice. Much of the student writing is college level, but this is a good writing book for the middle level teacher.

Murray, D. (1982). *Learning by teaching*. Portsmouth, NH: Heinemann. 184 pp.

This is Tom's favorite book on the writing process, writing, and teaching writing. Murray covers ownership, conferencing, pre-writing ideas, responding, researching, and the idea of craft in writing.

The best subscription either of us has found, one which will enhance the writing workshop and keep the classroom fresh is:

Curriculum Innovations Group. *Writing!* Columbus, OH: Author.

Published monthly and now in its sixteenth volume year, *Writing!* is a great little classroom magazine. I used it about 13 years ago with seventh and eighth graders and it was a definite asset. Filled with language activities, with ways to connect reading and writing, with relevant kinds of writing focuses each month taught through a process and developmental approach, the magazine can be used flexibly. Classroom sets can be worked in any time that the themes of study and magazine content mesh nicely, or it can just be a regular part of the curriculum. Enough variety allows for effective use either way.

Tom's right about Ken Macrorie's *The I-Search Paper* being a book about doing real research papers with real voices. I would throw in another book which is about real observing and researching, collaboratively, or individually:

Moffett, J. (1992). *Active voice* (2nd ed.). Upper Montclair, NJ: Boynton/Cook. 216 pp.

This is a K-12 writing program based squarely on the notion that writing is a process and also on Moffett's ideas on language and intellectual growth as delineated in his *Universe of discourse* so long ago. While the book is sequenced along the abstraction levels Moffett notes, it's really a book of ideas and approaches that will fit with the many individual needs and levels of writers and readers in a choice-driven classroom.

At the end of chapter 8, Tom gives you a list of publishers of children's and adolescents' writing. It's a pretty thorough list of outlets, and, of course, if you want to publish "in-house," he's given you some good suggestions for how to do that. One resource we've found that handles nearly all our questions for publishing is:

King, L., & Stovall, D. (1992). *Classroom publishing: A practical guide to enhancing student literacy.* Hillsboro, OR: Blue Heron Publishing. 212 pp.

This book is filled with samples of teachers' and students' publishing projects (for real audiences) from K-college levels, across all regions of the country as well as international areas, including all kinds of diverse topics, with all types of publications. Good middle level examples include an ethnography project, historical research, and doing multi-lingual folktale books. The guide is not restricted to language arts; its conception is a "publication across the curriculum" one, making it ideal for teams. The second part of the guide focuses on background to publishing and some resources for publishing student work in addition to the ones that Tom mentioned. All you need to know on publishing is really found here!

Chapter 9: Talking It Out: Oral Language

Several fairly new resources address the role of talking and listening in the classroom. They're worthwhile checking out as you think about integrating oral language naturally into the language environment or across your team's interdisciplinary works:

Booth, D., & Thornley-Hall, C. (Eds.). (1992). *Classroom talk: Speaking and listening activities from classroom-based teacher research*. Portsmouth, NH: Heinemann. 120 pp.

This collection of seventeen essays includes teachers at all levels contributing their projects and activities involving talking and listening in the whole curriculum, including special education and ESL contexts. The overall effect is the creation of many models and examples of using talk to help create the interactive classroom.

Phelan, P. (Ed.). (1989). *Talking to learn*. Urbana, IL: National Council of Teachers of English. 145 pp.

This one, volume 24 in the "Classroom Practices for Teaching English" series, has 24 good articles which are detailed oral language strategies teachers are already using successfully with all ages. But most are very adaptable to classroom settings in the middle.

Hynds, S., & Rubin, D. (Eds.). (1990). *Perspectives on talk and listening*. Urbana, IL: National Council of Teachers of English. 305 pp.

Another volume dealing with the role of talk in writing, conferencing, and with second language learners. The authors share their strategies for keeping track of meaningful talking and listening events in class. Some middle school examples, but other levels can be adapted to the middle.

Sheppard, R. (1985). *Enhancing learning through oral and written expression.* Columbus, OH: National Middle School Association. 108 pp.

This is exclusively a middle level book. Ronnie Sheppard offers many strategies and suggestions for planning to integrate oral language into interdisciplinary curricula as well as into the regular language arts classroom alone. It's best characterized as a content-area and language book. Although it is currently out of print, it is a good resource for those of you working on teams, and worth searching for in a library.

As you probably already know, there's an awful lot out there on small groups and on collaborative and cooperative learning. There are some very basic resources that provide a very sound background on the "how to's" of setting up a good small group structure and good collaborative or cooperative learning situations. Plus, they'll tell you why you should:

Johnson, D., Johnson, R., Holubec, E., & Roy, P. (1984). *Circles of learning: Cooperation in the classroom.* Washington, DC: Association of Supervision and Curriculum Development. 89 pp.

One of the briefer texts on cooperative learning, but inclusive of all the key concepts, processes, and solutions in setting up and managing a cooperative learning based classroom.

Sharan, S., & Sharan, Y. (1976). *Small group teaching.* Englewood cliffs, NJ: Educational Technology Publications. 237 pp. Hardback.

A classic in the field now. Covers assumptions behind using groups, types of groups, and how to organize them. What's still very useful about this book, especially for active learning at the middle level, is the Sharans' linkage of small groups to learning centers, activity centers, role playing and simulations. Theoretical, yet very practical, and still timely.

Slavin, R. (1987). *Cooperative learning* (2nd ed.). Washington, DC: National Education Association. 31 pp.

Another concise book outlining Slavin's basic cooperative learning approaches. Adaptable to the middle grades classroom easily, especially if you want to use specific group forms like STAD, TGT, or Jigsaw variations.

Middle school educators have been writing prolifically about cooperative learning in their classroom, too:

Middle School Journal. (1993) 24 (3).

In this edition, there is a focus section entitled "Cooperation in the Classroom." The section includes five articles examining the latest questions, issues, concerns, and future directions for cooperative learning. One article does deal directly with cooperation and literacy:

Klemp, R., Hon, J., & Shorr, A. Cooperative literacy in the middle school: An example of a learning-strategy based approach. 19–27.

Also in this edition is an ERIC/EECE clearinghouse column on cooperative learning resources:

Rothenberg, D. Cooperative learning in middle level education. 73–74.

While no resources list middle grades language arts documents specifically, other subjects are represented with ideas for potential integration into team approaches.

A slightly older piece provides a sound rationale for cooperative learning, especially for middle grades students:

Jones, M. G. (1990). Cooperative learning: Developmentally appropriate for middle level students. *Middle School Journal*, 22(1), 12–16.

Gail Jones matches the historical middle level goals with those of cooperative learning, showing clearly how compatible this powerful strategy is with the direction of middle level education. If you need a convincing statement on the worth of small group collaboration as a staple in the classroom, this is it.

We don't talk a lot in this book about formal drama and speech in the classroom, but if you're interested, there are a number of sources you could check out. These few seem promising starts:

English Journal. (1993). 82 (2). Focus section on speech in the middle.

In this edition, the editors created a whole section with six articles focusing directly on issues and strategies surrounding talking and listening and its importance in developing 10-14 year old language users. Contributors cover theory and strategies for discussions, doing drama, and structuring classrooms differently to accommodate a curriculum honoring talking and listening effectively.

English Journal. (1987). 76 (5). Focus section on drama.

This focus section centered on drama in the classroom with several articles about dramatic activity in the middle level classroom.

Sklar, D. (1991). *Playmaking: Children writing and performing their own plays*. New York: Teachers and Writers Collaborative. 169 pp. Hardback.

From start to finish, from introducing theater to exploring acting techniques, rehearsing, and performing, Sklar tells, in 20 lessons, stories of putting together dramatic lessons and plays with students in grades 4–12. Sklar's story-lessons focus on student-written plays as well as student-acted ones. Entertaining and fast reading.

Spolin, V. (1963). *Improvisation for the theater*. Evanston, IL: Northwestern University Press. 399 pp. Hardback.

Although this is an old one, it's a really good source for all kinds of informal dramatic activity in the classroom. Kids I've worked with from middle to high school have always really liked this involvement. It is full of exercises for beginning actors, from warm-ups on using the body, to speaking roles and exhibiting emotions. A section on children and theater personalizes the book for younger audiences. A final part on the formal theater describes how to do plays well with young people.

Walker, P. (1993). *Bring in the arts: Lessons in dramatics, art, and storytelling for elementary and middle school classrooms*. Portsmouth, NH: Heinemann. 207 pp.

This is a book about the natural link between drama and visual art and storywriting. Walker starts with seven lessons based on method improvising as a way to introduce and familiarize all students with drama. The next seven lessons build student confidence with visual art using the same approaches. The final part on storytelling relies heavily on the dramatic and artistic techniques as students develop their stories. The realization that storywriting is an art form and is a creative pleasurable process would be hard to escape when using Walker's method.

Most of the books mentioned earlier for small group teaching have sections on problems that come up in group work. Many stop short of discussing issues with gender and talk, or that very sensitive of issues in communicating—dialect differences. These others might give you some insight into such concerns:

McCracken, N., & Appleby, B. (Eds.). (1992). *Gender issues in the teaching of English*. Upper Montclair, NJ: Boynton/Cook. 220 pp.

Although gender issues in literature, writing, researching and teaching English are also considered, there is a separate section on gender and language in general. Nothing in the language section specifically touches middle level, but teachers should be thoughtful about the issues discussed there. A good book to sensitize yourself to the communication issues really existing between the lines and in the air.

Frequently *English Journal* focuses on gender issues in English, and in this one, it is:

Nelson, K. (1990). Gender communication through small groups. *English Journal,* 79 (2), 58-61.

Nelson admits the obvious—that sex-role stereotyping in language arts curriculum still exists in the 1990's. She advocates using the strategies of cooperative learning groups to help focus gender-mixed groups of students on literature and language issues from which discussions on gender roles and equity problems arise. While her examples focus on literature typically used in high schools, much is to be gained by the middle grades teacher who can easily adapt these ideas to a different set of young adult novels.

Even more recently, *English Journal* featured another focus on the issue of gender and talk:

Opalenik, M. (1993). Recognizing and providing an audience for female voices. *English Journal,* 82 (7), 61–62.

Written from an international school and cultural perspective, the article probably deals with the silence of older adolescent girls, yet the themes of silence and disempowerment, if we are to believe the research on 12-year-old girls and "voice," are quite pertinent. Opalenik outlines a strategy she used which worked to help quiet, insecure girls assert their own opinions and voices through their own reading and writing.

Middle level authors are dealing with such themes, however:

Dillow, K., Flack, M., & Peterman, F. (1994). Cooperative learning and the achievement of female students. *Middle School Journal,* 26 (2), 48–51.

The authors give justification for the powerful effect of cooperative learning groups, where talking and listening can be much more collaborative, on female achievement. Not focused on language arts per se, but convincing nevertheless.

Some "must read" background pieces on dialect issues should include:

Butler, M., Chair, and members of the Committee on the CCCC Language Statement. (1974). *Students' right to their own language.* Urbana, IL: National Council of Teachers of English. 32 pp.

From a fall, 1974 edition of *College Composition and Communication*, this resulting paper looks at issues around dialect and affirms the student's right to use his or her own dialect. A classic statement from NCTE still relevant today.

Shuy, R. (1967). *Discovering American dialects*. Urbana, IL: National Council of Teachers of English. 68 pp.

A good background for teachers because this quick overview of the many varieties of American dialects helps us appreciate the integrity of each person's speech. Another classic to be familiar with.

Chapter 10—Messing Around with Media

As you noticed in Chapter 10, many of the pages were overtaken by the computer in the language arts classroom. And much of what's out there now does deal with writing and the computer, both process and collaboration. If you're looking for ideas along those lines, try:

Rodriguez, D., & Rodriguez, R. (1986). *Teaching writing with a word processor, grades 7–13*. Urbana, IL: National Council of Teachers of English. 83 pp.

If you have not worked very much with student writers composing with word processing programs, this book will be helpful. The authors describe how to set up lesson files for computer writing sessions, how to conference using the computer, how to initiate electronic journal-writing, and how to do research and collaborative writing tasks. Always keeps sight of the computer as a tool in the process.

Wresch, W. (Ed.). (1991). *The English classroom in the computer age*. Urbana, IL: National Council of Teachers of English. 145 pp.

Wresch organized these 30 classroom teaching ideas around those with little, more, and substantial computer experience. So wherever your students' levels of familiarity are (and your own), there's a section for you. Anywhere from two to five articles (or lesson descriptions) per section describe middle level appropriate activities integrating language arts with computers. You'll find lessons on doing class poems or computer journals, doing a "create your own adventure" on computers, or using modems for global telecommunications and tapping into electronic networks. A useful list of helpful software concludes the text.

Until you read about Tuttle Middle, you would have thought that this text was futuristic:

Hawisher, G., & LeBlanc, P. (Eds.). (1992). *Re-imaging computers and composition.* Upper Montclair, NJ: Boynton/Cook. 222 pp.

You should know what "virtual" means in computer terms before you pick up this book. Be ready for articles on hypermedia, computer conferencing, and teaching composition in networked classrooms with multi-media. Chapters 11 and 12 cover authoring software and computer terms respectively. Almost no mention of the middle level, but as Tom's chapter shows, all this is in the middle already. ("Virtual" refers to text which exists only in computer memory [p. 210].)

Even more sophisticated for many of us is *NCTENet,* an electronic communications network that has the ability to link users with NCTE Headquarters and with other members. Contacts can be made through America Online, 800-827-6363, ext. 5670, or those with Internet access may contact 202-466-0533 to find out how this works.

But there are still some general texts out there full of ideas for incorporating lots of technology into the language arts classroom. One of my old favorites is:

Murray, M. (1974). *The videotape book.* New York: Taplinger. 248 pp. Hardback.

I used this book as a guide to assist my junior high students to plan and shoot video shows in English class. It is a very thorough book about using the video camera to create visual texts. Step by step, Murray tells you how to organize a video workshop, how to script, storyboard, and handle light and settings. Editing techniques are covered too.

Kelley, P., & Self, W. (Eds.). (1990). Technology in the English language arts. *Virginia English Bulletin.* 40 (1).

Articles describing lessons and units with every kind of media appear here, articles describing use of film, animation, television, audio cassettes, newspapers, video, computers, and printed advertisements. Some articles are about ideas in the middle level classroom; many that are high school could be easily adapted.

Another focus section holds some interesting ideas:

The English Journal. (1994). 83 (1). Focus section on media in the middle.

This focus section captures articles on developing critical viewers and listeners, on how to accommodate technological change in the language curriculum, and on the integration of media with language, literature, reading, and writing for young adolescents.

Chapter 11—Assessment and Evaluation

Naturally, the extensions here will give you more ideas about handling assessment and evaluation yourself. A good general one to start with is:

Goodman, K., Goodman, Y., & Hood, W. (1989). *The whole language evaluation book*. Portsmouth, NH: Heinemann. 280 pp.

Two sections at the beginning lay out the assumptions behind evaluation and assessment in a whole language setting. The next three sections offer portraits of evaluation systems at each schooling level, including the middle level. Lots of sample recording sheets, and some good discussion on how assessment works within an integrated and interdisciplinary setting. Other sections are informative, too, and the ideas are quite adaptable.

And you may pick up some good ideas from a focus section on assessment:

English Journal. (1992). 81 (2). Focus section on evaluation and assessment.

Six articles center on alternative evaluation modes, especially for writing; portfolios, conferencing, self-assessment measures, and response groups dominate. Three of the articles involve middle grades classrooms and writers.

Dickinson, T. (Ed.). (1993) Alternative assessment. *Middle School Journal*, 25 (2).

This is a whole issue devoted to various approaches middle level teams and teachers of all subjects (including language arts) currently take with alternative assessments. Some good recent work on portfolios.

Another general text derives from some ideas that are classic in the field:

Moffett, J. (1992). *Detecting growth in language*. Portsmouth, NH: Heinemann. 88 pp.

One of the best sections of *Student Centered Language Arts and Reading, K-13* was always the last section on evaluating students and managing a comprehensive evaluation system for individualized curricula. This short guide is really a companion to those sections, but can be used by someone unfamiliar with the larger text to establish an assessment plan based on literacy growth in individual students. The set-up makes most sense in relation to Moffett's concept of the "universe of discourse," but he gives explanations of the key ideas at the beginning of the volume. Ideal for looking at language growth across a curriculum, too.

Good texts for natural reading and writing will display sections that are helpful with evaluation and assessment. A good example is:

Valencia, S., McGinley, W., & Pearson, P. D. (1990). *Assessing reading and writing.* In G. Duffy (Ed.), *Reading in the middle school* (2nd ed.) pp. 124-44. Newark, DE: International Reading Association.

The authors make a plea for allowing middle grades teachers and students to reclaim classroom literacy assessment. They offer suggestions for the types of activities that could be included in portfolio assessment for reading and writing in the middle. The ending uses real examples of portfolio-keeping in the middle grades to answer questions.

And although this one just deals with writing, it gives some good tips for teams concerned with assessment:

Wood, K. (1993). Assessing writing performance across the curriculum. *Middle School Journal,* 24(3), 67-72.

Wood acknowledges the proliferation of writing likely to occur when the writing process governs writing in middle level classrooms. She gives us three categories of ways to assess writing in all content areas: a teacher assessment "checkpoint scale" from Kirby and Liner and peer assessment forms and strategies as well as self-evaluation strategies. Her ideas are easily usable by any teacher on a team.

More specific resources for portfolios exist too. These are very useful:

Graves, D., & Sunstein, B. (Eds.). (1992). *Portfolio portraits.* Portsmouth, NH: Heinemann. 212 pp.

These are really just pictures of teachers using portfolios at all levels of teaching and how they manage it, and of students keeping portfolios as well as how they learn and grow from the experience. There are two sections specifically written about fifth and eighth grade classrooms, but in general, the insights from the book are very adaptable to the middle grades.

Kent, R. (1997). *Room 109: The promise of a portfolio classroom.* Portsmouth, NH: Boynton/Cook Publishers.

While written from this high school teacher's experiences, the text offers many adaptable ideas for reconstructing a classroom around portfolios even at the middle level. Kent shares stories from his experiences teaching, and while doing so, shares with readers the possibilities for meaningful classroom writing—from journal-keeping, to writing center use, and through various assignments and projects he found workable with his students. The last four chapters explore the portfolio as it is developed with students, used for feedback, evaluation, and as a means of teacher and student reflection on learning.

Tierney, R., Carter, M., & Desai, L. (1991). *Portfolios in reading/writing classrooms.* Norwood, MA: Christopher Gordon Publishers. 200 pp.

This is one of the most comprehensive "how-to" books on portfolios for reading and writing. Tierney and colleagues leave nothing uncovered. They answer lots of questions, and show you how to start, how to use, analyze, evaluate, and conference with portfolio systems set up in reading/writing classrooms. Lots of good real life examples. Although K-12 focused, many examples are middle level, but all are adaptable to all levels.

Yancey, K. (Ed.). (1992). *Portfolios in the writing classroom: An introduction.* Urbana, IL: National Council of Teachers of English. 128 pp.

While Tierney's whole book is a single, detailed set of guidelines, this book offers multiple examples of systems through portraits of existing portfolio systems in English/language arts classrooms. Of the ten articles here, two are portraits of portfolio systems in middle level rooms.

Chapter 12—Dealing with the Nasty Realities

Grammar and Dialects:

English Journal. (1990). 79 (1). Focus section on language study in the middle.

Six articles in this section focus on alternatives to traditional grammar teaching in the middle grades language arts classroom. *English Journal* editors set out to find out how language studies (grammar study, dialects, language history) were taught to 10-14 year olds. The six articles, as a whole, explore how some teachers are teaching about language in the context of classrooms designed to allow language ability to grow naturally.

Strom, E. (1960). Research in grammar and usage and its implications for teaching writing. *Bulletin of the School of Education, Indiana University*, 36 (5), 1-23.

Strom's piece might not be recent, but it does a thorough job of reminding us how long we have known that direct study of grammar does not improve reading, writing, or speaking ability and skill. If you need a database of studies to make a point, here is a great starting place.

Tchudi, S., & Mitchell, D. (1989). *Explorations in the teaching of English* (3rd ed.) New York: Harper and Row. 430 pp. Hardback.

This is a comprehensive English teaching handbook full of useful ideas for both the middle and secondary teacher. In particular, you will find a wealth of creative ideas for teaching language in their chapter 11, "Exploring Language."

Weaver, C. (1979). *Grammar for teachers*. Urbana, IL: National Council of Teachers of English. 166 pp.

Weaver has one chapter entitled "What to do with Grammar," and in it she states that there is no justification for teaching grammar as a way to improve a student's use of language. There may be other reasons for teaching it, she states, such as providing interesting studies of grammar as a human phenomenon, or for teaching a process of scientific thinking, but the data simply does not support the usual reasons for teaching it and the usual strategies. On the other hand, the rest of the book is information every teacher should know about the grammatical system and its relation to the reading and writing processes.

Tracking/Ability Grouping, and Other Unfriendly Rules, Schedules—and Adults!

Erb, T. (1992). Encouraging gifted performance in middle schools. *Midpoints*, 3(1). 24 pp.

Although a general description written as an occasional paper for a multi-subject middle level audience, this paper is very pertinent for middle level language arts teachers. We all teach gifted students and supposedly we all are teaching (or about to) in middle level schools. And as Erb says, these two concepts, giftedness and middle level schooling, are often at odds. He examines both areas, bringing us all up to speed on the state of gifted education and middle level education, and laying out clearly the possible compatibilities between programs suggested for the gifted students and the structures and assumptions underlying middle level schools and curricula. When Erb finishes, we're all able to see how middle level schools could serve all kids, including the gifted.

George, P. (1993). Tracking and ability grouping in the middle school: Ten tentative truths. *Middle School Journal*, 24(4), 17–24.

George, who has elsewhere written on this issue, too, summarizes important research explaining why the practice of tracking is particularly harmful for young adolescents. His strikes against the practice resoundingly echo Weaver's against standardized testing (see chapter 11): it's related to self-esteem problems; it stratifies kids and labels them permanently; it destroys a sense of collaboration and community which middle level educators and whole language educators strive to cultivate. George includes a good short bibliography of sources, some of which back up his point, some of which support tracking for gifted students. Atwell's book, *In the Middle,* is part of the group which does not support tracking.

Lotan, R., Swanson, P., & LeTendre, G. (1992). Strategies for de-tracked middle schools. *Middle School Journal*, 24(1), 4-14.

So if you believe you should get rid of tracking, the big question remains "Where do we go from there?" The authors worked with several schools that committed to de-tracking, and what's presented here is the thinking (via a journal) and questions of one seventh grade teacher going through the transition. After each issue, question, or concern, the authors respond with possible solutions, strategies, and rationales for their ideas. A good discussion of the real problems arising from such a change.

Smith, F. (1986). *Insult to intelligence*. New York: Arbor House. 289 pp. Hardback.

The subtitle to Smith's book, "The Bureaucratic Invasion of Our Classrooms," gives you a good idea of what the book includes. Smith defines the nemesis of meaningful education in schools as the "r-bbit." What the "r-bbit" stands for is the "drill and kill" approach to teaching, a pervasive approach based on the underlying principles of behaviorism. In particular, programs relying on this approach "do not reflect normal reading, writing, or language" (p. 11). Smith then proceeds to explode a lot of mythology: that learning and instruction are necessarily congruent, for instance; that testing is a relevant means of assessment; that pre-packaged programs necessarily contain anything of value for learners. He even warns educators of the potential (and currently real) misuses of the computer. The last one-third of the book asserts what good teaching-learning alternatives are available, and how parents and teachers can help ascertain that a real learning environment is available to every student.

Wheelock, A. (1992). *Crossing the tracks*. New York: The New Press. 312 pp. Hardback.

In this groundbreaking text, Wheelock addresses the toughest issues in de-tracking schooling for young adolescents: handling decriers, involving parents in the process, and effects of a more democratic school structure on ethnically diverse populations. Much of the book, much to her credit, covers strategies and ideas for organizing for, and teaching and evaluating, heterogeneous groups.

Some middle level educators are alleviating many potential problems as well as positively involving adults as models and learners through various parent initiatives. The following newsletter is one of many of these types of positive involvements:

Carter, C., & Brazee, E. *The in-between years*. Orono, ME: Zeiter, Inc.

This quarterly newsletter to parents provides information on growth and development of young adolescents as well as on educational ideas. A positive focus on 10–14 year old students and their issues.

Exceptionalities, At-Risk, Non-Readers and Writers, and Other Problems Kids Have

Tom talks about a lot of problems kids have in school. As their teacher, these sources might help them—and you!

Rhodes, L., and Dudley-Marling, C. (1988). *Readers and writers with a difference.* Portsmouth, NH: Heinemann. 329 pp.

Rhodes and Dudley-Marling write for the holistic teacher of language arts who is concerned with all students, and who sees language arts as extending to all parts of the curriculum. The key is meaningful learning. Although each of the book's parts (for example, observation as assessment of literacy, meaningful activities of reading and writing, composition choices and conferencing, and thematic teaching) could be in many good whole language books, ideas for the remedial student and the LD student are integrated throughout each section.

Stires, S. (1991). *With promise: Redefining reading and writing for "special" students.* Portsmouth, NH: Heinemann. 180 pp.

A book about special needs students in reading and writing process classrooms at both the elementary and the middle levels. At least seven of the sixteen pieces involve portraits of, and ideas and strategies for, working with special needs middle grades kids with whole language approaches.

Weber, K. (1974). *Yes, they can: A practical guide for teaching the adolescent slower learner.* Toronto: Methuen Publications. 195 pp. Hardback.

A really old book, but one that made a difference to me as a younger teacher, and to, I hope, my students. This may be out of print, but it's worth finding in a good library. Weber's book assumes, unfortunately but probably realistically, that slower students will be grouped together. He sets about creating a meaningful reading, writing, speaking, and listening-based curriculum resting clearly on the assumption that slower kids can and will develop their cognitive thinking abilities when they learn through the study of relevant materials. Not an easy curriculum, not all non-traditional, just relevant studies. This text could still have some insights and ideas for those working in tracked situations and who want to make sure challenge occurs for students along with good self-esteem building.

The Diverse Language User: ESL and Multicultural Learners:

Brooks, C. (Ed.). (1985). *Tapping potential: English and language arts for the black learner.* Urbana, IL: National Council of Teachers of English. 330 pp.

Some very good and still timely suggestions about teaching African-American students. The parts of Brooks' book include sections on language, reading, writing, and literature. Helpful articles exist on black dialect, black learning styles, problems of minority readers, black dialect writers and their composing processes, and she includes a list of black YA literature.

Freeman, Y., & Freeman, D. (1992). *Whole language for second language learners.* Portsmouth, NH: Heinemann. 257 pp. Hardback.

Both Freemans are emphatic—a whole language classroom is essential for second language or bilingual learners. Given what is known about the problems with school for second language learners (fragmented curriculum and disempowerment) and their learning needs (learner-centered and real, authentic lessons, acknowledgement of culture and language difference, engagement with others, oral and written activity), the Freemans propose that whole language approaches would facilitate these learners powerfully. Each section of this book examines whole language key ideas and suggests ideas that would work especially well for the bilingual learner. Middle level students are included in their many examples and portraits of classrooms.

Rigg, P., & Allen, V. (Eds.). (1989). *When they all don't speak English.* Urbana, IL: National Council of Teachers of English. 156 pp.

These 10 articles explore programs that enhance the learning process for ESL students. All the programs are based on principles of learning language consistent with those of a whole language philosophy. All the general articles are relevant to the middle grades teacher, and the Edelsky article in particular offers several authentic learning possibilities a middle grades teacher would find useful.

Standardized Testing

Taylor, D. (1990). *Learning denied.* Portsmouth, NH: Heinemann. 112 pp.

Taylor's little book is a nightmare of "commonsense" teaching gone totally awry. She tells the story of second grader Patrick and his parents' war with the special education forces in public schooling, forces that labeled Patrick negatively, and often wrongly, and as a consequence, ensured his status as a "disabled" student. Although Denny Taylor's work at home with Patrick clearly showed his reading and writing growth, the school continued to ignore this evidence as batteries of tests, drills, and pull-out programs dominated his life at school.

Index